Lifelong Learning

Lifelong learning increasingly dominates discussions of post-compulsory education and training policies. Although the idea of lifelong learning has been most frequently used in discussions of higher and adult education and vocational training, it further provides a framework for debating and analysing the front end of education as well as its post-school phases.

Lifelong Learning examines the issues in four sections: Theoretical Perspectives; Curriculum; International Perspectives and Widening Participation. Such a mix serves to enrich the readers' interdisciplinary perspectives on contemporary initiatives. These sections include studies on important topics such as:

- community education
- popular education
- higher education
- the corporate university
- the school curriculum
- vocational studies

With contributors from China, Africa, USA, Canada, UK and other European countries, *Lifelong Learning* offers a comprehensive and challenging account of issues arising from varying lifelong learning decisions, and exposes the impact these decisions have on such a large majority of the population.

John Field is Chair of Lifelong Learning, University of Warwick. **Mal Leicester** is Chair of Adult Learning and Teaching, University of Nottingham.

Lifelong Learning

Education across the lifespan

John Field and Mal Leicester

London and New York

First published 2000
by RoutledgeFalmer
11 New Fetter Lane, London EC4P 4EE

Simultaneously published in the USA and Canada
by RoutledgeFalmer
29 West 35th Street, New York, NY 10001

RoutledgeFalmer is an imprint of the Taylor & Francis Group

Typeset in   10/12 pt Baskerville   System 3B2 6.03 [ADVENT] by
Keyword Publishing Services Ltd
Printed and bound in Great Britain by
T J International Ltd, Padstow, Cornwall

British Library Cataloguing in Publication Data
A catalogue record for this book is available
from the British Library

Library of Congress Cataloging in Publication Data
Lifelong learning : education across the lifespan / [edited by] John Field and
Mal Leicester.
        p. cm.
     Includes bibliographical references and index.
     1. Adult education. 2. Adult learning. I. Field, John, 1949– II. Leicester, Mal.

   LC5215.L497 2000
   374–dc21   00-036601

ISBN 0-750-70990-1

Contents

Tables and figure

Tables

Figure

Contributors

David Aspin is presently Professor of Philosophy of Education at Monash University, Melbourne, where he was formerly Dean of the Faculty of Education. Prior to his appointments in Australia, he was Professor of Philosophy of Education at King's College, London, working also in the Department of Philosophy at the London Institute of Education. Previous appointments included positions at Manchester and Nottingham Universities. His main interests are in epistemology and methodology, ethics and social philosophy, and the philosophy of mind and language, and their relation to issues and problems in education and its institutions. He has published widely on these matters.

Robin Barrow is Professor and Dean of Education at Simon Fraser University (British Columbia, Canada). He was previously Reader in Philosophy of Education at the University of Leicester. Educated at Westminster School and Christ Church, Oxford, Dr Barrow is the author of 21 books and a hundred or so articles in the philosophy of education, philosophy, and ancient history, including *The Philosophy of Schooling: A Critical Dictionary of Educational Concepts* (with Geoffrey Milburn), and *Giving Teaching Back to Teachers*. In 1996 he was elected a Fellow of the Royal Society of Canada.

Stephen Brookfield holds the title of Distinguished Professor at the University of St. Thomas in Minneapolis, Minnesota. Since beginning his teaching career in 1970 Stephen has worked in England, Canada, Australia and the United States, teaching in a variety of college settings. He has written and edited nine books on adult learning, teaching and critical thinking, three of which have won the World Award for Literature in Adult Education (in 1986, 1989 and 1996). He also won the 1986 Imogene Oaks Award for Outstanding Research in Adult Education. His work has been translated into German, Finnish and Chinese. In 1991 he was awarded an honorary Doctor of Letters from the University System of New Hampshire for his contributions to understanding adult learning. He currently serves on the editorial boards of educational journals in Britain, Canada and Australia, as well as in the United States. His most recent books are *Becoming a Critically Reflective Teacher* (1995) and *Discussion as a way of Teaching* (co-authored with Stephen Preskill) (1999).

Judith Chapman is currently Dean of the Faculty of Education at Australian Catholic University. Prior to this appointment she was for six years Professor of Education at the University of Western Australia and before that, Director of School Decision Making and Management Centre in the Faculty of Education at Monash University. Her main interests are in education policy analysis and policy administration, teaching and learning, improving the quality of education, and the meta-theory of educational administration; she has published widely in all of these fields. She has close connections with international agencies and has worked with OECD, UNESCO, IDEP and APEC on projects of national and international significance.

Jack Cohen is an internationally known reproductive biologist. His present position at Warwick University bridges the Ecosystems Unit of the Biology Department and the Mathematics Institute; his brief includes bringing more science to more public awareness. His books include several in reproductive biology (including *Living Embryos and Reproduction* and, with the mathematician Ian Stewart, *The Collapse of Chaos* (Viking/Penguin, 1994), and *Figments of Reality: The Evolution of the Curious Mind* (Cambridge University Press, 1997); which have received favourable reviews in *Nature* and the popular press. He is consultant to science fiction authors, designing alien creatures and ecologies. His most recent book is *The Science of Discworld*, with Stewart and Pratchett. He has initiated and participated in the production of several TV programmes, including *The Natural History of an Alien* (BBC and Discovery, 1998). His hobbies include boomerang-throwing and keeping strange animals (from hydras to mantis-shrimps, and octopi to llamas).

John Collard has been recently attached to the Faculty of Education, Australian Catholic University, on secondment from a position in the Catholic Education Office of Victoria. He has been involved in education for over 20 years and was principal of leading secondary schools in the Catholic education sector in Victoria. He is currently working on a doctoral thesis on education policy and management at the University of Melbourne.

Kathryn Ecclestone worked with young unemployed people on government training schemes in the 1980s before moving into further education for eight years to teach and manage vocational and access to higher education courses. She then moved into higher education to run teacher education and continuing professional development programmes for further and adult education teachers and trainers in the public and private sectors. She is now lecturer in post-compulsory education at the University of Newcastle and visiting research fellow for the City and Guilds of London Institute. Her research interests and publications encompass the policy and practice of assessment throughout the post-compulsory sector. At present, she is researching how current assessment policy and practice, in the context of debates about lifelong learning, affect learner autonomy and motivation. Publications include *How to Assess the Vocational Curriculum*, Kogan Page, 1996.

Richard Edwards is Reader in Education at the Open University, UK. He is involved in the production of distance learning courses for those working in the post-school area of education and training. He has written extensively on lifelong learning, in particular its relationship with postmodern social theory. His research interests include social theory and educational change, policy analysis, open and distance learning, and guidance. He has published widely in academic and professional journals. His most recent books are: *Changing Places: Flexibility, Lifelong Learning and a Learning Society* (1997, Routledge); with Robin Usher, *Globalisation and Pedagogy: Space, Place, Identity* (2000, Routledge). He is currently editor of *Studies in the Education of Adults*.

Konrad Elsdon is a product of adult education and has been variously active in it and in voluntary organizations as student, member, tutor, trainer, organizer, adviser and researcher for some 60 years. Since his retirement from HM Inspectorate (old style) he has been a special professor in what is now the School of Continuing Education at the University of Nottingham. His publications include books and articles on various topics, including teaching methods and training in the education of adults and development education. During the last 11 years he has concentrated on adult learning in voluntary organizations and its individual and social effects and implications. His forthcoming books are on self-help groups and, a new field for him, a historical theme.

Penny Enslin is Professor of Education at the University of the Witwatersrand, Johannesburg, where she teaches philosophy of education. Her research and teaching interests are in the fields of democracy and citizenship education, with particular reference to gender and democracy, and to citizenship in liberal democracies.

John Field became first Professor of Lifelong Learning in the UK when he moved to the University of Warwick in 1998. Previously, he was a professor in the School of Education at the University of Ulster, Jordanstown; he has also worked at the University of Bradford and Northern College, Barnsley. He has worked in adult education and training since 1978. His research interests include a variety of social, economic and historical perspectives on lifelong learning in Britain, Ireland and Germany. With Tom Schuller and Steve Baron, he edited *Social Capital: Critical Perspectives* (Oxford University Press). His other books include *European Dimensions: Education, Training and the European Union*. He serves as a governor for Tile Hill College in Coventry, and chairs the Executive Committee on Research for the Universities Association for Continuing Education.

Janet Hannah is senior lecturer in continuing education and deputy director of the Centre for Comparative Education Research in the School of Continuing Education at the University of Nottingham. Prior to joining the University of Nottingham, she held a number of positions including adult education outreach worker, lecturer in industrial relations at Newcastle Polytechnic, and research officer in the Trade Union International Research and Education Group (TUIREG) at Ruskin College, Oxford. Her teaching and research interests are in the field of comparative education, and in recent years she has engaged in research and published on workers' education and higher education in Britain and Brazil, and refugee education in the UK and Australia. In late 1996, she was awarded the Commonwealth Relations Trust adult education bursary with which she spent a sabbatical at the University of Technology in Sydney, undertaking the Australian research presented in this chapter.

Terry Hyland is Professor of Education Research at the Bolton Institute for Higher Education. Until autumn 2000, he was a lecturer in the Department of Continuing Education, University of Warwick. He qualified as a teacher in 1971 and has taught in schools, further, adult and higher education. Following a two-year secondment as Lecturer in Education Studies at University of Sokoto, Nigeria, he worked in post-school professional education at Bristol Polytechnic and Mid-Kent College before moving to Warwick. Key research interests lie in vocational education and training, professional studies, values education and the post-school curriculum. His book *Competence, Education and NVQs: Dissenting Perspectives* was published by Cassell in 1994 and *Vocational Studies, Lifelong Learning and Social Values* was published by Ashgate in October 1999.

Peter Jarvis is Professor of Continuing Education and a member of the Lifelong Learning Research Group in the School of Educational Studies, University of Surrey. He is author and editor of many books and articles on learning and education. Among his most recent are *Ethics and the Education of Adults in Late Modern Society* (NIACE), *The Teacher Practitioner and Mentor in Nursing, Midwifery, Health Visiting and the Social Services* (with Sheila Gibson) and *The Theory and Practice of Learning* (with John Holford and Colin Griffin). He is joint editor of the *International Journal of Lifelong Education*.

Rennie Johnston has worked in schools, further education and community adult education in the UK, Europe, Africa and Australia. For the last 15 years he has been based at Southampton University where has been involved in action research projects with unwaged adults; outreach and educational development work with adults from under-represented groups; and staff development and research with community adult education practitioners. He was Director of the Southampton Widening Provision Project from 1995 to 1999 and has recently been appointed Coordinator for Research and Development at the newly instituted University of Southampton New College with its specific mission to promote Widening Participation and Lifelong Learning. He is co-author of *Adult Education and the Postmodern Challenge* and has written widely on community adult education, experiential learning and adult learning for citizenship.

Patrick Keeney teaches at Okanagan University College (British Columbia, Canada). His academic interests are mainly in the areas of the history of education, philosophy of education, and educational law, particularly the effects of the Canadian Charter of Rights and Freedoms on educational governance. He is currently deputy editor of *Prospero: A Journal of New Thinking in Philosophy for Education.*

Klaus Künzel was born in Dresden 1945. He graduated from Bochum University in Philosophy, German and Education after an intermittent period of study at Merton College, Oxford. While completing his doctorate on the University Extension Movement in England he obtained a lecturership in Comparative Education at the University of Liverpool (1971–1973). On his return to Germany he became Wissenschaftlicher Assistant at the Institute of Education at Bochum University where he taught Adult Education and Educational Politics in its MA programme. In 1976 he was appointed Professor of Education at the University of Dortmund, a post he held until 1991 when he moved to his present post as Chair of Continuing Education at the University of Cologne. He was Head of the School of Education from 1994 to 1997, served on various faculty committees and was responsible for providing conceptual lead in the development of a continuing education service (UNIVATION) at Cologne University. He travelled extensively and spent sabbaticals in Oxford and Vancouver (University of British Columbia). His main research interests focus on historical, comparative and curricular aspects of continuing adult education; he is editor of the *International Yearbook of Adult Education* and *Kölner Studien zur Internationalen und Vergleichenden Weiterbildung*. Publications include extensive studies on educational marketing and advertising as well as a number of contributions on theoretical and political implications of continuing and lifelong learning.

Kenneth H. Lawson, now retired, holds an appointment as Special Professor in the School of Continuing Education at the University of Nottingham. Formerly he was Assistant Director in what was the Department of Adult Education at Nottingham. Previously he had been Warden of the University's Adult Education Centre as well as the Department's Administrative Secretary. His first appointment in adult education was Warden of the Wilmslow Guild Adult Education Centre in Cheshire, having been an adult student in WEA classes, and at Fircroft College, Birmingham and Ruskin College, Oxford. He entered the University of Oxford as a senior student at St. John's College in order to take a BA in Philosophy, Politics and Economics in two years. He was later awarded a PhD by the University of Nottingham. Throughout his professional career he taught adult education courses, first in economics and then in philosophy. For many years he taught philosophy of education on diploma and higher degree courses at Nottingham. He has published many articles and three books on philosophical issues relating to the education of adults.

Mal Leicester is Professor of Adult Learning and Teaching at the University of Nottingham and Director of The Educational Inclusion Research Centre. Previously, she was at the University of Warwick; she has taught at all levels of the education system and was Avon LEA Advisor for Multicultural Education. She has published extensively in philosophy of education, continuing education, values education and in relation to ethnicity and disability. Falmer Press have recently published her co-edited six volumes, *Education, Culture and Values* and Jessica Kingsley her book, *Disability Voice: Towards An Enabling Education.*

John McIlroy is Reader in Sociology at the University of Manchester. Previously, he worked in the University's adult education department, with responsibility for trade union studies. His research interests include work and industry, industrial relations, trade unions, labour education and adult education. He has published widely on adult education, labour education and trades unionism. He has edited *British Trade Unions and Industrial Politics: The High Tide of Trade Unionism, 1964–79* (Ashgate, 1999) and *Border Country: Raymond Williams in Adult Education* (National Institute of Adult Continuing Education, 1993). His book, *Trade Unions in Britain Today* (2nd edition Manchester University Press, 1995), is a standard text.

Jane McKie is a Lecturer in Continuing Education, University of Warwick, and has worked in the Department since 1995. She teaches courses in equal opportunities, study skills, theories of adult learning and teaching, and aspects of religious studies and mythology, and contributes to the administration of the Open Studies programme. She has particular responsibility for managing Open Studies certificates, which includes directing the Certificate in Philosophical Studies, the Certificate in Good Teaching Practice with Adult Learners, and codirecting the Certificate in Religious Studies. With a background in psychology, social anthropology, and religion and philosophy, her research is interdisciplinary. Recent projects have included looking at media representations of technology and education, and approaching the philosophy of education through myth and literature. She is a member of the Philosophy of Education Society of Great Britain.

Alyson Malach is Research and Development Officer for Black and Other Minority Communities. She worked in the social work sector for a period of 10 years and has 14 years experience of further education teaching and management. The majority of her teaching work was carried out in the north west of England. Since 1984 She has held a number of teaching and managerial posts in a range of curriculum areas. Her experience of teaching and management was gained in tertiary, community education, further education and sixth form colleges. She also has four years experience of working in higher education in the north west on staff and continuing professional development for further education and community sector staff. She has extensive experience in delivering and establishing mentoring systems for support staff and learners and has worked as a mentor to a range of learners' and individuals. During 1997/98 she served on the FEFC Inclusive Learning Committee and was lead writer for the Northwest College's partnership in producing the Inclusive Learning Materials on teaching and learning. She is also an experienced trainer on race equality issues.

Val Millman is an Education Adviser with Coventry City Council. Her responsibilities include careers education, work-related learning, equality of opportunity, and personal and social development. She has taught in both primary and secondary schools, and has undertaken a number of research and curriculum development projects that seek to embed these areas of teaching and learning across the 5 to 16 school curriculum.

William John Morgan is Professor of Comparative and International Education and

Director of the Centre for Comparative Education Research and the Commonwealth Education Documentation Centre, University of Nottingham. Between 1995 and 1998 he was also Director of the University's Institute of Asian Pacific Studies and was Director of the Centre for Research into the Education of Adults. He has been joint editor of the *Bulletin of the International Congress of University Adult Education* and is currently a member of the editorial boards of *Grundlagen der Weiterbildung (Foundations of Further Education)*, the *International Journal of University Adult Education*, and *Revista Internacional Paedia* (Argentina). He was a Visiting Fellow in the School of Professional Continuing Education, University of Hong Kong in 1991 and visited the People's Republic of China in 1993 at the invitation of the Department of Training, Ministry of Labour, and Japan in 1998, as guest of the Comparative Education Society of Asia and the Japan-UK Education Forum. He was elected in 1996 to a British Academy Sino-British Fellowship in the Social Sciences and has a collaborative link with the Institute of Higher Education, Peking University.

Shirley Pendlebury is Professor of Education at the University of the Witwatersrand in South Africa. She teaches courses in curriculum, teacher education and philosophy of education. Her main areas of research and publication are on practical wisdom in teaching and democratic theory and its implications for education.

Peter Scott is Vice-Chancellor of Kingston University. Previously he was Pro-Vice-Chancellor and Professor of Education at the University of Leeds where he was also founding director of the Centre for Policy Studies in Education. He was Editor of the *Times Higher Education Supplement* from 1976 until 1992 and was a Visiting Scholar at the Graduate School of Public Policy at the University of California at Berkeley from 1973 to 1975 while holding a Harkness Fellowship from the Commonwealth Fund of New York. He is a member of the Academia Europaea. He was originally a historian, and his main research interests are in higher education policy, in particular the governance and management of universities, links between further education and higher education, and in knowledge production. He is the author of, among other books, *The Meanings of Mass Higher Education* and (with five colleagues) *The New Production of Knowledge: The Dynamics of Science and Research in Contemporary Societies*. He has recently edited a book in the Falmer Press Millennial Series *Higher Education Re-formed* and is about to publish, together with Helga Nowotny and Michael Gibbons *Re-thinking Science: Knowledge Production In an Age of Uncertainities*.

Mary Stuart is Assistant Director in the Centre for Continuing Education at the University of Sussex. She has a background as practitioner and manager in the arts, the voluntary sector and in education. She has managed a range of projects in higher education funded by the Higher Education Funding Council and the Department for Education and Employment. She has worked with people with learning difficulties both as a teacher and as an advocate and continues to support the inclusion of people with learning difficulties through the European Citizenship programmes based in the Centre for Continuing Education. She has worked nationally with the Universities Association for Continuing Education as secretary to their educational equality network and is currently chair of the staff development network. She has worked with a number of organizations developing educational provision and consultancy to meet their development needs. She has a DPhil in social policy and has done research in the field of partnerships and social exclusion both in this country and in Eastern Europe and South Africa. She has published a range of materials relevant to her interests including work on social exclusion, people with learning difficulties, partnership, advocacy, and empowerment and organizational practice.

Jane Thompson worked in the Department of Adult Continuing Education at the University of Southampton and Ruskin College, Oxford where she was Director of Studies, before joining NIACE in May 1999. Her specialist teaching interests include women's studies and adult and community education. She has taught courses in community education and the sociology of education at postgraduate level and has supervised students writing MA dissertations and PhD theses. She is currently an external examiner at the University of Edinburgh and the National University of Ireland as well as Research Associate at the University of Warwick. At NIACE she is working on educational responses to the social exclusion, community regeneration and empowerment agendas. She has written widely about the theory and practice of adult continuing education. Her most recent publications include *Adult Learning, Critical Intelligence and Social Change* (1995); *Words in Edgeways: Radical Learning for Social Change* (1997); *Ruskin College: Contesting Knowledge, Dissenting Politics* (1999); and *Women, Class and Education* (2000).

Alexandra Withnall is a non-clinical lecturer in the Department of Geriatric Medicine, School of Postgraduate Medicine and a member of the Centre for Social Gerontology at Keele University. In 1998, she spent a month as a Visiting Lecturer in the School of Community Health at Charles Sturt University, NSW. She previously worked in the Department of Continuing Education at Lancaster University and was a Research Officer at the National Institute for Adult Continuing Education from 1979–90. Prior to this, she taught at the former Wolverhampton Polytechnic and in further education. Her interest in later life learning stems from a review of research on education and elderly people which she carried out as part of a larger DES-funded study of research in adult education in 1979–82. She is a founder member of the Association for Education and Ageing (formerly the Association for Educational Gerontology) and was elected to the chair in 1999. Combining her existing research interests in continuing education with newly developed insights from the field of ageing, Alex currently holds research grants from the EU, from the North Staffordshire Medical Institute and from the Economic and Social Research Council (ESRC) under its Growing Older: Extending Quality Life Programme.

Introduction

Lifelong learning or permanent schooling?

John Field and Mal Leicester

The rise of lifelong learning up the policy agenda has been a remarkable one. For much of the 1990s, it dominated discussions of post-compulsory education and training policies across an extraordinary range of organizations and nations. Although the idea of lifelong learning has been most frequently used in discussions of higher and adult education and vocational training, it increasingly provides a framework for debating and analysing the front end of education as well as its post-school phases. It recurs in the most surprising variety of contexts cropping up in debates over social exclusion, both urban and rural policy public health, multiculturalism, professional development and environmental conservation as well as in more familiar settings such as competitiveness and economic growth. And it appears to command respect among those who are otherwise political enemies.

Among policy makers, the consensus appears to be that lifelong learning is both necessary and desirable. It is easy to produce evidence that lifelong learning is now the common policy framework for debating and defining the post-school education and training system. National policy papers favouring lifelong learning have been published by the shelfload since the early 1990s. There have also been influential reports from the Organisation for Economic Co-operation and Development, the European Commission, and the G8 group of governments from the eight largest economies, as well as from UNESCO, which brings together a much wider group of nations than the other three intergovernmental bodies. For the most part, these documents place economic issues at the foreground of the argument, but few if any are solely concerned with vocational education and training. Even a cursory glance at the scope of the debate shows that the implications of lifelong learning appear, potentially, to be far-reaching.

This almost bewildering variety of far-reaching contexts sometimes leads to a blurring of boundaries, such as those between vocational and liberal, leisure and work, and even learning and education. Such blurrings may have their uses. On the other hand, does lack of discrimination cover meaninglessness? What are we to understand by the term 'lifelong learning' and how does it relate to that other widely used notion—'lifelong education'? In the past schooling has sometimes been seen as preparation for the (adult) life to come and post-school education either as compensation for inadequate or incomplete schooling or as concerned with learning that is somehow distinctive of adulthood. 'Lifelong Learning', however, cuts across this school and post-school distinction to suggest a learning process which spans the whole of one's life. This learning through(out) life leaves open the question of whether learning is also 'through' life in the sense of 'based on life experiences'. Richard Bagnall has pointed out that if lifelong education is seen as education from the whole of life's experiences then 'education' has indeed become vacuous.

It seems to us however, that when either term ('lifelong learning' or 'lifelong education') are used they are almost always used approvingly. There is, therefore, a normative dimension. Of course, this is not surprising given that both terms originated in policy discourse, and more particularly in the deliberations of intergovernmental agencies such as UNESCO and the educational research centre of the Organisation for Economic Co-operation and Development. They are mainly concerned with planned, purposeful, systematic, *worthwhile* learning—not just with any or all learning. Indeed, it may be that it is because 'lifelong learning' carries approval, and suggests a learning throughout life which is worthwhile, that it tends to be used interchangeably with 'lifelong education', though the later term may, perhaps, be less likely to include non-formal and informal learning.

Because 'lifelong learning' is used both normatively and widely, to include liberal, vocational and social aspects, we would suggest that it goes beyond a blurring of boundaries to a recognition that these aspects of learning/education are, in practice, interrelated. The agenda for lifelong learning encourages education for citizenship (political), seeks for wider participation (social), and emphasizes the importance of learning for economic prosperity (vocational) while recognizing the importance of individual choices and personal development (liberal).

'Lifelong learning' then, though comprehensive, is not meaningless. It serves to reject the school and post-school division to endorse learning across the lifespan, a learning which is worthwhile to the individual citizen and, therefore, to the society of which she is a part. Lifelong learning is thus often linked with the notion of a learning society—society which will, that is to say, be so organized as to provide (maximum) learning opportunities for each of its members, and also so as to value a broad range of that learning.

Modern societies also seek for a general flourishing and prosperity in the face of competition with other such societies. It is true that the current debate starts out with an interest in and an emphasis on maintaining economic competitiveness and growth. As well as pursuing a broadly similar approach, all the policy documents provide a largely shared analysis of the context. As the G8 charter for lifelong learning puts it,

> The challenge every country faces is how to become a learning society and ensure that its citizens are equipped with the knowledge, skills and qualification they will need in the next century. Economies and societies are increasingly knowledge-based . . . everyone should be encouraged and enabled to continue learning throughout their lives, not just in the years of compulsory schooling. (G8 1999).

Lifelong learning therefore arises, according to this perspective, primarily from changes in the economy. Such developments as the rapid diffusion of information and communications technologies, the constant application of science and technology to new fields, and the globalization of trade in goods and services have made it impossible to rely on existing ways of educating and training the workforce. Hence the need for constant investment in human capital, not simply so that firms and nations can compete but also in order that individuals and regions do not fall behind in the jobs race.

However, even this is too limited a view of the policy debate. Although traditional economic concerns provide its starting point, much of the debate has moved beyond the established solutions. Rather than limiting itself to proposals for reforming the training system, for instance, the UK government's Green Paper spoke ambitiously of 'transforming learning in the workplace' and 'supporting learning businesses', calling for employers to enter partnerships with unions and share responsibilities with individuals in order to take these ideas forward (DfEE 1998, 33–6). Rather than training policy, the Norwegian parliament published proposals for 'competence reform' (Storting 1998).

This also has far-reaching implications for the vocational education curriculum. In his attempt to sketch a social philosophy for 'third way' politics, Anthony Giddens (1998, 125) argued briefly that 'Although training in specific skills may be necessary for many job transitions, more important is the development of cognitive and emotional competence'.

In short, the sheer pace of change is such that it increasingly appears to require a holistic policy response if individuals and organizations are to cope, not only in terms of acquiring new and relevant skills and knowledge, but in having the personal qualities required to live with constant uncertainty and innovation.

Thus far, the policy debate might appear to be concerned solely with growth and competitiveness. Yet while it is certainly true that economic issues are commonly foregrounded in debates over lifelong learning, they are by no means the only policy preoccupation. In 1997, UNESCO placed great emphasis on the relationship between lifelong learning and equality in its international congress on adult education. Perhaps this might be expected from a body whose membership encompasses the poorer as well as the richer nations. But similar concerns play a part, if a more muted one, even among the advanced capitalist nations. The G8 charter emphasises the role of regional and social inequalities. The UK government's Green Paper on lifelong learning stressed the connections with social cohesion, community-building and individual development and freedom:

> Learning offers excitement and the opportunity for discovery. It stimulates enquiring minds and nourishes our souls. It takes us in directions we never expected; sometimes changing our lives . . . [It] contributes to social cohesion and fosters a sense of belonging, responsibility and identity.
>
> (DfEE 1998, 10–11).

So the policy debate has extended far beyond economic competitiveness and growth. If it was concerned solely with these relatively narrow fields of human activity, its implications would be much more clear-cut and obvious than they are, and it would affect far fewer people.

Clearly, something is afoot. But are the changes seismic ones, or are they rather cosmetic in nature? Is this simply a politician's fad, or a recognition that the world is indeed changing? Does the idea of lifelong learning represent largely a rebottling of stale and watery wine, or does it present more fundamental challenges to the way that we do things? Are we witnessing the logical extension of well-defined trends in education and training, or does lifelong learning mark a decisive turning point in the way that people and organizations define and manage their learning? And if the changes are important ones (as, by and large, the contributors to this volume believe that they are), are they entirely positive or, on the contrary, do they pose new and alarming threats?

In the essays that follow, we try to provide answers to these questions—although, in keeping with the very notion of lifelong learning, the answers are mostly provisional and open-ended. A third of our contributors provide an international perspective (from South Africa, China, Australia, US, Ireland, UK, and elsewhere in Europe). In all cases there is agreement that lifelong learning, particularly with its vocational and economic impulse, is very much on the agenda. Many contributors point to the three stranded liberal, vocational and social aspects and overall the consensus seems to be "two cheers" for governmental initiatives. There are real opportunities but . . . Often the 'but' is allied to fears that in spite of the 'widening participation' rhetoric, some groups may be excluded. Will the tendency to concentrate on employment-related education and training exclude older learners? Will the emphasis on assessment penalize the disabled? Is enough in train to include and benefit the voluntary scholar? Will the information flow about new opportunities reach into minority communities?

There is some discussion about how much real difference the initiatives are making or will make. And there are good grounds for scepticism. Although the discourse of lifelong learning has embraced both breadth and humanity, much of the policy thrust has so far focused on two areas of intervention: reform and growth in vocational training and the prolongation of initial education. There is a strong risk, then, that governments will treat lifelong learning as a form of reschooling for adults.

On balance, though, we come down on the side of those who believe that something is indeed happening. While the current popularity of lifelong learning owes much to fashion, as well as to the rather loose nature of the term itself nevertheless, 'lifelong learning' is pregnant with meaning for the ways in which learning is defined, recognized, valued and promoted. And if we shift attention away from the term itself for a moment, we can also discern real shifts in people's beliefs and behaviour: no one today acts as though all their important learning is over when they quit school for the last time.

References

DfEE (1998) *The Learning Age: A Renaissance for a New Britain*, Department for Education and Employment, Sheffield
G8 (1999) *Köln Charter: Aims and Ambitions for Lifelong Learning*, G8 Summit, Cologne
Giddens, A. (1998) *The Third Way: The Renewal of Social Democracy*, Polity Press, Cambridge
Storting (1998) *Competence Reform*, Storting, Oslo

Part 1

Theoretical perspectives

1 Lifelong learning, lifelong learning, lifelong learning

A recurrent education?

Richard Edwards

Marx once wrote memorably that history repeats itself, the first time as tragedy, the second time as farce. As a description, this is inaccurate, but nonetheless, it is a fine rhetorical flourish, one which points to two aspects of the 'historical' consideration of lifelong learning to be undertaken within this chapter. First, the continuities and discontinuities that weave and are woven into historical events. Second, the rhetorical power of the statement is suggestive of the discursive power and fabricated nature of 'the historical'. The meanings of the notion of lifelong learning across time therefore need to be explored for the various significations in play. This chapter does not offer therefore a simple historical narrative, a diachronic story of the emergence and progression of lifelong learning as concept, policy and practice—themselves very different types of history. It engages rather with the historical as a multiple text and considers some of the more general moves in the emergence of lifelong learning and what can be learnt from this. In this way, it might be considered a work of historical sociology (Dean 1994).

Thus, when asked to write a chapter giving a 'historical overview' of lifelong learning, I find a series of issues in play that suggests the farcical nature of such an endeavour. Maybe that is the tragedy of history. It is in that spirit that I fabricate a mapping of lifelong learning. Given that I occupy certain spaces and places, it is perhaps less an overview and more a glimpse.

Lifelong learning

Different stories might be told about the emergence of lifelong learning as a notion. Whether it is a notion, concept, arena for debate, a discursive practice, and the range of individual, social and institutional practices encompassed by it, might be part of such stories. Lifelong learning is fabricated as an idealized goal for education (Parson 1990), a process (Parson 1990), a product (Hatton 1997), a moral duty (Wain 1991), an empirical reality to reconstruct (Belanger 1995). For some, it has a long history going back to Plato (Jarvis 1988)—although both the types of learning and its confinement to the cadres of philosopher kings suggest something very different from more contemporary notions, as does Jarvis' section on 'man as a lifelong learner'. Yet it is also absent from the text, if not the index, of a contemporary history of British adult education (Fieldhouse *et al.* 1996). It can also be said to be largely a 'boy's (own) history' given the gendered nature of its construction to which this chapter is yet a further contribution of course!

A search for 'lifelong learning' on the ERIC database elicited 1741 references between the years 1932 to 1983, an average of 34 per year. Between 1984 and 1998, the number of references to lifelong learning was 1581, an average of 112 per year. This is crude, and more refined searching, although still within the parameters of what is held on the ERIC database, would trace the historical and to a certain extent geographical emergence of lifelong learning more fully. However, it gives us the possibility of saying that there has been a developing interest in the academic study of lifelong learning throughout the twentieth century, and this has increased significantly over the last fifteen to twenty years. A comforting thought for those of us who work within this space.

However, this would be too easy, as a closer look at many of the papers identified as lifelong learning show them to be about related and differing notions, such as adult education, lifelong education, *education permanente*, continuing education. These related concepts might well be considered aspects of or strategies for lifelong learning, but the latter largely remains absent—lifelong learning is implied rather than explicit—a point to which I shall return. This is complicated further by language, insofar as lifelong learning is an English construct. Its historical emergence may differ therefore from related concepts and practices emerging in other parts of the globe. Sutton (1994) points out that lifelong education appeared in the English language in the 1920s. He also suggests that the various terms and their formulations in different languages has caused problems, as international organizations such as UNESCO and the OECD have promoted certain concepts in more than one language. Indeed much of the literature in the 1970s and 1980s has been generated or sponsored by UNESCO, with the OECD playing a more prominent role in recent years.

This absent-presence of lifelong learning is to be found elsewhere. A search on the *British Educational Index* for 'lifelong learning' showed that between 1986 and 1998 there were no references. Similarly, a review of a range of dictionaries and encyclopedias of education and education research brought up only four references to lifelong learning (Page and Thomas 1977, Kallen 1979, Jarvis 1990 and Sutton 1994). Interestingly, while some took the view that lifelong learning was interchangeable with lifelong education, others did not. There are also differences in the conceptualization of the family of concepts, of which lifelong learning is a part. Some (Sutton 1994) suggest a spectrum from lifelong education, lifelong learning, recurrent education and continuing education, while others (Tuijnman 1991) see lifelong education as offering a holistic and humanistic philosophy, strategies for the implementation of which are developed through the policies of recurrent education. Earlier, Kallen (1973: 62) argued for recurrent education as a planning strategy for 'lifelong or permanent learning'. By contrast, Gustavsson (1997: 238), eliding any distinction between lifelong education and life-long learning (and what does the hyphen signify?), sees recurrent education as reductive, focusing on the economic while lifelong education is 'idealistic ... applicable for any purpose'. Hatton (1997: 363) suggests that with lifelong learning 'living becomes an open metaphor for learning', which suggests that rather than dying we may simply stop learning!

Kirpal (1976: 110) distinguishes between the 'lifelong education of the emerging future and the cultural learning of traditional societies . . . lifelong cultural learning'. He associates the latter with religion and ritual and contrasts it with the challenges of contemporary society which demand lifelong education, the main quest of which must be a 'global humanism'. Here lifelong education takes on a mission which would seem to threaten the cultural lifelong learning already in existence. The traditional forms of the latter also need to be contrasted with the forms of reflexive individualism associated with more current and Western views of lifelong learning. Cropley (1980: 1) argues that 'lifelong learning existed before the emergence of current interest in it, and would continue to occur even if educators ignored it'. However, in glimpsing the history, without being named, can it be said to exist, as the only evidence we have is that which is documented? Lifelong learning might be inferred from historical descriptions, but how do we evaluate them as learning rather than other processes and practices?

It is unsurprising perhaps that Giere (1995: 387) is particularly scathing about the conceptual confusion surrounding the literature in this area:

> [An] even closer look at the concepts makes them blur. It brings into sharp focus their
> vagueness, their atheoretical nature . . ., their arbitrary quality, their inherent tensions

and contradictions. This has split the lifelong education publishing community into believers and non-believers.

Similary, Larsson (1997: 251) bemoans the loss of richness and precision in the diversifying meanings of lifelong learning. More controversially, Boshier (1998: 8) asserts that lifelong learning is a regressive notion in comparison to the idea of lifelong education:

> lifelong learning denotes a less emancipatory and more oppressive set of relationships than does lifelong education. Lifelong learning discourses render social conditions (and inequality) invisible.

This suggests that in the English-language global academic literature, lifelong learning may be emerging as a conceptual space of its own having previously been implied by other concepts—the absent-presence mentioned earlier. In a sense then, it has been fabricated through its absence to take account of changing economic, political and cultural practices. Lifelong learning has not been the focus for study, although studies of particular organizational and curricula practices have implicitly engaged with aspects of lifelong learning. The latter has been subsumed within the literature. Its emergence as the key framing mechanism in certain countries and international organizations signifies and is part of the challenge to established institutional structures associated with trends towards greater individualization and marketization and ambivalence. In a sense, its emergence points to that which it is posited as being the answer to—uncertainty and change, for it is itself an uncertain and troubled conceptual space.

Lifelong learning

Yet in many eyes this may not be the case, as the above offers tracings from within certain academic literature within which there is no shared disciplinary affinity nor unified community of practice. Indeed, the relative lack of literature both illustrates the relatively recent emergence of lifelong learning as a framing mechanism and a certain slowness to engage with it from within the academic community.

In many ways, lifelong learning has emerged from within policy and as a policy concept influenced initially to a great extent by the work of the international bodies UNESCO (Faure *et al.* 1972) and the OECD (1973) and their respective prescriptions for lifelong education and recurrent education. As such, it is more proscriptive and prescriptive than descriptive and analytical, an attempt to reform the post-school arenas of education and training by harnessing them to a different agenda, to rethink their roles and contributions to lifelong learning and a learning society. Tracing the emergence and migrations of this agenda through the policy texts of local, national and international governments and organizations, public and private, would be an intriguing task (Lingard and Rizvi 1998). In some ways, it appears almost to be the equivalent of a computer 'flaming', or in more earthy terms, a volcanic eruption. The focus in policy moves to lifelong learning as a pragmatic and desirable means to further ends and the strategies to achieve it, displacing to a certain extent such previous strategies as lifelong education, continuing education, *education permanente*.

However, caution and analysis are still necessary, as the space of lifelong learning bounded within policy texts is itself diverse. In some, lifelong learning is focused on post-compulsory education and training, while others embrace aspects of schooling. In principle, it could provide a framework, like health, for considering learning from the cradle (or earlier) to the grave. Indeed lifelong learning increasingly carries with it the health warning, 'learn or else', a less than humane side to its conceptualization as the flourishing of human potential. Thus, a European Union White Paper (Commission of the European Communities 1995) sets out as its objectives: to encourage the acquisition of new knowledge; promote closer relations between schools and business; combat exclusion; develop proficiency in three Community languages; and treat investment in training on a par with capital investment. As Hake (1999) argues, there is a significant emphasis on initial education and training in this agenda. Similarly, the OECD (1996) calls for a strengthening of the 'foundations of lifelong learning' and for schools to become 'community learning centres', for more supple frameworks which 'permit a more flexible response to the diverse aptitudes and backgrounds of student'. Here the OECD has moved from its notion of recurrent education which excluded initial education, to a view more in line with that of UNESCO which embraces lifelong education.

By contrast, the various reports in the UK (Kennedy 1997, NCIHE 1997 and Fryer 1997) which fed into the government's Green and White Papers on lifelong learning (Secretary of State for Education and Employment 1998 and 1999) all identify the latter as concerned with the post-school sectors of education and training. In his useful summary of these documents, Tight (1998a: 484) suggests their message to be that:

> lifelong learning for all is the new imperative. Its curriculum is primarily vocational in content and intent. It is our fault if we have not participated to date. We risk social and economic exclusion if we do not participate in the future. We must pay directly for our participation.

This somewhat overstates it, but it is suggestive of the ways in which a more explicit policy focus on lifelong learning by national governments has reconfigured its conceptualization, embracing a different prescriptive framework to that articulated within the earlier documents, for instance, on lifelong education from UNESCO.

This is reflected in the alignment of lifelong learning with changes in the economy and workplace, the need to invest in human capital to ensure economic competitiveness in conditions of increasingly globalized capitalism. This maps lifelong learning to that required for employment and the workplace, the vocational and the accredited. While subject to much criticism for its limited and limiting perspective, the space of human capital may be broader than is often suggested. Two examples are suggestive. First, some, but by no means all, workplaces in parts of the globe are changing to involve team-based practices, involving a wider range of skills, a focus on self-management, interpersonal skills, etc. In some ways, this brings educational principles into the workplace and elides a certain elitist and radical dismissal of training. In certain contexts, there is a social aspect to the development of human capital. Second, where partnership rather than conflict models are to the fore, the support for trade unionism and learning opportunities provided through trade unions can be promoted as a significant part of lifelong learning. Policy spaces and policy implementation are chaotic and messy rather than rational processes. Thus, critiques of policies as merely or mostly vehicles for the development of human capital can be overstated.

A further area of concern in the policy formulations of lifelong learning is to do with its adherence to certain institutional structures. Thus, while there has been increased concern given to individuals as consumers in many countries and areas of policy, and individuals as learners, the focus has remained on reforming established structures to reconcile the agendas of different stakeholders—individuals, governments, employers, etc. For Tight (1998), this means that, for instance, the UK government Green Paper, *The Learning Age*, focuses on lifelong learning as participation in vocational and accredited courses rather than taking the full diversity of people's lifelong learning for granted. Of course, while at one level a fair criticism, it also overlooks the legitimate role of government in governing and organizations in managing the production of services and goods. Adults may not need structural and organizational supports to engage in learning, but governments and societies do, to pattern social and economic practices according to conditions, prognostications and possibilities. The extent to which these match the aspirations of populations and benefit them is obviously subject to analysis and contest. It is the re-patterning of those opportunities which results in certain radical propositions concerning lifelong education (Gelpi 1985), although this can be subject to the critique offered by Tight of more contemporary policies towards lifelong learning in its valuing of only certain forms of learning, those aimed at an under-theorized notion of 'liberation'.

Lifelong learning ...

There would appear to be many manifestations of lifelong learning in the glimpses we have taken of it. The above has brought to the fore human development, human capital and liberation as at play within the texts of lifelong learning—implied or explicit. No doubt we see and experience different aspects of it in our daily lives. Academics and policy makers are discussing and debating its range and significance, ways of promoting it, etc. There are professorships in lifelong learning being established. Above I have briefly explored some of the academic and policy tracings that are and can be made. With that in mind, I now want to provide a further glimpse, to begin to fabricate a recent history of lifelong learning, as it has emerged like a chrysalis from its predecessors to become a powerful family member—at least for the present.

Since the economic crises of the mid-1970s, there has been a growing interest in the development of lifelong learning opportunities among policy formers and makers in many of the industrialized countries. This has developed from and to a certain extent displaced earlier discourses of lifelong education as a condition of and for equality and (usually liberal) forms of democratic politics and citizenship. It has become a governing principle of much discourse that lifelong learning is necessary for 'successful'—competitive—economies as we move into the twenty-first century. International organizations, national governments, employers and trade unions, as well as those involved in working with adults articulate support for the development of lifelong learning. This discourse is no longer restricted to those who have used the notion to support the provision of education and training for adults. As we have seen, this increased visibility and importance given to lifelong learning is marked by shifts in its conceptualization and increased contestation. Here lifelong learning is marked by the genetic traits of its various lines of ancestry.

Earlier implied and explicit notions of lifelong learning developed alongside those of lifelong education and recurrent education, the former providing a more holistic view than the latter. In such discourses, lifelong learning was to be achieved through strategies aimed at providing opportunities for adults to learn what, when and how they wished. These were to result from national policies and plans to maximize the learning opportunities and potential of the population as a whole. Strategies were particularly needed for those adults 'disadvantaged' by lack of success in initial education. Thus, lifelong learning was constructed as integral to what might more accurately be termed an 'educated society', 'an education-centred society', 'an educative society' or, as Abrahamsson (1993) refers to it when discussing post-Second World War Sweden, a 'lifelong educated society'. 'We propose lifelong education as the master concept for educational policies in the years to come' (Faure *et al.* 1972: 182), a proposal which continued the modernist, gendered claim for mastery and mastering in the construction of learning practices.

In such discourses, the role of education is to provide opportunities for adults to be educated to enable them to be active as citizens in the social formation. In other words, lifelong education is aimed at creating the conditions for self-realization and citizenship within a liberal democracy. A seamless web of personal and social development are the goals within the institutional and value frameworks of liberal democracy, with differing stances as to their compatibility with a capitalist economy. UNESCO proved more critical of the latter, while it is inscribed in the mandate of the OECD which promoted policies of recurrent education to support economic development, something which may reflect the global membership and remit of the former and the more restricted membership and remit of the latter.

The perceived success of the Swedish example was for a long period marked by favourable reporting and dissemination through such bodies as the Organisation of Economic Co-operation and Development and the European Commission. However, it was also built upon relatively secure economic prosperity, a dimension which seemed to be assumed as an ongoing rather than contingent condition. In this sense, lifelong education would seem to assume and produce a certain stability and order, which contemporary globalizing tendencies, including the promotion of lifelong learning as a global policy strategy, challenges.

Sutton (1994: 3418) suggests that the notion of lifelong education 'lies within the tradition of the notion of the perfectibility of man' (*sic*). Recurrent education had a more restricted focus on the perfectibility of human potential in the workplace. However, both support learning and participation. The emphasis is highly normative, with a focus on structures and strategies for provision, very much situated within a view of the assumed inherent worth of education. Little is done in these early advocacies to explain the paradox that social formations which are experiencing greater levels of education and training than in previous generations do not necessarily witness a revitalization of political participation in formal politics. There has been the election of governments which institute market-based policies which progressive supporters of an educated society largely view as opposing the teleological goals of reason and emancipation. Societies would not appear to be operating within the teleologies prescribed within these discourses of recurrent and lifelong education.

As the economic security and ethical certainties underpinning earlier discourses of lifelong education have been challenged, the substance of the notion and who articulates it have changed in three significant ways. First, a greater emphasis is placed on the economic relevance of learning: certain forms of lifelong learning are constructed as conditions for economic competitiveness in a globalized economy. Second, greater emphasis is placed on the learners to secure their lifelong learning in a marketplace of opportunities throughout their lives. Third, it is not simply educators and particularly adult educators who engage in debates, but policy-makers, employers, trade unionists, etc. Thus, the notion of lifelong education which largely lacked influence in government, has been displaced by more powerful discourses of a lifelong learning market in which individuals are constructed as having to take responsibility for their own learning. For some, this is liberating, as it 'frees' them from the 'deadening hand' of the collective and the bureaucratic management of the state-funded and administered institutions. For instance

> in a society characterised by lifelong learning, knowledgeable and mobile consumers will shake and shape educational institutions, and those which have been sheltered from the marketplace will be challenged as never before.
>
> (Hatton 1997: 371)

However, such a view may be at the expense of a conception of the collective, of society, as having the possibility for being a shared condition and one of mutual interests and responsibilities. This indicates a notion of lifelong learning which embeds market principles, economic relevance and individualism. A learning market, servicing the market economy and acting in market-like ways, both reflects and contributes to processes of social differentiation within the contemporary globe. This is a view promoted by national governments and international organizations such as the OECD who have moved from articulating polices for recurrent education to those for promoting strategies for lifelong learning. Thus, discourses of lifelong learning displace and disrupt notions of lifelong and recurrent education. Here self-reliance and economic competitiveness are the goals and the strategies attempt to embed those goals promoting market-like reforms.

Lifelong learning is promoted through initiatives which give individuals 'choice' and 'consumer power'. For instance, in a range of European countries the notion of the individual credit/voucher/loan to buy one's own learning has been adopted (Van Der Zee 1991). In the United Kingdom, vouchers, both for learning and guidance, have been provided as a basis for increasing the market responsiveness of providers of services. In this way, individuals are said to have been 'empowered' in relation to the 'bureaucratic' and 'unfriendly' providing institutions (Hand *et al.* 1994). However, as with all forms of 'empowerment' it is fraught with contradictions, as it is only those with the necessary cultural and other capital who are likely to benefit from such developments. These trends result both from and in a fragmentation of social relations in which 'society' is reconfigured as the contractual and consumer relations of individuals.

However, there are also social and cultural challenges to society and these underpin a further dimension of lifelong learning, of social and cultural practices which are often— although not always—outside its recent policy framings. The study of societies has largely been conducted on the basis of nation states. In other words, societies have been considered to be a correlate of the boundaries of the nation state, itself historically a very recent arrival. National education systems have played a central role in providing cohesion and cultural hegemony within nation states (Green 1994). However, the boundaries of the nation state have been breached by globalizing trends in the economy, communications, migration, tourism, etc. Alternative identities to those of the nation have been asserted, for example, around gender, religion, ethnicity, region. The notion of society, therefore, has come to be seen as problematic in itself, with concerns for cross-cultural and inter-cultural understanding as people migrate as a result of war and hunger, for the purposes work, learning and leisure, and the media bring the globe to people's homes. Assumptions about nationhood, society, and culture as bounded constructs have come under scrutiny.

In this situation of less bounded sociality, what are the boundaries of collective self-interest to which 'we' belong that 'we' can call 'our' society? Given the heterogeneity and differences of those living within the boundaries of a nation state, who is the 'we' that is referred to in discourses of 'social and/or national interest'? A sense of 'bounded place' is displaced by a notion of 'spaces of interaction' (Massey 1991). Rather than being members of a single society, it is suggested we are part of a heterogeneous series of overlapping and inter-related local, regional, national, international, global societies. Here it is persons participating in a range of learning networks or communities of practice with which they identify and through which that identity is constituted that traces a space for lifelong learning. This might be thought to be the space for Kirpal's (1976) traditional lifelong cultural learning, the silent learning that takes place in societies regardless of its inscription in texts. However, as lifelong learning might be said to be the absent-presence in many of the texts of lifelong education, recurrent education, adult education, etc, so learning networks might be said to be the absent-presence in many of the texts of lifelong learning.

The discourse of learning networks is one that locates lifelong learning in ways which problematize the notion of society. Its antecedents lie in community and popular education and those concerned to 'deschool' society (Illich 1970). They have tended to have an over-arching moral or political purpose that is not necessarily to be found in all notions of lifelong learning, which may embrace consumer, lifestyle and affective practices as networks of learning.

Deschooling 'opposes lifelong and recurrent education as a form of compulsory lifelong schooling and suggests replacing it by lifelong completely voluntary access to learning exchanges or "educational webs"' (Giere 1995: 386). However, while deschoolers see webs as alternatives to schooling and remain bounded by modernist emancipatory ethics, they can be taken to exist alongside markets and more formal educational provision.

A recurrent education?

Lifelong learning is an English-language construct, part of a family of related notions, largely, but not solely fabricated by male educators within the contexts of Northern Europe and America. Depending upon one's conception of it, lifelong learning might be said to be part of all human societies across time, or be restricted to those societies which have structures for the provision of learning opportunities beyond initial schooling. In glimpsing its emergence in policy from the 1970s to the present I have attempted to suggest some of the differing formulations to be found and with that the differing practices enfolded by lifelong learning. I have attempted also to give some insights into how and why these emergences have developed. It is a process which will go on—a form of lifelong learning itself—for the recurrence of educational endeavours is as important as those of learning itself. In a sense, the work within this chapter illustrates the need for more work on the history of lifelong learning, fundamental to which is further elucidation of the object of study. However, in such a proposition, there is a reflexive paradox, as objects of study are constituted by, rather than pre-exist, social and textual practices. The historical overview of lifelong learning within this chapter therefore constitutes its own object of knowledge. It tells tales. How telling those tales are I leave to others, as part of their education and learning.

References

Abrahamsson, K. (1993) 'Concepts, organisation and current trends in lifelong education in Sweden', *International Journal of University Adult Education* 32, 3: 47–69.
Belanger, P. (1995) 'Lifelong learning: the dialectics of "lifelong education"', in P. Belanger and E. Gelpi (eds) *Lifelong Education, Education Permanente*, Dordrecht: Kluwer Academic Publishers.
Boshier, R. (1998) 'Edgar Faure after 25 years: down but not out', in J. Holford, P. Jarvis and C. Griffin (eds) *International Perspectives in Lifelong Learning*, London: Kogan Page.
Commission of European Communities (1995) *Teaching and Learning: Towards a Learning Society*, Luxembourg: Office for Official Publications of the European Commission.
Cropley, A. (1980) 'Lifelong learning and systems of education: an overview', in A. Cropley (ed) *Towards a System of Lifelong Education: Some Practical Considerations*, Oxford: Pergamon Press.
Dean, M. (1994) *Critical and Effective Histories: Foucault's Methods and Historical Sociology*, London: Routledge.
Faure, E., Herrara, F., Kaddoura, A.-R., Lopes, H., Petrovsky, A., Rahnema, M. and Ward, F. (1972) *Learning To Be*, Paris: Harrap/UNESCO.
Fieldhouse, R. and Associates (1996) *A History of Modern British Adult Education*, Leicester: NIACE.
Fryer, R. (1997) *Learning for the Twenty-First Century*, London: National Advisory Group for Continuing Education and Lifelong Learning.
Gelpi, E. (1985) *Lifelong Education and International Relations*, London: Croom Helm.
Giere, U. (1995) 'Lifelong learners in the literature: a bibliographical survey', in P. Belanger and E. Gelpi (eds) *Lifelong Education, Education Permanente*, Dordrecht: Kluwer Academic Publishers.
Green, A. (1994) 'Postmodernism and state education', *Journal of Education Policy* 9, 1: 67–83.
Gustavsson, B. (1997) 'Life-long learning reconsidered', in S. Walters (ed) *Globalization, Adult Education and Training*, London: Zed Books.

Hake, B. (1999) 'Lifelong learning policies in the European Union: developments and issues', *Compare* 29, 1: 53–69.

Hand, A., Gambles, J. and Cooper, E. (1994) *Individual Commitment to Learning: Individuals' Decision-making about Lifetime Learning*, Sheffield: Employment Department.

Hatton, M. (1997) 'A pure theory of lifelong learning', in M. Hatton (ed) *Lifelong Learning: Policies, Practices and Programs*, Toronto: APEC.

Illich, I. (1970) *Deschooling Society*, New York: Harper and Row.

Jarvis, P. (1988) *Adult and Continuing Education: Theory and Practice*, London: Routledge.

Jarvis, P. (1990) *International Dictionary of Adult and Continuing Education*, London: Routledge.

Kallen, D. (1973) 'Recurrent education', in R. Ryba and B. Holmes (eds) *Recurrent Education: Concepts and Policies for Lifelong Education*, Proceedings of the Comparative Education Society in Europe.

Kallen, D. (1979) 'Recurrent and lifelong learning: definitions and distinctions', in T. Schuller and J. McGarry (eds) *World Yearbook of Education: Recurrent Education and Lifelong Learning*, London: Kogan Page.

Kennedy, H. (1997) *Learning Works: Widening Participation in Further Education*, Coventry: FEFC.

Kirpal, P. (1976) 'Historical studies and the foundations of lifelong education', in R. Dave (ed) *Foundations of Lifelong Education*, Oxford: Pergamon Press.

Larsson, S. (1997) 'The meaning of life-long learning', in S. Walters (ed) *Globalization, Adult Education and Training*, London: Zed Books.

Lingard, R. and Rizvi, F. (1998) 'Globalisation, the OECD, and Australian Higher Education', in J. Currie and J. Newson (eds) *Universities and Globalisation: Critical Perspectives*, London: Sage.

Lyotard, J.-F. (1984) *The Postmodern Condition: A Report on Knowledge*, Manchester: Manchester University Press.

Massey, D. (1991) 'A global sense of place', *Marxism Today*, June, 24–9.

National Committee of Inquiry into Higher Education (1997) *Higher Education in the Learning Society*, London: NCIHE.

OECD (1973) *Recurrent Education: A Strategy for Lifelong Learning*, Paris: OECD.

OECD (1996) 'Meeting of the education committee at ministerial level: making lifelong learning a reality for all', http://www.oecd.org/news_and_events/reference/nw96-/a.htm

Page, G. and Thomas, J. (1977) *International Dictionary of Education*, London: Kogan Page.

Parson, S. (1990) 'Lifelong learning and the community school', in C. Poster and A. Kruger (eds) *Community Education in the Western World*, London: Routledge.

Secretary of State for Education and Employment (1998) *The Learning Age: A Renaissance for a New Britain*, London: HMSO.

Secretary of State for Education and Employment (1999) *Learning to Succeed*, London: HMSO.

Sutton, P. (1994) 'Lifelong and continuing education', in T. Husen and T. Postlethwaite (eds) *The International Encyclopedia of Education*, volume 6, Oxford: Elsevier Science Ltd.

Tight, M. (1998) 'Bridging the "learning divide": the nature and politics of participation', *Studies in the Education of Adults* 30, 2: 110–19.

Tight, M. (1998a) 'Education, education, education! The vision of lifelong learning in the Kennedy, Dearing and Fryer reports', *Oxford Review of Education* 24, 4: 473–85.

Tuijnman, A. (1991) 'Emerging systems of recurrent education', *Prospects* 21, 1: 17–24.

Van Der Zee, H. (1991) 'The learning society', *International Journal of Lifelong Education* 10, 3: 213–30.

Wain, K. (1991) 'Lifelong education: a duty to oneself?', *Journal of Philosophy of Education* 25, 2: 273–8.

2 Community education and lifelong learning

Local spice for global fare?

Rennie Johnston

'Community Education' and 'Lifelong Learning' have clear similarities. They are both broad, imprecise and 'elastic' terms which can appeal to a wide range of people and perspectives. In particular they offer a strategic flexibility which makes them attractive to politicians, policy-makers and practitioners alike—they can embrace a multitude of sins!

This chapter aims to clarify the conceptual confusion of Community Education and Lifelong Learning, examine their similarities and differences and investigate their inter-relationship. It will focus initially on the theory and practice of Community Education, exploring its values and purposes, curriculum and policy contexts, then try to reframe and recontextualize it within a contemporary Risk Society where traditional concepts of community are being challenged by a growing individualization, an emphasis on diversity and plurality and new understandings of social welfare. It will examine whether and to what extent, Community Education's social purpose can be sustained and adapted to take account of the new and powerful discourse of Lifelong Learning which is underpinned by a clear economic rationale, which focuses on human capital and employability and which is flourishing within an increasingly marketized and consumer-oriented world. It will conclude by examining what a social purpose Community Education approach can offer the wider discourse of Lifelong Learning through a critical analysis of key issues within the relationship. It will argue that a particular emphasis on social purpose Community Learning can serve to challenge, diversify and radicalize Lifelong Learning.

Sketching the territory, testing the elastic

Before looking in greater depth at Community Education and Lifelong Learning, it may be necessary to sketch out the territory for discussion. This is necessary precisely because they are such elastic and flexible terms—the pragmatic and political advantages this offers can easily be offset by the conceptual confusion it causes. For the purposes of this chapter, we need to map out, clarify and delimit what these terms mean. Of course, this clarification will, of necessity, be sketchy in that there can be no definitive understanding of such everyday terms as community, lifelong, education or learning

While it would be a mistake to focus too much on single constituent parts of such complex ideas, it is clear that the meaning of 'community' is central to any clarification of Community Education. Indeed, in its literature there has been extensive discussion of the significance of education in relation to identifiable geographical communities, occupational communities, interest communities and cultural communities. What all these understandings of community appear to have in common is a reference point, a sense of place or space, in some way separate or distanced from mainstream education or schooling. This in itself reflects another key and useful distinction which serves both to complicate and clarify the discourse of Community Education, that between community as fact and community as value (Plant 1974). One of the obstacles to greater clarity within Community Education has been the inevitable inter-mixing of 'community' used in a descriptive and in a normative, evaluative sense. For example, a key criticism of many constructions of Community Education has been that they often assume a 'Gemeinschaft'-type of reciprocating community where there is an essential complementarity of interest, whereas the reality is more likely to be a more formally-organised and atomistic 'Gesellschaft', if not even a conflict model of (local) society.

This chapter will return later to the issue of different constructions of community. However for reasons of both clarity and economy, it will see a key aspect of Community Education as being the educational reference point which it offers beyond institutional education and the contrast this implies with the values, purposes and organizational structure of conventional schooling. This reference point is physical but also ideological. In his study 'Community Education: The Dialectics of Development', Martin (1996: 109) makes the point that in relation to education 'community' should be viewed as an ideological construct which is both historically and contextually specific. Thus, Fletcher suggests that the moral base of Community Education is located in '. . . a common opposition to centralization, be it of political control over communities or administrative control over opportunities for learning' (Fletcher 1987: 46) and Martin believes that within Community Education, community '. . . implies a critical choice between an essentially hierarchical, socially regressive and static model of social relations and one that is progressive, emancipatory and dynamic' (Martin 1987: 12). Here 'community' provides the context for a more radical questioning of the role and purpose of education. This highlights the specific social purpose of Community Education which will be a major focus within this chapter.

In contrast to *Community* Education, *Lifelong* Learning seems to be more straight-forward—it traces and promotes a lifelong process of learning, 'from cradle to grave'. However, even at its simplest, Lifelong Learning has a horizontal as well as a vertical dimension—its comprehensiveness embraces learning that occurs in every aspect of life, at work, in the home, at leisure, at play. While this includes formal learning in educational institutions, the very choice of the term 'learning' also has a normative dimension. This implies a plurality of learning approaches and learning situations, some distancing from the primacy of formal education and certainly a move away from front-end models of institutional learning. To this extent, it has some interconnections and common ground with Community Education.

However, it is possible to identify further normative threads within the broad discourse of Lifelong Learning and some significant differences from Community Education. These relate to its extensiveness and its reference points. Unlike Community Education which takes place mainly in local and informal contexts and therefore is concerned predominantly with local narratives, Lifelong Learning is ubiquitous, embracing all kinds of learning, everywhere. Whereas the outside reference points for Community Education are communities, localities and a social purpose, Lifelong Learning looks to a bigger stage, nothing less than that of globalization! This in turn highlights a second, even more fundamental difference—with its particular focus on learning for work within the global marketplace—pride of place within Lifelong Learning is given to economic rather than social purposes. The discourse of Lifelong Learning is redolent with references to human capital and employability and it appears to flourish within an increasingly marketized and consumer-oriented world. In contrast to the possible marginality of Community Education, Lifelong Learning is located very much within the educational and political mainstream.

Community Education: unpacking its values, purposes, curriculum and context

Because of the many different meanings and constructions of community, it is possible to identify a very wide, and often conflicting, range of values and purposes within Community
Education. This ambiguous situation has led to the development of a plethora of models of
Community Education, which distinguish between, for example, universal, reformist and
radical perspectives (Martin 1987), liberal and liberating approaches (Fletcher 1980) and different forms of education of, in and for the community (Brookfield 1983). Whilst this chapter
acknowledges that this diversity of models is an attempt to make sense out of a plurality of practice, for the purposes of this discussion, it will focus on Community Education which identifies
a specific social purpose, identified by Fieldhouse as:

> providing individuals with knowledge which they can use collectively to change society if
> they so wish, and particularly equipping members of the working-class with the intellec-
> tual tools to play a full role in a democratic society or to challenge the inequalities and
> injustices of society in order to bring about radical social change.
>
> (Fieldhouse 1992: 11)

Community Education provides a localized focus for a social purpose education whose key
values are a commitment to social justice, greater social and economic equality, and a more
participatory democracy. Following Freire (1972), social purpose Community Education is
unequivocally and explicitly political, combining a critical understanding of the ideological
function of the education system in supporting the status quo and in maintaining cultural
reproduction, with a dynamic theory of oppositional cultural action. For this reason, this chapter will concentrate predominantly on community *adult* education which allows the greatest
scope and space outside the educational system for such cultural action.

Of course, the concept of social purpose within Community Education still needs to be problematized and deconstructed further. This relates both to its analysis and its prospective action.
A key issue has been that of social class. Whereas an emphasis on community has been seen as
an important counter-focus to challenge the prevalent 'ideology of individualism' within conventional adult education, it has also been criticised for its quietism, for the way that 'The
idea of community often obscures the most important social and economic relations'
(Jackson 1980: 42). The economic dimension of social class cannot be ignored, yet neither
can it be over-simplified. An increased diversity of society in the late twentieth century and,
alongside it, the existence of multiple forms of inequality, exploitation and discrimination
has prompted a growing recognition by many social purpose educators, that 'the working-
class has never been a single unitary subject but has been simultaneously fractured by
skill, gender, ethnicity, region and the cultures engendered by these divisions' (Westwood
1992: 234).

Such a perspective over the years has translated incrementally into curriculum development and change within Community Education and a closer interaction with a variety of
social movements. Thus, for example, Taylor and Ward, in revising their conception of social
purpose, community adult education in the context of the mid 1980s, have explicitly recognized five aspects of social structure which reproduce inequality, namely education, gender,
race, age and geography. In responding to these factors they advocate two key principles: the
necessity for in-depth, preliminary groundwork and dialogue to co-investigate the real 'felt
needs' of target groups in local communities; linked to educational approaches centred on
local manifestations of structural issues rather than conventional academic 'subjects' (Taylor
and Ward 1986: 172). This revised approach to social purpose adult education accords with

similar community-based approaches across the world (see Peters and Bell 1987, Wildemeersch and Jansen 1992, Meekosha 1993, Walters 1997) and highlights two particular curricular issues within social purpose community adult education—its distinctive epistemology and the idea of needs identification and needs-meeting.

In constructing 'A Theory of Community Education and its Relation to Adult Education' in 1980, Fletcher identified as a central premise:

> Educational resources are to be dedicated to the articulation of needs and common causes. Articulation does not mean mobilization or publicity: it means rather joining ideas and analysis and being disposed to seek for needs rather than wait for demands.
>
> (Fletcher 1980: 67)

This focus on needs rather than demands has served as an important way of distinguishing Community Adult Education from the consumerist culture of mainstream adult education, seen to be based too uncritically on the market place. It implies a recognition that the identification of need involves a longer-term process of dialogue and negotiation between educators and prospective learners. As such it provides a clear rationale for reaching out to communities beyond educational institutions and for moving beyond conventional constructions of knowledge.

Of course the concept of need is neither exclusive to Community Education nor unproblematic. In social policy, there is a whole literature focusing on issues like the inter-relationship of normative needs, expressed needs, felt needs and comparative needs. Views of needs and hence methods of needs identification depend crucially on the way in which needs are understood to be socially-constructed. In this context, Welton poses the problem that:

> . . . need is not separable from socio-historical constitution. Unless need articulation is mediated by critical ethically normative reflection deepened by theory, individuals will tend to need what the professionals provide.
>
> (Welton 1987: 55)

The issue of needs articulation and needs meeting is clearly a key one for both Community Education and Lifelong Learning and worthy of further consideration and exploration.

This connects with a similar need to explore and clarify social purpose community adult education's distinctive epistemology. The influence of Paulo Freire pervades the discourse of Community Education and this is nowhere more important than in his theory of knowledge. Freire's understanding of the dynamic relationship between knowledge and education underpins his very influential approach to educational praxis which he defines as 'reflection and action upon the world in order to transform it' (Freire 1972: 28).

The role and status of knowledge has provided an area of wide-ranging debate within Community Adult Education circles. Much has been made of Johnson's historical distinction between traditional, 'value-free', 'merely useful knowledge' and 'really useful knowledge', that serves practical ends for the knower. As Johnson puts it 'The real point, the real practicality, was learning how to change your life. Really useful knowledge is knowledge calculated to make you free' (Johnson 1988: 21–2). At issue here has been the predominant status of culturally-valued knowledge, the power of community-based knowledge and the role of knowledge in maintaining and transforming social relations. Freire's contribution to this debate was to offer a new paradigm in distinguishing between the 'banking' concept of education and 'problem-posing education'. In contrast to the former, where 'knowledge is a gift bestowed by those who consider themselves knowledgeable upon those whom they consider to know nothing', a problem-posing approach was intended to help people to '. . . develop their power to perceive critically the way they exist in the world in which they find themselves; they come to see the world not as a static reality, but as a reality in process, in transform- ation. . . . Education is thus constantly remade in praxis' (Freire 1972: 56–7). Of course, ques- tions remain from both inside and outside the discourse of Community Education about the whole process of Freire's 'conscientization' and about the implications for practice of his polar- ization between 'education for liberation' and 'for domestication' and this will be discussed later. What is, however, readily apparent is the fundamental impact that a Freirian epistemol- ogy has had on Community Education theory and practice and its adoption and development of an issue-based curriculum.

A problem-posing approach to knowledge and the curriculum provides social purpose educators working in communities with a different status (teacher/learners alongside learner/ teachers) and with a dynamic methodology which seeks out meaningful, practical starting points for curriculum negotiation within a critical structural analysis. Arising from Freire's philosophy and methods and incorporating some ideas from Illich, community adult educa- tion has developed a distinctive methodology which involves outreach, target groups, net- works, negotiation, participation and empowerment (Lovett 1975). Significantly, many of these terms have now been incorporated within a broader Lifelong Learning discourse and this conjunction will be explored further in the second half of this chapter.

Having briefly reviewed social purpose community adult education's values and purposes, its curriculum and its epistemological foundations, a final aspect for critical analysis is its pol- icy context. While this investigation has identified social purpose community adult education as being expressly political and in some ways distanced and oppositional to the discourse and practice of schooling, it also recognises that community adult education cannot be viewed or practised in complete isolation from mainstream educational and political systems. While Community Educators may be tempted to operate primarily in the autonomous territory of civil society, largely divorced from the controls, constrictions and restrictions of the state and the economic imperatives of the marketplace, few are in a position to do so completely or to ignore the broader policy context.

This whole relationship of community adult education to policy developments immedi- ately raises two key problems—the ambiguity of the term 'community' and the gap that can exist between Community Education's radical rhetoric and its often conservative prac- tice. In relation to the former, in a UK context, Martin (1996: 119) identifies within the his- tory of Community Education both the notion of sponsorship through the 'ideological construction of homogeneous communities' (Westwood 1992: 234) and the idea of the co-option of deficient or disadvantaged communities into some kind of compensatory or deficit model of education. At the same time, radical critics have noted that despite the out- reach methods, community development and non-formal focus, the actual content of most community adult education provision is very similar across the UK, reflecting only a slightly localized response to the needs of marketplace. Indeed, this very outcome may be the result of an over-professionalized needs-meeting approach which amounts only to the 'domestication' of a Freirian agenda and its reduction to a mere method stripped of its essen- tial ideological underpinnings (Allman 1987, Westwood 1992). In similar vein, Vincent (1983) counsels against the dangers of a romantic 'community' localism serving only to make more palatable an educational approach which has increasingly been controlled from the centre. Despite its rhetoric and its focus on community issues, culture and knowl- edge and a more active and participatory education for citizenship, social purpose commu- nity adult education has often promised more than it has delivered, foundering on its proximity to mainstream education, professional colonization and an unwarranted

'Gemeinschaft' view of community which privileges consensus and sameness over structural inequality and difference. In this context, Field asserts that:

> Unless we are clear what our organising values are—in other words, we pay attention to the philosophy which informs the educational intervention, and the kind of social movements and groupings we wish to empower—Community Education's contribution is liable to be hijacked by the new individualism.

(Field 1989: 26)

The whole link to policy development is another area where the inter-face between Community Education and Lifelong Learning needs to be further explored. A starting point might be to re-view the idea of community and locating a Community Education approach within the context of contemporary society.

Re-viewing community and Community Education within a Risk Society?

Ulrich Beck identifies a Risk Society as being typified by uncertainty and risk, a new phase of late modernity, 'reflexive modernization', where the very conditions that facilitated the development of modern industrial society become problematic themselves and where modern institutions increasingly struggle to cope with the global insecurity of life (Beck *et al*. 1994). In exploring contemporary risk, Anthony Giddens has made an instructive distinction between 'external', often predictable, risk and 'manufactured' risk which is created by human development and increasingly intrudes directly into personal and social life (Giddens and Pierson 1998: 210). Indeed, confirming evidence of the impact of such 'manufactured' risk can readily be drawn from a range of developments across the world, for example, environmental problems like nuclear power and global warming, increasing health and food scares, issues related to genetic engineering, and recent and imminent government retreats from (universal) welfare provision and redistributive taxation policies. Certainly, coping with risk has become a key imperative of a Learning Society and is central to the rationale for Lifelong Learning. This paper recognizes the existence of some kind of Risk Society and looks to explore critically its particular implications for both Community Education and Lifelong Learning.

A key aspect of a Risk Society is its focus on 'individualization': 'the disembedding and re-embedding of ways of life by new ones in which individuals must produce, stage and cobble together their biographies themselves' (Beck *et al*. 1994: 13). This process of 'individualization' sits alongside a growing emphasis on difference as promoted through global communication systems and consumerism, a greater awareness, understanding and fostering of cultural diversity, and new forms of association, as exemplified in a growth of a range of different social movements. It is also clearly reflected in social and economic policy in the USA, UK and increasingly elsewhere in Europe with the encouragement and development of active labour market strategies, a focus on individual responsibility or 'employability' and a responsive welfare state geared to draw people away from the identified evils of a 'dependency culture'.

In the light of increased individualization allied to a growth of diversity and pluralism, attempts have been made to try to reassert and reinvent the notion of 'community' as a way of maintaining a broader, more communal reference point. It is increasingly recognized that this needs to move beyond the cosy, inward-looking conservatism of 'Gemeinschaft', yet, at the same time, avoid the anomistic and atomistic bureaucratization of life implicit in

'Gesellshaft'. Two influential but very different contemporary approaches to this reassertion of 'community', which have clear implications for adult learning approaches, are those shaped by transatlantic ideas of communitarianism and by the more European concept of 'aesthetic communities'.

Communitarianism, as espoused most notably by Etzioni (1993), draws from both conservative and liberal traditions. It stresses personal responsibility, the family, a reciprocating community and social cohesion with a strong underpinning of moral rearmament, which appeals to traditionalists and consensualists alike, but offends more libertarian, especially feminist interests, particularly through its reassertion of the nuclear family and the implicit role of women within it. Education in this context is often seen as a vehicle for the rebinding of individuals to the moral obligations and social norms considered inalienable from communal life (Jansen and Van der Veen 1997: 271). Thus, educational applications inspired by communitarian values include predominantly school-centred initiatives on family literacy and family learning, the mobilization of more community-based citizens' or youth action groups working for the common good, in opposing social ills like crime, prostitution and local environmental problems and the support of projects to improve inter-cultural relations and try to integrate 'outsider' groups. Such approaches to community learning appeal to governmental agendas of social cohesion and social inclusion, if not social control, as can be demonstrated in their active promotion by a UK government as part of its 'non-ideological' Third Way policy framework.

In contrast to communitarian approaches to politics and education is the emerging European concept of 'aesthetic communities'. Owing much to postmodern understandings, 'aesthetic communities' are seen as organic, creative and affective; to embrace alternative frameworks of values and ideals; to emphasize care for the self and empathy for the other; and to focus on everyday life and lifestyle rather than more macro concepts of institutional and societal power (Jansen *et al.* 1998). Their orientation is more towards heteronomy than autonomy which, in terms of adult learning translates, into a modest, limited and reflexive agency allied to an interpretative consciousness which is expressed in both social learning and biographical learning (Jansen *et al.* 1998: 246–7). Such a learning focus accords with a growing 'politics of identity and difference' and involves learning processes and environments which flourish largely outside the ambit of formal education. In this context, one of the key issues within 'a Learning Society' is how to fill and shape the important space between macro systems and structures and the socio-biographical micro-world, prompting, amongst other things, an educational exploration at the meso level, of institutional and non-institutional learning environments (Alheit 1999: 77–9).

Clearly in invoking and operationalizing the concept of 'community' within the wider contemporary context of a Risk Society, educators will need to make new sense of the impact of individualization and communality, of identity and difference on adult learning. In promoting and developing community adult education, they will need to try to develop a social purpose which makes critical connections between the common but conformist purpose of communitarianism and the diversity and heteronomy of 'aesthetic communities', which recognizes the broad process of 'individualization' yet also highlights the limitations on choice and autonomy afforded by material poverty and social exclusion. In the context of a Risk Society, this may involve a review and reframing of their values and purposes, their curriculum approaches and, in particular, their attitude to mainstream policy developments. In doing this, it may be useful now to reconsider in greater depth the similarities and differences between Community Education and Lifelong Learning and reconceptualize their interrelationship. This can be done through a focus on three shared aims: combatting social exclusion, widening participation and encouraging active citizenship.

Exploring the spaces, tightening the elastic

At a macro level, there seems to be a broad consensus about the 'facts' of social exclusion. Evidence from across the world highlights growing social and economic inequality within and between nations (Delors 1996, UNESCO 1997, Korsgaard 1997: 10–15, Baptiste 1999: 95–6). There is also some kind of consensus about the macro effects of this, with a range of social commentators concerned about the decline in social cohesion as demonstrated by growing global crime rates, the exclusionary, disenfranchising and alienating impact of the privatiza- tion of previously public services, the dangers of increasing welfare dependence within an overall questioning of the contemporary funding basis and role of the welfare state (see Giddens 1998). Perhaps there is even a consensus about how an educational approach can help to combat it. As UNESCO puts it:

> While there is a growing demand for adult education and an explosion of information, the disparities between those who have access and those who do not are also growing. There is therefore a need to counter this polarity, which reinforces existing inequalities by creat- ing learning structures and Lifelong Learning environments that can help to counter the prevalent trend.
>
> (UNESCO 1997: 2)

There are, however, significantly different emphases on the reasons for combatting social exclusion and, more particularly how this might be done in practice. Those who take a more mainstream Lifelong Learning perspective tend to want to combat social exclusion for a mix- ture of social, cultural and economic reasons. They may well want to promote social cohesion and cultural integration but their primary reason is economic. Tony Blair says it all when he asserts that: 'Education is the best economic policy we have' (DfEE 1998: 9). These new materi- alists see the main strategy as the development of 'human capital' and 'employability'. Education and training, that 'new mantra of social democratic politicians' (Giddens 1998: 109) is a central aspect of supply-side manpower planning (*sic*) which will bring greater eco- nomic prosperity and a more flexible workforce ready to respond to the imperatives of the global marketplace.

The idea of investment in human capital is immediately attractive to educators, but we also need to examine this investment critically, in particular how the returns on investment are distributed (Schuller 1998: 160). We need to note that educational investment often amounts to a covert form of regressive taxation (Johnston 1999), with comparative research in the US and Europe demonstrating that education tends merely to reflect wider economic inequalities (Giddens 1998: 109–10). We also need to note the complex inter-relationship between human capital, cultural capital and social capital, 'features of social organization, such as norms, networks and trust, that facilitate coordination and cooperation for mutual benefit' (Putnam 1995: 67). While it would appear to be self-evident that there is a clear correlation between levels of formal education attainment and social inclusion (Field 1998, Schuller and Field 1998), within the discourse of Lifelong Learning, there is a real danger of reducing educational responses to social exclusion merely to questions of access and participation within the formal education system or the labour market. Critics from across the world (Baptiste 1999, Van der Veen 1998, Jackson 1997) have identified that access pro- grammes by themselves will not foster civic change, equalize power distribution or meet the needs of socially excluded groups. On the contrary, there is a real danger that it will only increase the number of people 'Imprisoned in the Global Classroom' (Illich and Verne 1976), where they can easily become enmeshed in new forms of governmentality and surveillance, bounded by linear notions of guidance, progression and competence and controlled by quality assurance procedures which are mechanistic, monolithic and conform-ist (Johnston 1999).

Based on his own community-based research, Van der Veen puts the point simply:

> Formal courses and training don't make any sense for people in danger of becoming social excluded [*sic*] when they don't see a connection to (the) underlying learning process [of social learning]. (1996: 5)

This takes us back to the place and role of Community Education in relation to social exclu-sion. Here, Community Education practitioners cannot afford to ignore or completely oppose the powerful discourse of Lifelong Learning with its macro analysis, primary economic purpose and widespread political support. Nevertheless there is space within it to argue for the injection of a different ethic and a more critical social purpose in tackling social exclusion, and for the extension of praxis at a community or meso level. This can be carried out mainly in civil society within the space between economy and state, and there are many current examples of such work taking place at community level involving the more process-centred social learning (see Van der Veen 1998, Elsdon 1998) and the more overtly political Popular Education (see Crowther *et al.* 1999, CREA 1999).

While such a Community Education approach can serve to problematize, possibly radic-alize the broad discourse of Lifelong Learning, this does not mean that it does not itself need to be reflexive and self-critical in changing times. Thus, in responding to social exclusion in the context of globalization, any idea of social purpose must also engage with the economic. At a macro level, global exclusionary issues like land rights, the North–South terms of trade and environment sustainability and protection are all clearly very closely tied to economic considerations. At a meso level too, there is space within the growing societal concern for and practice of economic regeneration and vocational education for a Community Education approach, its values, its epistemology and its methodology. It is reassuring here to note the increased development of both social learning and popular education initiatives with an eco-nomic as well as a social purpose (see Twelvetrees 1998, von Kotze 1998, MacPhail 1999). Even at a micro level, the place of 'desire' needs to be taken account of when educational activ-ities are increasingly being seen as consumer (and positional) goods in a marketplace empha-sizing educational choice as part of individual consumption (Field 1996: 137–8). Furthermore, in the context of a complex Risk Society, Community Educators, while maintaining their polit-ical commitment and value base, may also need to review the implications for contemporary practice of such stark polarities as Freire's 'education for liberation' versus 'education for domes-tication'. Indeed, in doing this, they may need to take greater account of a postmodern de-centred understanding of oppression where one person's domestication can also be another's liberation, for example in both the labour market and the extension of housing provision (see Johnston 1999: 177). Within the discourses of Community Education and Lifelong Learning, there are sufficient similarities, common ground and space for Community Educators to explore and develop their dialectical relationship in combating social exclusion. This also applies to another key aim: widening participation.

The discourse of Lifelong Learning emphasizes the need for widening participation, in the labour market, in education and training, as a consumer, as a responsible citizen. The issue of participation is also central to the discourse of Community Education: participa-tion in informal, non-formal and formal learning as well as community development and community action. Here, O'Hagan raises a critical question for Community Education about the link between participation and empowerment. In identifying differing participa-tory methods and structures within Community Education, ranging from an essentially conservative community consultation to more radical community control, he makes the point that an emphasis on participation does not necessarily mean greater social justice, equality, even democracy: '. . . by recasting the debate as between 'more participation' and 'less participation', attention is again diverted from examination of the ideological base of the type of participation proposed' (1987: 76). This might equally apply to a Lifelong Learning approach based on a Third Way philosophy. Its predominant focus on inclusion and participation has been criticized as involving too much of a slippage from economic to political equality (Phillips 1999). While all those educators with a commitment to greater democracy can agree with Giddens that all members of society should have civil and political rights and opportunities for involvement in society (1998: 102–3), this in itself may not lead to greater social justice or equality. It depends on the circumstances and context of this involvement, on the *terms of participation.*

In advocating 'life-long education', Giddens stresses the need for the development of 'cognitive and emotional competence' (1998: 125) as a way of ensuring greater and more effective participation within the labour force. On the face of it, this concept is not so very different from a contemporary Community Education focus on 'social learning':

> . . . learning how to build personal networks, learning to communicate about the dynamic and complex social conditions of late modern life and learning to develop new interactive routines
>
> (Van der Veen 1996: 6)

Van der Veen identifies two distinct discourses on social participation: a predominantly vocational one involving 'homo economicus', playing her/his part in maximizing material profits and a more liberal one, concerned with 'self-actualization' (1998: 180) which he believes has some relevance for Community Education. Of course, it is not just a question of vocational versus liberal or community approaches. In the context of widening participation, all of these can easily become over-paternalistic and prescriptive, if not patronizing. This can be equally true for the development of top-down labour market schemes which attempt to foster essentially adaptive 'social and life-skills' as for similarly adaptive and tokenistic approaches to participation within liberal or even Community Education. For this reason, in his attempts to renew the mission of Community Education in the context of global individualization, Van der Veen emphasizes key questions about links between lifestyle, personal networks and community participation, about competencies for participating in new forms of community and about the inter-relationship between informal learning and self-actualization (1998: 184) The key, once again, is the nature of the learning environment and its underlying values.

In the growing debate about widening participation, it is noticeable that old established Community Education terms like outreach, networks, target groups, learning from experience and a negotiated curriculum have been widely integrated into the more mainstream discourse of Lifelong Learning with its different emphases and purposes. There are clear dangers of incorporation and co-option here, with target groups becoming pathologized, networks professionalized, outreach reduced to mere technique, experience asset-stripped into disciplinary knowledge or mere competence and the curriculum negotiated only around the fringes as some kind of 'technology of consent' (Usher *et al.* 1997). In such a context, it ill behoves Community Educators to be too dogmatic about education or 'liberation' versus 'domestication', or to be over-purist or precious about their key values and language. As identified earlier these may well need to be re-viewed in the context of the increased individualization and pluralism of a Risk Society. However, this does not mean that this is not a vital site for struggle. On the contrary, a key contemporary task for Community Educators is to engage in both ideological and practical action in relation to Lifelong Learning.

In the case of the former, Foucault's analysis of the power/knowledge relationship offers some hope for counter-action:

> We must make allowance for the complex and unstable process whereby discourse can be both an instrument and an effect of power, but also a hindrance, a stumbling block, a point of resistance and a starting point for an opposing strategy.
>
> (quoted in Ball 1990: 18)

Within the discourse of Lifelong Learning, there is scope for Community Educators to tune in to, but also influence contemporary debates about widening participation and to place greater emphasis on informal, experiential and community-based learning. Key to this, of course, is the recognition and continued development of a more open-ended, egalitarian and reflexive epistemology, drawing from ideas of 'really useful knowledge', a problem-posing approach to learning and an issue-based curriculum. Such an emphasis can serve as a counter-point to more tokenistic or manipulative methods of participation or co-option and to re-emphasize the concept of cultural difference rather than deficit. It can also confirm:

> the view that adults bring something which derives both from their experience of adult life and from their status as citizens to the educational process; that adult education is based on dialogue rather than a mere transmission of knowledge and skill; that education is not only for personal development and advancement; that adult education constructs knowledge and does not merely pass it on; that adult education has a dialectical and organic relationship with social movements.
>
> (Jackson 1995: 184)

In this way, a Community Education approach can support and foster 'associations... [where] men and women learn to respect and trust others, fulfil obligations and press their claims communicatively' (Welton 1997: 72). This connects with the aim of fostering active citizenship.

One of most important agendas for Lifelong Learning is education for active citizenship. This can focus on the citizen as consumer, as was the case with the promotion of an essentially consumerist Citizen's Charter by the UK Major government in the mid 1990s; it can comple-ment efforts towards decentralization and the devolution of power from central to more regio-nal government where different models and processes apply in the UK, US and the European Union; and it can apply to efforts to make local government more responsive and accountable to its citizens. There is some overlap here with Community Education's traditional focus on active citizenship in relation to community development, community action and community empowerment, with both looking to extend and develop different forms of partici-patory democracy in new situations. However, there is a difference in the primary context for developing active citizenship. Whereas the main reference point from a Lifelong Learning per-spective is that of the economy and the state, Community Education's starting point is in civil society.

Here it may be useful to look more closely at civil society as it is beginning to attract increas-ing attention from a Lifelong Learning perspective. Giddens sees the renewal of civil society as being a key aspect of the Third Way he advocates, involving, amongst other things, commu-nity renewal through harnessing local initiative, support of the work of the third sector, and government and civil society working in partnership (1998: 78–86). This emphasis seems to accord very largely with the aims and purposes of social purpose Community Education, so the promotion of learning for active citizenship within civil society may be a key area of mutual interest and synergy. In exploring this possible common ground, it may be useful to identify and problematize different understandings of civil society.

Historically there have been different understandings of and emphases in civil society between Right and Left, between the former East and former West. For example, those towards the Right are interested in civil society as it reflects a primarily apolitical arena to develop civic virtues like self-sacrifice, duty and service for others, an arena separate from but still understood to be within the overall framework of a free market society (Green 1993: ix). In contrast, the Left, drawing more directly from Gramsci (1986) identifies civil society as a sector of public life outside of the directly regulated political and economic spheres where there is sufficient relative autonomy and subversive space to develop counter-hegemonic action. Equally, in post-communist East Central Europe, there is an emphasis on civil society providing a venue for rediscovering individual civil rights and space for the development of an entrepreneurial spirit and culture after the passive dependency engendered by communist state centralism (Bron *et al.* 1998), while in parts of Western Europe and the USA, there is a concern with community and public space as a way of counteracting an excessively individualistic ideology and an emphasis on the role and potential of quasi-political social movements in helping to change society (Gustavsson *et al.* 1997: 522). While the discourse of Lifelong Learning looks to transcend traditional divisions between Left and Right (and for that matter, East and West), it could be said that its emphasis on active citizenship in relation to social inclusion and human capital draws largely from the first and third of the understandings above. Equally social purpose Community Education, with its longstanding interest in and connections with social movements is more rooted in understandings two and four. However, the main thrust of this chapter is not to over-polarize the perspectives and approaches of Lifelong Learning and Community Education. Thus, this analysis will be used as a basis for exploring both similarities and differences in their respective engagements with active citizenship.

One area where Community Education can perhaps key into the Lifelong Learning agenda is in relation to the concept of 'voice'. Speaking from an ideological standpoint similar to that social purpose adult education, Aronowitz and Giroux make the point that:

> voice provides a critical referent for analysing how people are made voiceless in particular settings by not being allowed to speak, or being allowed to say what has already been spoken, and how they learn to silence themselves... voices forged in opposition and struggle provide the crucial conditions by which subordinate individuals and groups reclaim their own memories, stories and histories as part of an on-going attempt to challenge those power structures that attempt to silence them.
>
> (Aronowitz and Giroux 1991: 101)

Community education offers a place and space for the 'voice' that is a crucial part of participation and active citizenship. Such an approach and emphasis on 'voice' might also impact on the more mainstream and marketized discourse of Lifelong Learning within an increasingly diverse Risk Society, where there is scope within an increasingly differentiated consumerism for educators to work with and respond to the particular demands, interests and circumstances of new social movements. This holds out the prospect of a more critical and participative approach to the conventional wisdom of needs-meeting and a way of connecting the agendas of new social movements to wider social, economic and cultural inequalities and the polarization of the marketplace.

In fostering learning for active citizenship, a further investigation may also be necessary into different understandings of and responses to the idea of a 'democratic deficit'. A recent UK government research programme sees this 'democratic deficit' as being characterized by: widespread citizen distrust in the institutions and actors of the state; a growth in protest activities; a lack of public confidence in existing official procedures for participation and consultation; citizen apathy and a lack of voluntary activity in communities exposed to high levels of unemployment and social deprivation (ESRC 1998: 3). Indeed, this analysis strikes a chord with similar concerns arising from the 1996 US Presidential campaign (Henderson and Salmon 1998: 3) and from the 1999 elections to the European Parliament where several national voting figures reached an all-time low. Of course, it is in complete contrast with behaviour in newly democratic, or would-be democratic states like South Africa or East Timor!

In relation to ideas of a growing democratic deficit, certainly in the more affluent North, crucial questions are whether voter apathy only reflects wider cultural changes in civic activity within a contemporary Risk Society, what this means for the development of active citizenship and what is the role of learning in promoting this. Certainly, within civil society, there is growing evidence (see Dekeyser 1999, Elsdon 1998, Walters 1997, Merrifield 1997, Crowther *et al*. 1999) to suggest a current growth in active citizenship within community and voluntary organizations, social movements and social action groups which belies any idea of a democratic deficit. This also raises questions about the place of adult learning in relation to active citizenship, the different approaches of Lifelong Learning and Community Education and their respective relationships to mainstream policy. In differentiating between, and learning from their different approaches, a key issue is the tension between technical agency and political agency in working in civil society. The former approach is more obviously compatible with a Lifelong Learning perspective. It means working on a 'consultancy-type' basis, providing predominantly technical and methodological skills when they are requested. In such a vein, Elsdon (1998) suggests that voluntary organizations in the UK are in need of further information and training, and, in the community/voluntary sector in the UK, this way of working is reflected in a growing emphasis on 'leadership training', 'needs analysis' and 'capacity building' where a new industry of outside consultants has grown up to provide technical and managerial support to a range of organizations, predominantly within civil society.

This approach has the advantage of explicitly recognizing and respecting the autonomy and integrity of learners in civil society. However, its market perspective makes it more difficult to succeed in engaging with those who are not yet in a position to identify or articulate their needs in the first place, or just cannot afford to engage with such consultants except on a subsidized, and potentially colonized basis. In contrast to this technical/functional role is a more explicit and interventionist political agency, more akin to the values and purposes of social purpose Community Education. Here, a notable development is the recent resurgence of Popular Education movements. The Popular Education Forum for Scotland identifies itself as being 'overtly political and critical of the status quo' and seeks to forge a direct link between education and social action, pursue a collective pedagogy and develop a curriculum which comes out of the concrete experience and material interests of people in communities of resistance and struggle (Martin 1999). Indeed, this approach is similar to other Popular Education movements in, for example, Spain, Australia and Northern Ireland. This approach has the advantage of more directly addressing inequality while also more explicitly recognizing experience and working with difference. However, it may be susceptible to charges of preaching only to the converted, of following its own predetermined agendas, if it does not also engage democratically, reflexively and humbly with the agendas of different groups within civil society. Furthermore, its explicitly collectivist focus may also mean that it misses out on engaging critically with certain aspects of the individualization of a Risk Society and its very specific focus on civil society may mean that it does not impact on the relationship between civil society and the state.

In relation to the fostering of active citizenship through learning, there are clear differences in the respective approaches of Lifelong Learning and Community Education. Nevertheless, a Lifelong Learning perspective, in moving beyond mere market 'neutrality', might usefully learn from a Community Education methodology and epistemology in the way it can engage with and respond to excluded groups in civil society and beyond. Equally Community Educators might also learn from a broader, more market-related Lifelong Learning to extend its field of operations beyond an over-separatist conception of civil society, engage with a wider range of learners, for example some of those in work-related learning, and try to respond more directly to the individualization of society.

In the context of individualization, there is also further scope for broader educational networking and animation work within a Community Education approach. This can serve, on the one hand, to acknowledge and build on different individual pursuits and explore common interests and common ground, and, on the other, to pick up on the phenomenon that, within a Risk Society, individuals may need to get together to respond collectively to new and changing circumstances, threats and opportunities in 'acting in defence of the public realm' (Jarvis 1997: 63). At the same time, in exploring and problematizing the relationship between civil society and the state, it may be advisable to try to reframe the inter-connections between Community Education's primary focus on informal, experiential and often collective learning in civil society and Lifelong Learning's broader connections with more formal, individualized and state-controlled learning. There is scope to tune into and try to recast the current discourse of Lifelong Learning to place greater emphasis on informal, experiential and community-based learning as a way of inspiring, influencing and revitalizing formal education and with a view towards its further democratization, and diversification.

Conclusion

The idea of Lifelong Learning is attractive, powerful and politically expedient... but still developing. Community Educators should welcome its growing prominence and influence for the new emphasis it places on learning, particularly learning beyond the formal education system; and for the opportunities if offers for discussion and development of a diversity of learning approaches, new constituencies of learners and closer connections between learning and action. While its underlying values and policy reference points are different from those of Community Education, there is sufficient common ground with the aims, starting points and methods of Lifelong Learning for a useful interchange to be established and developed, both at a theoretical and practical level. In this process, Community Education can be proud of its values and historical social purpose, its distinctive epistemology and methodologies yet also self-critical and reflexive about their development in the context of a contemporary Risk Society. In this way, it may be possible to engage critically but productively with the discourse of Lifelong Learning and in so doing, serve to challenge, diversify and radicalize it.

References

Alheit P, 1999, 'On a Contradictory Way to the "Learning Society": A Critical Approach' in *Studies in the Education of Adults* 31.1, 66–82

Allman P, 1987, 'Paulo Freire's Education Approach: A Struggle for Meaning' in Allen G, Bastiani J, Martin I and Richards K (Eds) *Community Education: An Agenda for Educational Reform*, Milton Keynes, Open University Press, 214–37

Aronowitz S and Giroux H, 1991, *Policy and Policy-making in Education*, London, Routledge

Ball SJ, 1990, *Politics and Policy-Making in Education*, London, Routledge

Baptiste I, 1999, 'Beyond Lifelong Learning: A Call to Civically Responsible Change' in *International Journal of Lifelong Learning* 18.2, 94–102

Beck U, Giddens A and Lash S, 1994, *Reflexive Modernization*, Cambridge, Polity

Brookfield S, 1983, *Adult Learners, Adult Education and the Community*, Milton Keynes, Open University Press

Bron A, Field J and Kurantowicz E (Eds) 1998, *Adult Education and Democratic Citizenship II*, Krakow, ESREA/Wroclaw University

CREA, 1999, ' "Educacion Popular" and the Development of Spanish Communities', Barcelona, Popular Education Network

Crowther J, Martin I and Shaw M (Eds) 1999, *Popular Education and Social Movements in Scotland Today*, Leicester, NIACE

Dekeyser L, 1999, 'Adult Education and Social Movements: the significance and workings of social movements as part of the civil society, an approach from the angle of adult and continuing education' in Merrill B (Ed) *The Final Frontier: Exploring Spaces in the Education of Adults*, Warwick, Proceedings of the 29th SCUTREA Annual Conference, 69–76

Delors J, 1996, *Learning: The Treasure Within*, Paris, UNESCO

DfEE, 1998, *The Learning Age: A Renaissance for a New Britain*, London, DfEE Publications

Elsdon K, 1998, 'Voluntary Organisations and Communities: A Critique and Suggestions' in Bron A, Field J and Kurantowicz E (Eds) *Adult Education and Democratic Citizenship II*, Krakow, ESREA/ Wroclaw University, 143–56

ESRC, 1998, *Programme Specification for Democracy and Participation Research Programme*, Swindon, ESRC

Etzioni A, 1993, *The Spirit of Community*, London, Fontana

Field J, 1989, 'Citizens, Enterprise and Community' in *Journal of Community Education* 7.3, 23–26

Field J, 1996 'Open Learning and Consumer Culture' in Raggatt P, Edwards R and Small N (Eds) *The Learning Society: Challenges and Trends*, London, Routledge, 136–50

Field J, 1998, 'Globalization, Social Capital and Lifelong Learning: Connections for Our Times?' in Bron A, Field J and Kurantowicz E (Eds) *Adult Education and Democratic Citizenship II*, Krakow, ESREA/Wroclaw University, 27–40

Field J, 1999, 'Human Capital and Social Capital in Northern Ireland: Linking Schools Achievement and Lifelong Learning' in *Irish Educational Studies*, 18, 234–47

Fieldhouse R, 1992, 'Tradition in British University Adult Education and the WEA' in Duke C (Ed) *Liberal Adult Education: Perspectives and Projects*, Warwick, Continuing Education Research Centre, University of Warwick, 11–14

Fletcher, C, 1980, 'The Theory of Community and its Relation to Adult Education' in J L Thompson (Ed) *Adult Education for a Change*, London, Hutchinson, 65–82

Fletcher C, 1987, 'The Meaning of Community' in Allen G, Bastiani J, Martin I and Richards K (Eds) *Community Education: An Agenda for Educational Reform*, Milton Keynes, Open University Press, 33–49

Freire P, 1972, *Pedagogy of the Oppressed*, Middlesex, Penguin

Giddens A, 1994, 'Living in a Post-Traditional Society in Beck U, Giddens A and Lash S, 1994, *Reflexive Modernization*, Cambridge, Polity, 56–109

Giddens A, 1998, *The Third Way: The Renewal of Social Democracy*, Cambridge, Polity

Giddens A and Pierson C, 1998, *Conversations with Anthony Giddens: Making Sense of Modernity*, Cambridge, Polity

Gramsci A, 1986, *Selections from Prison Notebooks*, edited and translated by Q Hoare and G Novell Smith, London, Lawrence and Wishart

Green DG, 1993, *Reinventing Civil Society*, London, IEA

Gustavsson B, Larrson S and Rubensen K, 1997, 'Civil Society and Swedish Popular Adult Education', in Armstrong A, Miller N and Zukas M (Eds) *Crossing Borders, Breaking Boundaries*, London, SCUTREA/Birkbeck College, 522–30

Henderson P and Salmon H, 1998, *Signposts to Local Democracy*, London, Community Development Foundation

Illich I and Verne E, 1976, *Imprisoned in the Global Classroom*, London, Readers and Writers Co-operative

Jackson K, 1980, 'Some Fallacies in Community Education and Their Consequences in Working-Class Areas' in Fletcher C and Thompson T (Eds) *Issues in Community Education*, Lewes, Falmer

Jackson K, 1995, 'Popular Education and the State: A New Look at the Community Debate' in Mayo M and Thompson J (Eds) *Adult Learning, Critical Intelligence and Social Change*, Leicester, NIACE, 182–201

Jackson K, 1997, 'The State, Civil Society and the Economy: Adult Education in Britain' in Walters S (Ed) 1997, *Globalisation, Adult Education and Training: Impacts and Issues*, Leicester, NIACE, 47–56

Jansen T and Van Der Veen R, 1997, 'Individualization, the New Political Spectrum and the Functions of Adult Education' in *International Journal of Lifelong Education* 16.1, 264–6

Jansen T, Finger M and Wildemeersch D, 1998, 'Reframing Reflectivity in View of Adult Education for Social Responsibility' in Wildemeersch D, Finger M, Jansen T (Eds) *Adult Education and Social Responsibility*, Frankfurt am Main, Peter Lang, 237–48

Jarvis P, 1997, *Ethics and Education for Adults*, Leicester, NIACE

Johnson R, 1988, 'Really Useful Knowledge 1790–1850: Memories for Education in the 1980s' in Lovett T (Ed) *Radical Approaches to Adult Education*, Routledge, London, 3–34

Johnston R, 1999, 'Adult Learning for Citizenship: Towards a Reconstruction of the Social Purpose Tradition', in *International Journal of Lifelong Education*, 18.3, 175–90

Korsgaard O, 1997, 'Internationalisation and Globalisation' in Korsgaard O (Ed) *Adult Learning and the Challenges of the 21st Century*, Odense, Association for World Education, 10–15

Lovett T, 1975, *Adult Education, Community Development and the Working Class*, London, Ward Lock Educational

MacPhail I, 1999, 'History, Justice and the Law: The Struggle of the Assynt Crofters' in Crowther J, Martin I and Shaw M (Eds) *Popular Education and Social Movements in Scotland Today*, Leicester, NIACE, 175–85

Martin I, 1987, 'Community Education: Towards a Theoretical Explanation' in Allen G, Bastiani J, Martin I and Richards K (Eds) *Community Education: An Agenda for Educational Reform*, Milton Keynes, Open University Press, 9–32

Martin I, 1996, 'Community Education: The Dialectics of Development' in Fieldhouse R (Ed) *A History of Modern British Adult Education*, Leicester, NIACE, 109–41

Martin I, 1999, 'Introductory Essay: Popular Education and Social Movements in Scotland Today' in Crowther J, Martin I and Shaw M (Eds) *Popular Education and Social Movements in Scotland Today*, Leicester, NIACE, 1–28

Meekosha H, 1993, 'The Bodies Politic: Equality, Difference and Community Practice' in Butcher H, Glen A, Henderson P and Smith J (Eds) *Community and Public Policy*, London, Pluto, 171–93

Merrifield J, 1997, 'Finding Our Lodestone Again: Democracy, the Civil Society and Adult Education' in Armstrong P, Miller N and Zukas M (Eds) *Crossing Borders, Breaking Boundaries*, London, University of London, 321–5

O'Hagan B, 1987, 'Community Education in Britain: Some Myths and Their Consequences' in Allen G, Bastiani J, Martin I and Richards K (Eds) *Community Education: An Agenda for Educational Reform*, Milton Keynes, Open University Press, 70–82

Peters J M and Bell B, 1987, 'Horton of Highlander' in Jarvis P (Ed) *Twentieth Century Thinkers in Adult Education*, London, Routledge, 243–64

Phillips A, 1999, *Which Equalities Matter*, Cambridge, Polity

Plant R, 1974, *Community and Ideology*, London, Routledge and Kegan Paul

Putnam D, 1995, 'Bowling Alone; America's Declining Social Capital', in *Journal of Democracy* 6(1), 65–78

Schuller T, 1998, 'Three Steps Towards a Learning Society' in *Studies in the Education of Adults* 30.1, 11–20

Schuller T and Field J, 1998, 'Social Capital, Human Capital and the Learning Society' in *International Journal of Lifelong Education* 17.4, 226–35

Taylor R, and Ward K, 1986, 'Adult Education and the Working Class: Policies, Practice and Future Priorities for Community Adult Education' in Ward K and Taylor R (Eds) *Adult Education and the Working Class*, London, Croom Helm, 169–91

Twelvetrees A (Ed) 1998, *Community Education Development: Rhetoric or Reality*, London, Community Development Foundation

UNESCO, 1997, *Confintea V: Agenda for the Future of Adult Learning*, Hamburg, UNESCO Institute

Usher R, Bryant I and Johnston R, 1997, *Adult Education and the Postmodern Challenge*, London, Routledge

Van der Veen R, 1996, 'The Risk of Social Exclusion and Informal Learning' in *International Conference on Experiential Learning*, Cape Town, South Africa

Van der Veen R, 1998, 'The Transformation of Community Education' in Wildermeersch D, Finger M and Jansen T (Eds) *Adult Education and Social Responsibility*, Berlin, Peter Lang, 175–85

Vincent C, 1983, 'Education for the Community' in the *British Journal of Educational Studies* 41.4: 366–77

Von Kotze A, 1998, 'Adult Education and Training in the Framework of Reconstruction and Development in South Africa', in Wildemeersch D, Finger M, Jansen T (Eds) *Adult Education and Social Responsibility*, Frankfurt am Main, Peter Lang, 151–74

Walters S (Ed) 1997, *Globalisation, Adult Education and Training: Impacts and Issues*, Leicester, NIACE

Welton M, 1987, 'Vivisecting the Nightingale: Reflections on Adult Education as an Object of Study' in *Studies in the Education of Adults* 19.1, 46–69

Welton M, 1997, 'Repair, Defend, Invent: Civil Societarian Adult Education faces the 21st Century' in Korsgaard O (Ed) *Adult Learning and the Challenges of the 21st Century*, Odense, Association for World Education, 67–75

Westwood S, 1992, 'When Class became Community in Adult Education' in Rattansi A and Reeder D (Eds) *Rethinking Radical Education*, London, Lawrence and Wishart, 222–48

Wildemeersch D and Jansen T (Eds) 1992, *Adult Education, Experiential Learning and Social Change: The Postmodern Challenge*, Belgium, VUGA Gravenhage

3 The death of mass higher education and the birth of lifelong learning

Peter Scott

The argument set out in this chapter can be starkly stated. Between the late 1970s and early 1990s Britain was persuaded to accept mass higher education—absent-mindedly, reluctantly and incompletely. But, almost before it has been properly established, this new form of higher education now runs the risk of becoming an anachronism, over before it has properly begun. Although still regarded by many traditionalists as an oxymoron ('higher education' cannot be 'mass'), it is not sufficiently flexible to accommodate new demands which can no longer even approximately be labelled 'academic' but instead reflect the urgent and volatile imperatives of the emerging Knowledge Society. Mass higher education remains rooted in institutions—it has boundaries however extensive and however permeable. As a result it is being superseded by 'lifelong learning', although how long even this diffuse but discrete category can survive in a society in which 'learning' is just one element within wider patterns of individual identification, social realization, economic actualization and cultural consumption (all, of course, intertwined) is doubtful.

This is not a sudden departure but the continuation of a long revolution in British post-secondary education. Until 1960 university education was clearly distinguished from other forms of post-secondary education. During the 1960s a new administrative category 'higher education' emerged which embraced the traditional universities, advanced further education (colleges of technology, business, and art and design, many of which were amalgamated to form the new polytechnics) and teacher training (initially provided in freestanding colleges of education). In the late 1980s many further education colleges, which provided lower level vocational education, absorbed adult education institutes which up to that time had been an independent sector. By the 1990s, therefore, Britain possessed a two-tier system of post-school education—higher education, embracing both the university sector (now enlarged to include the former polytechnics) and other smaller and more specialist colleges; and further education into which many of the adult education colleges (and other providers of continuing education) had been absorbed. Most recently, since the election of a New Labour Government in 1997, these two categories—higher education and further education—have begun to be subsumed into a new, and transgressive, category 'lifelong learning'.

This chapter is divided into three sections. First, the evolution of new administrative and institutional classifications within, and of new conceptualizations of, post-secondary education in Britain will be discussed. Why is 'higher education' running up against the limits of its conceptual (and practical?) usefulness? Next a series of contemporary developments will be considered which go beyond 'mass higher education', at any rate as currently conceived and constituted—the creation of the new University for Industry (UfI); the growth of so-called corporate universities (which, in many respects, are anti-universities); the growth of higher education 'outside higher education' (in other words, higher education courses which are offered by institutions other than universities or other recognized higher education institutions); and the development of 'learning partnerships' and other forms of collaboration between further and higher education, between public and private sectors and between education and other sub-systems of modern society. The concluding section will discuss whether the impact of these changes on existing institutional structures justifies the view that a new paradigm of 'lifelong learning' is emerging which will supersede the traditional taxonomies of post-secondary education in Britain.

New maps of sectors and institutions

Comprehensivization has been creeping up the British education system during the past half century—from primary education to secondary schools and finally into further and higher education. Primary schools have always been comprehensive institutions, in the sense that they enrol pupils of all abilities and from all social and ethnic groups; they have never been truly comprehensive because they reflect the different social compositions of the communities they serve. In the 1960s as a result of the Plowden Report even greater emphasis was placed on the comprehensive—and egalitarian—character of primary education by discouraging the separation of pupils into separate 'streams' according to their ability. Although in recent years this process has been partially reversed, the primary school remains a stronghold of comprehensive values.

Secondary education, in contrast, has been a battle-field where enthusiasts for comprehensive schools and defenders of selective schools have frequently clashed. In the 1960s all local education authorities were required to reorganize their schools on a comprehensive pattern; in most cases they complied and grammar and secondary modern (and a very few secondary technical) schools disappeared to be replaced by comprehensive schools for all pupils in their areas regardless of academic ability. In essence this was a bi-partisan policy on which both Conservative and Labour parties were agreed. It was Margaret Thatcher, in her first Cabinet post as Secretary of State for Education between 1970 and 1974, who closed most grammar schools. However, in secondary education pockets of selectivity remained. Independent schools continued to select their pupils. Although the former direct-grant grammar schools were absorbed into the state system in the 1960s, grant-maintained schools independent of LEA control were established two decades later (only to be reabsorbed into the LEA system after 1997). Although not overtly selective on academic grounds, many GM schools acquired at least the aura of 'social selectivity'. More important perhaps was the persistence of 'streaming' of pupils by ability within secondary schools. The egalitarian practices still common in many primary schools never took such deep root in secondary education.

Education beyond the age of 16, when compulsory schooling ends, appeared for many years to be the exception to the comprehensive rule. Universities remained aloof from the rest of higher education; higher education continued to be distinct from further education; the education of 16- to 19-year-olds was divided into an academic stream, typically provided in school sixth forms, and a vocational stream, provided by technical colleges; in the education of adults a similar division persisted between liberal adult education and continuing professional development; and, outside the formal education arena, there was a parallel system of training in industry, business and the professions. Post-school education appeared to be characterized not only by a diversity of institutions and sectors but also by a heterogeneity of educational values and missions.

However, the same pattern of convergence can also be observed in post-secondary education. Until the early 1960s 'higher education' was purely an administrative category; it did not describe a distinctive and coherent sector of the educational system. The traditional universities received their funding from the Treasury through the (former) University Grants Committee (UGC); the then Ministry of Education had no competence in the area of university affairs. In the post-secondary arena the Ministry's remit only extended to further and adult education, although a distinctive sector of so-called 'advanced further education' had developed since 1945 which provided courses and qualifications equivalent to those offered in the universities. In 1961 the Government established a Committee of Inquiry into Higher Education chaired by Lord Robbins; this was the first occasion when higher education as a whole—advanced further education and teacher training as well as universities—was considered (Robbins 1963). Three years later, largely in response to the Robbins report, the Ministry of Education was replaced by the Department of Education and Science (DES) which took over the Treasury's previous responsibility for funding universities. As a result, for the first time the budget for universities formed part of the state's overall budget for education. In a further move towards greater integration the new DES was also made responsible for funding research in universities, through the research councils which previously had been responsible to other ministries. So it can be argued that only in the 1960s did a distinctive higher education sector come into existence.

In the course of the 1970s and 1980s the new sector further cohered. Many of the colleges of technology and art which had comprised 'advanced further education' had been amalgamated to form the new polytechnics which were established as complementary (and, later, rival) institutions to the traditional universities. The polytechnics were further strengthened by the acquisition of many formerly independent colleges of education. In the 1980s their status was enhanced when they were removed from the control of local education authorities and established as independent corporations. During the same period the tempo of national planning in the higher education sector increased. At first two parallel agencies operated—in the case of the traditional universities the UGC which already existed; and the new National Advisory Body for Public Sector Higher Education (NAB) in the case of the polytechnics and other higher education colleges. These agencies were later replaced by the Universities Funding Council (UFC) and the Polytechnics and Colleges Funding Council (PCFC) respectively. But the case for a single agency was growing stronger all the time. Eventually in 1992 the UFC and the PCFC were replaced by the Higher Education Funding Council for England (HEFCE), although separate councils were established in Scotland and Wales. At the same time the polytechnics were re-designated as universities bringing to an end the so-called the binary system of higher education and ushering in instead an age of comprehensive higher education.

However, throughout this period (non-advanced) further education remained a separate sector. Until the 1990s further education colleges remained subject to the control of local education authorities, providing not only vocational education of a traditional variety but increasingly also an alternative to upper-secondary education in school sixth forms. In addition some FE colleges offered courses leading to more advanced qualifications, so giving rise to the confusing in-between category of 'higher education in further education'. In 1992, like the polytechnics in the 1980s, they were established as independent corporations and a national agency, the Further Education Funding Council (FEFC), was set up to manage the new sector; local particularities were sharply reduced and a more homogeneous, and more distinct, sector emerged.

At the same time the rapid expansion of higher education also stimulated the growth of advanced courses in FE colleges. As a result the once-clear demarcation between further education and higher education tended to become much fuzzier. As organizations FE colleges and universities now had much more in common, and the colleges acquired a more significant stake in higher education. This process of convergence has continued. In the post-school arena less emphasis is now placed on the 'level' of courses (i.e. advanced or non-advanced) and on their institutional setting (i.e. whether provided by FE colleges or universities) and more on credit frameworks and progression pathways which focus on the needs of the learner. The effect has been to produce a shift away from sectoral and institutional categories, such as 'higher education' or 'further education', towards broader classifications of educational activity, such as 'lifelong learning'.

The third sectoral category, adult education, has also tended to be absorbed into this broader classification. Until the 1960s a clear distinction was drawn between liberal adult education, provided by universities in separate extramural departments, independent (but state-sponsored) agencies such as the Workers Educational Association (WEA) or local education authorities, and continuing education with a more distinctive vocational focus, much of which was provided in FE colleges and universities. During the next two decades this distinction tended to disappear and a new category—adult and continuing education—became established. The special earmarked funding which some universities had received for providing liberal adult education through their extramural departments was abolished. Instead it was included in general university funding. This process of 'mainstreaming' led to fears that the distinctive ethos of liberal adult education in which individual enlightenment rather than certification was the goal would be lost. In practice many of the students who previously would have taken adult education courses had now been absorbed into an expanding higher education system, typically in arts and social science faculties.

At the same time the distinction between continuing vocational education programmes and postgraduate courses has also become blurred. Many postgraduate courses are no longer taken by students who intend to embark on academic or scientific careers; instead they offer a continuation of undergraduate study or post-experience learning opportunities. During the 1990s many FE colleges, in order to increase student numbers (and so budgets), have taken over formerly independent adult education institutions. In higher education the increasing number of older students and the growing popularity of part-time study have tended to erode the distinction between 'initial' and 'continuing' education. As a result, even the wider category of 'adult and continuing education' has become more anachronistic, yielding (as 'further education' and 'higher education' have done) to a catch-all classification of 'lifelong learning'.

Post-secondary education, therefore, does not appear to be an exception to the general drift towards comprehensivization which has been characteristic of British school education. First, there has been a clear trend towards the establishment of more comprehensive institutions. There are many examples. In the former non-university sector of higher education specialist colleges were amalgamated to form more comprehensive multi-faculty polytechnics. Later the polytechnics were redesignated as universities, so enlarging the scope and mission of universities. Similarly FE colleges have evolved from being narrowly based technical colleges offering vocational courses into community colleges providing a variety of academic, vocational and adult education programmes. The same trend can be observed in changing policy, funding and management frameworks. The UGC and NAB were succeeded by the UFC and PCFC, to be succeeded in turn by the HEFCE. Most recently plans have been announced to abolish the FEFC along with the Training and Enterprise Councils (TECs), which had been responsible for articulating public and private provision for vocational training. As a result the demarcation between the public education system and what Americans call the 'corporate classroom' has been effectively abandoned. Indeed the broader distinction between all education and training on the one hand, and, on the other, processes of business re-engineering and economic development, is also being eroded.

Second, the various categories of post-secondary education have been incorporated into wider and more comprehensive classifications. Indeed it can be argued that the seven (or more) categories which were used in the 1960s—universities, teacher training, advanced further education, further education, liberal adult education and continuing education—have been reduced to, in effect, a single classification—lifelong learning. So comprehensivization has operated both at the organizational and conceptual levels. This conceptual reordering has been at least as significant as the administrative and institutional reorganization of the post-school system. Indeed it can be argued that it was the former, the increasingly comprehensive images of post-secondary education, which determined the latter, the drive towards more comprehensive patterns of organization, rather than the other way round. The growing recognition of the interconnections between different sectors first eroded the boundaries between these sectors and is now leading to their abandonment.

Beyond mass higher education

During the last decade—and with increasing velocity since the election of a Labour Government in 1997—a number of specific initiatives have been taken which have tended to reinforce this dissolution of traditional demarcations in post-secondary education. Some, such as the University for Industry, have been high-profile 'headline' initiatives deliberately conceived as radical departures—ruptures, even—from the 'old order'. Others have arisen through the accumulation of specific measures which together reflect broad policy thrusts; a good example is the government's determination to give priority to sub-degree two-year diploma courses in higher education which, in turn, has focused attention on the role of FE colleges within a mass system. Others again have been a combination of aspirational rhetoric and organizational tinkering; a good example here is the high-level emphasis on collaboration between agencies, institutions and sectors which has been reflected—imperfectly—in new bureaucratic regimes comprising new funding and administrative arrangements.

The University for Industry (UfI)

The UfI is a misnomer—in the sense that it is not intended to be, even in the most approximate sense, a university and 'university' is unlikely to be included in its final title. But the use of 'university' in its working title and initial prospectus is both suggestive—and, arguably, transgressive. It is suggestive because it indicates the growing emphasis on 'branding', a common even obsessive preoccupation in the 'market' sector but a new departure in the public sector; 'university' is an instantly recognizable and highly prestigious brand. It is transgressive because it reveals a willingness to use the 'university' title to draw attention to the needs of previously neglected forms of education and training—and even to subvert traditional hierarchies of institutional esteem.

The UfI was launched shortly after the Labour Party's 1997 election victory. A prospectus (again, the corporate language may be suggestive) was issued in 1998. Potential partners were invited to express their interest in working with the UfI. The formal launch of the UfI is scheduled to take place in 2000. It has two strategic objectives:

- To stimulate demand for lifelong learning among businesses and individuals;
- To promote the availability of, and improve access to, relevant, high-quality and innovative learning, in particular through the use of information and communications technologies (UfI 1998).

Both objectives need to be decoded to reveal the intentions that lie behind the establishment of the UfI. Two words in the first objective are significant—'stimulate' and 'businesses'. The former suggests the crucial importance of marketing in the conception of the UfI. Indeed, it has been argued that the UfI is essentially a marketing organization; the actual delivery of courses and training will be undertaken by the UfI's partners (sub-contractors? suppliers?) which will be predominantly FE colleges but will also include some private and corporate training organizations and a few universities. At the heart of the UfI is the belief that the application of state-of-the-art marketing techniques can dramatically increase the demand for lifelong learning. Certainly impressive targets have been set. The aim is that by 2002, 2.5 million people will be using the UfI as a source of information about educational and training opportunities and more than 600,000 will be following UfI-branded or commissioned programmes.

The second word 'businesses' (before 'individuals') suggests the intimate links between the UfI project and the government's drive for greater economic competitiveness (skills rather than people are the primary focus) and also its commitment to stimulating partnerships between the public and private sectors, as opposed to concentrating on the development of the state system of education. The list of UfI priorities underlines the emphasis on economic development. In the first few years these priorities are expected to be remedying deficits in basic skills, upgrading skills in information and communications technologies, stimulating demand for training in small and medium-sized businesses, and meeting the needs of specific industrial sectors (such as automotive components, multimedia, environmental technology and services, and distributive and retail trades). This list demonstrates how distant the UfI's mission is from that of the 'university', even in the context of mass higher education.

The key words in the second objective are 'access', 'high-quality', 'innovative' and—inevitably—'information and communication technologies'. There is little space in the UfI vision for conventional delivery of education and training, whether in terms of institutional settings or traditional face-to-face teaching. Instead the emphasis is all on 'distributed' delivery at a diversity of 'sites', many of which will not be colleges or universities, and on 'distance' delivery through computers and other media. The emphasis on quality is not simply a ritual mantra; instead it suggests another role which the UfI will play, as the provider of quality kite-marks for the training programmes it brands and/or commissions.

There continues to be considerable scepticism about the future of the UfI. Serious doubts have been expressed about the project's capacity to increase demand when most indicators suggest that, in many key areas, the supply of education and training opportunities already exceeds the demand from both individuals and employers. These doubts about the UfI brand's ability to attract new customers have tended to undermine the enthusiasm with which training providers, colleges and universities will enter into partnerships with the UfI. The reliance on 'distributed' delivery and information and communications technologies has also been questioned. Although access to computers and use of the Internet are both increasing at a rapid pace, those people with the most limited access may represent the largest pool of unsatisfied demand for lifelong learning; those best equipped to access UfI resources are also best placed to benefit from existing, and more conventional, education and training opportunities. Finally, the sheer diversity of potential UfI programmes, it is argued, may undermine the establishment of a clear UfI brand (on which increased demand relies) and also the UfI's ability to maintain the quality of those programmes. Critics point out that frequent attempts have been made to reproduce the success of the Open University in a wider post-secondary domain, so far without clear success. However, there can be no doubt about the Government's determination to ensure the success of the UfI. Substantial resources have been allocated and high-level appointments have also been made—Lord (Ron) Dearing, chairman of the recent National Inquiry into the Future of Higher Education as chairman, and Dr Anne Wright, a successful vice-chancellor, as chief executive.

Corporate universities

Recently a great deal of interest has been expressed in the development of corporate universities, although the scale of corporate intervention in higher education remains comparatively modest and its scale limited. Corporate universities, like Internet companies, have received perhaps disproportionate attention—and for the same reason: both are presumed to represent the wave of the future. There are four prominent examples of corporate universities in the United Kingdom (Middlehurst 2000).

1.   Unipart U (University) was established in 1993 and offers about 200 courses, all work-related and concentrated in areas such as IT, supplier management and customer service. The philosophy of Unipart U is neatly summed up in the following quotation: 'The courses are designed to be practical so that attendees "train for work" and can apply "this morning's learning to this afternoon's job"' (Unipart 1990).
2.   British Aerospace Virtual University is a more ambitious project, although still in the early stages of development. Although it has much in common with Unipart U, there are important differences. First, because of its commitment to advanced technologies (and, indeed, its engagement with cutting-edge science), the Virtual University offers a wider range of, arguably more sophisticated, programmes. Second, for this reason, more of its work is done in partnership with existing universities. Third, the aim is to maintain 'a balance between academic content and the unique requirements of the company' (BAVU 1998).
3.   British Airways Engineering Programme, as its title suggests, is more limited in scope. The company recruits a small number of trainees who will go on to fill senior engineering management positions. They follow an HND programme, with a top-up BEng option. The programme is conceived of as an alternative to conventional engineering provision by universities.
4.   Cable and Wireless College was founded in 1950 and now occupies high-quality accommodation a stone's-throw away from the campus of the University of Warwick. It offers courses ranging from a single day to an MBA in Telecommunications which is offered jointly with Henley Management College. Employees of other companies also attend courses at the college.

There are other examples of corporate universities such as Lloyds / TSB University, the Ford Employee Development Programme, the Marriot Virtual University, the Peugeot Employee Development Programme and the Rolls Royce Academy. Although included within a single category, they have different aims. Some are tightly linked to the specific and immediate training needs of the company; others are designed to enrich the job experiences of their employees by offering opportunities for complementary study in other areas. Most operate in partnership with existing universities, which makes it difficult to distinguish corporate universities from more conventional forms of university–industry collaboration (such as the highly successful Warwick Manufacturing Group) or indeed between two universities where the focus of that collaboration is on the development of advanced technologies (such as the partnership between the University of Cambridge and the Massachusetts Institute of Technology announced in 1999).

It is misleading to concentrate on corporate universities for two reasons. First, they are part of a spectrum of what has been called 'borderless higher education' (although, as the case of Cable and Wireless College demonstrates, some corporate universities are—designedly—campus-bound). This spectrum includes:

•   Distance learning offered by traditional universities. The Open University, of course, is the pre-eminent distance learning institution in Britain (and beyond), but most other universities have developed some distance learning provision;
•   University-to-university partnerships and consortia, many of which now transcend national boundaries. The Cambridge–MIT partnership is one example; another is

Universitas 21, a world-wide consortium of elite universities. But there are also interesting examples in further education such as the combination of colleges into the
University of the Highlands and Islands in Scotland;

• University–industry collaboration, of which there are many examples in fields such as
business and engineering. Corporate universities have most in common with this
category because of their reliance on the academic resources (and often the staff) of
existing, universities;

• For-profit universities, the most notorious example of which is the University of
Phoenix in the United States. Although the penetration of for-profit universities into
Britain's higher education market remains limited, such enterprises have much in
common with the mass media's growing involvement in higher education. The BBC,
of course, has a long-standing stake in education. More recently Pearson and the
Financial Times have begun to develop management education programmes.

The evidence suggests that these different forms of 'borderless higher education', public and
private, not-for-profit and for-profit, local and global, will tend to converge, so reducing the
distinctiveness of corporate universities in their pure(er) form.

Second, although corporate universities represent an alternative to the traditional organization of higher education into discrete and autonomous institutions, they remain heavily
dependent on existing universities for their intellectual resources. Many of their training programmes are offered in partnership with universities. In most cases corporate universities
depend on universities for accreditation even of in-house programmes (although there are
signs that alternative forms of—non-academic—accreditation are developing based on the
power of global brands such as Microsoft). They also depend for much of their teaching on university staff. For all these reasons it is difficult to regard corporate universities as rivals to traditional universities. Rather they add to the diversity of higher education, while demonstrating
the increasing permeability of the frontiers of traditional systems. But these frontiers are
being crossed not only from outside-in, by corporate or for-profit universities, but also—perhaps more—from inside-out, as traditional universities develop new forms of collaboration
with non-academic partners.

Higher education in further education

Approximately 10 per cent of students on higher education programmes are enrolled not in
universities and other designated higher education institutions but in further education. The
total number of students in what is often called HE-in-FE now exceeds 150,000. To place this
total in perspective, it is equivalent to the total number of students in higher education in the
early 1960s at the time of the Robbins report, or to ten average-sized universities today. Two-
thirds of FE colleges offer some advanced, i.e. higher education, courses and more than half
receive funding directly from one of the higher education funding councils. The remainder is
indirectly funded through partner higher education institutions. So it is a substantial enterprise. Among the colleges is a small number which have a substantial stake in higher education
with more than a thousand students on advanced programmes. They are usually described as
mixed-economy colleges, i.e. part-FE and part-HE.

Most of these courses are at sub-degree level, typically Higher National Certificates
(HNCs) or Higher National Diplomas (HNDs). HNCs are studied part-time, while HNDs
are two-year full-time courses. FE colleges also offer two-year Diploma of Higher Education
courses in less vocational subject areas where HNCs and HNDs are not available, and also
Access and Foundation programmes which are usually one-year full-time courses and are

designed to prepare students for degree-level courses. Some FE colleges do offer degree-level courses, often as the junior partner of a higher education institution but occasionally on their own account. Many of these courses are 'franchised' by universities, because FE colleges cannot award diplomas or degrees, but in some cases colleges have been 'licensed' by EdExcel, the national agency responsible for awarding HNCs and HNDs.

In the past decade greater attention has been focused on HE-in-FE for two main reasons. The first has been the need to regularize the relationship between the two sectors in terms of control, funding and quality assurance. Initially the presence of HE-in-FE was regarded as an anomaly—or, at any rate, as a residue. The emphasis was on clarifying the distinctive territories of FE and HE and, in particular, of their respective funding councils. For example, it was originally agreed that HNCs should be funded through the Further Education Funding Council because they were seen as largely of local significance, and that HNDs should be funded through the HEFCE because they recruited students from a national constituency. Similar attempts were made to demarcate responsibilities for quality assurance, although this presented difficulties because of the tension between the peer-review self-regulatory ethos of quality assurance in higher education and the inspectorial regime which generally prevailed in further education.

More recently, as it became more difficult to treat HE-in-FE as an anomaly or a residue, the emphasis has switched. The HEFCE has now assumed responsibility for funding all higher education courses regardless of the type of institution in which they are provided. Because of the scale of HE-in-FE and the number of FE colleges involved this change has substantially increased the potential administrative load on the HEFCE. To cope with, or reduce, that load the funding council is encouraging FE colleges to form funding consortia with universities as a compromise between direct funding and indirect funding through higher education institutions. Meanwhile the Government has announced that the FEFC is to be abolished and be replaced by a Learning and Skills Council in a far-reaching reform of all post-16 education (see below). Different arrangements are proposed in Scotland and Wales, both of which now enjoy devolved government with a separate Parliament and Assembly respectively. The effect of this changed approach is to recognise that FE-in-HE has an important and permanent place within a wider post-secondary education system in which traditional demarcations between higher, further and adult education are rapidly becoming anachronisms.

The second reason is that, although committed to a further expansion of higher education from an age-participation-index of 34 per cent to 50 per cent, the Government expects—and, indeed, requires—the bulk of that expansion to be in two-year sub-degree programmes with a strong vocational bias. FE colleges' share of such programmes is more than half the total, as opposed to only 10 per cent of all higher education programmes, which means that they will have a very important role to play in the further development of a mass system of higher education in Britain. The importance of this role has been reflected in the additional student numbers which the HEFCE has agreed to fund, the bulk of which have been for two-year diplomas rather than three- or four-year bachelor's degrees. As a result, a disproportionate share has gone to FE colleges. Although traditional undergraduate education continues to be the core of British higher education, there are already signs of a shift to a more American pattern in which two-year associate degrees are a more standard qualification. Such an arrangement could also be aligned with the first cycle of higher education in many continental European systems.

The next step would be to combine HNC/Ds and DipHEs into Associate Degrees, suitably differentiated into vocational and academic variants but within a common qualifications framework. Such a development would be compatible with the long revolution through which post-war British education at all levels has passed, in which fragmented provision has been superseded by comprehensive arrangements. The increasing frequency with which the phrase 'associate degree' is now used may also support the argument, advanced earlier in this article, that conceptual reordering often precedes (and, therefore, shapes) administrative reorganization. Indeed the Government announced in January 2000 that it favoured the development of two-year 'Foundation Degrees' with a pronounced but generic vocational orientation. There are signs that the traditional taxonomies of post-secondary education— not simply the demarcations between sectors and the categorization of institutions but also the classification of courses and qualifications—are coming under sustained challenge. One of the arenas in which that challenge is most intense is in the confused borderland between further and higher education.

Learning partnerships

Between the 1979 election when Margaret Thatcher came to power and the 1997 election when almost two decades of Conservative rule came to an end with the triumph of Tony Blair's New Labour, competition had been one of the most powerful motifs of educational policy. Greater emphasis on parental choice, the publication of comparative performance indicators (notably examination results), the creation of new types of school (such as grant maintained schools) and changes in funding regimes—all tended to stimulate greater competition between schools. If anything, competitive pressures were even more intense in post-secondary education. Universities, of course, had always accepted a degree of genteel competition bureaucratically mediated through the common admissions systems and its carefully graded hierarchy of institutional esteem and, more recently and perhaps more roughly, through the periodic research assessment exercises. So the shift towards a more overtly competitive culture in the 1980s could be accommodated without too much dislocation in higher education's underlying value structures. In further education the transition was much brusquer—from a planned local authority environment inimical to most forms of institutional initiative to an intensely competitive post-incorporation culture in which institutional success was judged by crude 'market' criteria. Not surprisingly, abuses proliferated with phantom students being enrolled and costs—and corners—ruthlessly cut. Unlike higher education, further education went through a crisis of identity in the 1990s characterized by a radical dislocation of values.

However, since Labour's victory in 1997, a further shift has taken place. The rhetoric—and, to a large extent, the apparatus—of competitiveness have not been dismantled in post-secondary education. But the discourse is different. Now more emphasis is placed on collaboration. Indeed the vigour and success of institutions are now more likely to be judged by their participation in creative partnerships with other institutions—not only other colleges or universities but other public institutions and private organizations as well. Stand-alone beggar-my-neighbour success, so celebrated during the Thatcher period, is no longer rewarded. Instead networks of all kinds are politically correct. In the case of higher education part of this change had occurred during the dog-days of the Tory dominance when John Major was prime minister. The headlong expansion of student numbers during the late 1980s and early 1990s was curbed—mainly on the insistence of the Treasury. But the end of expansion also sharply reduced opportunities for competitive behaviour. In a reversion to pre-Thatcher planning each institution was given a student number target, to be met but not exceeded. Competition was confined to the periphery as institutions competed for limited additional sums made available under various special initiatives. This retreat from competition was much less pronounced in further education where competition continued upto, and beyond, the Labour election victory.

Two years after that victory the new Government is finally developing a clearly articulated alternative to the competitive culture of the 1980s and 1990s. That it has taken so long is not surprising; it took Margaret Thatcher and her Conservative colleagues several years to slow and reverse the momentum of the welfare-state culture they had inherited from (Old) Labour. Two key documents have helped to clarify this alternative. The first was the Green Paper *The Learning Age* which was published in 1998 and was principally concerned with higher education (DfEE 1998). Although immediate reaction to the Green Paper concentrated on the degree to which the Government had accepted the recommendations made in the Dearing report, its canvass was much wider. The ambitious aim was to move away from an old-fashioned preoccupation with institutions and sectors (and so their organization, management and funding—which had remained the central concerns in the competitive climate of the Thatcher period) and instead focus primarily on, in this case, lifelong learners. The emphasis, in other words, was on a re-conceptualization of post-secondary education, which may prefigure a reconfiguration of its institutions (now, of course, networked) and sectors (increasingly anachronistic?). If the focus is on meeting the needs of lifelong learners, competition between institutions may actually be dysfunctional.

The second key document was the 1999 White Paper *Learning to Succeed: A New Framework* which was published following a far-reaching review of post-16 education and training (excluding higher education) (DfEE 1999). This paper went beyond the earlier Green Paper because it made concrete proposals to dismantle the apparatus of competition built up during the years of Conservative rule—notably the Further Education Funding Council and the Training and Enterprise Councils (TECs)—and to create instead new, and more collaborative, structures—of which the centrepiece will be the Learning and Skills Council. The new council incorporated the responsibilities of both the FEFC and the TECs, but also had new responsibilities for working with LEAs in the area of adult and community education. Its expanded remit suggestively supports two of the theses put forward in this article—first, the slow but sustained movement towards more comprehensive configurations in post-secondary education and training; and, second, the new emphasis on collaboration. The council's agenda is driven by the needs of learners not the requirements, or demands, of institutions. Not only are there local councils, working closely with the recently established Regional Development Agencies (RDAs), local Learning Partnerships were also established. Again the emphasis on 'partnership' is explicit.

This last example reinforces the argument in the first part of this chapter, namely that traditional taxonomies of post-secondary education are breaking down in Britain. The UfI is perhaps the most dramatic example of how these taxonomies are being transgressed. To some extent it can still be treated as an exceptional policy intervention rather than a harbinger of wider-scale transgressions. However, the discussion of HE-in-FE where these transgressive tendencies have to be translated into routine policy-making suggests that it may be complacent to regard the UfI as a one-off rather than a, perhaps bizarre, symptom of long-term reconfiguration of the system. The last example, of how these changes are being represented through high-level policy-making, also suggests that a fundamental shift in the constitution of post-secondary education is already well under way.

Conclusion

In the first section of this chapter it was argued that the *longue durée* of British post-secondary education is towards the integration of separate sectors which formerly were regarded as having little in common; and that this trend has much in common with the comprehensive movements in both primary and secondary education. There are differences, of course; the most notable is that in schools (and especially in secondary schools) comprehensive reorganization was a deliberate act of State policy, while in the post-secondary arena integration has been produced by the accumulation and aggregation of disparate policy initiatives by successive Governments and uncoordinated sectoral and institutional responses to changes in the external environment. Nevertheless the final effect has been to similar—to produce a coordinated, and even comprehensive system of post-secondary education. First higher education coalesced out of the traditional universities, advanced further education (which was given a much sharper focus by the establishment of the polytechnics in the 1960s), and teacher training. Next, further education took on a much wider role as the provider of open-access and community-oriented education rather than simply of narrower vocational training. Finally, (liberal) adult education and continuing (vocational) education came together, only to be absorbed (or 'mainstreamed') in further or higher education. Most recently there have been clear signs that the frontier between further education and higher education is crumbling.

In the second section, four examples of this larger reconfiguration of post-secondary education in Britain were considered: the creation of the UfI, the rise of corporate universities, the growing importance of HE-in-FE, and the development of 'Learning Partnerships'. What they have in common is that they cannot easily be analysed, or implemented, within the traditional taxonomies of adult, higher and further education. Nor are they isolated examples. The abolition of the FEFC demonstrates that further education can no longer reasonably be regarded as a stand-alone activity provided by special-purpose institutions organized in a clearly demarcated sector; instead it is embraced in a much wider and looser 'system' comprising other organizations and programmes designed to enhance economic development or to combat social exclusion. Although higher education was deliberately excluded from the most recent White Paper, it is unlikely that this apartheid will be maintained. Already the boundaries are breaking down at institutional level as universities and colleges form increasingly comprehensive partnerships. Although speculation about a possible merger between further and higher education funding councils proved unfounded (and has now been overtaken by events), it has been succeeded by active discussion about the merits of regionally based funding structures for both further and higher education.

This remapping of British post-secondary education, in both conceptual and policy terms, may justify the claim that a new paradigm has emerged—which, in shorthand, can be labelled 'lifelong learning'. Lifelong learning, of course, extends far beyond the frontiers of formal education. Bound up in it are not only educational issues but also issues of cultural, social and economic policy. In some respects lifelong learning is better seen in the wider arena of changing patterns of 'private' consumption than within the traditional context of providing 'public' education—or, even, learning opportunities. A recent report from the Organisation for Economic Co-operation and Development (OECD) emphasized the diversity and pluralism of lifelong learning and, consequently, the need for coordination across many policy arenas (OECD 1996). The report also asserted that the State's role was to steer and facilitate, rather than to manage or control, this boundless 'system' of higher education. For governments in Britain and elsewhere, this represents a significant change—first, because existing policy instruments are essentially concerned with management and control, and these 'administrative' instruments must now be succeeded (or supplemented) by subtler 'cultural' instruments; and, secondly, because coordination across the various departments of government has never been easy.

The National Advisory Group for Continuing Education and Lifelong Learning (NAGCELL) produced two reports in 1997 and 1999 which tried to encompass the complexity of lifelong learning (NAGCELL 1997 and 1999). In the process the group struggled to define the new paradigm that is replacing the traditional taxonomies of adult, higher and further education. Its members emphasized the articulations between lifelong learning on the one hand and on the other employment patterns, family structures, social security—and, wider still, notions of social justice, political participation and community involvement. By emphasizing the need for cultural change (rather than relying on administrative intervention) and for voluntarism (rather than State action), they also seemed to be raising fundamental questions about the continuing viability of the bureaucratic welfare state which has dominated the public arena for much of the twentieth century—but which now is challenged both by its insufficiencies, as exposed most sharply by the processes of globalization, and its successes. Its most relevant success for the purposes of this discussion (but also perhaps its most notable) has been the radical extension of opportunities for post-secondary education; here the State's success in stimulating, and for a long time satisfying, the appetite for continued learning has created a demand that now outstrips the state's capacity, not so much to provide the resources but to offer the appropriate policy parameters and administrative structures. Such speculation, although far beyond the scope of this chapter, demonstrates the unboundedness of the idea of lifelong learning—and may help to explain the dynamic underlying the past and future integration (or comprehensivization) of post-secondary education in Britain.

Two conclusions—or, rather, questions—are suggested if this analysis is accepted. The first is that there is a choice of interpretations. The growth of more comprehensive forms of post-secondary education can be regarded as a reactionary—or, at any rate, conservative project. Just as (so it is alleged) comprehensive secondary schools took grammar schools as their model, so the university will become the dominant institution even in much extended systems of lifelong learning. Mass higher education has been unable to break the university's monopoly. Why should it be different with lifelong learning? The rival interpretation is that the shift to lifelong learning is a 'bridge too far'. Not only have higher education institutions and systems, certainly as presently constituted, reached the limits of their own usefulness; they are also being actively subverted by new conceptions of learning, knowledge and organization. In practical terms, this suggests that while a relatively conventional higher education, such as Britain still has, can comfortably cater for up to a third of the age group, new approaches and institutions are needed if participation is to be widened to half or more of the eligible population. In other words higher education can be 'mass' (despite the oxymoronic complaints of those who have always argued that more-means-worse), but it cannot be 'universal'.

The second conclusion, or question, follows logically. Again there is a choice of interpretations. The first is that new forms will be additional to old ones. The core of university provision will remain comparatively untouched, but will be surrounded by a penumbra of new kinds of institution including virtual and corporate universities. Although there will be active trading between old and new institutions, as there currently is between traditional and corporate universities, the latter must remain firmly subordinated to the former. The penumbra is also the periphery. Logically, therefore, the most urgent need is to (re?)stratify the higher education, or lifelong learning, system and to regulate relations between its different components. The second interpretation is based on more radical premises. The present combination of organizational roles and cognitive functions in the modern university is historically contingent. It reflects a particular configuration of technological capabilities, professional values and organizational economies. Therefore, to take the most obvious and controversial example, teaching and research have been bundled together for reasons of convenience. But that configuration may change and the present combinations of roles and functions may become dysfunctional. As a result they may have to be unbundled—and also rebundled, because there is already evidence that clear-cut demarcations between education and training, between education and training together and economic and social development, can no longer be safely made. If this second interpretation is preferred—as it is, in broad terms, by me—lifelong learning becomes a much more radical project. The pattern of higher education development with which we have been familiar in the twentieth century—in effect, the expansion and (limited) liberalization of the university core combined with the development of 'additional' rather than alternative, and therefore firmly subordinated, forms of higher education—may become an anachronism in the new century.

References

British Aerospace Virtual University (1998) *Achivement through Knowledge*, Farnborough: BAe

Department for Education and Employment (1998) *The Learning Age*, London: Stationery Office

Department for Education and Employment (1999) *Learning to Succeed: A New Framework*, London: Stationery Office

Middlehurst, Robin (2000) *The Business of Borderless Education*, London: Committee of Vice-Chancellors and Principals

National Advisory Group for Continuing Education and Lifelong Learning (1997) *Learning for the Twenty-First Century*, Sheffield: Department for Education and Employment

National Advisory Group for Continuing Education and Lifelong Learning (1999) *Creating Learning Cultures: Next Steps in Achieving the Learning Age*, Sheffield: Department for Education and Employment

Organisation for Economic Co-operation and Development (1996) *Lifelong Learning for All*, Paris: OECD

Robbins (1963) *Higher Education*, Report of the Committee on Higher Education appointed by the Prime Minister under the chairmanship of Lord Robbins 1961–63, London: HMSO

UfI (1998) *Pathfinder Prospectus*, Department for Education and Employment, Sheffield

Unipart (1999) The Learning Organisation (http://www.ugc.co.uk/learning.htm)

4 The corporate university

Peter Jarvis

The dominant institutions in society have always generated and controlled knowledge, as Foucault (1972) has demonstrated. We only have to look back to the formation of the universities to see the validity of this statement; before the Enlightenment their founders were the churches and after it, the State. But now the newest universities are being established by the large transnational corporations, reflecting another major shift in social and political power. In this chapter, we shall show that these corporate universities illustrate the manner in which both the power structures of society and its knowledge base have changed. At the same time, we will suggest that it is not an entirely new phenomenon since the professions have had their own professional training and their own schools for many years. The chapter has four major sections: the changing infrastructure of society; the nature of knowledge and the emergence of the learning society; the university as a corporation; the corporate university. In the final section, we shall examine some of the most recent research on the corporate universities which has been conducted in the United States, where there are more of these universities than anywhere else in the English-speaking world. Finally, a number of questions about higher education in this new era will be raised.

The changing structures of society

Sociologists have long been concerned about the structure of society, but one thesis that attracted considerable attention in the 1960s and 1970s was that of the logic of industrialization. This was first published at the beginning of the 1960s in *Industrialism and Industrial Man* (Kerr *et al.*, 1973). Like Marx, but from an entirely different viewpoint, these authors implied that each society has an infrastructure and a superstructure. The infrastructural driving force of change was the industrialization process itself. However, it was the identification of this infrastructural force that was a major weakness in the thesis; they did not foresee the changes that were to occur in the 1970s which were to alter the face of the industry and commerce itself.

But another aspect of their argument which is also important for this chapter is where they located higher education in their framework. They regarded it as part of the superstructure, as the handmaiden of industrialism:

> The higher educational system of the industrial society stresses the natural sciences, engineering, medicine, managerial training—whether private or public—and administrative law. It must steadily adapt to new disciplines and fields of specialization. There is a relatively smaller place for the humanities and the arts, while the social sciences are strongly related to the training of the managerial groups and technicians for the enterprise and

for government. The increased leisure time, however, can afford a broader public appreciation of the humanities and the arts.

(Kerr *et al.*, 1973, p. 47)

They claimed that the higher educational system would have to expand to meet the needs of industrialization, and this would create an increasing level of education for all citizens, albeit there would be greater emphasis on those subjects relevant to the infrastructural demands.

Industrialization is not now, however, the driving force of change, although there are still infrastructural forces. They are now global rather than State or country-wide. These forces lie in the control of capital and the utilization of information technology. The process of globalization, as we know it today, began in the early 1970s; corporations began to transfer capital around the world, seeking the cheapest places and the most efficient means to manufacture, and the best markets in which to sell their products. This resulted in the continued decline in manufacturing industries in the First World and new occupational structures emerged. Theorists began to suggest that there is actually a world economy (Wallerstein, 1974, *inter alia*) based on the capitalist system of exchange. This theoretical approach was questioned by Robertson (1994) who was more concerned to show that globalization is a cultural phenomenon and, partially, by Castells (1996) who has argued that the State still has a role to play in a not-completely free global market. Even so, the world market has expanded rapidly, aided and abetted by the development of electronic communication systems. The information technology revolution began in this same period and took off, with one development leading to another. Castells claims that 'to some extent, the availability of new technologies constituted as a system in the 1970s was a fundamental basis for the process of socioeconomic restructuring in the 1980s' (Castells, 1996, pp. 52–3).

Another factor that reinforced this process was the Fall of the Berlin Wall for, from that time, there has literally been 'no alternative' (Bauman, 1992) to capitalism; the global economic infrastructure was both a cause of and reinforced by these cataclysmic political events. Now the world-wide infrastructural driving force of social change is information technology (a new means of production) in association with those who control capital (the social relations of production). Castells (1996, p. 145) states that this has resulted in three major economic regions, Western Europe, America and the Asian Pacific—with other areas of the world associated with them—although he sees Russia as a fourth potential region.

These processes changed the structure of the workforce with a decline in manufacturing jobs and an increased demand for knowledge-based workers in some countries, but with new industrial workers in others. Indeed, Reich postulated that there would be three major groups of workers—knowledge-based, service-based and routine production. Castells (1996, p. 147) also suggests a similar division of labour to Reich, with four main types: the producers of high value (knowledge workers); producers of high volume (based on low cost labour—service and production workers); producers of raw materials (based on natural products); redundant producers (devalued labour). He maintains that at both the global level, and within the economic regions, there is this division of labour, with differing proportions occurring in each country and region. Reich (1991, pp. 179–80) has indicated that the proportion of symbolic analysts (knowledge workers) has increased in the American work force from 8 per cent in the 1950s to about 20 per cent in the 1980s. He argued that it will continue to increase. Knowledge workers are

> ... the creators, manipulators, and purveyors of the stream of information that makes up the post-industrial, post-service global economy. Their ranks include research scientists, design engineers, civil engineers, software analysts, biotechnology workers, public

relations specialists, lawyers, investment bankers, management consultants, financial and tax consultants, architects, strategic planners, marketing specialists, film producers and editors, art directors, publishers, writers, editors and journalists.

(Rifkin, 1995, p. 174)

It is very significant that many of the forms of knowledge work indicated here fall into the category of occupation to which the title 'profession' has generally been assigned, although the concept of profession has always been rather ambiguous. Professionals have always been knowledge workers and the professions have both traditionally established their own professional training schools, and then sought to get them associated with a university. Indeed, this has been built into some of the models of professionalization of these occupations and Wilensky argued that every occupation could professionalize (Wilensky, 1964). However, the professional bodies have never had the control of capital, so that their power has been eclipsed by the transnational companies who both control capital and employ the professionals as part of their staff of knowledge workers. Independent professional practice still has a place in contemporary society, but the large companies employ many more knowledge workers.

The wealthiest countries have a large proportion of knowledge workers, but they are still concerned about the social exclusion of the redundant workers. As other countries industrialize, they generate more knowledge-based workers but their work force remains predominantly agricultural and manufacturing. Additionally, other countries are socially excluded with most of their work force being redundant labour and they have subsistence economies; these are among the world's poorest. This is the inevitable result of globalization (Bauman, 1998).

However, it is the fact that there are increasing number of workers utilizing knowledge that has led to the emergence of the knowledge society—but education still remains part of the superstructure. Indeed, the newly emerging learning society as a whole is in a sense superstructural in itself.

The nature of knowledge and the learning society

With the increase in knowledge-based workers or professionals, it is now important to see how knowledge itself has changed during this process. Indeed, there have been a multitude of books published in recent years about knowledge (Hamilton, 1974; Popper, 1979; Scheler, 1980; White, 1982; Gergan, 1994; *inter alia*). It would take a book in itself to explore the changing nature of knowledge, although this is not the intention of this chapter. Rather we want to demonstrate how certain forms of knowledge are changing and how this relates to the formation of corporate universities. As early as 1924, Max Scheler (1980) began to explore knowledge from the perspective of the different speeds by which it changed or, as he called it, its level of artificiality. He suggested that there were seven different types of knowledge: myth and legend knowledge implicit in everyday language; religious knowledge; mystical knowledge; philosophical-metaphysical knowledge; positive knowledge; technical knowledge.

The last two forms of knowledge are most relative and artificial, and by this Scheler meant that they changed so rapidly that they did not have time to become embedded in a society's culture. In the 1920s, he (1980, p. 76) wrote that the recognition and validity of positive and technical knowledge changes from hour to hour. Now it might have been second by second! The level of artificiality of positive and technological knowledge is even greater today. The knowledge society is utilizing these more relative forms of knowledge (Stehr, 1994, p. 6).

Since these forms of knowledge are changing rapidly, it is necessary for individuals to keep on learning in order to keep abreast, so that it is understandable why Kerr *et al.* relegated all non-industrial knowledge to leisure-time pursuits. Even so, it is still necessary to ask how this knowledge is legitimated. There are three main ways of doing this (Scheffler, 1995): through logical reasoning, through empiricism or through pragmatism. It might also be argued that truth can be reached through revelation, although it is beyond the scope of this chapter to explore the implications of this position.

Philosophy and pure mathematics are examples of subjects that demand logical reasoning. Habermas (1984) has suggested truth can be reached through argumentation and the reaching of an agreement—a modification of logical reasoning. However, any agreement reached might still be regarded as being relative to the context and not actually a legitimation of truth. Empiricism is the recognition of fact through the senses, although no fact has meaning in itself. Meaning, or interpretation, is a more subjective process, even though the meanings are often presented as if they were intrinsic to the fact itself. Significantly for the learning society, both of these forms of knowledge can be taught and learned.

However, it is pragmatism, a philosophy that claims that knowledge is valid—in the sense of functionality—if it works, that has come to the fore in recent years. Now, knowledge is only genuine for practitioners if it works for them and they have to learn that for themselves. This cannot be taught. They have to generate this knowledge for themselves—they are learners and, consequently, researchers as well as practitioners. The work place has become a site for learning and research, and the knowledge society the learning society.

At the heart of the knowledge society lies positivist and technical knowledge. However, it is important to distinguish between these two forms of knowledge: much of the research leading to the development of technical knowledge is undertaken in the laboratory and then tried out in practice to see if it works and if its products can be marketed. By contrast, a great deal of positivist knowledge is actually generated through pragmatic means in practice itself and then utilized by knowledge-based industries in the global market. Both knowledge and service workers use both forms, but some knowledge workers also use more technological knowledge. Both forms are changing with great rapidity, so that both categories of workers need to keep on learning new knowledge.

These rapidly changing forms of knowledge have to be learned and practised by all workers. Failure to compete in the global market means that the transnational companies will not survive and this will result in the relative impoverishment of the countries in which the companies are located. Consequently, the main emphases of government strategies to introduce the learning society are placed upon the need to learn in order to remain competitive. The UK Government White Paper (DfEE, 1999) demonstrates this thesis very clearly. In addition, most of them make some reference to the need for people to learn so that they can grow and develop and participate more in the democratic processes of their society. For example, in the introduction to an OECD report (1996, p. 13), the following occurs:

> Success in realising lifelong learning—from early childhood education to active learning retirement—will be an important factor in promoting employment, economic development, democracy and social cohesion in the years ahead.

The redundant workers—the socially isolated—are the other major concern in most of these documents. In the above cited UK Government White Paper there are numerous references to the socially disadvantaged, demonstrating the welfare role of government, something not so significant in the original logic of industrialism thesis, or in the way that right wing governments promoted it. However, it is a welfare to work programme.

The dominant discourse of the learning society has become equated with the working society and lifelong learning with work-life learning. This is what is to be expected since it reflects the demands of the infrastructural forces of the global world. Much more learning probably occurs outside the world of work—with some being generated by employers themselves through employee development programmes (see Thompson, 1999).

Each of Castells' (1996, p. 147) four types of worker is to be found in most societies. Indeed, in any large company there will be at least the producers of high value (knowledge workers) and producers of high volume (based on low cost labour). Their education and training needs are different, but both need to keep abreast with all the changes that are occurring—they all need to be lifelong learners. Traditionally in the United Kingdom, the first would have been educated in higher education and be regarded as professional, and the second trained in further education—although this division is increasingly hard to maintain, as we shall show in the next two sections. In the first, we shall discuss the way that universities have been forced to change to respond to the changing demands of the knowledge workers in the learning market and, in the second, we shall discuss the corporate universities which actually relate much more closely to further education and indicate where one of the major shifts have occurred with the development of the knowledge society.

The university as a corporation

Universities, founded by Church and State, have traditionally taught a wide range of subjects—many of which change much more slowly than do the positive and technical forms of knowledge. They have also been supported financially by their founders, especially the State, so that they have not had to compete in a competitive global market. There is a sense, therefore, in which they reflect post-Enlightenment modernity, but not the post-1970s late modernity. Since the 1970s, they have been exposed to the infra-structural pressures of society to change. This process was exacerbated at the beginning of the 1980s in the United Kingdom by a right-wing monetarist government decreasing the funding levels of the universities so that they had to become more competitive. This has resulted in many of the traditional universities assuming a more corporate form and functioning more like them, with vice-chancellors becoming chief executive officers, collegial governance disappearing, and so on (Brandon, 1999). They have become a very heterogeneous group now, especially since the creation of the new universities. Consequently, something of a crisis in the academy has occurred (Lucas, 1996).

The universities have been forced to respond to the demands of the global infrastructure at both undergraduate and post-graduate levels, which they have partially done especially through the expansion of post-graduate education for the professions. While these changes have subsequently occurred in other countries of the world as well as in the United States and the United Kingdom, e.g. Australia, it is not true everywhere. In some instances governments have continued to support a more traditional elitist university structure. We will examine the ways that those universities which are changing are responding to the infrastructural demands.

Undergraduate education

Reich predicted that about one-third of the work force in the United States would be knowledge workers by the end of the century. Traditionally, universities have not admitted such a high proportion of the population. However, in those societies exposed to the demands of the infrastructural need for an educated work force, more higher education places are being created. In some Western countries as many as half of all young people leaving school have the opportunity for higher education. In the UK, one-third of all young people enter higher education (DfEE, 1999, chap 4/30). A mass higher education system is being created, similar to that which has been operating in the United States for a considerable period of time. Undergraduate education is becoming part of the initial education system, thereby creating a crisis in the higher education system (Lucas, 1996, p. 63). The failure of some governments to recognize this and have a ready-prepared work force might also inhibit investment by transnational knowledge-based companies in their countries.

One of the social pressures on universities is for them to recognize that the school system has not always enabled the most able children to achieve, and that many people who failed, or had little or no opportunity, in the initial school system, have the ability to make a success in higher education later in life. Once this has been recognized, some universities have introduced access-type courses, or modular market-type systems, that allow individuals to study at higher education level without having first achieved their school leaving certificate. Although there have not been sufficient opportunities at this level, the colleges of further and higher education have cooperated closely with universities; universities have franchised some of their undergraduate courses to further education and both have expanded their curricula to meet these demands. This is increasingly necessary as people's work is being upgraded and changed. At this point further and higher education overlap and in the not too distant future, we can expect to see mergers between universities and colleges, so that they can become more efficient providers of work-life learning.

Postgraduate education

Once these young people have graduated and entered employment, their education must continue so that they can keep abreast with all the innovations being created by advanced technology and with rapidly changing knowledge. Universities have, therefore, begun to adapt to the demands for continuing professional education for these workers. There are more facilities to study part-time for higher degrees, many of which are work-based. For instance, Campbell (1984) records that since 1974 there have been more adults in universities in Canada than traditional-aged undergraduates. This is true of most North American and UK universities. In the UK, for instance, the Higher Education Funding Council reported that there were many more people studying in universities who were over the age of 21 than there were traditional undergraduate students in 1993. These are professionals (knowledge and service workers) studying for undergraduate and post-graduate degrees part-time, and even at a distance. New post-graduate courses are springing up for different knowledge-based industries—from management to consultancy, from medicine to journalism, and so on, but nearly all of them are relevant to the workplace. Universities in the West are beginning to change and to place a great deal more emphasis on higher degrees having a work-based learning format, that are modular in structure and can be studied part-time at a distance—including electronic modes of delivery.

However, this expansion of higher education into lifelong learning is not just a trend for taught courses, it also occurs in research. An increasing number of people researching for PhDs are part-time; their research is work-based and they are often funded by their employers. The idea that the doctorate is a route into university employment has changed. Doctorates are being undertaken during, and even at the end of, work-life and much of the research is based on their researcher's own work. Practitioner researchers (Jarvis, 1999) are becoming a relatively common phenomenon in the universities of knowledge societies. It is also significant that the need for these higher qualifications is felt by the knowledge workers in other countries where the opportunities are less common, so that they are looking to the West for further opportunities.

It is not only the way that knowledge has changed that has generated change in education and learning. It is the fact that the learning society has also become a learning market. Schumpeter (1976) actually argued many years ago that one of the strengths of the market is that it has necessarily to be innovative. In order to compete in the global learning market, there has been an expansion of all forms of provision of learning opportunities world-wide, both in what it offered and how it offered it: from traditional face-to-face teaching in a 'real' time situation to the utilization of a variety of methods, in a realignment of time and space. An expansion not only made possible by the advance of information technology but also by the globalization of the English language.

Universities that have become corporations are responding to the demands of the infrastructure at an academic level with which they have always worked, utilizing information technology and extending their clientele by attracting learners from all age groups to an expanding post-graduate programme. As Kerr *et al.* (1973) suggested, they are offering learning opportunities that are vocationally orientated and relegating non-vocational subjects to the margins. They are becoming work-lifelong learning institutions. Universities, however, have a more traditional culture and have taught a wider range of subjects than those which are demanded by the global infrastructure, so that they may not always respond to the market demands sufficiently quickly, a point stressed by Niebuhr (1984) who called for a revitalization of America's learning in which he regarded industry and commerce as the agents of change.

The corporate university

As the learning society has emerged and corporations have become more involved in the education and training of their staff there have been many calls for partnership between the corporations and the education system. But Eurich (1985, p. 15) has suggested that in the United States this has not always been feasible:

> Differences in mission between the two systems have led, however, to marked contrast in styles that hamper co-operation. Higher education enjoys a more leisurely and wider time frame.... To the corporate world, 'time frames' are costly and company controls well understood.
>
> Frequently, starting from opposite poles, co-operation has proved to be neither feasible nor desirable—certainly not mutually satisfactory. It has engendered distrust and discomfort, if not disdain; it has often been abandoned as not worth the effort on either side.

Even so, she went on to point out that there have been many areas of cooperation in the United States, especially with the community colleges—similar to the colleges of further education in the UK. At the same time, Carnidale *et al.* (1990a, p. 106) noted that educational institutions provide a great deal of the training and upgrading of the American workforce, although many universities 'have not moved to create special offices that work specifically on customized training programs within industry'. They (1990b, p. 69) suggested that the two-year colleges were much more aggressive in developing their links with industry and commerce.

It is significant to note here that the area where there has been most response to the corporate demands for more education has been further education, since the universities have partially responded to the continuing education demands from the professions. This is not to defend the universities, since they tend to be extremely conservative as Eurich claims, but some of them have gradually been forced to expand their post-graduate and research programmes in response to these demands.

Eurich (1985, p. 48) also recorded the fact that by the time she was writing there were approximately 400 companies in the US that had their own learning centres, many of which were called universities. But this figure has grown rapidly and by 1995 there were over 1000 corporate universities and corporate training budgets totalled $52 billion—an increase of 15 per cent since 1990 (Rowley *et al.*, 1998, p. 34). (The exact amount of money spent on training in America appears to be something of an estimate, since Carnidale *et al.* (1990b, p. xi) suggest that it is $210 billion annually). In the UK, there have been similar developments—such as the British Aerospace Virtual University, the University of Lloyds TSB (a bank), and other major companies having their own training centres, academies, and so forth. Research into the British corporate universities has not really happened yet, although it is beginning with a project at the University of Surrey, following some work developed but not yet published by the University of Queensland (*THES*, 1999), so that the following paragraphs concentrate on the research in the USA. However, it has to be recognized that research into these universities might not be entirely open or value-free, since these companies may be competing with each other in a very competitive global market. For instance, Lyotard (1984, p. 5) wrote:

> Knowledge in the form of an informational commodity indispensable to productive power is already, and will continue to be, a major—perhaps *the* major—stake in the world-wide competition for power. It is conceivable that the national-states will one day fight for the control of information, just as they battled in the past for the control of territory, and afterwards for the control of access to and exploitation of raw materials and cheap labor. (emphasis in the original)

Now it is the transnationals that might do battle with each other rather than nation states, and industrial espionage is certainly no new phenomenon!

Research into these corporate training programmes began in the 1980s in the USA—not only with Eurich's work but with others, such as Castner-Lotto (1988). But in 1994, Meister published the first research work about the 'corporate universities'. She examined 30 corporations, which she regarded as having corporate quality universities, all of whom emphasized employee lifelong learning as essential to building a work-force able to compete in the global market. Significantly, it is not only the workforce; Motorola, amongst others, also expects its supply and distribution chain to participate in its programmes, and its university is also involved in the hiring of employees and with working with those agencies likely to refer potential employees to the corporation. Castner-Lotto (1984, p. 22) suggests that:

> The goal has become to instill the entire chain with an understanding of the company's quality vision as well as a passion to continuously learn, so that learning happens as a part of an individual's job, either at a computer work station, working with a team of suppliers, in customer forums, or alone via a self-paced workbook or audio/videotape. The emphasis on promoting a spirit of continuous lifelong learning is what makes Corporate Quality Universities so different from the traditional corporate classrooms of the past decade.

She (1984, p. 23) goes on to isolate the essence of these universities, which is fourfold:

- building a competency-based training curriculum for each job;
- providing all employees with a common vision of the company;
- extending training to the company's entire customer/supply chain;
- serving as a learning laboratory for experimenting with new approaches and practices for the design and delivery of learning initiatives.

The work force of these large companies comprises more than the knowledge workers so that the idea of the elitist university has disappeared. The workers being educated in the corporate universities need to be able to do and to know, so that teaching theory has disappeared to a great extent and practical knowledge lies at the heart of the curricula. Programmes have been designed for their function within the company, concentrating on aspects of education and training that would have traditionally been the preserve of further education but also straddling the divide between it and higher education. Each module is specifically designed for a specific job or procedure, based in practice, and involves practical knowledge. It is summed up with the 'three C's' of the core curriculum:

- corporate citizenship—know how the company works, and its values and vision;
- contextual framework—know the company's customers, competitors and their best practices;
- competencies—know and practise both established and new job competencies.

The fact that all workers should be learners all the time underlies the idea that the corporate quality university should be a learning laboratory, but then it will be recognized that one of the faculties in the British Aerospace Virtual University is the Faculty of Learning. Research into learning in corporate universities is not really involved in the biology, sociology or psychology of learning, but in ways that employees may learn more efficiently what they need to know for their work at the time when they need it. Gradually, that learning will be under the employees' control and will be provided in 'modular multisensory instructional modules' (Meister, 1994, p. 121) of between five and ten minutes each. Indeed, much of this learning will be what the Corning Education and Training Center calls the SMART Process (self-learning, motivation, awareness, responsibility and technical competence). (Meister, 1994, p. 129). Transnational companies will research learning styles to see, for instance, if the same instructional material can be provided in different counties and cultures, or whether it will be more efficient to prepare different material for different cultures.

Finally, corporate quality universities are also focusing on recognition of achievement and qualifications. Employees who are learning and are being good servants of the companies need recognition, something that companies are often poor in doing. Having recognized this, some of the companies are teaching their staff to recognize the achievement in others. One such programme in training in recognition is the STAR programme, run by Texaco:

- S—state precisely what learning is being praised;
- T—time the recognition close to the point of achievement;
- A—express your admiration for the achievement;
- R—show the relevance of the learning/achievement.

(Meister, 1994, p. 184)

Other companies are training their management to recognize learning in a variety of different ways, such as the presentation of instant recognition cards by management in order to recognize achievement; these entitle the employee to some small reward in cash or kind. These cards are awarded 'on the spot' when managers see good practice which they want to recognize.

It must be emphasized that much of what has been described above might be regarded from a very traditionalist perspective as sophisticated training, or further education, rather than higher education. Indeed, the University of Lloyds TSB does regard most of its work as being at this level (*THES*, 1999). But a clear distinction between these levels is now hard to maintain. The learning that occurs might be cognitive or practical or both; it might be personal or advantageous to the corporation as a whole; it might occur as a result of teaching or discovery, and so on. But it is not restricted to any specific level of knowledge, and should be regarded as transferable. The corporate university must reflect the practices of a learning corporation (Senge, 1990; Pedlar *et al.*, 1997). Apart from this recognition, are there other forms of recognition, such as educational-type qualifications?

Some of the programmes from the corporate quality universities are getting college credit. The manager of the American Express Quality University said:

> We hope that if employees get college credit for training programs they complete, they will be more motivated to further their education and pursue two- or four-year degree programs as deemed appropriate for their jobs.
>
> (Cited by Meister, 1994, pp. 162f.)

New degree programmes are also beginning to emerge and a partnership between the American Express Quality University and Rio Salado Community College led to an associate degree in customer relations. This reflects the same movement in further education in the UK, where colleges have sought to offer undergraduate qualifications.

But long before the transnational corporations were calling their sophisticated employees' learning centres universities, other corporations, working at the cognitive end of the learning market, were already awarding their own qualifications.

> A new development on the scene of business and education is the growing number of corporate colleges, institutes, or universities that grant their own academic degrees. It is the Rand PhD., the Wang or Arthur D Little Master of Science degree. No longer the purview of established educational institutions alone, accredited academic degrees are being awarded increasingly by companies and industries that have created their own separate institutions and successfully passed the same educational hurdles used to accredit traditional higher education.
>
> (Eurich, 1985, p. 85)

By 1985, Eurich had discovered 18 institutions offering academic qualifications at associate, bachelors, masters and doctoral level. The first academic award was offered as early as 1945. However, she goes on to make the following point:

> All 18 corporate institutions operate what may be called an 'open admissions' policy. They are open, quite literally, to all qualified persons *outside* the sponsoring corporation. While this is literally true, one exception requires notice: McDonalds' Hamburger University basically only serves its own employees, but it admits students from its supplier organizations and has perhaps eight or so a year.
>
> The important point is that these are not typically 'in-house' educational programs for employees. The Rand, Wang and Arthur D Little institutes do not serve employees of their parent organizations; each admits students who meet the admissions requirements from any college or university, any company, or from any country. Their graduates cannot expect employment by the sponsoring firm.
>
> (Eurich, 1985, p. 97; emphasis in the original)

These are, then, universities in the more traditional mode but founded by the corporations. But all of the developments described here point in the direction that knowledge-based corporations are probably going to take education and training in the near future.

Concluding discussion

The corporate university symbolizes quite clearly that we have entered a new era, in which the information technology empowered by those who control capital determines the shape of the society's superstructure. Although, as Castells (1996) has pointed out, the State may still perform a significant role if it seeks to do so. In this case, for instance, the State might fund some of those cultural and other elements of the established system of higher education that Kerr *et al.* (1973) suggest will otherwise be relegated from its core curriculum.

Earlier in this chapter, we focused on practical knowledge as the basis of the new corporate universities' work. It is not a new concept but one which has been foreign to universities since they have traditionally embraced the sciences and humanities as a result of the Enlightenment. In *Nicomachean Ethics*, for instance, Aristotle developed an analysis of practical wisdom that is really quite crucial to thinking about the future of education itself. Having distinguished between science and art, Aristotle notes that practical wisdom is neither the one nor the other. Scientific knowledge is knowledge of universals, devised from first principles and is demonstrable, whereas art is concerned with coming into being—with creating. Practical wisdom, by contrast, is not only concerned with universals, it is also concerned with the particular and, with great insight he wrote:

> ... nor is practical wisdom concerned with universals only—it must also recognize the particulars; for it is practical, and practice is concerned with particulars. This is why some who do not know, and especially those who have experience, are more practical than others who know...

(Aristotle: Book VI.7, p. 146)

Not only is practical wisdom concerned with experience and that is why, he claims, that younger people have little practical wisdom, for it also comes not from scientific knowledge but from perception of the particular—from having engaged in the art of practice. Aristotle, then, differentiates practical wisdom from scientific knowledge, philosophic wisdom and intuitive reason, but in no place that we can find does he place them in a simple hierarchy with scientific knowledge or philosophical wisdom at the top and practical wisdom at the bottom. He notes that wisdom must be based on scientific knowledge plus intuitive reason, but that some people can exhibit practical wisdom without possessing scientific knowledge since they have learned this knowledge from practice. In every instance, however, he claims that the ensuing action should be for the good of humankind.

We have seen throughout this chapter that the contemporary emphasis is on practical knowledge. Universities, whether they are corporate or traditional, have to rethink the place of practical knowledge, or wisdom, in their curricula and how they assess it both in the work place and in other learning sites. However, the new corporate universities might seek in the future to develop their own theoretical basis for the practices with which they are concerned and about which they offer opportunities to learn—and if they do that they might begin to develop new theory (meta-practical theory). But in so doing, they might create the same gap between theory and practice that many students in the traditional universities have experienced and about which they, and their employers, have been critical (Jarvis, 1999).

Corporate universities will almost certainly develop in some ways in the same direction as the 18 discussed by Eurich above, and will no doubt soon award their own degrees since the qualification is the symbol of participation (and consumption) in the market (Baudrillard, 1988). They might also seek to enter into partnerships with the established universities so that there can be a mutual recognition of qualifications. At the same time, the Australian study suggests that they will almost certainly become competitors with further and higher education for the same students who currently seek their qualifications (*THES*, 1999). At present they are better funded, are able to offer extremely good support services for their learners, and more able to adapt to the demands of the infrastructure than the established colleges and universities which themselves need to become learning universities (Duke, 1992), rescoping and restructuring themselves (Gray, 1999) to respond to the infrastructural demands of the global market. But the universities' planning in the future must be against a broad backcloth, as suggested in Gray's book, since they will have to take into consideration the inevitable emergence and development of corporate universities in the United Kingdom. The Committee for

Vice-Chancellors and Principals in the UK has already recognized this by sponsoring some of the current research into the corporate universities in America.

Acknowledgement

I am grateful to my colleague Dr Colin Griffin for reading and commenting on an earlier draft of this chapter.

References

Aristotle (1925) *Nichomachean Ethics* (trans Davis Ross) Oxford: Oxford University Press
Baudrillard J (1988) The System of Objects, reprinted in Poster (ed) op. cit.
Bauman Z (1992) *Intimations of Postmodernity* London: Routledge
Bauman Z (1998) *Globalization: The Human Consequences* Buckingham: Open University Press
Brandon P (1999) Salford University: An Historical Industrial Partnership, in Grey (ed) op. cit.
Campbell D (1984) *The New Majority* Edmonton: University of Alberta Press
Carnidale A, Gainer L and Villet J (1990a) *Training in America* San Francisco: Jossey Bass
Carnidale A, Gainer L and Villet J (1990b) *Training the Technical Work Force* San Francisco: Jossey Bass
Castells M (1996) *The Rise of the Network Society* Oxford: Blackwell (vol. 1 of *The Information Age: Economy, Society and Culture*)
Castner-Lotto and Associates (1988) *Successful Training Strategies* San Francisco: Jossey-Bass
Collomb B and Seidel H (1998) Foreword, to Otala L op. cit.
Delors J (Chair) (1996) *Learning: The Treasure Within* Paris: UNESCO
DfEE (1999) *Learning to Succeed: A New Framework for Post-16 Learning* London: Department for Education and Employment
Duke C (1992) *The Learning University* Buckingham: SRHE and Open University Press
Eurich N (1985) *The Corporate Classroom* Princeton, NJ: Carnegie Foundation for the Advancement of Teaching
European Union (1995) *Teaching and Learning: Towards the Learning Society* Brussels: European Union
Foucault M (1972) *The Archaeology of Knowledge* London: Routledge
Gergan K (1994) *Toward Transformation in Social Knowledge* London: Sage (2nd edn)
Gray H (ed) (1999) *Universities and the Creation of Wealth* Buckingham: SRHE and Open University Press
Gray H (1999) Re-scoping the University, in Grey (ed) (1999) op. cit.
Habermas J (1984) *The Theory of Communicative Action* (2 vols) Cambridge: Polity
Hamilton P (1974) *Knowledge and Social Structure* London: Routledge and Kegan Paul
Jarvis P (1999) *The Practitioner Researcher* San Francisco: Jossey Bass
Kerr C, Dunlop J T, Harbison F and Myers C A (1973) *Industrialism and Industrial Man* Harmondsworth, Penguin (2nd rev. edn)
Lucas C (1996) *Crisis in the Academy* London: MacMillan
Lyotard J-F (1984) *The Post-Modern Condition: A Report on Knowledge* Manchester: Manchester University Press
Meister J (1994) *Corporate Quality Universities* Alexander: ASTD and Burr Ridge, Illinois: Irwin
Niebuhr H Jr (1984) *Revitalizing American Learning* Belmont: Wadsworth
Organization for Economic Cooperation and Development 1996 *Lifelong Learning for All* Paris: OECD
Otala L (1998) *European Approaches to Lifelong Learning* Geneva: European University-Industry Forum
Pedlar M, Burgoyne J and Boydell T (1997) *The Learning Company* London: McGraw Hill
Popper K (1979) *Objective Knowledge* Oxford: Oxford University Press
Poster M (ed) (1988) *Jean Baudrillard: Selected Writings* Cambridge: Polity
Reich R (1991) *The Work of Nations* London: Simon and Schuster
Rifkin J (1995) *The End of Work* New York: G.P. Putnam's Sons
Robertson R (1996) *Globalization* London: Sage

Rowley D J, Lujan H D and Dolence M G (1998) *Strategic Choices for the Academy* San Francisco: Jossey Bass

Scheffler I (1965) *Conditions of Knowledge* Chicago: University of Chicago Press

Scheler M (1980) *Problems of a Sociology of Knowledge* edited by K Stikkers London: Routledge and Kegan Paul

Schumpeter J (1976) *Capitalism, Socialism and Democracy* London: George Allen and Unwin

Senge P (1990) *The Fifth Discipline* New York: Doubleday

Stehr N (1994) *Knowledge Societies* London: Sage

Thompson A (1999) A Beautiful Paradox, in *Lifelong Learning in Europe* 2/99 pp. 96–91

Times Higher Education Supplement (1999) Corporate Unis Muscle in 9 July, p. 3

Wallerstein I (1974) *The Modern World System* New York: Academic Press

White A (1982) *The Nature of Knowledge* Totowa, NJ: Rowman and Littlefield

Wilensky H (1964) The Professionalization of Everyone? *American Journal of Sociology* 70(2)

5 Rights and obligations

Values in lifelong education as a political programme

Kenneth H. Lawson

This chapter identifies and discusses some of the values embedded in literature on 'lifelong learning and education' which suggest that it contains an implicit political programme or agenda. Wain (1987) appears to recognize this when quoting Faure *et al.* (1972) as saying that the idea of a 'learning society' may be seen as '. . . one of the slogans on the banners in a rough political, social and cultural battle, leading to the creation of objective conditions, a call for effort, imagination, daring ideas and actions'. Further quotations make it clear that the context is 'liberal democratic' and egalitarian. Education cannot be a privilege or a gift, it 'has to be a right of citizenship'.

Suchodolski (1976), writing under the auspices of UNESCO, takes 'certain values and principles of life as absolute' and specifies three goals for lifelong education. It can lay 'the foundation for a happy and dignified life for every individual' and the '. . . overcoming of three basic types of alienation'. Moreover, 'the realisation of lifelong education finally depends on the outcome of the great social struggle about reform of contemporary civilisation'. The economic dimension is stressed by references to 'the prospects for man in a society centred on production and consumption'.

In order to make the following discussion manageable we shall concentrate upon such UNESCO sources in an attempt to set out a UNESCO programme and concept although this procedure risks attributing to UNESCO a position which it might not be happy with. Nevertheless its literature and some of its spokespersons do appear to support as foundational values, concepts which are consistent with the values of (1) political or democratic liberalism, or (2) the neo-liberalism of free enterprise market economics. These will be shown as complementary systems up to a point but they are also in tension. Both are founded on particular views of individual freedom and both attempt to secure political commitment by explaining in their different ways, how self-interest can best be served by cooperating in preserving communal interest. A foundation idea is that of a 'mutual' or stakeholder society.

Dave (1976) is explicit when he sees 'lifelong education [as] a process of accomplishing personal, social and professional development throughout the life-span of individuals in order to enhance the quality of life of both individuals and their collectives . . . [which] is connected with both individual growth and social progress'.

Lifelong education has clear instrumental purposes but within a defined ethical dimension based on liberal values. It is no accident therefore that Suchodolski locates origins of the idea of lifelong education in the report of the Adult Education Committee in the United Kingdom (the 1919 Report). This is the report which substantially influenced the development of 'liberal adult education' and for Suchodolski it is the egalitarian strand which is important. The report stressed that 'Adult education is not a luxury for a limited, exclusive group of specially selected individuals, but an integrated part of social life.' Suchodolski follows this then by seeing the education of adults as 'a constant effort towards the breaking down of the class barriers of the school system, by means of which an "elite-conscious" society tries to exclude the lower classes'. In his view lifelong education is a complex idea and a complex process but it brings much closer the relationship between 'education on the one hand and the individual as well as society on the other'. Lifelong education in Suchodolski's view has a profound overall purpose because it is based on the assumption that 'man's chief purpose in life is to exceed the limits set by the necessity of taking care of his own material and spiritual needs ... first by renewing, extending and deepening his contacts with other people and secondly by a profound commitment to social tasks'. Suchodolski's mood is both egalitarian and social.

Both Dave's and Suchodolski's tone is individualistic and commercial and other writing under UNESCO auspices show this perspective. Legrand (1975) describes lifelong education from the standpoint of the individual as representing 'an effort to reconcile and harmonise different stages of training in such a manner that the individual is no longer in conflict with himself'. He also quotes Jessop as saying that lifelong learning 'is a temper, a quality of society that evinces itself in attitudes, in relationships and in social organisations'.

In the same publication, Kirpal makes a more explicit political statement, noting that: 'nowhere has class and privilege been completely eradicated ... [therefore] equality of access to education and culture become socially acceptable goods and the essence of democratisation of man in all his activities and the broadening of his scope and horizons in all directions of his own choice'.

In the Hamburg Declaration of July 1997 presented to the fifth UNESCO international conference on adult education and embodied in the Mumbai Statement (1998) we read: 'Adult education thus becomes more than a right, it is a key to the twenty-first century. It is both a consequence of active citizenship and a condition for full participation in society. It is a powerful concept for promoting justice, gender equality and scientific and social development.'

These might be seen as overly optimistic claims and a rather utopian view of the effectiveness of educational solutions but the politically relevant values are clear. The Mumbai Statement emphasizes the key purpose of lifelong learning as 'democratic citizenship' but it also takes into account the importance of economic development, the interests of the least powerful, and the impact of industrial processes on the caring capacities of our common home, the planet.

The prospective is both local and global, it addresses the interests of civil society, the abstraction known as the economy and not least the interests of the less powerful in our societies. This means that however lifelong education is defined, its scope is wide and there can be no curriculum defined in advance, as in more conventional concepts of education. As the Mumbai Statement notes '... when we focus on the word "life" within the concept of adult learning we are drawn towards understanding learning as part of and related to, the full ecological dimensions of our existence'.

The emphasis on democratic citizenship is also important as a status which is connecting individuals and groups to the structures of social, political and economic activity, which 'highlights the importance of women and men as agents'. That implies responsibility, a duty to understand political, social and economic issues and a responsibility to act on the basis of what is learned. This all suggests that thinking about lifelong learning and education (the terms are frequently seen together) is by no means value neutral, it is both ethically and politically loaded. Moreover, it is clearly directed towards the interests both of individuals and communities. Education seen from these perspectives is not merely an activity throughout life, it is for life. Moreover, the evidence strongly suggests that a particular model of life is intended. It is a form of life which recognizes a mutuality between the personal and the social. The values are highly consistent with the values of a liberal democratic society and it is the furtherance of these values by educational means which may be seen as the political programme inherent in UNESCO concepts of lifelong education.

Some key concepts

These include: 'individuality', 'citizenship', 'rights', 'equality', 'justice', 'community' and 'democracy' all of which are from the vocabulary of 'democratic' or 'social' liberalism.

A second set of concepts which derive from the vocabulary of economics, includes 'competition', 'the workforce', 'training', 'professional currency', and 'human captial'. These as Vinokur (1976) puts it are part of 'the material base of society', i.e. the articulated whole of its productive forces. In this context education, itself a non-economic activity, has economic functions which include the transmission of value systems and the formation of a labour force.

By conflating the two aspects of liberalism together, the values associated with lifelong education as a UNESCO concept are quite specifically instrumental and they are directed to such general goals as 'adaptation to more rapid economic and social change'. From a social point of view lifelong education is an investment but from this point of view it is what is sometimes called a 'positional good' which helps to locate individuals within economic and social structures by virtue of saleable skills. Lifelong education becomes an instrument of social mobility. It also helps to guarantee employment in a world of rapidly changing technology.

From an individual point of view, the economic aspect of lifelong education, that is to say its training function, provides the motivation for engaging in lifelong education. This is a problem discussed by both Dave and Kirpal (1976). They recognize that some individuals might have no wish to engage in education throughout life and that there are problems of alienation to be overcome. One way in which interest in lifelong education might be engendered is by helping individuals to recognize that self-interest is involved and this is precisely the motivation embodied in theories of free market economics. Neo-liberalism in keeping with political liberalism is based on an assumption that the private and public domain coincide at some point. A personal choice has public repercussions and the public affects the private therefore both parties to an agreement agree precisely because there is some mutual gain. A contract is entered into. This is a simplistic view but it is in essence at the heart of liberalism in both its political and its economic forms. A contractual relationship is embodied in the concept of citizenship and the citizen as a private person also has an interest as a public person. The liberal state is deemed to exist for the benefit of its citizens who in turn are deemed to have a commitment to the governance of the state. The private and public domains coincide.

In liberal terms therefore, lifelong education is seen as mutually beneficial, and self-interest, in theory, becomes the motivator. On this view liberalism is an attempt to justify the exercise of authority by mutual consent. It is based on a contractual theory of politics with an individualistic ethic and authority is derived from consent. We put forward the hypothesis therefore that lifelong education in its UNESCO formulation is intended to secure commitment to lifelong education by mutual consent which brings together both private and mutual interests. It is based on agreement between contracting parties, who bring together both private and public interests. Individuality is deemed to be reconcilable with mutuality and we conclude with an outline of the liberal foundations of these assumptions.

Control of agreement: individuality and community as foundations of the theory of liberal democracy

Classical liberalism may be seen as an attempt to justify political power by locating it in the ideas of assent and agreement, manifest in a hypothetical 'social contract'. Its values are there located in the foregoing account of lifelong education and they include 'rights', 'equality', 'justice' and 'choice'. The concept of 'citizenship' is central as a device for conjoining the private domain with the public domain, but it starts from a position which emphasises the value of 'individuality' as an ethical principle. This is clearly set out by C. B. MacPherson (1962) writing on Locke's theory of 'possessive individualism' which begins from an assumption that a foundational possession is the power to choose.

MacPherson sets out the following propositions relevant to our present discussion:

1   What makes a man human is freedom from dependence on the wills of others.
2   Freedom from dependence on others means freedom from any relation with others except those which the individual enters voluntarily with a view to his own interests.
3   The individual is essentially the proprietor of his own person and capacities for which he owes nothing to society.
4   Since freedom from the wills of others is what makes a man human, each individual's freedom can rightfully be limited only by obligation and rules as are necessary to secure the same freedom for others.
5   Political society is a human contrivance for the protection of the individual's property in his person and goods and for the maintenance of orderly relations of exchange.

A central principal in liberal theory is the one contained in 4 above which recognizes the mutual dimension of self-interest. My freedom depends in part on freedom from interference from others. Likewise their freedom is dependent on freedom from interference by me. There is a mutual obligation to maintain each other's freedom and the protection of self-interest is dependent on this mutual obligation which produces a joint public interest. A right (to personal freedom) generates an obligation, and it is a recognition of this which produces the so-called 'liberal dilemma'. Individual freedom depends upon public acknowledgement and defence of a right to be free, and this right depends upon acceptance of public regulation. A liberal democratic society and state has to be seen as a 'mutual' or stakeholder society in which regulation has to be accepted in order to defend individual freedom. Recognition of this produces the concept of 'citizenship' which entails both rights and duties. It represents both freedom and constraint.

Historically this set of ideas was embodied in the city state of classical Athens which as Kitto (1964) expresses it 'was the means by which the Greeks consciously strove to make life both of the community and of the individual more excellent than it was before (and what began as) a local association for common security became the focus of man's moral, intellectual, aesthetic, social and practical life, developing and enriching them in a way in which no form of society had done before or has done so since'.

Farrar (1988) reinforces this view when she says that Athenians 'did not continue the good in terms of direct material advantages. Political life expressed . . . an ordered self-understanding not a mere struggle for power.' Moreover, 'political status, the status of the citizen both marked and shaped man's identification with those aspects of human nature that made possible a reconciliation of personal aim and social order'.

Writing in the context of modern liberalism but from an extremely individualistic point of view emphasizes the tension between the individual and society. Nozick (1974) writes ' . . . there is no social entity with a good to which individuals contribute. There are only individual people, different individual people with their own individual lives. Using one of these people for the benefit of others, uses him and benefits others . . . To use a person in this way does not sufficiently respect and take account of the fact that he is a separate person and that his, is the only life that he has.'

Nozick goes on to argue that if an individual makes a sacrifice for the benefit of others 'he does not get some overbalancing good from his sacrifice', and ' . . . there is no moral outweighing of one of our lives by others so as to lead to a greater overall social good. There is no justified sacrifice of some of us for others.'

Such arguments present a particular perception of individuals as 'persons' that is to say being entitled to the utmost respect and freedom from responsibility for others. It is a view that gives priority to the idea of 'authority', although interestingly, the terms do not appear in the index to Nozick's book.

Nozick's view as simply stated appears to make no allowance for the fact that individuals derive benefit from society and where fixed or limited resources are concerned, in purely economic terms the consumption of goods by one person necessarily means that they are not available for others and there is mutual self-sacrifice in many fields. Nevertheless, Nozick's purpose is to emphasize the importance of individuals as ethical subjects entitled to respect and consideration by others.

In the concept of liberal thought overall, the purpose of arguments for a strong conception of individuality is to demonstrate that there is no 'good' beyond individuals and to which they contribute and owe allegiance. There is no universal and ordering 'social good' or 'good of the state' beyond the sum of individual goods freely chosen. What matters are our personal scales of preference and these order our choices but they are choices which make demands upon a common pool and as individuals we are interrelated and interdependent. Our language, our culture are acquired from others and what we call our values are developed and ordered within a social context.

Sandel (1982) observes that views such as Nozick's presuppose a very rarified and abstract notion of the self which is defined independently of its attributes. It is more like the unlocated Cartesian 'I' who thinks. In reality 'thinking' is a rational rule-governed process. It involves the ordering of thoughts, and we learn from others what the rules are and how to apply them. In short we are, in some sense of the word 'educational', socialized beings owing allegiance if not gratitude to our society. In a sense individuality already presupposes communality, but there are tensions and some are created by our perception of self interests, but such a term has meaning only in a communal context—which allows individuals to identify their interests from the interests of others.

In Taylor's (1991) view, we regain 'horizons' in order to construct our own authenticity, and 'defining myself means finding what is significant in my difference from others'. In Rawls' (1973) terminology, 'we do not start *de novo* without a structure or fixed contours, there is no algorithm for settling upon our good, no first person procedures of choice'. The necessity of a 'community' as a precondition for the development of individuality seems to be obvious and it is a recognition of this which produces the liberal dilemma. How can private space be reserved within a community in which each individual is believed to have a right to choosing and pursuing a personal idea of the good?

Rephrased, the question addressed is how can self-interest be protected without some form of regulation. Self-interest has to be compromised in some way because it is in everyone's interest to accept a form of governance. A form of governance which does not contradict the idea of free choice is the specification therefore it must rest upon choice, and its role a minimum one—the protection of individuality. The argument leads to a liberal democracy, based upon consent, and an implied social contract.

In such a form of government (which in theory reconciles the private and the public domain) can be seen the logic of a UNESCO concept of lifelong education. That too is in the interests of individuals but what they learn is deemed to be of value to the community of individuals and to each member of it. Self-interest is seen to work in a shared public interest from which everyone benefits. It is an idealised model designed to remove the problem of alienation and to secure commitment to education as a private and public good.

The claims of 'citizenship'

The concept of 'citizenship' has two dimensions. It implies 'membership' as a status which is an entitlement to protection and is a main reason why refugees are so anxious to be recognized as citizens in a host country. Citizenship carries 'privileges', 'entitlement' and 'rights' (to which we shall return). Citizenship also carries corresponding 'responsibilities', 'obligations' and 'duties'. The latter are constraints but they do not necessarily run counter to individual self-interests. As Parfit (1984) puts it, we need not assume that ' . . . if I am self-interested I shall *always* be trying to do whatever will be best for me'. It is sufficient that 'I never do what will be wrong for me'; 'I try to choose the least worst option in the circumstances.'

A citizen in accepting responsibilities, obligations and duties, is sacrificing some freedom and self-interest and judgements have to be made on such things as:

1 legislation, political and economic policies
2 procedures for resolving conflicts and for reconciling disagreements
3 the grounds and limits of political and ethical values and decisions.

These issues are both abstract and concrete. They are abstract in the sense that they raise questions about generalized and universalized principles and about particular concrete cases. Not only willingness and a commitment to participate in procedures and decision-making processes is involved. Information skills are also necessary. An appropriate education is necessary. It is not an optional extra. A knowledge of the reasons for particular procedures and an ability to make use of them are both necessary as is a knowledge of the nature of and reason for particular duties and the basis of obligations.

On a strict interpretation of democratic liberal principles, the force of particular obligations can be challenged but only on good grounds. This means that a stronger obligation must be cited and an understanding of the rationale behind a more extensive framework of obligations is required. This framework includes values such as 'justice', 'fairness', 'equality' and 'rights'.

The concept of 'rights' is essential and they play an important role in Rawls' (1973) theories of liberalism. He attributes to individuals the right 'to determine the grounds and limits of political obligation and duty'. The nature of an obligation in a particular case has to be judged; and although principles such as 'fairness' and 'justice' become relevant, the wider network of values which created the particular obligation are questionable.

Despite such considerations 'obligation' remains as a central value. It has moral force only because it is accepted as having moral force, but in the end its force lies in its role within a system which rests on actions and legislation being based on what are seen ultimately as being 'good reasons', one of which is the furtherance of human welfare and dignity and mutually agreed self-interest. A consensual system of interlocking values is presupposed.

Rights, justice and fairness

All three concepts are based on the notion of 'equality' and the idea of a 'contract' which is equally binding upon the partners of the contract. In liberal theory the total structure of society and the state is a series of mutually advantageous contracts. Individuals implicitly contract to respect each other, and the social contract embodied in the total structure. The basis of each agreement still resides in the notion of self-interest and personal choice and commitment. It is still the individual as the basic ethical value.

In such a system or framework 'rights' are an entitlement which in Dworkin's (1981) view are 'political trumps held by individuals (who) have rights when for some reason, a collective goal is not a sufficient reason for denying them what they wish as individuals to have or to do'. Once again we can discern a commitment to individual freedom and especially freedom to choose, as the final liberal principle. Rights must be equally held by everyone and justice is defined partly in terms of 'fairness'. Therefore, the most fundamental right is the right to equal treatment in like cases. This is a statement of principle.

Dworkin (1981) notes the difficulties in distinguishing 'rights' from 'goals'. Thus the right to the freedom of speech, is also an objective or goal to be embodied in policies and all putative rights and claims to rights must be similarly embodied. There has to be agreement on what entitlements are so strongly justifiable that they warrant the status of being a right.

To conclude this section we may note that the purpose of rights, justice and fairness are all intended to make the private and the public interests converge. It is only then that universal commitment to government and the whole apparatus of a state can be recovered. Rationality and consistency in relationships at all levels are required and the modern view of democratic liberalism, finally attempts to reproduce the Athenian ideal. There should be shared and agreed social and political vision based upon shared values and goals. The individual good coincides with the public good.

It must be noted that it is a theoretical justification of liberal democracy and the assumption on which it rests that has been outlined. It is not a descriptive account but it is being suggested that something like the above theory is implicit in UNESCO thinking about lifelong educa- tion. The abstract nature of the account may be illustrated further by using some of the assumptions in Rawls' (1973) theories in which he defines liberal democratic principles on the basis of their inherent rationality.

Rawls' intention is ' . . . to present a conception of justice which generalises and carries to a higher level of abstraction, the familiar theory of the social contract as found, say, in Locke, Rousseau and Kant'. Rawls' guiding idea is that the principles of justice for the basic structure of society are the object of the original (hypothetical) agreement. 'They are the principles that free and rational persons concerned to further their own interests would accept in an initial position of equality'. The conclusion drawn is that it would be rational, that is to say, it *would* be in their self-interest to recognize a mutual obligation to rules which ensure fairness, as the foundation of 'justice' and a system based on equal rights and equal obligation.

A point to be noted in our context is that the initial position assumes the importance of indi- viduality and a respect for persons and their interests. From the initial position, the argument takes us to a final position in which individuality is recognized and a respect for it is main- tained within 'the bonds of civic friendship'. Out of this bond, a social commitment is deemed to arise and it is this sense of commitment which may be seen both as an assumption and a goal implicit in UNESCO conceptions of lifelong education.

The neo-liberal stand

This strand in liberal thought has been described by Marshall (1890, 1952) as being embodied in a system of economic freedom within a framework of laws. In this context, freedom is embodied in freedom to buy and to sell, and also as workers, property owners and organizers they should be free to seek maximum reward. For Adam Smith (1776) in his *Wealth of Nations*, 'self-interest' and 'mutual liberty' are fundamental ideas. In neo-liberalism 'justice' and 'fair- ness' are best achieved by process of supply and demand and as for Marshall in the concept of 'economic equilibrium'. Such values are also embodied in the Mumbai Statement which emphasizes 'human capital', the 'labour market' and the need for 'greater flexibility', greater responsiveness and a greater participation by the private sector in all parts of the educational system. There is an emphasis upon the need for vocational education and training in the inter- ests of greater competitiveness. This indicates what Forrester (1998) calls a 'vocational logic'. Nevertheless, the Mumbai Statement, despite its emphasis upon the need for a competitive workforce, is concerned with the welfare aspects of economic activity including, unemployment, uneven development and economic inequality. In this way, private and public interests converge and there is a call for 'broader forms of community engagement or partnerships with both the world of work and with diverse groups of learners'.

A connection between private and commercial interest is presupposed and the underlying but unspoken assumptions are consistent with those which underpin political liberalism. It is in Adam Smith's terminology an assumption that cooperation and competition are each necessary to the working of what he calls 'the invisible hand' which produces economic prosperity through the separate endeavour of individuals. This view is presented by Robbins (1952) in discussing the German concept of 'Harmonielehre' which expresses a sense of purpose, a teleology of economic activity.

As Robbins put it 'the purpose of exchange' in the classical economic model 'is to surrender something which one prefers less to obtain something that one prefers more'. There is a balance of the need to give up something of value in order to acquire something of greater value. This parallels the sacrifice of self-interest in political terms in order to produce a greater sum of communal security. This is an argument for regulation and government as necessary both to private and public welfare. Neo-liberalism expresses the same idea in economic terms.

In Marshallian economics of perfect competition which presupposes that the equation of marginal utilities or gains is balanced against marginal cost or sacrifice in order to maximize utility or satisfaction. This is the economic equivalent of the political benefits of personal sacrifice and mutual gain in accepting the role of democratic citizenship. The limitations of free competition were already recognised by Smith in the eighteenth century and given technical precision in the 1930s by Robinson and Chamberlin respectively in their theories of imperfect and monopolistic competition.

It may be said therefore that neo-liberal economics recognizes the need for regulation and constraint by individuals in the interest of a greater good. In more personal terms, individuals sacrifice time and effort in economic roles in order to secure personal goods. An economic system, however unfairly weighted between labour and capital and governed by regulations and constraints, is in the end a system based on ideas of mutuality and a conjunction of private and public interest.

It is in such a context that the necessity to learn may be seen as being both a private motivation in order to keep one's place in an economic system and as a public gain as a consequence of engaging in education. No judgement is being made here of the enormous simplifying assumptions behind political liberalism and economic neo-liberalism. The present purpose is to suggest only that these political, social and economic value systems appear to underpin UNESCO thinking about lifelong education.

Postscript

Two distinct but related forms of liberalism have been identified, both postulated on the assumption that 'individuality' is a fundamental value. In political liberalism and in economic neo-liberalism a beneficent form of individualism is based on the liberal concept of an 'individual'. It hinges on the belief that individuals are also persons and part of our concept of a 'person' is that as a rights-bearing individual with corresponding social obligations, we are dealing with a moral concept. 'Individuality' is a socially located concept inseparable from ideals of 'community'. It is assumed that logically and pragmatically the idea of being an individual as a person has to be socially located. Languages, cultures and economic welfare are all in some sense of the word acquired from and within a context of community. Taylor (1991) has called this view of individuality and individualism a 'moral ideal'. It contrasts with an 'amoral phenomenon' something like what we mean by egoism. This he regards as a 'phenomenon of breakdown . . . which leaves anomie in its wake'.

Taylor's view derives in part from de Tocqueville and he uses it to good effect in arguing for inescapable horizons of significance which he calls 'authenticity'. This idea has already been alluded to above, but it is worth further emphasis.

In much of the literature on education, especially the education of adults, 'self-development' and 'self-discovery' are common terms, but they raise questions about the nature of 'development' and the form of what is discovered or realized.

Taylor points out that one approach is Nietzschean with a 'vocabulary' of 'self-making'. The other is John Stuart Mill's approach. Here the individual is sovereign and autonomous but Mill places restrictions on the extent of permissible liberty which define morally and politically acceptable limits. Such views are consistent with what has been said above and they can be seen rightly as within the domain of lifelong education, not only as economically relevant, but as morally and politically relevant. The limits where 'individuality' and the authority of society meet are not fixed and that is Mill's point. We need to know our rights and duties. We have to learn when to fix the shifting boundaries as social, political and economic conditions change. This entails continuous learning and relearning. This could be one of the strongest justifications for lifelong education. Another justification is that learning can also be interesting, exciting and enjoyable. No one appears to suggest that lifelong education might be fun.

References

Chamberlin E (1957) *The Theory of Monopolistic Competition*. Harvard University Press, Cambridge MA (8th edn).

Dave R H (ed.) (1976) *Foundations of Lifelong Education*. UNESCO Institute of Education, Pergamon Press, Oxford.

Dworkin R (1977) *Taking Rights Seriously*. Duckworth, London, pp. 169–71.

Farrar C (1988) *The Origin of Democratic Thinking*. Cambridge University Press, Cambridge.

Faure E *et al.* (1972) *Learning To Be*. Harrop, London.

Forrester K (1998) 'Adult learning: a key for the Twenty-first century' *International Journal of Lifelong Education*, November–December 1998.

Kirpal P N 'Historical studies and the foundations of lifelong education' in (Dave Ed. 1976) *Foundations of Lifelong Education*. UNESCO, Institute of Education, Pergamon Press, Oxford, p. 102.

Kitto H D F (1964) *The Greeks*. Penguin, Harmondsworth.

Legrand P (1975) *An Introduction to Lifelong Learning*. Croom Helm, London, p. 54.

MacPherson C B (1962) *The Political Theory of Individualism*. Oxford University Press, Oxford, p. 3.

Marshall A (1890, 1952) *Principles of Economics*. Macmillan, London.

Mumbai Statement on Lifelong Learning, Active Citizenship and the Reform of Higher Education (1998) *International Journal of Lifelong Education*, vol. 17, no. 6, November–December, pp. 359–60.

Nozick R (1974) *Anarchy, State and Utopia*. Blackwell, Oxford, pp. 32–3.

Parfit D (1984) *Reasons and Persons*. Oxford University Press, Oxford, pp. 5–6.

Rawls J (1973) *A Theory of Justice*. Oxford University Press, Oxford, pp. 3 and 11.

Robbins L (1952) *The Theory of Economic Policy*. Macmillan, London.

Robinson J (1933) *The Economics of Imperfect Competition*. Macmillan, London.

Sandel M J (1982) *Liberalism and the Limits of Justice*. Cambridge University Press, Cambridge.

Suchodolski in (Dave Ed. 1976) *Foundations of Lifelong Education*. UNESCO, Institute of Education, Pergamon Press, Oxford, pp. 77–8.

Taylor C (1991) *The Ethics of Authenticity*. Harvard University Press, Cambridge, MA.

Vinokur A 'Economic analysis of lifelong education' in (Dave Ed. 1976) *Foundations of Lifelong Education*. UNESCO, Institute of Education, Pergamon Press, Oxford, p. 314.

Wain K (1987) *Philosophy of Lifelong Education*. Croom Helm, London.

6 The evolution of the learning society

Brain science, social science and lifelong learning

Jack Cohen and Mal Leicester

The single most far-reaching consequence of the Standard Social Science Model has been to intellectually divorce the social sciences from the natural sciences, with the result that they cannot speak to each other about much of substance.

(John Tooby and Leda Cosmides 'The psychological foundations of culture')

The movement towards lifelong learning

'Lifelong learning' in 'the learning society' is currently a hot issue for educators worldwide. In Britain the Government has issued a Green Paper (consultative document) on lifelong learning (1996), the European Commission has published a White Paper (considered statement) on the learning society, and Japan has its Lifelong Learning Act. In Britain the University of Industry, the expansion of further and higher education by 500,000 places and a national system of Individual Learning Accounts are proposed. While gratified by this current rhetoric, we wonder whether the expansion of educational job opportunities and government publicity, are not more potent motivators than the liberal philosophy to which the rhetoric pays lip service.

There are, if we take them at face value, two linked motivating ideas in this movement for increased learning across the lifespan, which Taylor untangles as 'the perceived needs of an increasingly sophisticated economy for a more skilled and educated workforce, and the desire, within a context of greater accessibility, for wider participation' (Taylor, 1998). Lifelong learning is presented as having the potential to maximize the proportion of citizens able to contribute to their society's economic and political well-being. This ideal, that all citizens should continue to develop their skills, their knowledge base and their intellectual performance after mandatory education has finished, is widespread. Ancient Athens has been presented as such a participatory society, but there are few, if any, rival claims; and the slightest historical knowledge casts doubt even on this claim—women, slaves and even many men were not counted as citizens and were not part of the philosophical discourse which has dominated our picture of their city. The evidence seems to suggest that with models of societal educational provision favoured in the past, including the recent past, only a small proportion of the population participate to any substantial degree in post-mandatory formal learning. Indeed, the 'universal participation in mandatory learning' for the young was rarely universal and never mandatory. Our picture of the past of our own and other societies too often has our assumptions—children at school is a common one, but see Dickens' portrayals of the London poor—imputed to it.

What these 'past' societies have actually done is to have provided a common 'Make-a-Human-Being' kit (Cohen, 1989) using fairy tales, songs, myths and tales and a shared experience of a succession of social roles. In societies where many or most children were schooled, this has usually been followed by some sectors of young people following one of a number of apprentice learning opportunities in early adulthood (e.g. army training, medical training, car mechanic apprenticeship, teacher training). This is a model for the majority of people in our own society, of course.

However, these models cannot provide a lifelong learning society in which all adults fully participate, for three reasons. First, they still incorporate the notion of 'the educated man' (Peters, 1966). In other words, there is thought to be an end-point which can be attained at a particular age (say 21) such that one is now equipped for life and need not continue to learn. Second, their vocational/professional programmes are progressively divorced from everyday life, since they specialize in some small segment of adult activity. Third, as we argue in the coming section, both schooling and post-school professional development start from a mistaken view of how the brain works and thus of how we actually learn.

Many critics have commented on the potential bias in these forms of vocational lifelong learning against liberal forms of education which emphasize 'learning for its own sake' and 'the development of individual potential'. In the model of educational provision we will propose, we acknowledge both the need for a skilled workforce linked to economic prosperity *and* the value of many liberal forms of education. Our perspective on lifelong learning reconciles this classical distinction by relegating it to history: self-realization as a citizen can synthesize and continue both ideals. Whereas current conceptions of post-school educational provision tend to emphasise either vocational training (University for Industry, National Vocational Qualifications, human resource development, work-based learning, etc.) or personal development (extra-mural or leisure courses, self-directed learning, etc.) our approach to lifelong learning, though radically individualistic, will also be a fruitful way of encouraging a maximized contribution to a society's economic well-being. Not only will what we propose incorporate the development of individual portfolios of skills, the sheer variety of these will lend itself to vocational flexibility. Moreover, precisely because all citizens can develop congenial combinations of skills, we have a more motivating approach for a larger proportion of citizens than the current uniform expectations of standardized competencies (Hyland, 1998). Our proposals, in other words, inter-relate the vocational and the liberal conceptions of 'lifelong learning' and do so in such a way that mass participation is more likely to be achieved.

A new approach to lifelong learning

What is new about our approach to lifelong learning is that it is based on important new insights about the nature of the human brain, a neglected domain in the current debates about the learning society—indeed in educational thinking per se.

Much educational theorizing is partial—both in the sense of incomplete and in the sense of biased. This lack of breadth and balance in educational thinking and educational provision arises because ideas from the natural sciences are simply neglected by those supposed to be trained in education. Philosophical, psychological, socio-psychological and sociological research and understandings, and increasingly, the actual experience of 'the reflective practitioner' (Schon, 1983) are much more educationally influential, despite the inevitable distortions which arise from their inattention to most modern science. Yet the study of the brain is surely particularly relevant for education. Since we learn with our brains, or, at least, to put that less contentiously (because at this point we are not considering the relation of mind and brain), since our brains are significantly involved in our learning, new ideas in the brain sciences must play their part in illuminating how to facilitate worthwhile learning.

In what follows, we have taken ideas associated with the important notions of the 'interactive brain' and the 'adapted brain' in order to explore their potential for education at two levels— the level of the individual learner and the level of social policy. In more concrete form, given that there are strong grounds for these particular accounts of the nature of brains, what are the policy and pedagogic implications?

Models of the brain

A common assumption has been that the brain is a sort of general computing device (Greenfield, 1997). This assumption was commonest with early models of the brain. Marcello Malpighi, for instance, in the seventeenth century, saw the brain as functioning homoge- neously as one huge gland. A little later, in the first part of the eighteenth century, Jean-Pierre Flowers also concluded that the brain was homogeneous. He removed parts of the brains of laboratory animals and found that all functions grew progressively weaker rather than select- ive functions being specifically impaired.

This idea of a uniform brain with no specialist parts has left a legacy in our educational thinking, about a general IQ for example. And it seemed to make sense to feed the same body of knowledge into all learners, whose brains would learn/process/compute the data in the same way. Those who assimilated the requisite amount of knowledge by adulthood (whether attained at 16, 18 or 21) counted as 'educated'. This idea perpetuates the 'front-end' model of edu- cation, as equivalent to 'schooling', rather than encouraging notions of learning across the lifespan.

Even when these early ideas were discredited the notion of a unitary centre of operations proved difficult to let go. It was still felt that there must be some kind of mini-super brain, or ultimate controller, in charge of more discrete functions. Or the brain unity was seen like a sponge cake, in layers: thus, Maclean (quoted by Greenfield, 1997) suggested in the 1940s and 1950s a three-tier brain, composed of the most 'primitive, reptilian', the 'more advanced, old mammalian' and the 'most sophisticated, new mammalian' layers responsible for instinctive behaviour, emotional behaviour and rational processes as one proceeds upwards.

At the beginning of this century, neurophysiologists began to use electrodes and oscillo- scopes to investigate the workings of nerve cells. Until then their star-like shapes and connec- tions had been indicative of their network and messaging functions, but the discovery of the nerve impulse was a quite remarkable revelation. After clockwork and other mechanical models, all later models were imbued with the magic of electricity. But this also has been grossly misunderstood. Confusions have continued into the modern teachings about brain function, because electricity is good modern magic which matches the mystery of brain function; it com- pounds the confusion. The nerve impulse is primarily a movement of ions, accompanied by electrical events; ion pumps then use energy to return the system to its original state; a nerve impulse is much more like a line of falling dominoes than like an electric current in a wire. It is slow, it is repetitive and it is emphatically not digital in its effects (although nerve impulses themselves are something like all-or-nothing). The effect is nearly always analogue, the infor- mation is carried in continually-varying frequency of impulses. There are a few nerve cells which are off-on, and some very complex ones may indeed be able to count, but their action is not digital. Therefore our present reductionist models of brain working, which model brains on digital computers, are probably as confused as the early electrical and even the clockwork ones. The idea that sense organs are like mechanical cameras or microphones, which plug into the idea of the digital computer, and that muscles and other effectors function similarly, are equally false-to-fact. We now know that the development of brain, sense-organs and effectors proceeds by continual interaction, the brain tuning the sense organs, and the feedback from effectors and sense organs recursively determining the new states of the brain.

In the nineteenth century, functions of the brain were argued from accidental or surgical deletions, but unlike Flowers in the eighteenth century, more differentiated function was argued from the lesions; brain areas for language and for movement of the limbs were mapped. Apart from the odd phrenologists, who took this idea much too far, and produced a generation of scientists holding to the old one-brain picture because they did not wish to be tainted with phrenological superficiality, brain scientists working with animal and occasionally human brains mapped many and diverse areas and tied them to functions. This mapping met the brain-electrode science of the neurophysiologists and contrived between them a kind of imagined brain circuitry, where the anatomists' picture of 'nuclei' and 'tracts' made a structure like an old-fashioned television set circuit (we would say 'wireless set', but do not wish to lose our readers into history) with components like the high-voltage producer and the cathode ray tube representing 'organs' and the bundles of wires between them representing their informational interactions. It is very important to realize that our new model of the brain is very different again (see, for example, Pinker, 1997): the 'hard-wired television-circuit' idea has been replaced by a much softer view, of a malleable structure reconfiguring itself as it functions.

More recently, techniques enabling much less invasive explorations of the brain than the surgical, or even the finest and most well-positioned electrode, have been developed. These include Positron Emission Tomography (PET) and Magnetic Resonance Imaging (MRI). What these new methods do is to render visible the metabolically active—functioning—parts of the brain, as high-lighted areas on a picture of the whole brain, usually as a two-dimensional scan. (The patient has to receive specific radioactive or slightly-poisonous substances, so one might wonder, after the first task has been performed and the area has lit up, whether the patient would be quite as good at it *again*!)

With these, and many other, modern techniques it has become apparent that for any specific task several different brain regions are working simultaneously. Scientists have discovered that there is not just one brain area for one function, and are developing a much more complex model of an interactive brain. The brain uses a different complex set of 'organs' for each of its functions and, just as with body organs like the liver, each brain organ may play a part in more than one function. In order for an individual to live in the world successfully several brain areas tend to act in parallel, in complex ways, constantly shifting with our ongoing tasks in the world. Instead of control centres or tiers, Greenfield's metaphor is 'a cocktail of brain soup and spark' (1997). This captures the fluidity, the diversity and the recursive interactions of brain functioning. However, our own unease with this metaphoric mixture of fluids and electrics suggested to us an alternative metaphor—of permeable, branching and flexible moving pathways criss-crossing and recursively interacting with each other and with incoming information from the external world (imagine Spaghetti Junction 'reeling and writhing' and repeatedly re-assembling).

However, let us return to the view that, as different individuals interact with the world, they recursively develop these parallel brain processes in separate brain regions in differing ways. We have a picture of the making of a different brain for each developing individual. And when a particular brain region is damaged, for example by a stroke or a brain tumour, other areas of the brain develop to replace the lost functions.

What is the structure of this complex of organs in the brain? How did evolution equip us with this amazing learning device? Our brains were probably adapted to an omnivorous existence in the savannah environment, presumably mostly for individual survival and reproductive success (Foley, 1987), but with some specializations for inclusive fitness (saving our cousins from drowning if there are more than four of them?). Thus, it seems, we have developed a complex collection of separate brain processes for dealing with an individual's interactions with that potentially dangerous outside world. There are four rather problematic arguments from this image of our ancestors on the savannah. To some extent the same problems arise if we substitute the seashore, or even a carnivorous life in the margins of the early rainforest. We are not living there now, yet the brain still serves us well in today's very different world. What has happened to those special abilities which were honed then? We show many abilities, like higher mathematics, which it is totally unreasonable to suppose our brains to have been evolved to perform (how many of your near-ancestors failed to breed because they couldn't do a quick cube root of 46923 in their heads?). And how did the evolution of our complex languages, upon which so much of our culture is based, evolve? The original brain could not, it seems have evolved the complex machinery which we now use for our lexicon, our grammar.

The first two questions are topsy-turvy; put right-way-up, they have the same answer: instead of asking why our brains still operate in this very different environment, we should look at how the environment we have constructed, our extelligence (Stewart and Cohen, 1997), complements that intelligence which was developed by our ancestors. Put simply, our world fits our brains because we built that world to do so. How could we have built it any other way? But our brains are not 'fixed', as our limbs and livers are (nearly). Successive generations had progressively different brains because the environment progressively changed. It increasingly became one of social interaction and lost some of the old dangers. Each new generation's brains found new ways to develop, and this is still happening: your grandmother may be unhappy to do more than 60 miles an hour in a car, but you are blasé about speed; your children have grown up with video players and the Internet, and their brains may find the new environment much more comfortable than you do. We are suggesting that cars and the Internet would have been totally different if a different creature had evolved to invent them.

The higher mathematics question has a similar answer: the way that we phrase our questions to the universe depends upon both cultural and individual history, building upon that original savannah brain; our brain probably has not evolved much in the last 40,000 years (judging by the cast of the brain inside the skull) but its present functions would amaze even our recent ancestors. Our Mousterian (Middle Stone Age) ancestors carved tiny busts of women from reindeer antler, beautiful even to our eyes, but Cubist paintings would not appeal to them. In other words, sharing an evolutionary basis permits us to share items at its base, but we have moved so far along our cultural paths that they could not begin to follow (even if they weren't dead! Modern hunter-gatherers, of course, are no more representative of our ancestors than the writers are). We believe that mathematics, too, would be different if our brains had been differently adapted.

The language question is the most difficult. Pinker (1994) has addressed this question beautifully. He has emphasized that a brain with language has a process available to it, rather than a lexicon or even a grammar (thus departing somewhat from his mentor Chomsky). Arguing from the existence of a cryptic brain-language (that word is on the tip of my tongue) he sees the interactive origins of language processes in the child as our major clue. Children of all cultures learn their languages from those around them, from far too few clues. The information available to children is very sparse, particularly about rules of grammatical word usage. Yet after only one or two hearings, the child can accurately get noun-before-verb or invent reasonable past tenses even for invented words. This means that there were some processes, evolved within our early brain for quite different purposes (possibly for listing edible and inedible food items, and for planning actions and journeys) which were adapted for language use and development. Since then there has been a continual refinement and complicating of the language, and of the brains which use and produce it. Our Mousterian ancestor, again, would certainly not be able to follow modern speech, but there is an unbroken chain of

language-building, and progressively more involvement of more brain parts, as the generations passed. The Mousterian mind had no initial vocabulary or language structure, just as
we had no model of a car or of mathematics. We must have begun with a brain that was adapted
for other functions, and which has been recursively subverted to develop cars, mathematics
and language acquisition.

Our modern picture, then, sees the infant brain interacting with its environment as the child
develops, creating a differently programmed mind in each individual. That individual interaction alone explains our individual differences, but is not enough to explain evolution of society.
But that environment has itself evolved, as it has been changed by the succession of individuals
interacting with each other and with their children. In other words, the recursive interactions
of successive generations of adapted brains, subject to new stimuli, has mediated this progressive change. The original savannah-adapted brain, not much different in today's infants, is
now subjected to an enormously sophisticated Make-a-Human-Being kit in all cultures, refined
and complicated to produce the complex creatures we are—our extelligence is much more
complex even than our intelligence. Thus for us, our common environment, which has changed
across the generations as the extelligence evolved, provides a kind of changing common framework within which our individual experience personalizes our individual—but nevertheless
very similar—brains (Cohen, 1996, 1999).

This more complex model of the interactive and adaptive brain challenges many long-
standing educational assumptions. As we have said, there is not one main 'controller' to
'educate', by pouring in one body of knowledge for some pre-ordained end date, producing an
individual now able to cope with the world. Rather, as we can now see, there is a complex
array of evolved brain mechanisms which can learn to cope with a complex array of modern
tasks in differing ways, changing themselves in the process. While all human babies have similar 'organs', through developing some of these an individual may foreclose on others. Both
within and between cultures differentiated abilities develop and new potentialities and limitations emerge. We suggested that learning to read might compromise saga-learning. Well, it
might, but we actually don't know because we have insufficient evidence yet to specify such
actual examples of foreclosures. What we do know is that some foreclosures are likely. We
know this because we know that there is not always a coherence (congruence) between brain
development and external stimuli. For example, experiments with kittens have shown that, in
order for the brain/eye circuits to develop properly, light with images must fall on the retinas
as soon as their eyes open. If the eyelids are kept closed, even for one or two days at this time,
they cannot see properly later. This stimulus is not 'instructional', coherent (congruent) with
its effect; it makes the brain develop kittenly, its images do not instruct. We invent: not seeing
horizontal lines at three days doesn't mean they can never see horizontal lines; it might mean
that they can't see circles later, or distinguish textures! We also know that a Japanese speaker
cannot hear the difference between 'r' and 'l' as English-speakers say them. It seems that this
distinction has been foreclosed by the early 'learning' of Japanese; it happens between the
ages of six and twelve months. Thus the evidence is that early language 'learning' seems to
restrict pattern-perception to a sub-set from the full set of possible human language sounds.
These are our grounds for supposing that learning some kinds of things might well foreclose
on others: developmental learning seems to work by restricting options, by nerve cells losing
connections, refining rather than expanding our abilities.

We have said that as we live out our lives our evolved 'brain soup and spark' is developed in
unique, personalized ways. This continues across the lifespan. Even though the middle-aged
brain may be slowing down, it is still adapting and changing through interaction with the
environment. Indeed, when, with older age, loss of the neurons in the brain occurs, other
neurons can take over so that learning even into old age is both possible and desirable.

Of course, in the past, practical considerations have had more influence on educational provision than have assumptions about the brain: considerations such as the need to occupy children's time, or to 'civilize' the poor. The educators have often been but dimly aware of models of the brain and of changes in brain paradigms, from clocks to mechanical and electrical mechanisms and more recently to computers, and have not found these helpful in the classroom. In any case, what most educators know about the brain is the 'pop version', what Stewart and Cohen have called 'lies to children' (Stewart and Cohen, 1997). Some of these 'lies' about brains include the reptilian/primitive mammal/human layers, best portrayed by Carl Sagan in *Dragons of Eden*, and the left/right hemispheres story, best portrayed in W H Calvin's *The Throwing Madonna*. There is an element of truth, of honest explanation, in these stories but what most of us 'know' about the brain is wrong. However, now that scientists are in a position to check our theories and models of the brain against better empirical evidence, and we can actually 'watch' the brain work, this must change. We must take what brain scientists are more reliably discovering, and seek to work out its educational implications.

Educational Implications

The problem with working out the educational implications of the interactive and adaptive models of the brain is that we find it difficult to handle ideas that incorporate a notion of 'development', including the idea of a changing, developing brain. We tend to invent a preformation idea to explain the origin of the oak in the acorn, or of Maureen in her DNA (Cohen, 1999). We find it hard to accept that new properties can emerge, that they were not somehow already there in some primitive form. However, if we accept the notion of emergent properties, if we do not naively require that anything which is there must have been there from the beginning, then we may 'leap the hurdles' built into the suggestions of this section.

What, then, is the intellectual basis for our emphasis on emergent properties? It lies in the change of thinking about brain function which began with isolated thinkers like Wason in the 1960s and was illuminated with the 'adapted' brain models of Tooby and Cosmides (e.g. Barkow *et al.*, 1992) in the early 1990s. The Kuhnian notion of the paradigm shift is usually illustrated by reference to the shift in theoretical physics from Newton to Einstein. A similarly massive change in thinking, more relevant to this essay, occurred in biological thought. Until the 1950s, population geneticists had a very unitary view of the genetics of a species. It seemed obvious that all members of a species must have pretty well the same genetic base; they looked alike, they developed in the same way, they were manifestly one kind of life form. There were variations, of course, in such unimportant characteristics as blood groups, and some apparently useful polymorphisms (inherited variations in shape or colour) in some snails and in human skin colour. But, in general, the model was of uniformity within a species, with occasional aberrations derived from genetic mutations in a few individuals. A paper by J B S Haldane in 1956, called 'The Cost of Natural Selection', exposed the zenith of such thinking. It demonstrated mathematically that a population of about a thousand individuals could only 'tolerate' a few new gene versions entering the population (good mutations) and a few leaving (bad mutations) in individuals dying with inadequate offspring—say about ten of each, at most. With more deaths to permit more good gene entry or to remove more genetic mistakes, the population would be unable to retain its numbers. Of about 100,000 genes in the average mammal, then, only a very few, perhaps 20 would be 'mutant', for good or ill. (This model was the source of the myth of the science-fiction 'mutant'.) In the 1960s Lewontin and Hubby (1966), using a new technique which did not require lengthy breeding programmes (screening enzymes and other proteins directly to discover variants), made a radical set of discoveries which have been amply confirmed since. About one-tenth of the genes in an average individual were 'heterozygous' (a different version had been received from each parent), and about a third of all genes had a variant version somewhere in the population. Not 20 but 10,000 genes were mutant!

This discovery necessitated a complete rethinking. Instead of all rabbits, or all red deer, or human beings having the same basic blueprint, like Model T Fords, with occasional good mutations (like better headlamps) or bad mutations (like dents, or inferior bearings), we were all very different. We were like hand-built cars or hand-knitted sweaters, generally the same but different in many details. One school of geneticists dismissed this variety as unimportant, 'neutral', but the progressive revelation of correlations of the differences with environmental differences, differences of temperature tolerance, of digestive abilities, especially of resistance to disease, has made this dismissal untenable. We are indeed hand-made cars, all adjusted differently to give much the same phenotypic result. Because species have such a large reservoir of genetic adaptability, we do not now see evolution as awaiting the lucky mutation: there is ample diversity to be selected from today's variations recombined. Genetic innovation is not needed for novelty in phenotype, or for generation of new abilities.

This paradigm shift in biological thought illuminates the contentions we have made about individual brains adjusting differently to meet the same survival goal, resulting in differences in learning needs and styles, abilities and interests from person to person; each of us is a hand-knitted human being.

Once we recognize that our experience, always individual and unique, shapes the savannah-evolved micro-circuitry of the brain so that a unique brain evolves, assumptions that a uniform education should, or indeed could, be processed into these diverging centres of consciousness comes to seem more problematic. Indeed, if we take seriously this idea of complex brains, each of which has adapted to an individual's unique experience in personalized ways, a basic educational implication would seem to be that we should not, cannot, provide one general educational recipe for each individual across the lifespan. An attempt, for example, through basic education in adulthood, to attain universal literacy may prevent some adults from developing other skills and understandings, excluding them from real achievement. A society's policy of lifelong learning should surely be to develop a provision of maximum flexibility to cater for individual needs, interests, existing abilities and learning styles. And clearly such learning is an ongoing process, not one with an arbitrary end date coinciding with the finishing of school. There is some movement towards this with 'individual education plans' in schools and the proposed 'individual learning accounts' post-school, but we suggest that much more (and more consciously) such individualized learning routes and opportunities should be constructed. In addition, and this will be more difficult to accept, the practice of general testing, and the requirements for particular competencies, should be problematized; each educational trajectory must be shaped by its own rules.

All this, it must be said, has massive implications for the pre- and in-service training of teachers and 'adult' educators in the various fields. Teachers will first need to be aware of these recent findings and ideas in the brain sciences, and they must grapple in individual ways, for teachers too are individuals, with their educational implications. They would each need to work out how to facilitate highly individual learning within the particular groups of pupils/students for whom they are responsible.

It seems to us that such ideas are consonant with philosophical ideas currently pervasive and increasingly influential in the education literature—ideas which could loosely be characterized as post-modern. Although postmodernism is rarely defined (definition in any case running counter to the anti-essentialism of postmodernist epistemologies) there is certainly an emphasis on plurality of perspective and voice which seems to resonate with the notion of personalized brains and individualized ways of perceiving and interacting with the world, and with the idea of many 'truths' and a plurality of forms of knowledge and understanding (and with long sentences). Similarly, the abandonment of the notion of a homogeneous brain, a central controller, chimes with postmodernist ideas about the fragmented and multiple self (and with Dennett's (1998) influential views). And yet the modernist vision, the Enlightenment educational project, is preserved in terms of the value accorded to continuous learning for each individual—a post-postmodernism (Leicester, 2000).

Conclusions

We believe that our educational emphasis, not on a remedial 'filling of gaps' in a universal set of competencies but on promoting individual strengths, is consonant with what recent understandings in the brain sciences tell us about lifelong learning. Some good practice currently emphasizes individual learning—in school, the 'differentiated curriculum' and 'individual learning' plans, for example. But if learning models consonant with the notion of the adapted mind are to be successfully developed and implemented, greater individualization and a high degree of open-minded educational experimentation is required. Since the overall message is 'Don't fit square pegs into round holes', new teaching modes and learning structures will be based on the kind of open-ended notions characteristic of some 'adult education' ideas (for example, Mezirow's notion of perspective transformation (1991)) but applied to school as well as to post-school learning.

We do not know what skills and combination of skills, and what associated foreclosures an individual's ongoing development of an interactive/adaptive brain will bring. Until we try such methods, not like the 'free play' methods of the sixties but with observation and guidance towards new fulfilments and new learning trajectories, we will not know whether foreclosure is a real problem to be avoided in any particular case. Our perception of modern understandings in the brain sciences signals to us very strongly that this is the kind of brain we have, with foreclosure; but we could easily be wrong. All the better. But in case we are right, teaching needs not only to be guided but to be wise, to be informed by knowledge of the brain organs, their specializations and their capacities. Such 'teaching' must inevitably be less oriented to common or general goals and more facilitative of self-directed goals and perceptions; as always, the problem is where to get such wise teachers. . . . .

We suggest that the new technologies have a potentially significant role in this new kind of learning society. These technological developments readily allow for individual interests and learning directions. Watch any child at the Internet. But, in the educational establishments of the old societies, individual and collective human learning/knowledge has traditionally benefited from individual exposure to the work of communities of scholars. It seems to us that the new technologies will facilitate a fruitful interaction between individual learning—individual portfolios of skills—and established bodies of knowledge, and also facilitate communication with those having similar interests who would, in this process, be elected to the function of those 'wise teachers' whose absence we deplored. Thus collective bodies of knowledge, accumulated by the old ways, need not be lost to the personalized brains of individualized learners. The new ways make these established bodies of knowledge more readily available to more learners.

Finally, we want to point out that the kind of educational ideas and developments suggested in this chapter are inherently egalitarian in their valuing of all self-directed learning for its potential emergent fruits. No particular body of knowledge or set of skills (e.g. those currently offered in the National Curriculum) is elevated to *the* body of knowledge or *the* set of skills required for 'education'. Rather, although there will be much that is shared by groups of (or even by 'all') learners as we adapt to a common external world, nevertheless much adaptation/learning will be individualized and we will all be considered to be following valid directions in that each may be fruitful in terms of contributions to a shared society. Only in retrospect will we discover which of these paths bore most fruit. Brain studies of the future may well help to guide students more wisely, once the experimental trajectories have been mapped. Whether this prospect terrifies or appeals to each of us depends, we think, on our present differences of personality and history.

Interestingly, the movement towards lifelong learning, in the learning society, with which we began, already values 'learning' rather than 'education'; without justification being offered, they have been collapsed into one. However, traditionally, only 'worthwhile' learning qualified as educative (Peters, 1966). With our approach, however, we see that because the continuous adaptation and interaction of the brain is aimed at developing skills by which the individual copes with his environment, we have 'worthwhile' learning in survival terms built in, thus 'learning' and 'education' do justifiably merge. Again, watch children at computers, surfing the Net. And in proposing such a continuously evolving, learning society, the exciting fact is that we do not yet know what new, interesting and useful individual skills and combinations of skills will emerge.

References

Barkow J H, Cosmides L and Tooby J (1992) *The Adapted Mind: Evolutionary Psychology and the Generation of Culture*. Oxford: Oxford University Press

Calvin W H (1991) *The Throwing Madonna: Essays on the Brain*. New York: Bantam

Cohen J (1996) Who do we blame for what we are? In Brockman J and Matson K (eds) *How Things Are: A Science Tool-Kit for the Mind*. New York: William Morrow, pp. 51–60

Cohen J (1989) *The Privileged Ape: Cultural Capital in the Making of Man*. Carnforth, Lancs: Parthenon

Cohen J (1999) Becoming Maureen; a story of development. In Casti J L and Karlqvist A (eds) *Mission to Abisko: Stories and Myths in the Creation of Scientific "Truth"*. Reading, Mass: Helix Books, pp. 49–58

Dennett D C (1998) *Brainchildren: Essays on Designing Minds*. Cambridge: MIT Press

Foley R (1987) *Another Unique Species: Patterns in Human Evolutionary Ecology*. Harlow: Longman

Greenfield S (1997) *The Human Brain: A Guided Tour*. New York: Basic Books

Haldane J B S (1956) The cost of natural selection. *J Genet* **55** 511–24

Hyland T (1998) Morality and further education: towards a critical values foundation for the post-compulsory sector in Britain. *J. Moral Edn* **27** (special issue: life-long moral education) 333–4

Leicester M (2000) Post-postmodernism and continuing education. *International Journal of Lifelong Education* **19**(1) (Special issue: Philosophical issues in lifelong education)

Lewontin R C and Hubby J L (1966) A molecular approach to the study of genic heterozygosity in natural populations of *Drosophila pseudo-obscura*. *Genetics* **54** 595–609

Mezirow J (1991) *Transformative Dimensions of Adult Learning*. San Francisco: Jossey-Bass

Peters R S (1966) *Ethics and Education*. London: Allen and Unwin

Pinker S (1994) *The Language Instinct*. New York: HarperCollins

Pinker S (1998) *How The Mind Works*. London: Penguin

Sagan C (1966) *Dragons of Eden*. New York: Ballantine

Schon D A (1983) *The Reflective Practitioner*. New York: Basic Books

Stewart I N and Cohen J (1997) *Figments of Reality*. Cambridge: Cambridge University Press

Part 2

Curriculum

7 Care or control?

Defining learners' needs for lifelong learning[1]

Kathryn Ecclestone

Government policy for lifelong learning in the United Kingdom since 1997 has created a new and compelling policy discourse. Far from the hard-edged, arid economic instrumentalism of Conservative policy, New Labour emphasizes social inclusion and people's ability to survive in a ruthless global economy. It has been widely welcomed because, as Government policy proposals show, 'there are thoughts and ideas . . . which had not seen the light of day under recent governments—words such as citizenship and community, for example' (Standing Conference on University Teaching and Research in the Education of Adults (SCUTREA) 1998, p. 2). Policy now elides liberal, social justice and vocationally modernizing perspectives, thereby reconciling many educators to a move from 'equal opportunities' to 'inclusion' within existing social formations.[2]

However, despite its espoused commitment to diverse purposes for lifelong learning, policy continues to focus almost exclusively on learning for economic competitiveness. Although there is no clear evidence about the links between educational achievement and economic prosperity, fear of globalistion and of the future in general, has produced a consensus between growing numbers of supporters for education as a force for social justice, supporters of student-centred curricula and the vocational training lobby. This consensus assumes that education 'is the best economic policy we can have' (Blair in DfEE 1998). Policy and many responses to it therefore reflect a much wider shift from left-wing and right-wing politics, leading to what Avis (1998) calls a modernizing 'settlement' amongst many academics, policy-makers and educators which promotes incremental technical reform of qualifications, assessment and funding to erode divisions in a mass post-compulsory system. The promise of a democratic, more accessible assessment technology in the form of outcome-based assessment (OBA) and credit frameworks is central to such hopes.

Yet, behind much rhetoric about motivating and empowering learners to be more autonomous, powerful socioeconomic pressures are making many learners more pragmatic, instrumental and compliant in their attitudes to formal learning (Macrae *et al.* 1998, Bloomer and Hodkinson 1997). As more young people stay on in education, forms of assessment which reinforce these attitudes do not bode well for motivating them later on. In policy rhetoric surrounding lifelong learning, adults who do not participate in formal learning are transmogrified subtly as 'adults at risk' in numerous reports and policy documents (for example, Kennedy 1997, Fryer 1998, DfEE 1998, 1999). Such trends are likely to increase a temptation to see adult learners negatively and to have low expectations of them.

In this context, the chapter summarizes some responses to policy for lifelong learning, focusing on those which may indicate an emerging moral authoritarianism in the guise of liberal intentions. It then examines the origins of this ideological drift. Finally, it discusses the implications for curricula and assessment.

Responding to policy for lifelong learning

Attempts to make more learners participate in lifelong learning emphasize the need to prevent people from the risk of being marginalized (or excluding themselves). A caring concern and commitment to social cohesion are powerful antidotes to the crisis-ridden pessimism of Conservative policy which suggested that individuals should take responsibility for meeting the demands of global competiveness or suffer the consequences Nevertheless, many educators are pessimistic:

> In a rapidly changing, knowledge-based economy, many people's futures are at risk because of low levels of basic skills, inability to handle the new communication and information technologies, and poor management of many small firms. And while far too many people lack opportunity or motivation to escape from the low skills, low earnings trap, at the other end of the labour market we are engaged in an ever-faster race to keep up with technological change and change in global markets for which many of our educational systems are poorly equipped.
>
> (McNair 1998, p. 3)

Outside a consensus which links skills, motivation and economic survival, there are fears that instrumental, individualistic curricula reinforce compliance with the prevailing demands of capital (see, for example, Hargreaves 1989, Alexander and Martin 1995). Others object to making learners pay for their fate whilst having to be commited to lifelong learning for the sake of their employers (Coffield 1999, Tight 1998a). Based on fears that these trends erode democratic citizenship, critics call for: more critical, cognitively-challenging and reflective dimensions in the post-compulsory curriculum (for example, Avis *et al.* 1996); a reassertion of radical aims for adult and community education (for example, Ross 1995, Alexander and Martin op. cit.); for a critical pedagogy which uses social difference and antagonism as 'spaces' for generating critical reflection about their implications (Edwards and Usher 1996); curricula to focus more on students' needs and interests (Bates 1998, Eraut 1997, Swann 1998).

Meanwhile, critique based on theories of 'social capital' is a compelling alternative to self-interest and 'human capital', with its simplistic, causal links between individuals' motivation to develop skills, and social cohesion and economic prosperity. As Schuller and Field (1998) point out, the notion of human capital has been immensely influential at many levels, including political imagery. It emphasizes the importance of human beings as another capital investment:

> Just as physical capital is created by changes in materials to form tools that facilitate production, human capital is created by changes in persons that bring about skills and capabilities that make them able to act in new ways.
>
> (Coleman cited by Schuller and Field 1998, p. 227).

However, as Coffield (1998) argues, emphasis on human capital enables the problems of unemployment, job insecurity and continuous training to be 'privatised and handed over to individuals to solve' (p. 65). In contrast to the self-interest this produces, proponents of social motivation hope to encourage other obligations, such as the intrinsic motivation to improve one's skills, to solve a pressing problem or to promote a particular collective ethos (Fevre 1997). Linked to this, social capital theorists see learning as inspired from communal and social interests, thereby raising commitment to 'the features of social life—networks, norms and trust— that enable participants to act together more effectively to pursue shared objectives' (Putnam cited by Schuller and Field op. cit., p. 228, see also Kilpatrick *et al.*, 1999). Similarly, strands of communitarianism seek alternatives to socialism and liberal individualism (see Arthur 1998).

Following this argument, better understanding about these links, and the particular factors in specific communities (including organizations) which undermine or enhance social capital, could encourage more participation in lifelong learning (Schuller and Field op. cit.).

An emphasis on social capital seems to provide a positive, even liberating, focus on intrinsic, socially motivated lifelong learning. Nothwithstanding this, policy is influenced by reports which portray adults who do not participate in formal education as being 'marginalized' and 'at risk'. The idea that there should be more compulsion to encourage non-participants to take up learning opportunities therefore seems to be emerging, portrayed as a radical solution to problems of non-participation (Ecclestone 1999a for detailed discussion, Tuckett 1998, Ecclestone and Tuckett 2000). For those who believe that education is a force for social justice, the problem of giving people 'permission to have agency' is particularly acute when hope for the future is bleak if you do not have skills and where useful learning comes to those who have already had it. Following this argument, if education really *does* empower people, stronger direction may be needed to overcome a prevailing belief amongst those who do not participate in formal learning that education is 'not for the likes of us'. The logic of this view is that marginalized adults may need propelling into the liberating and empowering possibilities that education offers.

This benign, well-meant concern fits well with New Labour's much-vaunted 'moral purpose' and humanitarian objectives in all aspects of policy, from the Kosovo war in 1999 to welfare reform. Yet such responses sanction increased state intervention in private lives and, therefore, have potentially authoritarian tones. For example, financial incentives to motivate people to take up learning opportunities may precede stronger encouragement for them to make provisions through savings and to plan their long life of learning strategically so that they maximize opportunities for useful and relevant accreditation rather than frittering it on short-term courses without progression (see FEFC 1998a).

Meanwhile, increasing numbers of people experience such pressure to update and retrain that learning is becoming virtually compulsory (Tight 1998a), a trend also evident in parts of Europe (Coffield 1998). In addition, rhetoric about lifelong learning and learning organizations obscures how workers must be commited, flexible and, ultimately, dispensable, whilst employers cast them aside when the economic going gets tough (Coffield 1999a).

For some critics, trends towards more compulsion across welfare and social policy are a sign that New Labour is merely continuing authoritarian themes of 'neo-liberal' Conservative policy (for example, *Marxism Today* 1998, Hill and Cole 1999) and it has become commonplace amongst these critics to see New Labour as the latest manifestation of the New Right. However, moves to compulsion in lifelong learning may arise from wider ideological trends towards moral authoritarianism in the guise of liberal intentions: I explore this thesis below, drawing on Frank Furedi's analysis of a 'culture of fear and a climate of low expectations' (see also Elliott and Atkinson 1998, Heartfield 1998, Calcutt 1998).

An emerging morality?

Pessimism behind concern to protect marginalized adults from globalization reflects more profound doubts about links between knowledge creation, the benefits of technological progress and social cohesion. Arising from deeper fragmentation of philosophical and political beliefs, and a loss of faith in social institutions, discourses of 'crisis' and 'social transformation' provide a rhetorical legitimacy for political intervention in education structures, curriculum content and assessment regimes throughout Europe (for example, Field 1997, 1998, Brine 1995, Sultana 1995). It can also be argued that despair and pessimism pervade much academic response to educational policy and practice where postmodernist debates illustrate a flight from belief in changing the world (Edwards and Usher 1996).

Following this argument, discourses of fear and crisis, alongside fragmenting, even obsessive, notions of 'difference' and 'diversity', also create lower expectations about what can be done about social issues, other than to support employers in whatever they say they need to survive. Furedi (1997, 1998a, 1998b) argues that risk consciousness both creates, and arises from, a prevailing discourse of risk and a cautious, anxious outlook on the future. Through an analysis of diverse phenomena from media and political preoccupations in the UK and the United States, he proposes that a manifest lack of confidence about the future pervades all levels of society, affecting the most fervent supporters of capitalism and its one-time critics. To make his case, he synthesizes themes of fear, risk aversion and increased state regulation of lifestyle from apparently disparate examples: a myriad of health panics; campaigns for 'safe' sex and healthy living; concerns about correct parenting and children's safety; preoccupation with sexual abuse, family violence, work-place harassment and bullying; fear of environmental hazards; a morbid obsession with the fate of victims and survivors from disasters and people's emotional responses to them, rather than analysis of what causes these phenomena.[3]

Although New Labour's emphasis on personal responsibility continues themes in Conservative social and economic policy, Furedi notes a new tendency to see people as victims of fate and individual circumstance. This eulogizes the idea of victims by giving them a moral claim, not because of what they have done but because of what was done to them, whilst seeing them as scarred permanently by the events or abuse they have suffered in the past. The media reinforces this through an almost morbid fascination with human responses to disasters and personal tragedy, fostering images of damaged people who cannot help themselves or work out their own responses to problems.

In turn, this creates an insidious dependence on experts to 'help' people deal with their experiences 'appropriately', such as counsellors, advice workers and social services. In a society that is becoming more individuated and fearful, he argues that this dependency on professional helpers fuels mistrust of peers, neighbours and local communities—even the family itself. At the same time, attempts to create solidarity around tragedies—for example, Dunblane, disasters, sexual abuse, the deaths of famous people—foster the idea that such events can offer important warnings to us all, lending the events themselves, and their lessons, an apparent 'moral significance'.[4]

A consequence of fear and victimhood is to encourage dependency on experts which exacerbates the fragmentation of social communities. This leads Furedi to argue that a tendency to question the scope available for human action and intiative creates 'the diminished subject':

> Increasingly we feel comfortable with seeing people as victims of their own circumstances rather than as authors of their own lives. The outcome of these developments is a world which equates the good life with self-limitation and risk aversion.
>
> (Furedi 1997, p. 147)

The premise of a diminished subject is a misanthropic view of the world and of humanity's ability to solve problems at all levels, including personal life. This legitimizes state intervention in individuals' personal lives by initially encouraging, and then regulating, self-limitation and risk aversion, often presenting intervention sincerely and benignly as advice and guidance.

Following this argument, recent examples are proposals for the Home Office to issue guidelines to parents about how to protect children from paedophiles, from the Home Office to social services about voluntary parenting groups, from the Department of Health about being a good father, and from the DfEE about parent/school contracts. More subtly, soft forms of regulation and risk aversion also come from organizations who once campaigned for rights or equal opportunities, such as guidelines from the National Union of Students about the dangers of sex, drinking, drugs and potential violence from residents of university towns who may resent students, and from unions introducing codes of conduct for harassment at work. In these examples, 'risk' ranges from obviously dangerous ones of paedophiles (although perhaps 'stranger danger' is overplayed), to walking alone to halls of residence, men not being present at the birth of their children, to not doing your homework or being alone with colleagues.

Of course, guidelines are not moralistic per se and are often common-sense attempts to alert people to risks or to clarify protocols and expectations. Yet Furedi argues that they usually arise from mistrust and then reinforce it by anticipating and then formalizing expectations of transgression and misbehaviour. In this way, they transmogrify into rules and calls for legislation, thereby removing initiative and autonomy by codifying banal and common place behaviour whilst appearing to solve social problems. In a climate of fear and low expectations of human agency, 'risk' itself becomes redefined to mean almost any transgressional behaviour, including autonomy itself.

Citing the work of Ulrich Beck and Anthony Giddens, Furedi compares his thesis about the decline of 'subjectivity' (i.e. the potential for human action) to other accounts of risk consciousness which attribute its prevalence to technological advance and environmental hazards. Yet although fear based on risk consciousness appears to provide a provisional solution to problems of social cohesion, he argues that, instead of unity based on striving for a better future, we unite in averting risks associated with it.

Furedi also correlates risk awareness and low expectations about social and scientific progress to the decline of traditional moral values and growing uncertainty about personal and social issues. In the United States, for example, disagreement about the most elementary conduct of behaviour has been characterized as 'culture wars' and the fragmentation of moral values has become heavily politicized—illustrated, perhaps, by conflicting interpretations of Clinton's 'little local difficulty' in 1999 and a rising tide of moral censure and prurience, evident also in the UK.

Such uncertainty means that calls of traditional moralists for a resurrection of conservative values (for example, Tate 1998) have little resonance. Instead, Furedi sees the politicization of morality as the most insidious threat to beliefs in human agency, innovation and risk because it reinforces low expectations about human behaviour in all aspects of life. Belief in the power of fate, and doubts about people's ability to cope with life, undermine personal autonomy and responsibility whilst leading us to accept closer State regulation of our behaviour. He argues that the decline of traditional morality and the emergence of risk consciousness have created a moral vacuum, filled by a 'new etiquette for regulating the interactions between people' (1997, p. 150).

The idea of a 'new etiquette' is an important nuance in Furedi's thesis because it signifies a polite, caring, non-judgemental morality which seeks to empower, include and protect the powerless. Indeed, in its attempts to 'protect us from ourselves', it rejects conservative values as irrelevant whilst lecturing those who take risks. Importantly, its inclusive language reaches out to the marginalized and critics alike, appearing to confront problems of social division whilst not attaching itself directly to a system of values (a feature also evident in strands of communitarianism (Arthur 1998)). This relativism is partly a product of its own internal instability: reconciling people to a life of uncertainty cannot provide certainty of its own.

Stemming from genuine concerns about social fragmentation, the discourse of caring inclusivity which denotes the new etiquette is therefore far from a cynical hi-jacking of liberal values merely to disguise more sinister motives or to reconcile us to a gloomy future. Thus, my earlier phrase 'moral authoritarianism *in the guise of liberal intentions*' (new emphasis added) implies too much of a conscious conspiracy. Instead, any drift towards moral authoritarianism is *disguised* by liberal intentions but not deliberately. It is clearly much more subtle than this and, as Ball points out, shifts of ideology and moral economy are never clear-cut or uncontested, nor realized in standard ways (1997). Nor are they fully understood or even recognized by their exponents.

Of course, the growth of state regulation over the past twenty years is hardly a new observation. Nor is Furedi the first to note a growing celebration of 'victim' culture. However, such criticisms are normally associated with the libertarian Right (for example, Anderson and Mullen 1998). Furedi sees different roots for the phenomena he discusses from other neo-Marxist, liberal or leftist critics of New Labour's authoritarianism (see, for example, *Marxism Today* 1998, Pilger 1998). Indeed, he notes that such criticisms often object to the tone and presentation of state interventions, but not to the underlying rationale for them (see, for example, Tight 1998b). For him, the new moral authoritarianism is not New Labour's new version of conservatism or merely the individual Christian morality of individuals in the UK government. Instead, it is a logical outcome of the inability of traditional morality to address the social fragmentation of the past 20 years, and initiation, largely from the liberal Left, of a culture of fear and politicized morality. From this perspective, the new authoritarianism is not tied to neo-Liberalism or Conservativism but deeply implicated in New Labour's modernizing project.[5]

As I argued above, concern for marginalized adults 'at risk' in lifelong learning remains tainted with the profound pessimism and low expectations about solutions to social and economic problems which dogged the last two Conservative governments in the UK. Furedi argues that a new etiquette responds to pessimism by demanding that people subject themselves to the core values of safety, cautious and self-limiting behaviour and an obligation not to put others at risk. This is not to suggest that deliberately exposing people to harmful risk is acceptable but to reiterate that 'risk' can never be positive when it is associated with almost any transgressional or controversial action. In this way, a view that not learning at work risks others' jobs, or that non-participation in formal education is socially and economically irresponsible, extends moral judgments about what constitutes risky behaviour and encourages mistrust. This is especially suspect when all the formal learning and skills that individuals can accumulate does not stop high-tech employers leaving the UK (Coffield 1999a) or create new, stable jobs.

Despite this important but overlooked caveat about tenuous links between education, social cohesion and economic prosperity, the new etiquette avoids overt judgements about the causes of social problems. It offers instead a relativist, apparently liberal morality which helps people make sense of their individuation whilst suggesting that there are few radical answers except to increase individuals' accountablity for problems and make them pay more for apparent solutions (see Coffield 1998, Tight 1998a). It also justifies what Giddens calls 'a fundamental impetus towards the re-moralising of everyday life', producing a new morality that demands commitment to a lifestyle rather than to a community (Giddens cited by Furedi 1997, p. 163). In this context, education becomes redefined as a 'commodity' rather than a public good (Macrae *et al.* 1998).

In response to individuation, some critics link erosion of social commitments to the 'cult of the individual', exacerbated by human capital theory. Theories of social capital, social motivation and communitarianism are, therefore, based on a view that individualism undermines collective commitments. In contrast, Furedi argues that this emphasis misreads how faith in human agency is declining, especially amongst liberals and the Left.

Instead, people who are atomized and mistrust others are unlikely to have an elevated sense of individual aspiration, thereby diminishing rather than enhancing autonomy. This erodes possibilities for social aspirations. Following this argument, individuation implies a turning in on oneself and is not, therefore, synonymous with individualism. As a result, the type of communal motivation and trust necessary to initiate and sustain formal learning cannot be fostered when people are isolated. Yet arguments developed in this chapter show that it may be tempting to manufacture cohesion by inducing guilty obligation to others in the pursuit of social capital.

An important question for educators is whether Furedi's thesis suggests that liberal preoccupations with marginalization in lifelong learning could encourage a form of 'compulsory social motivation' to take root. Concerns to recreate collective responsibility by promoting social capital could be tainted with moral authoritarianism, albeit subtly, while this drift may be obscured by a tendency to associate authoritarianism with the 'New Right'. However, the thesis outlined here requires further theoretical development and empirical observation, as well as engagement with objections to it. As a basis for further debate, I want now to discuss some implications for teaching, learning and assessment for adult learners.

Creating compliance

It is easy, as Ball (1997) points out, to see current policy as somehow uprooted from what went before it, and unaffected by other shifts in ideology and values in public policy. Tracing such connections is particularly important after twenty years of Conservative education policy and the euphoria amongst the liberal Left for New Labour. At the same time, it is important to trace breaks with the past, particularly in terms of 'changing modes of regulation' since these create overt structures to implement policy together with much more subtle mechanisms and discourses to secure compliance (Whitty and Edwards 1994).

Ball proposes that 'the new moral economy of the public sector' is drawn from the market economy and rooted in a 'social pyschology of self-interest' (op. cit., p. 259) which has transformed our professional (and personal) subjectivities and values. Mechanisms such as inspections, quality assurance and outcome-based assessment systems all use 'micro-disciplinary practices' (p. 260) and total quality management as techniques of self-surveillance and mutual surveillance between peers (see also Hodkinson 1998). This is especially powerful as curriculum structures and assessment regimes increasingly adopt characteristics of audit, inspection and quality assurance, encouraging dependence on guidelines and regulations from a growing array of government bodies. An example is a 'code of conduct' which the Further Education Funding Council (FEFC) produced in 1998 for inspection in colleges. Partly a response to demands for more clarification but also, perhaps, a response to increasing numbers of formal, lengthy and increasingly acrimonious appeals from college principals about inspection grades, the FEFC's chief inspector stated that 'we have tried hard to get the right balance between *making rules and offering guidance*' (my emphasis) (FEFC 1998).

Of course, guidelines and clarifications are necessary in any assessment or quality assurance system based on outcomes and criteria. Nonetheless, although they seem to allow transparency about what is required, they conceal a deeper tension. Guidelines and continuous attempts to secure standardized interpretations through more 'clarification' soon become 'exemplars of good practice' and then rules, whilst criteria to clarify standards of quality become checklists for self and external regulation. Importantly for arguments about mistrust in this chapter, they also become a means of protection against challenge from learners (see Ecclestone and Swann 1999), or, in the case of FEFC inspection, from institutional managers unhappy with inspection decisions. An unintentional effect is to foster a climate of mistrust where people are increasingly reluctant to interpret independently what guidelines mean or to collaborate in order to define and solve problems for themselves. This tendency seems to feed a disempowered demand from those on the receiving end of guidance for more external prescription, followed by fear of transgression, and then resentful challenges to regulation.

Trends outlined here belie rhetorics of partnership, democracy and openness. It is therefore increasingly important to explicate how new forms of mistrust and low expectations in education might come to underpin our views about learning, assessment and quality assurance systems in new arrangements for lifelong learning.

First, expectations about higher achievement and participation for more adults in formal qualifications and programmes do not counter low expectations about the potential for human agency. If current targets largely constrain people in narrow forms of vocational training and prescriptive outcome-based assessment, lifelong learning becomes a very poor substitute for belief in the possibility of a creative life.

Second, lifelong learning seems to be evolving into lifelong assessment, based on codifying and standardizing practices hitherto at the discretion of educators and inspectors to disclose. There is, as the whole outcomes debate shows, important progressive potential in drives for transparency (see, for example, McNair 1995, Ecclestone 1999b). Yet as the systems become more complicated, they require new experts and bureaucracies to tell learners and educators how to use them 'properly', creating mistrust of deviations from the increasingly formalized learning and assessment they produce. Mistrust, not just from governments who do not trust educators, but increasingly between institutional managers and inspectors, educators and learners, becomes suffused with a fear of taking risks or innovating new ideas or practices.

Third, mistrust slowly confines spaces for innovation, creativity and risk. This problem is compounded by a circular logic of clarification and regulation. It is therefore difficult to reconcile espoused commitments to learners' autonomy and motivation when assessment increasingly confines these to pre-defined outcomes which encourage circumscribed forms of procedural autonomy (see Bates 1998, Ecclestone 2000). If educators and learners become less likely to take risks, to be innovative or to negotiate their own curriculum, there will be declining expectations that such activities are either possible—or desirable. This increases cynicism about the potential for voluntarism and instrinsic motivation amongst adults in formal learning programmes.

Fourth, a related effect is that nervousness about any learning which cannot be regulated in prescribed assessment regimes could relegate certain types of learning to the margins of traditional academic disciplines or non-vocational education, accessible by a shrinking elite, such as learners in the private sector or in the oldest universities. Hostility to 'elitism' implies that anything associated with it is irrelevant for other learners. It also produces a powerful, anti-intellectual discourse. Indeed, what is ironic about hostility to 'elitism' is that many educators accept instead tighter prescription and regulation from government agencies.

Fifth, commitments to 'inclusive', 'relevant' learning imply notions of 'deserving' and 'undeserving' learners and access to relevant (responsible) or irrelevant (irresponsible) types of learning. As Richard Edwards points out, it is possible that anything outside the learning market of current policy proposals will no longer be valued as learning whilst a discourse of participation labels as 'non-learners' those who do not subscribe to organized education and training (Edwards 1997). In a moral context which sees 'risk' as any transgressional behaviour, those who do not participate could be pressurized to do so. As Field (1999) shows, over-emphasis on social capital can lead to criticism of those who do not conform to types of learning seen as socially desirable by the rest of a community.

Sixth, Furedi's contention that the new etiquette detaches preoccupation with the minutiae of individual concerns from wider social explanations, is perhaps reflected in the way that new forms of assessment may also 'display lack of interest about deeper structures of individual development in a social context' (Ball 1990, p. 83). Ball argues that emphasis on personal responses in place of reason removes cognitively rigorous and rational appraisals of life and work (see also Hargreaves and Reynolds 1989). Meanwhile, modular assessment prevents learners from making connections between ideas and social issues or even between different modules (see Ross 1995).

Seventh, a desire to empower learners by exercising more control over them, combined with assessment systems based on increasingly prescriptive outcomes, exacerbate a tendency that different nannies 'know best' what learners need, often couching this, as Tight (1998b) notes about the Kennedy and Fryer reports, in caring but patronizing tones. This denigrates the idea that learners can express their own needs and wishes for learning, opt out of it, or define their own problems. The incursive morality I have explored not only implies that people's shortcomings make them responsible for their own economic fate but, more insidiously, for the fate of others. Notions of deficiency, remediation for learners 'at risk', together with compulsory feelings of social obligation could turn lifelong learning into a form of colonization over people's lives.

Last, targets for higher levels of achievement for more people conceal increasingly low expectations about the purpose of education and training. Instead of transformation, social change and intelligence, it makes people cope and adjust while a vocational, credentialist curriculum encourages extrinsic motivation and self-interest. This could encourage educators and learners to lower their horizons to getting through with minimum effort or engagement and undermines belief in potential for intrinsic motivation. The minimalist pedagogy that these trends produce could encourage growing scepticism that many learners are capable of such motivation at all.

Conclusion

In a climate where old political meanings of 'Left' and 'Right' are breaking down, traditional associations of authoritarianism, compulsion, social justice and autonomy with particular political standpoints all need radical examination. However, the arguments in this chapter should not suggest libertarian calls for unfettered individual freedom or the abandonment of a commitment to social justice. It calls instead for debate and further theoretical and empirical exploration of the ideas presented.

There is therefore a need to engage with philosophical and political detractions from the thesis of risk and low expectations explored here and the way that I have applied it to lifelong assessment. These can be summarized as: dismissal of the reality of a precarious future and the progressive potential of risk conciousness for new forms of democratic participation (Beck 1998a, 1998b); a need to rethink the moral implications of risk consciousness for the balance between individual freedom and State regulation, particularly in relation to definitions and control of risk (Beck 1998a); an underestimation of faith in human agency and the progressive potential of social capital; a lack of any constructive ideas to counter individualism and the socio-economic realities of people who are displaced economically, socially and politically.

Notwithstanding the gloomy possibilities explored here, the chapter does not suggest that supportive guidance, outcome-based assessment and inclusiveness in formal learning programmes are not important: there are strong progressive possibilities in new discourses of inclusiveness, as well as spaces for inspiring and empowering learners (and for them to inspire and empower us!). It is also important not to overlook the extent of self-intiated learning that people are involved in and its progressive potential (Tight 1998a).

Nonetheless, if the arguments here have any resonance, they suggest that we have to challenge the potentially constraining discourses and practices surrounding proposals for lifelong assessment and to resist their definition and regulation by government agencies. In addition, we have to be extremely wary of proposals for a formal citizenship curriculum for post-16 learners.

This requires countering the trend towards 'knowing best' what learners need. It also requires taking risks in debating with learners what their needs are and how they might be met. At the same time, a growing tendency to see adults 'at risk' means that we should also challenge a prevailing lack of faith in humanism which may be infecting educational debates (see also Harkin 1998). As a minimum, challenges to encroaching authoritarianism demand a belief that people can solve problems and define what these are for themselves: merely hoping for spaces in a risk conscious culture is likely to become more futile.

The arguments here are particularly relevant for further theoretical and empirical work on social capital. However, it may be that raising such issues is risky when the new inclusiveness of New Labour seems to create opportunities for dialogue with academic researchers about lifelong learning but only if any dissent is on government's terms (see also Coffield 1999b). In a consensus climate, we might become fearful of saying the wrong thing: risk aversion, low expectations and mistrust of peers who take risks could affect the academic community as well.

Notes

1 This chapter is adapted from an article published in the *British Journal of Educational Studies* (Ecclestone 1999a).
2 There is an interesting parallel here with the 'peace process' in Northern Ireland where Republican calls for equal opportunities in a united Ireland have become calls for 'parity of esteem' and 'inclusion' in formal bodies. In addition, in a speech by the UK Prime Minister to his party conference in 1999, the goal of 'equal opportunities' is equated with 'equal worth'.
3 This soft approach to news dominated coverage of the Kosovo war, particularly in its treatment of refugees, and has also been criticized by John Pilger (1998).
4 Examples have been coverage of the Dunblane murders in 1997, the death of Princess Diana, the *Guardian* newspaper's justification for explicit extracts on the West murders, and a general rising tide of censure in the media of public figures who transgress emerging codes of conduct, for example in relation to drug-taking.
5 This is becoming more apparent as the UK Prime Minister more overtly stigmatizes opponents of his moral crusade as 'the forces of conservativism' and, more insidiously, as 'elitists'.

References

Alexander, D and Martin, I (1995) Competence, curriculum and democracy, in Mayo, M and Thompson, J (eds) *Adult Learning, Critical Intelligence and Social Change* Leicester: National Institute of Adult and Continuing Education

Arthur, J (1998) Communitarianism: what are the implications for education? *Educational Studies*, 24, 3, pp. 353–68

Avis, J (1998a) (Im)possible dream: post-Fordism, stakeholding and post-compulsory education, *Journal of Education Policy* 12, 2, pp. 251–63

Avis, J, Bloomer, M, Esland, G, Gleeson, D, Hodkinson, P (1996) *Knowledge and Nationhood: Education and the Transfer of Work* London: Cassell

Ball, S J (1990) *Politics and Policy-making in Education* London: Routledge

Ball, S J (1997) Policy sociology and critical social research: a personal review of recent education policy and policy research *British Journal of Educational Research* 43, 3, pp. 225–7

Bates, I (1998) The empowerment dimension in GNVQs: a critical exploration of discourse, pedgogic apparatus and school implementation, *Evaluation and Research in Education* 12, 1, pp. 7–22

Beck, U (1998a) What is a risk society? *Prometheus* Winter 1998, pp. 75–9

Beck, U (1998b) Organised irresponsibility: reply to Frank Furedi *Prometheus* Winter 1998

Bloomer, M and Hodkinson, P (1997) *The Voice of the Learner in Further Education* London: Further Education Development Agency

Brine, J (1995) European and vocational policy and construction of the European Union *International Studies in Sociology of Education* 5, 2, pp. 145–65

Calcutt, A (1998) *Beat: The Iconograpy of Victimhood from the Beat Generation to Princess Diana and the Present Day* Sheffield: Sheffield Hallam University

Coffield, F (ed) (1998) *Why's the Beer Always Stronger up North? Studies in Lifelong Learning in Europe* London: Policy Press/Economic and Social Research Council

Coffield, F (1999a) Breaking the consensus: lifelong learning as a form of social control, *British Education Research Journal* 25, 4, pp. 479–99

Coffield, F (1999b) Introduction: Past failures, present differences and possible futures for research, policy and practice, in Coffield, F (ed) *Speaking Truth to Power: Research and Policy in Lifelong Learning* London: Policy Press/Economic and Social Science Research Council

Department for Education and Employment (1998) *The Learning Age: A Renaissance for a New Britian*, Green Paper, London: HMSO

Department for Education and Employment (1999) *Learning to Succeed*, White Paper, London: HMSO

Ecclestone, K (1999a) Care or control? defining learners' needs for lifelong learning *British Journal of Educational Studies* 47, 4, pp. 332–46

Ecclestone, K (1999b) Empowering or ensnaring? the implications of outcome-based assessment for higher education *Higher Education Quarterly* 53, 1, pp. 29–49

Ecclestone, K (2000) Autonomy and assessment in post-compulsory education in the UK *Journal of Education and Work* 13, 2, pp. 141–63

Ecclestone, K and Swann, J (1999) Litigation or learning? tensions in improving lecturers' assessment practice, *Assessment in Education; Principles, Policy and Practice* 6, 3, pp. 377–89

Ecclestone, K and Tuckett, A (2000) Does policy for social inclusion show signs of moral authoritarianism? *College Research Journal*, Further Education Development Agency, Summer 2000

Edwards, R (1997) *Changing Places? Flexibility, Lifelong Learning and a Learning Society* London: Routledge

Edwards, R and Usher, R (1996) *Post-modernism and Education* London: Routledge

Elliott, L and Atkinson, D (1998) *Age of Insecurity* London: Verso

Eraut, M (1997) Curriculum assumptions and frameworks in 14–19 education *Research Issues in Post-Compulsory Education* 2, 3, pp. 302–319

FEFC (1998) Press release for launch of new inspection handbook, August 18 Coventry: FEFC

Fevre, R (1997) *Some Sociological Alternatives to Human Capital Theory and their Implications for Research in Post-compulsory Education*, School of Education, University of Cardiff, Working Paper 3

Field, J (1997) The European Union and the learning society: contested sovereignty in an age of globalisation, in Coffield, F (ed) *A National Strategy for Lifelong Learning* Newcastle: University of Newcastle

Field, J (1998) *European Dimensions: Education, Training and the European Union* London: Jessica Kingsley

Field, J (1999) Schooling, networks and the labour market: explaining participation in lifelong learning in Northern Ireland *British Education Research Journal* 25, 4, pp. 501–17

Fryer, B (1998) *Learning for the 21st Century* Report of the National Advisory Group for Continuing Education and Lifelong Learning

Furedi, F (1997) *A Culture of Fear: Risk-taking and the Morality of Low Expectations* London: Cassell

Furedi, F (1998a) The fear of risk *Prometheus* Winter 1998, pp. 69–73

Furedi, F (1998b) Beyond the dramatic: reply to Ulrich Beck, *Prometheus* Winter 1998, p. 81

Further Education Funding Council (1998) *The 'Learning Age': Response from the Further Education Funding Council* Coventry: FEFC

Hargreaves, A (1989) The crisis of motivation and assessment, in Hargreaves, A and Reynolds, D (eds) *Education Policies and Critques* London: Falmer Press

Harkin, J (1998) In defence of the modernist project *British Journal of Educational Studies* 46, 3, pp.

Heartfield, J (1998) *Need and Desire in the Post-Material Economy* Sheffield: Sheffield Hallam University

Hodkinson, P (1998) Technicism, teachers and teaching *Journal of Vocational Education and Training* 50, 2, pp. 193–209

Kennedy, H (1997) *Learning Works: Widening Participation in Further Education* Coventry: Further Education Funding Council

Kilpatrick, S, Rowena, R, Falks, I (1999) The role of group learning in building social capital *Journal of Vocational Education and Training* 51, 1, pp. 129–45

McNair, S (1998) Editorial, *Adults Learning* July

Macrae, S, Maguire, M, Ball, S J (1998) Whose learning society? a tentative deconstruction, *Journal of Education Policy* 12, 9, pp. 499–507

Marxism Today, Special Edition, November 1998

Neal, M and Davies, C (1998) *The Non-Risk society* London: Social Affairs Unit

Pilger, J (1998) *Hidden Agendas* London: Hodder and Stoughton

Ross, C (1995) Sizeing the quality initiative: regeneration and the radical project, in Mayo, M and Thompson, J (eds) *Adult Learning, Critical Intelligence and Social Change* Leicester: National Institute of Adult and Continuing Education

Schuller, T and Field, J (1998) Social capital, human capital and the learning society *International Journal of Lifelong Education* 17, 4, pp. 226–35

SCUTREA (1998) Newsletter, April

Sultana, R G (1995) A uniting Europe, a dividing education? eurocentrism and the curriculum *International Studies in Sociology of Education* 5, 2, pp. 115–45

Swann, J (1998) How can we make better plans? *Higher Education Review* 30, 1, pp. 37–55

Tate, N (1998) *Authority in the Modern World*, Annual Memorial Lecture, University of Brighton, 10 March

Tight, M (1998a) Lifelong learning: opportunity or compulsion? *British Journal of Educational Studies* 46, 3, pp. 251–63

Tight, M (1998b) Education, education, education! the vision of lifelong learning in the Kennedy, Dearing and Fryer Reports *Oxford Review of Education* 24, 4, pp. 473–87

Tuckett, A (1998) Recruits conscripted for the active age *Times Educational Supplement* 22 May, p. 33

Whitty, G and Edwards, T (1994) Researching the Assisted Places Scheme, in Walford, G (ed) *Researching the Powerful in Education* London: University College London Press

8 Adult cognition as a dimension of lifelong learning

Stephen Brookfield

Adult education scholars currently find themselves in something of a dilemma. They have spent years striving to establish a theory of adult learning which they could claim represented their own empirical territory. The *raison d'être* of this effort has been to assert that adulthood as a time of life brings with it a way of learning (and a corresponding set of practices for facilitating this learning) that is not paralleled at earlier stages of the lifespan. Adult learning has been claimed to be a separate, distinct and discrete phenomenon, something that stands alone as the clear object of theory development. For many academics establishing the distinctive nature of adult learning has had important professional ramifications. If we could establish irrefutable proof that adults learned in a way that differed in kind from the learning undertaken by children and adolescents, then at a stroke we could lay claim to an area of research (adult learning) and a set of practices (adult education) that were undeniably our own. We could hold conferences, establish journals, write books, create departments and award doctorates—in short create a whole professional career structure—based on our familiarity with the conceptual and empirical territory that, clearly, was unique to us.

In the USA and UK this position was reached in the 1980s. Then, just as adult education scholars began to feel a pleasant sense of credibility and stability, along comes an American president (Bill Clinton) who talks about lifelong learning and uses this phrase in a way that emphasizes the connections between schooling and adult education. In Clinton's 1992 and 1996 Democratic presidential campaigns the ideas of lifelong learning, and the need to invest in the continuous retraining of adult workers, were continually invoked. Then, in 1997, came the publication in the United Kingdom of the Dearing report on lifelong learning, a major policy document with great ramifications for higher education. Universities begin to create chairs, institutes and departments of lifelong learning, and the idea that the provision of continuous learning opportunities is necessary to economic survival in the information age, becomes accepted as self-evident. So now those adult educators who nailed their colours to the mast of adult learning as a discrete domain are left shipwrecked.

As the discourses (and the jobs) shift to emphasizing lifelong learning as the organizing concept for adult education, this very discourse undercuts the separateness previously claimed for adult learning. Instead, learning now starts to be conceived as a lifelong process with important connections established between schooling, higher education, workplace learning, and colleges of the Third Age. So the very position that has ensured adult educators' professional credibility in the past—the position that adult learning is a discrete and separate domain—is now discredited. Yet, to abandon that position and embrace the concept of lifelong learning risks bringing with it accusations of a lack of integrity, fraud and intellectual opportunism.

It is in this uneasy situation that I want to suggest a possible resolution that acknowledges the value of the concept of lifelong learning (a phrase that I have always felt was more empirically accurate than 'adult learning') while allowing for the distinctiveness of the learning that does occur in adult life. Although I believe it is wrong to argue that adulthood stands alone as a discrete, self-contained and separate stage of life, I do believe that there are forms of learning we engage in that are visible in a much more heightened form in adulthood as compared to childhood and adolescence. In other words, while these forms of learning are discernible at earlier stages of life, it is in adulthood that they stand out in particularly sharp relief. In this chapter I want to examine four strands of empirical research into adult learning that, taken together, hold the promise of establishing just what it is that is distinctive about the adult dimension to lifelong learning. These four strands will be discussed in terms of capacities that seem to be observeable chiefly in adult learners: the capacity to think dialectically, the capacity to employ practical logic, the capacity to know how we know what we know, and the capacity for critical reflection.

The capacity to think dialectically

Dialectical thinking as a distintively adult form of reasoning was first proposed by Riegel (1973) and further elaborated by researchers such as Basseches (1984, 1986, 1989), Allman (1985) and Irwin (1991). As conceived by these writers dialectical thinking is a form of adult reasoning in which universalistic and relativistic modes of thought co-exist. Its essence is the continuous exploration of the interrelationships between general rules and contextual necessities with the realization that no fixed patterns of thought or conduct, and no permanent resolutions to intractable problems, are possible. In dialectical thinking the chance to explore the contradictions and discrepancies between the general and particular is regarded as an opportunity for personal development rather than a depressing and confusing reality of adulthood. Adults think dialectically when they inhabit the arena of decision-making in which an awareness of universal rules, general moral strictures and broad patterns of causal and prescriptive reasoning ('if this is the case then I should do that') is balanced against, and constantly intersects with, the contextual imperatives of a situation. The recognition and honouring of the importance of contextuality—the recognition that specific situations make nonsense of general rules or theories—is something that is learned developmentally. This balancing of the universal and the specific is identified by a cluster of developmental psychologists as one of the key indicators in their conceptualization of wisdom (Sternberg, 1990; Lee, 1994; Denney *et al.*, 1995).

Adults' capacity to think dialectically is not proposed as a rarified, higher order, intellectual activity. Rather, it is seen as much in studies of everyday decision-making (what Rogoff and Lave (1984) and Billig *et al.* (1988) call everyday cognition and the psychology of everyday thinking) as it is in studies of intellectual development among college students. As an example, consider the general rule of parenting invoked by parents where exercising authority, setting limits and administering discipline to children are concerned—the rule that success will only be achieved by 'being consistent'. Superficially this rule appears to remove most of the ambiguity from the business of disciplining children. Clinging to the rule that we should behave in the same way in whatever situation of disciplining children we find ourselves (difficult though we recognize that may be) holds the promise of providing us with a life preserver that will keep us afloat as we're tossed about on the roiling sea of family life. But early on in our effort to be consistent we realize that no two situations are alike and that the subtle shadings of family interactions mean that we have to vary our disciplinary approaches as situations change. Being consistent as parents (if this is interpreted to mean 'always behave the same way') strands us in limbo, since the multiple situations in which we're required to exercise discipline alter so frequently that they make a nonsense of standardized rules of parental conduct.

Basseches (1986) locates his work on dialectical thinking in the context of adults' involvement at their workplaces and in terms of how adults enter into, and disengage from, personal relationships. With regard to the latter he writes that 'a dialectical approach (to beginning a personal relationship) might begin with the assumption that my traits are not fixed and that the relationships I enter will change who I am and who my partner is' (p. 26). Should the relationship falter, 'I am likely to look for how experience both within and outside of the relationship has led us to grow in different directions, so much so that we would be hampered by remaining so tied to each other. The assumption is that a relationship can reach a point where it tends to interfere with the development of one or both of the partners rather than helping them to grow further and growing with them' (p. 27).

In terms of moral decision-making in adulthood, the relevance of the cluster of concepts with dialectical thinking at its centre is clear. The contextual contradictions and ambiguities faced in the making of moral choices and decisions—in particular the discrepancies between uncritically assimilated norms governing moral conduct and obligations in personal relationships, work and politics and our experience of these complex realities—impel us to find meaning and create order in the midst of this confusion. In trying to resolve these contradictions between ideals and actuality we think dialectically. We become attentive to the importance of context and the validity of situational or relativistic reasoning, while at the same time committing ourselves to those values and general beliefs we find most valid for our experience. In other words, adult moral learning focuses on exploring the contradictions involved in fusing universal moral standards with the pragmatic constraints and situational imperatives of relationships, work and community involvement. Adults become aware of how context alters the neat application of general codes, of how the rules of moral reasoning learned at earlier stages of life are reinterpreted and contextualized because of the moral complexities of adult life.

The capacity to employ practical logic

As we consider the phenomenon of lifelong learning as it relates to learning (rather than to educational policies, provision and practices with which it is often confused) it is important to note that several psychologists have identified a stage of adult intellectual development that extends Piaget's concept of formal operations identified as the end point of young adult development. Post-formal operations, as this stage has been called, emphasizes adults' ability to reason contextually. Dialectical thinking, in its focus on adults' capacity to move back and forth between objective and subjective frames of reference, universal and specific modes of decision-making, certainly fits within this framework. Practical logic, discussed later in this section, focuses more on adults' capacity to think contextually in a deep and critical way. It is more domain-specific than dialectical thinking, concerned with reasoning within a well-defined situation in a way that pays attention to its internal features.

One of the most complete statements on post-formal thought is that of Sinnott (1998) who sees it as endemic to the struggle of adult life 'to find existential meaning in life and to develop an adult logic of living in balance' (p. 10). To Sinnott there are two central components to post-formal operations; 'the ability to order several systems of formal operations, or systems of truth' (p. 24) and the use of self-referential logic. In a self-referential posture we are aware of the incompleteness of all knowledge and the subjectivity of logic yet we decide to act 'despite being trapped in partial subjectivity' (p. 34). Sinnott breaks down these two central abilities into 11 specific thinking operations, including such things as metatheory shift, problem definition, creating multiple solutions, acknowledging multiple causalities and recognizing paradoxes and contradictions. The ability to order several systems of formal operations, or systems of truth, seems to me to be close to dialectical thinking as outlined earlier. The idea of self-referential logic (in which we act according to a critical questioning of rules within a parti-cular framework) seems to me close to what others have called, variously, expertise (Tennant, 1991), practical intelligence and practical knowledge (Wagner, 1992, Chaiklin and Lave, 1996, Sternberg and Wagner, 1986; Scribner, 1984). Labouvie-Vief's (1980) work proposes the concept of 'embedded logic' to describe how adults 'achieve a new integration in which logic, initially decontextualized, is reembedded in its social context' (1980; p. 16). This idea is connected to the concept of situated cognition, which recognizes that 'cognition is a social activity that incorporates the mind, the body, the activity and the ingredients of the setting in a complex, interactive and recursive manner' (Wilson, 1993, p. 72).

It is important to repeat that, as with dialectical thinking, practical logic is not a form of rea-soning observeable only in academic settings. Indeed, studies of this way of thinking have focused very much on workplace learning in places such as dairies (Scribner, 1984) or the devel-opment of clinical judgement in nurses which 'resembled much more the engaged, practical reasoning first described by Aristotle, than the disengaged, scientific, or theoretical reasoning promoted by cognitive theorists and represented in the nursing process' (Benner *et al.*, 1996, p. 1). There have been studies of the workings of practical logic in the ways mothers and chil-dren solve problems together (Levine, 1996), in how sports fans understand the nuances of cricket or baseball games (Spilich, 1979), and in how punters make decisions in betting shops on which horses to back (Ceci and Liker, 1986). As Tennant and Pogson (1995) observe of the authors of the last study, 'they make a compelling case for their conclusion that racetrack handicapping is as intellectually demanding as the decision-making apparent among established professions such as science, law, and banking' (p. 51).

A logic that is practical is a logic that springs from a deep understanding of the context of the situation (whether this be placing a bet or deciding whether to alter a patient's medication). It is a logic that does not follow formal rules of deductive reasoning, but that is experiential and inferential. It involves being aware of, and attending seriously to, very subtle cues whose importance only becomes apparent to those who have the benefit of a lengthy and mindful immersion in experience. In my own field, when adult educators do something apparently spontaneously that contradicts established principles of good practice, they are often apply-ing a form of practical logic. For example, in one of my discussion-based courses a while ago I, seemingly unthinkingly, announced a 'no-speech allowed' policy at the first meeting of the class. In effect I said,

> I know that speaking in discussions is a nerve-wracking thing and that your fear of mak-ing public fools of yourselves can inhibit you to the point of nonparticipation. I, myself, feel very nervous as a discussion participant and spend a lot of my time carefully rehear-sing my contributions so as not to look foolish when I finally speak. So please don't feel that you have to speak in order to gain my approval or to show me that you're a diligent student. It's quite acceptable to say nothing in the session, and there'll be no presumption of failure on your part. I don't equate silence with mental inertia. Obviously, I hope you will want to say something and speak up, but I don't want you to do this just for the sake of appearances. So let's be comfortable with a prolonged period of silence that might, or might not, be broken. When anyone feels like saying something, just speak up.

Superficially, this looks foolhardy, since it raises the prospect that the class will spend an hour in silence. But, after this class, several students came up to me and told me that the fact that they had been allowed to stay silent actually took so much performance anxiety off their shoulders that they felt emboldened to speak. If I had been asked in the midst of my declaration why I was telling participants they didn't need to talk in the discussion I would have said that it seemed like a good way to defuse the anxiety that I felt in the room. I would also have elaborated on some of the signs of anxiety that I observed. I would have said that I was think-ing of my own autobiographical experiences of discussion participation where I felt a comba-tant in an intellectual arena that resembled the Algonquin roundtable or a Bloomsbury dinner party. I know that if a speech policy resembling the one above had been declared in my undergraduate or post-graduate seminars then it would have reassured me enormously and probably relaxed me enough to get into the conversation. So, though I did something that on the face of it looked like the error of a novice teacher, on closer examination it seems to me I was using a kind of practical logic. This logic combined an attention to cues in students' behavior (for example the way they entered the room, even the way they composed their bodies in the chairs) that were very clear because I'd observed them many times before, with a rapid autobiographical scanning of my own experiences as a learner to gain some insights for my own conduct.

The capacity to know how we know what we know

A third stream of research relating to the distinctively adult aspects of lifelong learning has evolved within the field of adult education research, and, as such, represents one of the few attempts to develop theoretical propositions about adult learning which does not rely on per-spectives drawn from an allied discipline. The central component here is learning to learn (Cell, 1984; Smith, 1990; Tuijnman and Van De Kamp, 1992), defined as the capacity adults pos-sess of becoming self-consciously aware of their learning styles and being able to adjust these according to the situations in which they find themselves. Fundamental to the concept is some form of epistemological awareness; that is, a self-conscious awareness of how we come to know what we know, and an evolved understanding of what it means for us to know something. Kitchener (1983, 1986) describes this as epistemic cognition; that is, 'knowledge of whether our cognitive strategies are sometimes limited, in what ways solutions can be true, and whether reasoning correctly about a problem necessarily leads to an absolutely correct solution' (1983, p. 226). Epistemic cognition 'includes the individual's assumptions about what can be known and what cannot (e.g., our knowledge of some things is ultimately uncertain), how we can know (e.g., by observing what exists; via authority), and how certain we can be in knowing (e.g., absolutely, probabilistically). Following from each form of knowing is an understanding of how beliefs may be justified in light of the characteristics of the knowing process' (Kitchener, 1986, p. 76).

King and Kitchener (1994) have developed a model of reflective judgment to measure the development of epistemic cognition in adults. They posit seven stages of intellectual develop-ment, the most advanced of which (stages 6 and 7) 'reflect the epistemic assumption that one's understanding of the world is not 'given' but must be actively constructed and that knowl-edge must be understood in relationship to the context in which it was generated ... true reflective thinking presupposes that individuals hold the epistemic assumptions that allow them to understand and accept real uncertainty' (p. 17). More recently Mezirow identifies epi-stemic critical self-reflection as an important domain of transformative learning. This occurs when the learner 'sets out to examine the assumptions and explore the causes (biographical, historical, cultural) the nature (including moral and ethical dimensions), and consequences (individual and interpersonal) of his or her frames of reference to ascertain why he or she is predisposed to learn in a certain way or to appropriate particular goals' (Mezirow, 1998, p. 195). The connections between epistemic cognition and work on critical thinking and critical reflection (Brookfield, 1995) and on the constructive ways of knowing observed in women learners (Belenky *et al.*, 1986) will be clear. Epistemic cognition clearly displays the use of self-referential logic that Sinnot identifies as one of the two key features of adult post-formal thought.

Epistemic cognition is clearly observeable in work on teacher thinking (Day *et al.*, 1993; Kincheloe, 1993; Carlgren *et al.*, 1994). This research looks at the ways adults as teachers make rapid, multiple decisions in classrooms in response to the cues they observe. When asked to state a rationale for these, teachers will display a form of epistemic cognition as they state the inferential chains of reasoning they use, the cues they attend to (and why these rather than others are worthy of their attention) and the grounds for their decisions. In our moral lives epistemic moral cognition involves us becoming aware of why we feel a strong sense of moral certainty about certain opinions or behaviours, and why we feel an absence of this about others. We can discuss the experiential evidence for these feelings rather than just insisting on their moral correctness. We are better able to make judgements regarding the relative validity of moral pronouncements made by others. A developed sense of epistemic moral cognition also helps us to decide which moral impulses should be followed as accurate guides to action, and which should be held in check.

In the field of adult education, Smith (1982, 1983, 1987, 1990) has argued that learning to learn is an important intellectual activity evident in adult students and, consequently, should be a major focus for adult education practice. Learning to learn is defined as the capacity adults possess to become self-consciously aware of their learning styles and to adjust their preferred ways of learning according to the situations in which they find themselves. In his last major publication, Smith (1990) placed this notion in the context of lifelong learning, defining it as 'knowledge, process and procedures which people come to and are assisted to make appropriate educational decisions tasks associated with successful lifelong learning' (p. 1). In terms of its positioning, he argues that learning to learn, while evident at earlier ages, is most fully realized in adults and is an important developmental process. Smith points out that metacognition and metalearning—the capacity to think about one's thinking—are terms used more or less interchangeably with learning to learn. The connections to epistemic cognition are clear to see. All these terms support the self-referential orientation mentioned earlier by Sinnot as crucial to post-formal thought. He cites research such as Danis and Tremblay's study of successful self-taught adults in which the authors found that their subjects were able to transcend their own learning process 'and are able to describe rules and principles pertaining to their own learning process and the act of learning itself' (Smith, 1990, p. 13).

Critical reflection

A final body of work focuses on adults' development of critical reflection, briefly defined as the process by which adults become critically reflective regarding the assumptions, beliefs and values which they have assimilated during childhood and adolescence. Becoming critically reflective involves assessing the accuracy and validity of these norms for the contexts of adult life. Put simply, it entails judging the 'fit' between the rules of life transmitted, assimilated, and evolved in childhood, and the realities of adulthood. Does what we were told in childhood about the nature of friendship, or the rules for a successful marriage, make sense for us in our own intimate relationships? Are the principles of democratic political living espoused in school and church evident in local and national politics? Does what we learned about the characteristics of a good worker hold true in the workplace? Are the television depictions of family, work and political life we grew up with of any relevance to our own experiences in these arenas of adult life? All these activities involve us moving between the universal and subjective modes of analysis involved in dialectical thinking. They all entail the use of a practical form of logic embedded in the contexts of adult life. And they all lead to the adults concerned having a more developed, self-referential understanding of how they come to decisions.

The argument is made by theorists of adult critical reflection (Mezirow, 1990, 1998; Brookfield, 1994, 1995) that this process can only occur as adults pass through experiences in their interpersonal, work and political lives which are characterized by breadth, depth, diversity and different degrees of intensity. This breadth, depth, diversity and differential intensity only come with time. We cannot critically scrutinize the validity of our unquestioned assumptions about interpersonal relationships, work and politics until we have lived through the building and decay of several intimate relationships, until we have felt the conflicts and pressures of workplaces, and until we have acted politically and lived with the consequences of our political actions. How can we assess the truth of rules we learned in childhood regarding relationships, work and politics until we have experienced directly these complex, contradictory and ambiguous realities? According to this interpretation of adulthood, what is distinctive about adult learning is the search for meaning in these complex, contradictory and ambiguous realities, and the process by which critically reflective capacities are developed in this search.

The pattern of critical reflection that emerges from studies of adult development is one comprising a praxis of action, reflection on action, further action, reflection on the further action and so on in a continuous cyclical loop. But these alternating phases need not be separated by extensive periods of time. Action can be mindful, thoughtful and informed. Weick (1983) describes this as 'acting thinkingly'. At any one point the phases described are engaged in a complex series of operations, some of which are scrutinizing past assumption, some of which are exploring new meaning schemes, some of which are trying on new identities and so on. As noted in a study of reflective thinking among Canadian teachers, 'emotions such as frustration, depression, love, shock, elation, hatred and fear interacted with cognitive components throughout the reflective process' (D'Andrea, 1986, p. 258). It should not be presumed that the following stages are neatly observable sequences or stages evident in each person's intellectual development.

The theorists of critical process discussed posit the following pattern. An episode of critical reflection within the context of adult life is prompted by some unexpected occurrence which occasions reflection on the discrepancy between the assumptions, rules and criteria informing our values, beliefs and actions and our experiences of reality. These trigger events are usually presented as traumatic or troublesome in some way, as disorienting dilemmas, cognitive dissonances, or perceptions of anomalies, disjunctions and contradictions between our expectations of how the world should work and actuality. Practically every theorist of critical thinking and change emphasizes how trauma triggers critical thought (what Belenky *et al.* (1986) describe as disequilibration studies) through such life shaking incidents such as divorce, bereavement, unemployment, disability, conscription, forced job change or geographical mobility.

A period of self-scrutiny and appraisal of the features of these anomalies follows the trigger event, in which periods of denial and depression alternate with attempts to understand the nature of the contradiction, dilemma or discomfort in their lives. During this period people seek desperately for others who are confronting similar anomalies. This appraisal is followed by an active effort to come to terms with the tension and discomfort that is felt. In this phase of exploration we interpret our experiences to make sense and create meaning from the apparent chaos through which we are passing. There is a hermeneutic quest to discover the meaning, reason and significance embedded within the dilemma as people try to reduce feelings of discomfort and alienation. This phase may be distinguished by a flirtation with new identities, by the contemplation of new role models, or by an effort to inhabit the perspectives of others so that the dissonance can be interpreted from another vantage point. This exploration will often involve a public admission of discomfort, dissatisfaction and the search for change.

At this stage people often join networks and peer support groups (for example, Alcoholics Anonymous, women's consciousness raising groups, community action movements, or gay rights initiatives). This phase entails a testing of new identities, beliefs, values and actions as people search for a 'fit' between these and reality.

Arising out of this process of exploring and testing new identities, assumptions, explanations, roles, values, beliefs and behaviours is the development of a changed way of thinking and acting which 'makes sense' or 'fits' the disorienting dilemma. This new perspective is constructed by the person involved; and is liable to be, initially at least, partial, tentative and fragile. Indeed, there is often a series of incremental confirmations of the validity of elements of this new perspective as people's actions are informed by this. The perspective becomes judged to be increasingly valid, and its features refined, as experience confirms its accuracy. Boyd and Fales (1983) write that 'the new insight or changed perspective is analyzed in terms of its operational feasibility' (p. 27). The outcome of this confirmation process is often described as a period of resolution or integration. Having decided that new norms, assumptions, beliefs and behaviours make sense in the context of our experiences, we seek for ways to integrate these permanently into our lives. These resolutions may be more or less tenuous, ranging from the development of tentative commitments to a heady rush of self-affirmation—a feeling that a person's 'real' or 'true' identity has been realized.

Understanding the affective dimensions to adult learning

One noticeable absence from the literature of adult learning is detailed attention to its visceral and emotional dimensions, to the ways in which epstemic cognition, practical logic, dialectical thinking and critical reflection are experienced as contradictory realities, at once troubling and enticing. Although writers frequently allude to the importance of understanding critical reflection as an emotive as well as cognitive process there are few grounded depictions of how adults feel their way through the process that so many adult educators have prescribed for them. The personal voice and subjective experience of the student is often curiously absent. In this section I want to summarize some of my own research into how adult students experience their own learning (Brookfield, 1994, 1995).

Five significant themes are highlighted in adult learners' generalized descriptions of how they experience learning, all of which stand out for two reasons: first, they represent the experiential clusters that emerge with the greatest frequency and the greatest validity across the diverse educational settings in which adults learn. Second, they contradict much of the inspirational rhetoric that surrounds discourse on adult learning. Although there are stories recounting heady moments of transformative breakthrough, of empowerment, of emancipation and of liberation, what figure equally strongly in adult students' accounts of learning, particularly those focused on critical reflection, are feelings of impostorship, acknowledgments of a disturbing loss of innocence, accountings of the cost of committing cultural suicide, descriptions of incrementally fluctuating rhythms of learning, and recognition of the significance that membership in an emotionally sustaining learning community has for those in critical process. These stories are the dark underside of the inspirational rhetoric of adult learning.

Impostorship

Impostorship is the sense adults report that at some deeply embedded level they possess neither the talent nor the right to become learners. As adults describe the beginnings of their journeys as critical learners, they speak of their engagement in critical process almost as a form of inauthenticity, as if they are acting in bad faith by taking on the external behaviours they associate with critical analysis without really feeling a sense of inner congruence or conviction about these. There is a sense of impostorship regarding the rightness of their taking critical perspectives on familiar ideas, actions and social forms. This feeling does decrease over time, but it rarely disappears entirely. Not all share this feeling, it is true, but amongst adults represented in my own research it does seem to cross lines of gender, class and ethnicity. The cultural roots framing impostorship are hard to disentangle, but most who spoke about impostorship viewed it as having been produced by their awareness of the distance between the idealized images of omniscient intellectuals they attached to anyone in the role of 'student', and their own daily sense of themselves as stumbling and struggling survivors. This contrast between the idealized and the actual was so great that the inference was made that aspiring to describe themselves in these idealized terms was unrealistic and unconvincing.

At the outset of critical episodes, the triggers that bring this sense of impostorship to the forefront of consciousness are seen at distinct times in adults' autobiographies. The first of these has to do with the moment of public definition as a student. The news that one has been admitted into an educational programme is greeted with a sense of disbelief, not entirely pleasurable. The second set of triggers refers to one's public definition or recognition as a learner, this time in a social setting. The experience beloved of so many adult educators of having participants introduce themselves at an opening orientation session as a way of relieving students' anxieties, seems to have the converse effect of heightening these same anxieties for many students. Rather than affirming and honouring their prior experiences, this round table recitation of past activities, current responsibilities and future dreams serves only to heighten adults' sense of impostorship.

Impostorship of a more complex and embedded nature manifests itself in a third way in the reverence adults turned learners feel for what they define as 'expert' knowledge enshrined in academic publications, or at least in the public domain of the published, printed word. When asked to undertake a critical analysis of ideas propounded by people seen as experts adults will often say that to do so smacks of temerity and impertinence. More particularly, they will report that their own experience is so limited that it gives them no starting point from which to build an academic critique of major figures in their fields of study. There is a kind of steam-rolling effect in which the status of 'theorist' or 'major figure' flattens these students' fledgling critical antennae. This is perhaps most evident when the figures concerned are heroic in their eyes but it is also evident when students are faced with a piece of work in which the bibliographic scholarship is seen as impressive. The sense of impostorship they feel in daring to comment critically on this makes their experience of engaging in critical analysis seem a rather unconvincing form of role-taking, even play acting. Their assumption is that sooner or later any critique they produce will be revealed to be the product of an unqualified and unfit mind.

Cultural suicide

Cultural suicide is what often happens to adults who are seen by those around them to be re-inventing themselves, to be in critical process. Cultural suicide is the threat adults perceive that if they take a critical questioning of conventional assumptions, justifications, structures and actions too far they will risk being excluded from the cultures that have defined and sustained them up to that point in their lives. The perception of this danger, and experience of its actuality, is a common theme in adult students' autobiographies. Students who take critical thinking seriously report that this often causes those around them to view them with fear and loathing, with a hostility borne of incomprehension. The adult in critical process who was formerly seen by friends and intimates as 'one of us', is now seen in one of two ways, both of which carry a real sense of threat to those who see themselves as being betrayed or left behind. On the one hand the person concerned may be viewed as taking on airs and pretensions, as growing 'too big for her boots', as aspiring to the status of intellectual in contrast to her friends and colleagues who feel that they are now somehow perceived as less developed creatures grubbing around in the gritty gutters of daily life outside academe. The adult who has come to a critical awareness of what most people accept as taken for granted, common-sense ideas can pose a real threat to those who are not on a similar journey of self-discovery, or who do no see themselves as engaged in the same political or intellectual project. In the eyes of those left behind the adult student is perceived as having 'gone native', to have become a fully fledged member of the tribal culture of academe.

On the other hand, adults in critical process are sometimes seen as turning into subversive troublemakers whose *raison d'être* now seems to be to make life as difficult and uncomfortable as possible for those around them. A common experience reported by adult students is of their rapidly being marginalized as a result of their slipping into a more critical mode in their daily work. They find out that their raising of critical questions regarding commonly held assumptions is met with resentment and suspicion, with a feeling that the person concerned has betrayed the group culture and has somehow become a pink-tinged revolutionary. Many students complain that being critically reflective only serves to make them disliked by their colleagues, harms their careers, loses them fledgling friends and professionally useful acquaintances, threatens their livelihoods, and turns them into institutional pariahs.

Incremental fluctuation

Mezirow's (1991) writings on adult perspective transformation have stressed how incremental movement through the various stages of critical reflection is much more likely than dramatic paradigm shifts. In speaking of critical reflection as a learning process, adults often describe a rhythm of learning that might be called incremental fluctuation; put colloquially, it can be understood as two steps forward, one step back, followed by four steps forward, one step back, followed by one step forward, three steps back, and so on in a series of fluctuations marked by overall movement forward. It is a rhythm of learning which is distinguished by evidence of an increased ability to take alternative perspectives on familiar situations, a developing readiness to challenge assumptions, and a growing tolerance for ambiguity, but it is also one which is characterized by fluctuating moments of falling back, of apparent regression. When learners are in the middle of these temporary regressions they report that they experience them as devastatingly final, rather than inconvenient interludes. They are convinced that they will never 'get' critical thinking, that 'it's beyond me', and that they may as well return to tried and trusted ideas and actions on the grounds that even if these didn't account for everything in life at least they were comfortable, known and familiar.

Lost innocence

Adults in critical process speak of the epistemological as well as cultural risks they run and they see their learning to think critically as a journey into ambiguity and uncertainty requiring a willingness to let go of eternal verities and of the reassuring prospect of eventual truth. In contrast to the relentlessly upbeat rhetoric surrounding much exposition on empowerment, liberation, emancipation and transformation, their descriptions of their journeys as learners are quite often infused with a tone of sadness. In particular, they speak of a loss of innocence, innocence being seen in this case as a belief in the promise that if they study hard and look long enough they will stumble on universal certainty as the reward for all their efforts. Although this kind of comment represents a loss of epistemological innocence, a disappearance of a previously felt faith in the impending revelation of certainty, it also signifies what could be viewed as a corresponding growth in wisdom, in wise action (Sternberg, 1990). People in critical process look back to their time as dualistic thinkers, and to their faith that if they just put enough effort into problem-solving solutions would always appear, as a golden era of certainty. An intellectual appreciation of the importance of contextuality and ambiguity comes to exist alongside an emotional craving for revealed truth.

As practically the only book addressing directly the connection between emotions and adult learning recognizes, the transformative dimensions of critical thinking involve, for an adult, 'the agonising grief of colluding in the death of someone who he knows was himself' (More, 1974, p. 69). In terms of schemas drawn from developmental psychology, people experiencing a loss of innocence are caught in the relativistic freeze between concrete and dialectical thinking (Basseches, 1984) or between dualism and multiplism (Perry, 1981). Despite the prevalence of a sense of epistemological loss, however, one can look long, hard and mostly unsuccessfully for themes of yearning, bereavement and sadness in reports of adult critical thinking found in professional journals and research conference proceedings.

Community

Impostorship, lost innocence, cultural suicide, moments of incremental fluctuation—these make for a pretty depressing rendition of the process of learning to think critically, and one which stands in marked contrast to the positive optimism of much transformative rhetoric. There is, however, a more hopeful experiential theme which emerges from adults' experiences as critical learners—the theme of community. As adults speak of their own critical process they attest to the importance of their belonging to an emotionally sustaining peer learning community—a group of colleagues who were also experiencing dissonance, reinterpreting their practice, challenging old assumptions and falling foul of conservative forces.

Given the fluctuating, emotionally complex and culturally punished nature of critical thinking it is not surprising to hear adults speak of the store they placed on their membership in a peer support group. As they talk and write about the factors that help them sustain momentum through the lowest moments in their autobiographies as critical learners, it is membership of a learning community—of an emotionally sustaining group of peers—that is mentioned more consistently than anything else. These groups are spoken of as 'a second family', 'the only people who really understand what I'm going through', 'my partners in crime', and they provide a safe haven in which adults in critical process can confirm they are not alone, and through which they can make sense of the changes they are experiencing.

Since learning to think critically entails so many tales from the dark side it is important that educators have the chance to gain accurate insight into the emotional and cognitive ebbs and flows of this process so that they can help adult students tolerate periods of confusion and apparent regression more easily. Through peer learning communities students can be encouraged to share their private feelings of impostorship in an attempt to help them realize that their private misgivings can coalesce into publicly recognized truth. Knowing that one is not alone in thinking or feeling something that seems divergent is an important step in coming to take one's own experience seriously, especially when that experience is of a critical nature and therefore likely to be devalued by mainstream theory and practice.

As Simon (1988, p. 4) points out, taking a critical perspective on commonly accepted ideas and practices can easily turn an educational setting into a council of despair as people start to realize the power of the forces and the longevity of the structures ranged against them. However, by using learning communities as the forum in which they can compare their own private journeys as critical thinkers, adults come to realize that what they thought were idiosyncratic incremental fluctuations in energy and commitment, morale sapping defeats suffered in isolation, and context—specific barriers preventing change, are often paralleled in the lives of colleagues. This knowledge, even if it fails to grant any insights into how these feelings can be ameliorated or how these barriers might be removed, can be the difference between resolving to work for purposeful change whenever the opportunity arises, and falling prey to a mixture of stoicism and cynicism in which staying within comfortably defined boundaries of thought and action becomes the overwhelming concern.

References

Allman, P. (1985). 'Dialectical Thinking: Our Logical Potential'. In, G.A. Conti and R.A. Fellenz (eds.). *Dialogue on Issues of Lifelong Learning in a Democratic Society*. College Station, Texas: Texas A & M University.

Basseches, M. (1984). *Dialectical Thinking and Adult Development*. Norwood, New Jersey: Ablex Publishing Corporation.

Basseches, M. (1986). 'Dialectical Thinking and Young Adult Cognitive Development'. In, R.A. Mines and K.S. Kichener (eds.). *Adult Cognitive Development: Methods and Models* (pp. 76–91). New York: Praeger.

Basseches, M. (1989).'Dialectical Thinking as a Metasystematic Form of Cognitive Organization'. In, M.L. Commons, F.A. Richards and C. Armon (eds.). *Beyond Formal Operations: Late Adolescent and Adult Cognitive Development*. New York: Praeger.

Belenky, M.F., Clinchy, B.M., Goldberger, N.R., and Tarule, J.M. (1986). *Women's Ways of Knowing: The Development of Self, Voice, and Mind*. New York: Basic Books.

Benner, P., Tanner, C.A., and Chesla, C.A. (1996). *Expertise in Nursing Practice: Caring, Clinical Judgment, and Ethics*. New York: Springer.

Billig, M, Condor, S., Edwards, D., Gane, M., Middleton, D., and Radley, A. (1988). *Ideological Dilemmas: A Social Psychology of Everyday Thinking*. London: Sage.

Boyd, E.M. and Fales, A.W. (1983). 'Reflective Learning: Key to Learning from Experience'. *Journal of Humanistic Psychology*, 23, 99–117.

Brookfield, S.D. (1994). 'Tales from the Dark Side: A Phenomenography of Adult Critical Reflection'. *International Journal of Lifelong Education*, 13(3), pp. 203–18.

Brookfield, S.D. (1995). *Becoming a Critically Reflective Teacher*. San Francisco: Jossey-Bass.

Carlgren, I., Handal, G., and Vaage, S. (eds.) (1994). *Teachers' Minds and Actions: Research on Teachers' Thinking and Practice*. Bristol, PA: Falmer Press.

Ceci, S. and Liker, J. (1986). 'Academic and Non-Academic Intelligence: An Experimental Separation'. In, R.J. Sternberg and R.K. Wagner (eds.). *Practical Intelligence: Nature and Origins of Competence in the Everyday World*. Cambridge: Cambridge University Press.

Cell, E. (1984). *Learning to Learn from Experience*. Albany: State University of New York Press.

Chaiklin, S. and Lave, J. (eds.) (1996). *Understanding Practice: Perspectives on Activity and Context*. Cambridge: Cambridge University Press.

D'Andrea, A.L. (1986). 'Teachers and Reflection: A Description and Analysis of the Reflective Process which Teachers Use in their Experiential Learning'. Unpublished doctoral dissertation, Ontario Institute for Studies in Education, Toronto, Canada.

Danis, C. and Tremblay, N.A. (1988). 'Autodidactic Learning Experiences: Questioning Established Adult Learning Principles'. In, H.B. Long (ed.). *Self-Directed Learning: Research and Application*. Athens, Georgia: Department of Adult Education, University of Georgia.

Day, C., Calderhead, J., and Denicolo, P. (eds.) (1993). *Research on Teacher Thinking: Understanding Professional Development*. Bristol, PA: Falmer Press.

Denney, N.W., Dew, J.R., and Kroupa, S.L. (1995). 'Perceptions of Wisdom: What Is It and Who Has It?' *Journal of Adult Development*, 2(1), pp. 37–47.

Irwin, R.R. (1991). 'Reconceptualizing the Nature of Dialectical Postformal Operational Thinking: The Effects of Effectively Mediated Social Experiences'. In, J.D. Sinnott and J.C. Cavanaugh, (eds.). *Bridging Paradigms: Positive Development in Adulthood and Cognitive Aging*. New York: Praeger.

Kincheloe, J.L. (1993). *Toward a Critical Politics of Teacher Thinking: Mapping the Postmodern*. Westport, CT: Bergin and Garvey.

King, P.M. and Kitchener, K. S. (1994). *Developing Reflective Judgment: Understanding and Promoting Intellectual Growth and Critical Thinking in Adolescents and Adults*. San Francisco: Jossey-Bass.

Kitchener, K.S. (1983). 'Cognition, Metacognition and Epistemic Cognition: A Three-Level Model of Cognitive Process'. *Human Development*, 4, 222–32.

Kitchener, K.S. (1986). 'The Reflective Judgment Model: Characteristics, Evidence, and Measurement'. In, R.A. Mines and K.S. Kitchener (eds.). *Adult Cognitive Development: Methods and Models*. New York: Praeger.

Labouvie-Vief, G. (1980). 'Beyond Formal Operations: Uses and Limits of Pure Logic in Life-Span Development'. *Human Development*, 23, pp. 141–61.

Lee, D.M. (1994). 'Becoming an Expert: Reconsidering the Place of Wisdom in Teaching Adults'. In, J.D. Sinnott (ed.). *Interdisciplinary Handbook of Adult Lifespan Learning*. Westport, Connecticut: Greenwood Press.

Levine, H.G. (1996). 'Context and Scaffolding in Developmental Studies of Mother–Child Problem-Solving Dyads'. In, S. Chaiklin and J. Lave (eds.). *Understanding Practice: Perspectives on Activity and Context*. Cambridge: Cambridge University Press.

Mezirow, J. (1990). *Fostering Critical Reflection in Adulthood*. San Francisco: Jossey-Bass.

Mezirow, J. (1991). *Transformative Dimensions in Adult Learning*. San Francisco: Jossey-Bass.

Mezirow, J. (1998). 'On Critical Reflection'. *Adult Education Quarterly*, 48/3, pp. 185–98.

More, W.S. (1974). *Emotions and Adult Learning*. Farnborough: Saxon House.

Perry, W.G. (1981). 'Growth in the Making of Meaning'. In, A.W. Chickering (ed.). *The Modern American College*. San Francisco: Jossey-Bass.

Riegel, K.F. (1973). 'Dialectical Operations: The Final Period of Cognitive Development'. *Human Development*, 16, pp. 346–70.

Rogoff, B. and Lave, J. (1984). *Everyday Cognition: Its Development in Social Context*. Cambridge, MA: Harvard University Press.

Scribner, S. (1984). 'Studying Working Intelligence'. In, B. Rogoff and J. Lave (eds.). *Everyday Cognition: Its Development in Social Context*. Cambridge, MA: Harvard University Press.

Simon, R.I. (1988). 'For a pedagogy of possibility'. *Critical Pedagogy Newsletter*, 1(1), pp. 1–4.

Sinnott, J.D. (1998). *The Development of Logic in Adulthood: Postformal Thought and Its Operations*. New York: Plenum Press.

Smith, R.M. (1982). *Learning How to Learn: Applied Theory for Adults*. New York: Cambridge Books.

Smith, R.M. (ed.)(1983). *Helping Adults Learn How to Learn*. New Directions for Continuing Education, No. 19. San Francisco: Jossey-Bass.

Smith, R.M. (ed.)(1987). *Theory Building for Learning How to Learn*. Chicago: Educational Studies Press.

Smith R.M. (ed.)(1990). *Learning How to Learn Across the Lifespan*. San Francisco: Jossey-Bass.

Spilich, G.J. (1979). 'Text Processing of Domain Related Information for Individuals with High and Low Domain Knowledge'. *Journal of Verbal Learning and Verbal Behavior*, 16, pp. 275–90.

Sternberg, R.J. and Wagner, R.K. (eds.) (1986). *Practical Intelligence: Nature and Origins of Competence in the Everyday World*. Cambridge: Cambridge University Press.

Sternberg, R.J. (1990). *Wisdom: Its Nature, Origins, and Development*. New York: Cambridge University Press.

Tennant, M. (1991). 'Expertise as a Dimension of Adult Development: Implications for Adult Education'. *New Education*, 13(1), pp. 49–55.

Tennant, M. and Pogson, P. (1995). *Learning and Change in the Adult Years*. San Francisco: Jossey-Bass.

Tuijnman, A. and Van Der Kamp, M. (eds.) (1992). *Learning Across the Lifespan: Theories, Research, Policies*. New York: Pergamon.

Wagner, R.K. (1992). 'Practical Intelligence'. In, A. Tuijnman and M. Van Der Kamp. (eds.). *Learning Across the Lifespan: Theories, Research, Policies*. New York: Pergamon.

Weick, K.E. (1983). 'Managerial Thought in the Context of Action'. In, S. Srivastva and Associates. *The Executive Mind: New Insights on Managerial Thought and Action*. San Francisco: Jossey-Bass.

Wilson, A.L. (1993). 'The Promise of Situated Cognition'. In, S.B. Merriam (ed.). *An Update on Adult Learning Theory*. San Francisco: Jossey-Bass.

9 Learning for living

Opportunities and approaches within the school curriculum 5–16[1]

Val Millman

Since lifelong learning begins in childhood . . . schools and teacher training establishments are crucial organisations for shaping those attitudes and values which prepare future adults for a world in which flexibility and adaptability are essential and in which enjoyment of learning may be a matter of personal survival

(Longworth and Davies, 1996, p. 166)

Introduction

The current lifelong learning debate poses a considerable challenge to a school curriculum that is traditionally founded on teaching compartmentalized knowledge and on assessing success or failure at fixed points in an individual's school life. Much change has yet to take place before schools can claim to foster lifelong learning cultures. Many contradictory educational policies have yet to be reconciled before such changes are possible.

In this chapter, I shall present two initiatives, implemented by the Coventry Local Education Authority (LEA) and its schools, which attempt to introduce lifelong learning perspectives and approaches into the school curriculum through career- and work-related learning. Though of course the whole school curriculum should be permeated with a lifelong learning perspective, in practice many schools begin with careers education. These are in-service training initiatives that I organized for Coventry primary and secondary teachers in my role as LEA education adviser for these curriculum areas. The main aim was to train teachers, as key agents of educational change, to support pupils' learning in ways that prepare them for the changing world of work. I shall try to show how teachers' ability to bring about curriculum change in this area may be either enabled or constrained by national and local education policies. I shall first describe the context into which these initiatives were introduced in Coventry schools, at a time when nationally determined education policies, including the National Curriculum, were marginalizing many teaching and learning experiences that are essential to effective lifelong learning. I shall also provide background information about the City of Coventry, its population, its education and employment contexts, in order to demonstrate how these career-related learning initiatives linked with city-wide plans for change and development.

Education Act 1988: introduction of the National Curriculum

Part of the Conservative government's impetus for the introduction of the National Curriculum in 1989, following its Education (Reform) Act of 1988, was the desire to equip Britain's future workforce for an increasingly competitive world economy. The Education Act required state-funded primary and secondary schools to teach ten subjects and Religious

Education. These subjects were: English, mathematics, science, history, geography, design technology and information technology, art, music, physical education and modern foreign languages, the last in secondary schools only. Accompanying the legislation were prescribed programmes of study and expected attainment levels for each of four key stages: Key Stages 1 and 2 (age 5 to 11) and Key Stages 3 and 4 (ages 11 to 16).

By the late 1990s, teachers had accepted the National Curriculum as the undisputed teaching agenda for schools. This followed a prolonged period of change demanded by on-going revisions of the National Curriculum, regular rigorous school inspections, and an increase in areas of responsibility and accountability. On the margins of these changes, other curriculum debates were taking place, one of which related to schools' legal requirement to provide a:

> balanced and broadly based curriculum that:
> a) promotes the spiritual, moral, cultural, mental and physical development of pupils at the school and of society: and
> b) prepares such pupils for the opportunities, responsibilities and experiences of adult life.
> (Education Act 1986, Section 351)

Preparing pupils for the opportunities, responsibilities and experiences of adult life

In the decade following the 1986 and 1988 Education Acts, most schools remained unclear as to how they were expected to meet their responsibilities for preparing 'pupils for the opportunities, responsibilities and experiences of adult life'. Following publication of the statutory National Curriculum programmes of study, a series of non-statutory guidance documents was published, relating to themes such as personal and social education (PSE), careers education, social, moral, spiritual and cultural education, and the work-related curriculum. But teachers found that there was insufficient time in which to teach non-statutory subjects and to organize extra-curricular activities that offered pupils rich opportunities for personal learning and development.

However, in the mid-1990s it became apparent that, although more pupils were performing at higher levels across National Curriculum subjects, many pupils were not developing the skills, qualities and attitudes perceived to be necessary for a socially coherent and economically competitive technological society. While the 1997 Labour Government consolidated many educational strategies established by its predecessor, it also more sharply defined schools' role in promoting the 'social inclusion' of pupils and in preparing them for their transition to adult life. It launched national strategies to raise achievement in skills such as numeracy, literacy, and information and communication technology (ICT), and gave increased recognition to vocational qualifications in secondary schools. The acquisition of key personal skills such as 'working together' was central to these vocational courses which also strongly emphasized work experience and out-of-school learning.

In 1999, the Secretary of State for Education and Employment proposed National Curriculum revisions that reflected this broader government agenda for schools. This new curriculum framework strengthens schools' role in 'Preparing pupils for the opportunities, responsibilities and experiences of life, through more explicit and coherent provision in the area of personal, social and health education (PSHE) and citizenship' (DfEE, 1999, p. 12). The framework clearly specifies skills, knowledge and understanding that children should acquire. These include: 'taking responsibility', 'making real choices', 'feeling positive about themselves', 'meeting and working with people', 'preparing for change' and 'finding information and advice' (DfEE, 1999, pp. 19, 22). This new curriculum provides a greater opportunity to embed lifelong learning principles in teaching and learning in both primary and secondary schools. But additional time, space and teacher training will be necessary for effective implementation of these changes.

The City of Coventry and its population

Coventry is a historic city, situated at the centre of the UK in the West Midlands. Having suffered devastating war damage during the 1940s, the city undertook extensive reconstruction and enjoyed an economic 'boom' during the 1950s. At this time, people migrated to Coventry from across Britain and from overseas, to join its expanding workforce. The city today (2000) has a multiethnic, multicultural and multilingual population of 306,000.

However, employment levels in Coventry have fluctuated over the past 40 years, with current trends reflecting the national pattern of a decline in manufacturing and a growth in distribution, business and public services which demand managerial, technical and personal skills. Working patterns have also changed, with an increase in self-employment, temporary, casual and part-time work, accompanied by increasing numbers of women entering the workforce (Coventry TEC, 1994). These changes have impacted significantly on families, communities and Coventry's school-leavers. There is increased family mobility, and, within families, changing roles for men and women, for parents and children. Young people are having to adapt to new social structures and seek new sources of identity and support. Their post-school routes to employment differ radically from those that their parents experienced, when they typically worked for one of a number of large local manufacturing employers (Quality Careers Service and Coventry LEA, 1997).

Coventry LEA and its Education Service

In the 1970s, the decline of the local economy and changing job market stimulated Coventry LEA to review the educational needs of 14- to 19-year olds. Its new policy document, *Comprehensive Education for Life* (Coventry City Council, 1982), stressed the importance of education as a lifelong process and recommended the extension of schools into community colleges and modular provision for post-14 pupils.

In recent years, Coventry LEA, like other local education authorities, has experienced diminishing powers and resources. As educational initiatives have become increasingly driven by external funding and by a diversity of stakeholder agendas, the LEA has become a source of support and influence rather than of control. However, in building new working partnerships with schools, further education colleges and universities, Coventry LEA has continued to prioritize educational approaches that are supportive of its earlier policies. The LEA works closely with employers and the Quality Careers Service (QCS) and has established five Education Business Partnership centres where pupils participate in learning modules at one of the company sites. Coventry's Strategic Director for Lifelong Learning asserts in the LEA curriculum policy (Coventry City Council n.d.)

> We are all of us employed so that children can progress from the dependence of childhood through the disturbed turbulence of adolescence until they can stand on the threshold of adult life. Their job is to grow up; our job is to help them do it. (p. iii)

At the start of the new millennium, there are 19 secondary schools, 89 primary schools and 11 special schools within Coventry LEA. These schools have a total of 50,000 pupils, 78 per cent of whom are white, and 22 per cent of minority ethnic origin. Twenty-three per cent are eligible for free school meals because of their low family income level. Each school is locally managed and its governing body is responsible for meeting its statutory requirements and for working in partnership with the LEA to deliver locally agreed plans such as that developed by the Coventry and Warwickshire Lifelong Learning Partnership. Other City Council plans, such as the 5-year Coventry Community Plan (Coventry City Council, 1998), also contribute to implementation of the lifelong learning plan through extensive youth, adult and community education service provision. Educational strategies are central to the Coventry Community Plan, which is based on the following six priority areas: to create more jobs for Coventry people, to tackle crime and make communities safer, to tackle poverty, to invest in young people, to create a vibrant city centre, and to meet the needs and aspirations of older people.

The LEA's Support and Advisory Service (SAS) provides advice and support to schools and monitors their performance on behalf of the City Council. It also organizes a teacher training programme at its Teachers' Centre. The SAS has developed the initiatives described in this chapter in partnership with local schools and Quality Careers Service. I shall now set these initiatives in context by outlining Coventry's careers education and guidance training strategy, entitled *Preparation for Adult Life* (Coventry LEA and Quality Careers Service, 1997), and by summarizing the findings of a survey of Coventry headteachers (Coventry LEA, 1998).

Preparation for adult life: Coventry's careers education and guidance training strategy

The speed of change taking place within Coventry's labour market and within the Education Service, recently pointed to the need for a city-wide strategy that would bring coherence to local education – industry initiatives. There needed to be a strategy for ensuring that children and young people were receiving clear and consistent messages about current labour market changes which would support them in their day-to-day living and in preparing for their transition to adult life. These messages are communicated to children and young people not only through teachers but also other service providers, many of whom are either employed by Coventry City Council or by organizations with which the Council works in partnership. What was needed was a strategy targeted at teachers and other 'key influencers', within and beyond schools, to achieve a greater shared awareness of labour market changes and their implications for children and young people.

In 1997, Coventry LEA and Quality Careers Service proposed a training strategy, targeted at 'key influencers', called *Preparation for Adult Life: Helping Coventry Children and Young People Anticipate the Changing World of Learning and Work in the 21ˢᵗ Century*. The strategy document was organized under the following headings:

- Defining the key messages
  What do children and young people need to know and understand, about the changing world of learning and work, to help them prepare for adult life?
  What barriers might prevent children and young people from receiving these key messages?
- The role of key influencers of children and young people
  Which adults are the key influencers? What are their areas of responsibility and influence?
  What do key influencers need to do to enable children and young people to understand and act on key messages?
  What barriers might prevent key influencers from getting these messages across to children and young people?
  What strategies need to be implemented to ensure that key influencers can successfully get across key messages to children and young people?

  (Coventry LEA and Quality Careers Service, 1997)

Primary and secondary school teachers were one of the strategy's main target groups. This was because of concerns that, given the speed of labour market changes, and the lack of time available to teachers over many years to look beyond immediate job responsibilities, they were unintentionally giving out-of-date and inappropriate advice to children and young people. Coventry LEA decided to use government funding for career-related teacher training to update teachers on the key messages identified in the above document (Coventry LEA, 1997).

Survey of Coventry headteachers

In 1998, the Support and Advisory Service undertook a headteacher survey about personal and social education (PSE) programmes in Coventry's primary and secondary schools. This survey confirmed that, although many headteachers think personal and social education is important, they think that careers education makes the least contribution, out of 18 cross-curricular elements, to the curriculum (Coventry LEA, 1998). Headteachers were asked to identify the skills, knowledge, understanding, attitudes and values that they thought were essential for children and young people growing up in the late 1990s and the new millennium. They were also asked to assess how effectively they were addressing these areas of learning in their own schools. Their responses can be summarized as follows:

Skills

Over two-thirds of responding primary schools identified cooperative working as most important for pupils. Other skills considered important were: communication (including listening), handling difference and conflict positively, interpersonal relationships, flexibility and the ability to adapt behaviour to different situations, independent working, and seeking help and advice. Although primary headteachers were generally dissatisifed with how effectively they were addressing pupils' skill development, they were quite pleased with the following: interpersonal relationships, cooperative working, taking initiative, seeking help and advice, communication, and seeking help when things go wrong.

Over half of secondary schools identified communication skills (including listening), interpersonal relationships and study/research skills as most important. A third of schools also identified as important handling difference and conflict positively, ability to adapt behaviour to different situations and cooperative working. Secondary schools were quite satisfied with how they were addressing pupils' skill development, with the exception of information seeking, debating, adaptability, analytical thinking and being enterprising and taking risks.

Knowledge and understanding

Over two-thirds of primary schools identified literacy and numeracy as the most important areas of knowledge and understanding for their pupils, and over half of schools identified an understanding of personal needs and feelings. These were areas that headteachers thought were being satisfactorily addressed. Areas that were considered less important and were not being well developed included: information technology, self-awareness (understanding of strengths and weaknesses), group and community awareness, an informed perspective about the role of the individual in society, and understanding the effect of people on the world in which we live.

Over half of secondary schools identified numeracy and literacy as of most importance for pupils, and over a third identified as important information technology and an understanding of personal needs and feelings. A quarter of schools identified self-awareness (strengths and weaknesses) and an informed perspective about the role of the individual in society as important. Secondary schools were generally satisfied with how they were addressing the development of pupils' knowledge and understanding.

Attitudes and values

Two-thirds of primary schools identified understanding, caring and respect for others as one of the most important attitudes and values for pupils. Over half of schools identified willingness to learn and self-confidence and self-worth as important. A third of schools prioritized having a view of others that is free from prejudice and discrimination, and taking responsibility for the physical and mental well-being of self and others. Primary schools felt they were addressing attitudes and values more effectively than skills, knowledge and understanding.

Although secondary schools were generally satisifed with how they were addressing pupils' development of values and attitudes, there was less consensus among them than among primary schools about their relative importance. Over a third of schools said that recognizing the social responsibilities that go alongside personal rights was most important and a quarter of schools identified understanding, caring and respect for others.

Addressing lifelong learning through LEA-led initiatives

The Support and Advisory Service used these survey findings to inform its programme of school support and teacher training. If LEA-led programmes are to successfully effect change, it is essential that schools see them as supporting their priorities rather than adding to pressures and workloads. The two initiatives described below were therefore presented to schools as means of motivating pupils through increased curriculum relevance, thus supporting schools' 'raising achievement agendas'. However, their longer-term aim was to stimulate schools to review their whole school ethos and working practices, and to identify new ways in which they could look outwards and better respond to their changing communities.

These initiatives focused on helping teachers and pupils to explore current changes taking place in the labour market and the impact of these on themselves, their families and their local communities. For far too long, careers education and guidance assumed a separation between people's employment experiences, domestic responsibilities, and personal learning and development. This distinction is unhelpful to individuals at a time when family structures and gender roles have significantly changed, and people are reviewing personal goals, routes and identities. The school curriculum needs to move beyond its recent emphasis on pupils' knowledge acquisition to incorporate pupils' understanding of individual and social change, their development of personal value systems and their capacity to actively engage in associated processes of learning and growth.

Two school curriculum initiatives: a focus on inservice training for teachers

I shall now describe the following initiatives:

1   The participation of primary school teachers in a *Preparation for Adult Life* course that develops approaches to addressing personal, social and careers education across the curriculum.

2   The participation of secondary school heads of subject departments in courses that use labour market information to raise their awareness and to encourage them to incorporate it into their teaching.

The participation of primary school teachers in a *Preparation for Adult Life* course that develops approaches to addressing personal, social and careers education across the curriculum

> Career-related learning in primary schools helps children to manage their progress in learning and work. It is part of a wider concern for 'Learning for living' which includes personal, social and health education, citizenship, environmental education and work-related learning ... The potential for career-related learning to motivate children and make their learning more relevant to them is an important contribution to tackling social exclusion. Early intervention to target children at risk of becoming disaffected can forestall the more intractable problems, which could arise later.
>
> (CRAC/NICEC, 1998).

My description of this primary teacher training course will be preceded by national and local background information relating to teacher-training and careers education, and followed by an analysis of the sorts of changes that teachers were able to carry out during a fifteen-month period following the course.

Background to the course

Coventry LEA, in collaboration with Coventry's Quality Careers Service (QCS), has continued to support school careers education programmes throughout the period of National Curriculum implementation. Between 1995 and 1998, Coventry LEA used a government training grant to pilot a course for primary teachers and to organize a conference for primary headteachers entitled *Preparing Children for Adult Life: How Their Future Will Be Different From Our Present*. Although these sessions focused on the importance of career- and work-related learning, they were presented within the broader context of pupils' ongoing personal and social development. Following the conference, eight headteachers agreed to release teachers to attend an 8-session course over two terms, and to undertake curriculum development in their schools. All eight teachers, who were middle or senior managers holding multiple areas of responsibility, expressed similar attitudes at the start of the course:

> 'I initially didn't apply because I thought it wasn't relevant to primaries.'
> 'I was probably nominated as 'the most suitable'—everyone was overloaded.'
> 'I did not know much at all about opportunities and destinations for Coventry's school leavers.'
> 'I'm not too sure about patterns of employment in the school's catchment area.'
>
> (Coventry LEA, 1997)

The pilot course

The three course aims were: to raise primary teachers' awareness of the relevance of careers education to their pupils; to secure their understanding and commitment; and to equip them to undertake curriculum development in their schools.

The course covered the following areas:

- Developing a broad definition of careers education as 'preparation for adult life'.
- Writing a school personal and social education policy that addresses 'preparation for adult life'.
- Understanding changing labour market trends and patterns and their implications for the learning needs of children and young people.
- Using employment-related data relevant to individual school areas to better understand and respond to pupils and their families.
- Involving teachers and pupils in action research relating to work-related aspirations and experiences.
- Addressing career- and work-related learning in different National Curriculum subjects.
- Developing pupils' skills, values and attitudes through extra-curricular experiences, such as 'jobs around the school'.
- Acquiring resources to support Personal and Social Education (PSE) and career- and work-related learning, such as the Education – Business Partnership Centre learning modules.

At the end of the course, teachers identified school-based activities that they aimed to undertake during the next school year. Fifteen months later, five of the eight teachers who were still teaching in the same schools, reported on how successful they had been in carrying out their plans and in making use of aspects of the course.

Changed practice in schools following the course

Table 9.1 summarizes the planned and unplanned careers education activities that teachers had carried out since attending the course.

Since the course, teachers had carried out more planned than unplanned careers education activities. They were most able to bring about changed practice in relation to careers education when their action did not make demands of other colleagues; they could build on existing work or make careers education part of a current school priority such as literacy; and when they had ready-to-use materials easily at hand. The activities they had been unable to carry out were those that created an additional school priority, demanded research and original thinking or extended written tasks, and those that needed other colleagues' involvement. All teachers cited lack of their own and other colleagues' time, and lack of curriculum priority as major obstacles to changed practice.

An example of a successful course-follow-up activity

There was one activity that all course members had successfully carried out. This activity was based on a course session where Quality Careers Service had raised teachers' awareness of the changing labour market and its implications for families and children, and had also given teachers materials for carrying out their own investigations. Table 9.2 summarizes their approaches and their findings.

Both the headteacher conference and the course for primary teachers were successful in transforming teaching colleagues' resistance to the relevance of careers education to primary school pupils. The presentation of labour market information in a way that can be directly related to the learning needs of pupils and families in individual schools, was the key to this transformation. Moving from this heightened awareness and commitment to changed practice

Table 9.1 Planned and unplanned careers education activities

Sch	Focus of planned activity successfully implemented	Focus of planned activity NOT successfully implemented	Focus of unplanned activity implemented using course material and ideas
1	1. Employment data 2. PSE policy	1. Additional cross-curricular policies 2. PSE teacher guidance for early years 3. Personal attainment descriptors for use with pupils 4. Links between PSE and Records of Achievement	1. Research into pupil perceptions of work 2. Key Stage PSE teaching plan 3. Personal attainment descriptors for use with pupils
2	1. Employment data 2. Co-operative games pupil materials	1. Technology/careers teaching units 2. PSE policy 3. Pupils use of Education Business Partnership Centres	1. Pupils' jobs and responsibilities 2. Personal attainment descriptors for use with pupils 3. Pupil materials on rights and responsibilities
3	1. Employment data 2. Personal attainment descriptors for use with pupils	1. Pupils' jobs and responsibilities 2. PSE policy 3. PSE/careers teaching units 4. Audit of teaching of cross-curricular themes	1. Careers/PSE Literacy links 2. Personal attainment descriptors for use with pupils 3. Purchase of new resources 4. Purchase of published schemes of work 5. Attended further training
4	1. Employment data 2. Records of achievement pupil materials 3. Personal attainment descriptors for use with pupils	1. PSE/careers education policy 2. Pupil's jobs and responsibilities	1. Personal attainment descriptors for use with pupils 2. School wall of achievement 3. Pupils' jobs and responsibilities 4. Industrial links 5. Paired work with younger children
5	1. Employment data 2. PSE policy	1. Staff training on PSE 2. Pupils' jobs and responsibilities 3. Teacher guidance on careers education	1. Pupils use of education business partnership centres 2. Talks by visitors to the school

in schools, with colleagues who did not yet share these new perspectives, was fraught with obstacles. Teacher training initiatives need to equip teachers with practical materials and strategies to help them overcome such obstacles, especially in areas such as careers education that do not share the same curriculum status as National Curriculum subjects.

The participation of secondary school heads of subject departments in courses using labour market information to raise their awareness and to encourage them to incorporate it into their teaching

> We could ALL do with the opportunity to stand still and reflect on the future that our young people will be involved in. (Head of post-16)
> I have plenty of ideas. The challenge now is to consider what we do to help equip students with key skills. (Head of geography)

Before describing the courses attended by heads of different subject departments from Coventry schools, I shall provide background information about career- and work-related learning in the secondary school curriculum which illustrates its increasingly vocational emphasis.

In 1996, the government published 'the first ever White Paper on the education and training of 14- to 19-years-olds in England' (DfEE, 1996) entitled *Learning to Compete*. A major focus of this, and subsequent documents, was how secondary schools should equip young people for adult and working life through improving all young people's 'employability'. The government also set national education and training targets, the aim of which was to improve UK international competitiveness by raising standards and attainment levels. All education and training was expected to develop self-reliance, flexibility and breadth, through fostering competence in key skills.

Coventry's secondary school teacher training initiative was part of the *Preparation for Adult Life* training strategy outlined above. Although this chapter focuses on the course for heads of subject departments from Coventry's nineteen secondary schools and six special schools, parallel training programmes, using similar training materials, were run for secondary headteachers and deputy headteachers, school governors, and school careers education coordinators. Courses were also run for parents, including parents of children with special educational needs.

Within secondary schools, heads of subject departments are the major influence on what and how teachers teach, and on what and how pupils learn. Given that pupils spend most of their time following the National Curriculum, it seemed essential to raise department heads' awareness of the implications of labour market changes for the different groups of young people they teach. In many subjects, there is subject content that bears directly on these issues. In almost all subjects, there are opportunities to draw pupils' attention to labour market changes through using particular teaching contexts and examples. Teachers, through the way they teach, all have the opportunity to develop skills, attitudes and values that will be more or less useful to young people when they leave school. And, consciously or unconsciously, teachers transmit to their pupils, messages about future routes and goals that may or may not be constructive and relevant to their individual abilities, aspirations and needs.

Although these arguments seemed irrefutable to course organizers, it was unlikely that most department heads would see it as their subject priority; they would probably not choose to attend a course of this kind. This 'labour market training module' was therefore incorporated into the following half-day subject training sessions for heads of department, organized by

Table 9.2 Teachers' approaches and findings

	School 1	School 2	School 3	School 4	School 5
What information did you collect?	1. Census data 2. Changes over time in social context of catchment area 3. Work done by families of year 6 boys	1. Years 5 & 6 pupils' perceptions of future 2. Data about years' 5 & 6 pupils' parents' occupations	1. Census data 2. KSI pupils' knowledge about parental occupations 3. KSI pupils' ideas about work they would like to do in future	1. The jobs which children's adult family members do 2. What careers year 6 children are hoping for	1. Census data 2. Year 6 pupils' work aspirations 3. Work done by adults living in year 6 pupils' houses
How did you collect this information?	1. Data already in school 2. Asked long serving governors and staff 3. Asked year 6 boys to fill in proforma	1 & 2. Teachers of years 5 & 6 talked to children using common headings	1. Data already in school 2 & 3. Children drew pictures and wrote about this in a PSE lesson	1. The children privately filled in a prepared questionnaire 2. The children interviewed each other as part of a newspaper project	1. Data already in school 2 & 3. Brief discussion preceded pupils filling in prepared worksheet
What did you find out?	1 & 2. Update of already familiar picture 3. Boys' views of work very underdeveloped and very sex stereotyped	1. About half of the boys wanted to be professional footballers 2. Children knew what their parents did but not where they worked. Not much unemployment	2. Nearly everyone had someone in their family in work although mostly low skilled. Children could name what their parents did and where they went to work	1. Most adults have a job, females mainly part-time 2. Children's expectations appear to reflect family's although most did not plan to follow in parents' footsteps	2 & 3. The local pattern reflected citywide pattern. Pupils had realistic view of what is available

Did any of the findings surprise you?	1 & 2. School population represents 'bottom end' of social population of catchment area (some pupils go to church schools) 3. Boys had such little knowledge of work	2. I was surprised by the extremely wide range of occupations of parents	1 & 2. I was surprised so many parents were employed (this had not been reflected in 1991 census info). 3. Children expected some kind of work or further education when leaving school	1. I was surprised to see how many parents and siblings were in employment given the number of free school meals and problems with money for school trips etc and my own perceptions of unemployment	3. I was very surprised by the high level of employment of adults in the area and by the wide range of jobs they were doing.
What issues did these findings raise for your school?	1. Need to draw on area's wider social population 2. Need for class teachers to have discussions with children		Need to raise expectations of adults in school and of children	We need to deal with parents' unrealistic expectations of children, either too high or too low	That staff have inaccurate perceptions of employment levels and patterns of parents
Have you shared your findings with anyone else in school? If so, who?	1. Shared data with staff in context of benchmarking and levels of attainment trends in test results (will also share data with new staff)	Not yet. This information needs to be shared with head and with staff	Have shared info. With senior management team. In future need to share it with governors and other staff	Not yet. Parental expectations need to be addressed	Report back to all staff at end of term meeting
What advice would you offer to other teachers thinking of carrying out a similar activity?	Home discussion needs to take place before accurate data about parents' occupations can be collected	Need to prepare children by having general discussion about work first. Need for sensitive handling of issues e.g. unemployment		Introduce through relevant curriculum context. Need to respect privacy and possible parental reactions	Minimum preparation meant that I did not 'lead' the children's thoughts or ideas in any particular direction

subject advisers: English, mathematics, geography, history, science, design and information technology, and heads of post-16. The approaches and materials used in these sessions, together with examples of teachers' responses, will now be described.

Training aims, materials and approaches

The training module aimed to raise department heads' awareness of labour market changes and convince them of their responsibilities for ensuring that subject teachers understood the implications of these changes and addressed them in their teaching. The module also aimed to demonstrate the relevance of labour market changes to individual subjects and the opportunities afforded by these subjects to draw pupils' attention to the changing world of education, training and work they would enter on leaving school.

Two sets of materials were used as a basis for these sessions: the *Preparation for Adult Life* strategy document referred to earlier, and a Labour Market Information (LMI) pack developed in collaboration with Coventry Quality Careers Service (QCS and Coventry LEA, 1997) This pack was designed as a flexible training resource, and copies were made available to each head of department to facilitate follow-up sessions with teachers. It contained 21 overhead transparencies (OHTs) and presenter's notes, grouped in three sections: 'The national and international picture', 'The local picture' and 'What this means for school-leavers'. The national/international and local pictures contained visual representations of past, present and future trends in the changing occupational structure. The final section contained recent evidence of school-leaver destinations, broken down by gender, ethnicity and qualification levels. It also presented key messages relating to lifelong career development and career plans, coping with change and transitions, and the identification of transferable skills. Details of further and higher education, and of local training provision were also included.

The training module was tailored to each head of department subject group, and its relevance to their current priorities was demonstrated. All subject heads were given extracts from the *Preparation for Adult Life* strategy document and they all took part in a short quiz entitled *'Preparing children and young people for adult life: how will their future be different from our present?'* In addition, OHTs from the LMI pack were individually selected, and new materials and training activities developed, for each subject group, as follows:

Mathematics

Focus:
How can mathematics teachers use labour market information directly in their teaching?
Stimulus materials:
Results of a national survey of employers and employees on the relevance of 45 National Curriculum mathematics topics to the world of work.
An example of a pupil activity based on one of the OHTs, using pie charts and graphs to represent data.
Learning activities:
Heads of department were asked to transform one of four OHTs containing labour market data into a pupil activity. Each head of department received copies of these activities.
Response and evaluation:
Quiz answers showed a good general awareness of current labour market changes although they were surprised at the employers' survey findings. They produced useful pupil materials after much initial resistance, criticisms of OHT data presentation and complaints about lack

of teaching time. Course evaluations acknowledged that it would be 'much better' to use real data in teaching than textbook figures.

English

Focus:
The widespread use of information and communications technology (ICT) across most areas of employment.
Stimulus materials:
Background information.
Presentation by an ex-Coventry pupil who now works for a marketing firm in London. She described a typical working week, highlighting her use of ICT and personal and communication skills.
Learning activities:
Heads of department were asked to identify curriculum opportunities where ICT applications could be more strongly developed.
Response and evaluation:
Quiz answers showed a general level of awareness of labour market changes. They were amazed at widespread and diverse uses of communications technology in the world of work. They only generated vague ideas of school follow-up work.

History

Focus:
Which skills, attitudes and personal qualities that are considered necessary, for employability and for entrance to higher education, are central to the history curriculum?
Stimulus materials:
Latest post-graduate destinations data.
List of employability skills identified through a local employers' survey, and key skills required by higher education.
Examples of National Curriculum opportunities for careers work, e.g. pupils researching the career of an individual in the past.
Learning activities:
Heads of department were asked to identify additional opportunities for including labour market data in their teaching.
They discussed ways of using this information with teachers, pupils and parents, to promote the study of history in their school.
Response and evaluation:
They had quite a good general awareness of labour market changes. They could see the relevance of this information to some aspects of their subject and were enthusiastic about using it in school.

Geography

Focus:
Which skills, attitudes and personal qualities that are considered necessary for employability and for entrance to higher education are central to the geography curriculum?
Stimulus materials:
Latest post-graduate destinations data.

List of employability skills identified through a local employers' survey, and key skills required by higher education.

Examples of National Curriculum opportunities for careers education work, e.g. pupils exploring employment trends and job classifications within primary, secondary and tertiary industrial sectors.

Results of local survey of pupil attitudes to geography.

Learning activity:

Heads of department were asked to identify additional opportunities for including labour market data in their teaching.

They discussed ways of using this information with teachers, pupils and parents to promote the study of geography in their school.

Response and evaluation:

They had a good, quite detailed awareness of labour market changes. They could see the relevance of this information to some aspects of their subject and were enthusiastic about using it in school.

Science

Focus:

What range of career options do science subjects prepare pupils for?

Stimulus materials:

Facts and figures about destinations of pupils leaving school with advanced level science qualifications.

Latest post-graduate destinations data.

Learning activity:

Discussion of current changes in manufacturing industry and the knowledge, understanding and skills required by employers, e.g. engineering works.

Response and evaluation

They had quite a good general awareness of labour market changes. They showed few insights into how they could use labour market data in their teaching but were keen to know what career-related information the Quality Careers Service would provide them with.

Information technology and design technology

Focus:

For what range of career options do information technology and design technology prepare pupils?

Stimulus materials:

Teachers accompanied pupils to an employers' open day which focused on these subject areas.

Learning activity:

Visits to local industry and workshops with local employers and with careers advisers to see how technology is bringing about workplace changes.

Response and evaluation:

They particularly valued the visits to industry to see technology applications in a variety of occupations.

Heads of post-16

Focus:

How will labour market changes effect 18 plus school leavers who go into higher education?

Stimulus materials:

OHTS from LMI pack.

Key skills required by higher education.

Employability skills identified through a local employers' survey.

Post-graduate destinations data collected from local University.

Learning activities:

Group discussion of issues for different groups of post-16 students and how this data could be used to raise student awareness.

Response and evaluation:

Their knowledge of labour market changes was poor compared with their knowledge of higher education opportunities. They were keen to use what they had learnt with students and parents.

Although different groups responded differently to stimulus materials, there were some common responses across all heads of department groups. All expressed surprise at one or more aspects of labour market information, particularly the fundamental structural nature of the changes and the increasing numbers of workers in small businesses. They found the breakdown of local employment data by gender, ethnicity and city area particularly interesting. They recognized the need to identify more explicitly with pupils those skills, attitudes and values associated with their subject areas and the personal qualities that they need to develop. However, no evidence is available of how heads of department subsequently disseminated course ideas and materials to subject teachers in their schools. Like their primary colleagues, these department heads thought they would only have time to implement activities that they could directly incorporate into their curriculum plans and for which teaching materials were already prepared.

Conclusions

In recent years, primary and secondary schools have been increasingly required not only to improve pupils' educational performance but also to work in partnership with other organizations to address a range of personal, social and economic problems exhibited in their local communities. Nationally determined policies and funding strategies, and time demanded by partnership initiatives, have driven individual school agendas in sometimes contradictory directions. Despite much rhetoric about local management of schools, many headteachers and teachers feel that they have lost control of the teaching curriculum, and of the time in which to respond to local and individual learning needs. While it is essential for schools and teachers to start redefining themselves as learning, changing and responsive organizations and individuals, they will not have the confidence or capacity to do this in an educational culture in which they feel disempowered.

National and local strategies for change must engage more effectively in the day-to-day realities of teaching and learning in schools. Well-resourced initial and in-service teacher training is an essential means of supporting teachers in improving classroom and whole school practice, provided that training objectives are realistic and approaches are consistent with its purpose. Career- and work-related training must offer teachers practical means of bringing about change at a number of levels. As teachers they must model a commitment to professional change and development, and must have the personal confidence to welcome and support this process in teaching colleagues, pupils and parents. As members of school communities they must create a school ethos that evolves and confidently responds to changing needs and circumstances. The training initatives described in this chapter demonstrate that teachers welcome change that they perceive as supporting their pupils needs and interests, provided that they can have control over how it is managed. In these training sessions, teachers' initial resistance to the apparent irrelevance of career- and work-related learning was transformed. Good lifelong learning practice is beginning to emerge in both primary and secondary schools and should be celebrated through widespread local and national dissemination.

Acknowledgements

I would like to thank colleagues from Coventry Education Service and Quality Careers Service who supported the initiatives described in this chapter. In particular I am grateful to Di Hatchett, Ashley Hayward and the teachers who so willingly shared their experiences of school-based curriculum development, and to Mal Leicester and John Field for their help in redrafting this chapter.

Note

1 The views expressed in this chapter are the views of the author and do not necessarily reflect those of the Coventry LEA.

References

Careers Research Advisory Council (CRAC) and National Institute for Careers Education Council (NICEC) (1998) *Career-related Learning in Primary Schools*, Cambridge: CRAC-NICEC
Coventry City Council (1982) *Comprehensive Education for Life*, Coventry: City Council
Coventry City Council (1998) *Coventry Community Plan*, Coventry City Council
Coventry LEA (n.d.) *Entitlement and Achievement*, Coventry LEA
Coventry LEA (1997) *Careers Education and Guidance Inservice Training Programme, 1996–1997*, Coventry LEA
Coventry LEA (1998) *Support and Advisory Service Survey of Personal and Social Education in Coventry Schools*, Coventry LEA
Coventry LEA and Quality Careers Service (QCS) *Preparation for Adult Life: Helping Children and Young People Anticipate the Changing World of Learning and Work in the 21st Century*, Coventry: LEA & QCS
Coventry and Warwickshire Lifelong Learning Partnership (1999)
Department for Education and Employment (DfEE) and Qualifications and Curriculum Authority (QCA) (May 1999) *The Review of the National Curriculum in England: The Secretary of State's Proposals*, London, DfEE & QCA
DfEE (1996) *Learning to Compete: Education and Training for 14–19 year olds*, London: DfEE
Coventry TEC (1994) *Labour Market Forecasts*, Coventry: TEC
Longworth, N. and Davies, W.K. (1996) *Lifelong learning* London: Kogan Page
Quality Careers Service (QCS) and Coventry LEA (1997) *Labour Market Information for Coventry 1997–2000*, Coventry: QCS&LEA

10 Learning, work and community

Vocational studies and social values in the learning age

Terry Hyland

The learning age

Under the umbrella slogan of *The Learning Age* the Labour government has over the last few years issued a number of documents (DfEE, 1998a,b,c) designed to explain and publicize its policy for post-school education and training (recently codified in the White Paper *Learning To Succeed*, DfEE, 1999a). The idea of 'lifelong learning' which figures prominently in all the official prescriptions (Fryer, 1997; Kennedy, 1997)—like its popular predecessor the 'learning society'—is, however, by no means a new one. Appropriated from the adult education tradition (Edward, 1997; Barnett, 1998) to prescribe a conception of learning from the cradle to the grave—or as Henry Morris once put it, with the aim of 'raising the school leaving age to 90' (Kellner, 1998: 15)—the lifelong learning slogan is once again being employed as a popular method of criticising the mainstream and dominant school-centred, so-called 'front-loading' model of education.

However, apart from this opposition to the traditional schooling model, contemporary conceptions of lifelong learning are rather different from those associated with the older adult education traditions of 'recurrent education' and *education permanente* (Lawson, 1975; Legge, 1982). In a recent editorial celebrating its seventeenth year of publication, the *International Journal of Lifelong Education* rejoiced in the fact that 'lifelong education has really come to the fore in the educational vocabulary in recent years' (*IJLE*, 1998: 69). The editors go on, however, to bemoan the fact that this concept of learning is 'increasingly being equated with continuing education and related rather specifically to vocational updating'.

Such comments reflect the policy trends of the last two decades or so which have resulted in the 'vocationalisation' (Hyland, 1991; Skilbeck *et al.*, 1994) of all education from school to university so that now the 'economistic' (Avis *et al.*, 1996; Armitage *et al.*, 1999) purposes of learning are given pride of place to the detriment of the broader social and cultural functions of state systems (Maclure, 1998). Tight (1998a) offers the view that the concept has become part of a trinity—lifelong learning, the learning organization and the learning society—aimed at 'articulating the importance of continuing learning for survival and development at the levels of the individual, the organisation and society as a whole' (254). This provides some useful insights though it seems more accurate to say that, whereas the notion of the learning organization applied to industry and businesses may have a justifiably vocationalist/economic thrust, we still need to account for the way in which the other two items of the trinity have also come to be defined in this circumscribed way. Lifelong learning, as Strain (1998) points out, does not naturally carry such instrumental and utilitarian connotations, and it is worth marking and interrogating the re-engineering of these latest educational shibboleths.

The policy slogan which immediately preceded the now ubiquitous lifelong learning mantra—the 'learning society' which grew to encompass far more than the trinity identified by Tight—serves to illustrate how the 'vocationalization of everyday life has functioned to disguise the complex and hugely problematic nature of the economizing of education' (Avis *et al.*, 1996: 166). Barnett (1998: 14–15) examines four different conceptions of the learning society in his critical analysis of the 1997 Dearing Report on higher education: the replenishment of human/economic capital, the maintenance of cultural capital, the inculcation of democratic citizenship and the fostering of self-reflexive and rational learners. He concluded his evaluation with the observation that the

> Dearing conception of the learning society is the *economic* conception . . . but with a human face. Individual learning and development are to be welcomed but principally for their contribution to the growth of economic capital.
>
> (*ibid.*: 15, emphasis in original)

Dearing's preference for an economistic model of the learning society—on the grounds that 'in the future, competitive advantage for advanced economies will lie in the quality, effectiveness and relevance of their provision for education and training' (Dearing, 1997: para. 34)—though some way short of the most extreme utilitarian conceptions of the learning society, reflects perfectly the culture shift in educational aims and values that has occurred in Britain over the last two decades. (Tight, 1998b, makes some interesting comparisons which highlight commonalities in this respect between the Dearing, Kennedy and Fryer reports.) The report on higher education produced by the Robbins Committee (1963)—though alluding to vocational preparation—was concerned principally with the intellectual, cultural and social aims of education, a perspective shared by the authors of the 1973 Russell Report (DES, 1973) on adult education. All this is a long way from current conceptions of educational aims and lifelong learning neatly summed up in the Secretary of State's comments on the 1998 Green Paper *The Learning Age*. Mr Blunkett observed that

> the ability to manage and use information is becoming the key to the competitive strength of advanced economies. With increasing globalisation, the best way of getting and keeping a job will be to have the skills needed by employers . . . For individuals who want security in employment and a nation that must compete worldwide, learning is the key.
>
> (Blunkett, 1998: 18)

Similar sentiments are clearly in evidence throughout all the official DfEE documents on lifelong learning and, at the level of overt sloganizing and propaganda, there is a high degree of continuity between New Labour policies for post-compulsory education and training (PCET) and those of their Conservative predecessors. However, when subjected to deeper scrutiny, lifelong learning policies can also be interpreted as an extension of the basic minimum economistic models to conceptions which point the way towards and help provide a foundation on which to build more wide-ranging social theories of lifelong learning which could bring about a 'new educational settlement' (Gleeson, 1996) and realize the Fryer (1997) vision of a 'new learning culture, a culture of lifelong learning for all' (para. 1.1)

Visions of the learning society

Although some commentators have described the idea of the learning society as, on the one hand, a 'myth' which has 'no real prospect of coming into existence in the forseeable future' (Hughes and Tight, 1998: 188) or, on the other, as an example of 'idealist educational discourse' (Rikowksi, 1998: 223) which is unhistorical and indeterminate, there is now sufficient policy documentation and analysis around to allow for the identification of distinctive models of education and training associated with the main themes. I will examine three of these models in particular in order to establish a conceptual framework within which to locate the later evaluation of emerging policy and practice in the field—with special reference to the emerging vocational education and training (VET) system since New Labour came to power—and to offer a critical alternative to current developments in the form of a social theory of lifelong learning.

Young (1998) is surely correct to characterize conceptions of the learning society as being 'essentially contested', reflecting 'different interests' and 'different visions for the future' (193). The contested nature of the general notion does not, however, seem to have stood in the way of either conceptual or policy analysis in the PCET sphere. It would be useful to examine brief outlines of three leading 'contestants' in the field.

Edwards' typology (1997: 175–84)

a) An educated society—drawn from the adult education tradition, this conception 'supports lifelong learning within the social policy frameworks of post-second World War social democracies'.

b) A 'learning market enabling institutions to provide services for supporting the competitiveness of the economy'. The primary objective is to 'meet the demands of individuals and employers for the updating of skills and competences'.

c) A learning society is one in which 'learners adopt a learning approach to life, drawing on a wide range of resources'. Both the liberal democratic conception and the learning market are 'displaced by a conception of participation in learning as an activity in and through which individuals and groups pursue their heterogeneous goals'.

Young's typology (1998: 194–9)

a) The schooling model stresses 'high participation in post-compulsory schooling as a way of ensuring that the maximum proportion of the population reach as far beyond a minimum level of education as possible'.

b) The credentialist model gives 'priority to ensuring that the vast majority of the population have qualifications or certified skills and knowledge and that the qualifications people achieve are related to their future employment'.

c) The access strategy represents a 'vision of a learning society of the future in which learning, after the phase of compulsory schooling, is increasingly freed from its ties with specialized educational institutions such as schools, colleges and universities'. This model stresses, learner choice and autonomy, credit transfer and access to a wide range of information and communication technology (ICT) resources.

d) Young's favoured perspective is what he calls the educative model which 'starts with a recognition that all social life involves learning, whether conscious or planned or not'. Within this framework the 'learner questions and begins to transform the context or community of practice in which the learning takes place. The ultimate end is the fostering of 'expansive learning' which can 'enable schools, colleges or training programmes to help students, teachers and people in the community to design and implement their own futures, as their prevailing practices show symptoms of crisis'.

Ranson's typology (1998: 2–10)

a) A society which 'learns about itself and how it is changing' in order to cope with structural social, political and economic change and temper the 'dynamic conservatism' of modern societies and allow for transformation 'without intolerable disruption'.

b)   A society which 'needs to change the way it learns' so as to support schooling/VET reforms which can accommodate 'massive expansion in participation' and keep pace with 'technological, communication and epistemological change'.

c)   A society in which 'all its members are learning' is one which 'recognizes that learning cannot be separated from society and is not just for the young but for all, throughout their lives'. The upshot is that 'diversity, accessibility, transferability, partnership and accountability become the defining characteristics of a comprehensive system of continuing education'.

d)   A final stage is a society which 'learns to democratically change the conditions of learning' and is informed by the idea that the task of 'reforming education from an elite (selective) to a socially just (comprehensive) system can never be a purely educational or pedagogical problem, but has to be conceived as a social and political one'. Such radical reform requires 'open public discourse' for the 'process of reasoning in public discourse helps to uncover common ends and thus to transform different groups into sharing a sense of the community, to become a public'.

Ranson's typology offers us a kind of stage-development model of how a learning society might be developed and structured; until the conditions of one stage are met, it is not feasible to try to deal with the requirements of the subsequent stage. In fact all three perspectives can be characterized in such developmental terms , and the key features and directions may be illustrated in terms of the following continuum:

Basic minimum curriculum → **Skills for employment** → **Narrow utilitarian ends**   **INDIVIDUALISM [Self]**

Updating skills for technological change → **VET for global economic competitiveness** → **Broad vocationalism**

A broad-based learning culture → **Unification of vocational and academic tracks** → **Educative learning**   **[Society] COMMUNITY**

Figure 10.1 Learning society: a developmental continuum

The general direction of policy and programme development is from narrow skills training for individuals towards a broader vocationalism linked to wider educational, social and moral objectives. Against the background of this continuum and the three typologies, it is now possible to attempt to analyse and characterize the various perspectives of the learning society contained in the New Labour *Learning Age* policy documents.

Emerging policy on VET in the post-compulsory sector

Commenting on the broad outline of recent policy, Coffield (1998) observed, ironically, that much of the many of the *Learning Age* documents have 'concentrated on how wonderfully different New Labour's plans for lifelong learning are from those of previous Conservative adminstrations' (27). Unsurprisingly, the new policies are introduced and justified in terms of the failure of previous reforms to tackle the main problems of VET and learning in the post-school sector. In explaining the need for a new body such as the University for Industry (UfI), for example, Hillman (1997) points to the fact that 'deficiencies in British education and training have been a cause for concern for policy-makers for 150 years', and that 'vocational learning... remains relatively low status in the UK' (29). Young (1998: 190) has also characterized the PCET sector as 'sharply divided' with 'vocational provision that carries little credibility'. In a similar vein, *The Learning Age* introduces the section on the principles of public funding and investment in learning with the observation that:

> After nearly two decades of inadequate investment in learning, we face a major challenge. The Government has already shown its commitment to education as a priority by announcing an additional £165 million for higher education and £100 million for further education in 1998–99, and by its pledge to support an extra 500,000 people in further and higher education by 2002.
>
> (DfEE, 1998a: 25).

The document goes on to describe the 'serious weaknesses' in the 'country's learning score-board'. In terms of individual learning these include seven million adults who have no formal qualifications at all and more than one in five adults with poor literacy and numeracy skills (12). In terms of work-based, or organizational learning, there has been a systematic under-investment by UK firms, especially small and medium-sized enterprises (SMEs), in comparison with our competitors (DfEE, 1998b; Hyland and Matlay, 1998; Matlay and Hyland, 1999).

The general solution to these problems is to be sought in the development of a culture of lifelong learning, a 'quiet and sustained revolution in aspiration and achievement' (DfEE, 1998a: 13) on the part of all stakeholders in the system. In order to develop such a culture emphasis is given to a number of flagship initiatives, and it is worth looking a bit more closely at two of these in particular the UfI and the New Deal Welfare to Work (WtW) project.

University for industry

Although the UfI *Pathfinder Prospectus* (DfEE, 1998c) was published in mid-1998 as a prelude to the official launch in 2000, the original UfI blueprint dates back to joint research and development by the Institute of Public Policy Research and the University of Sunderland in 1995/96 (Milner, 1998). The new body will perform the functions of an 'impartial broker' seeking to connect individuals and companies to training/learning programmes rather than being a principal provider, though the organization 'will commission initially a limited number of flagship packages in areas of strategic importance' (DfEE, 1998c: 27).

In order to achieve its two main objectives of stimulating the demand for lifelong learning amongst employers and employees and improving access to and availability of learning opportunities, the UfI will make extensive use of information and communications technology (ICT) to access learning networks. Through exploitation of the Internet and 'cyberspace' linked to the free phone helpline, *Learning Direct* (DfEE, 1998d), the plan is to enable users to gain access to a wide range of learning resources and packages offered through a network of learning centres such as the Learning World complex developed in the original Gateshead pilot.

New deal initiatives

The links between the New Deal and other lifelong learning projects are clear: schemes are specifically designed to be radically different from the past legacy of failed experiments and reforms in VET, its moral and political justification is provided by new emphases on co-operation, mutualism and social inclusion and, like the UfI and related projects, it is under-pinned by the 'third way' (Giddens, 1998) policy of public–private collaboration linked to attempts to reform the whole welfare and benefits system. In this respect, New Deal policy is epitomized in the *Target 2000* umbrella of initiatives, including National Traineeships suggested by Dearing (1996), New Start for disaffected 14- to 19-year-olds, and Right to Study which entitles all youngsters under 18 in employment to one day a week of study at a local college

(Training and Employment Network, 1997). In addition, it is possible to discern a number of different emphases and applications of the New Deal in the key policies:

1   New Deal refers specifically to the WtW scheme for unemployed 18- to 24-year-olds launched in April 1998 and extended in June 1998 to include long-term unemployed people aged 25+ (DfEE, 1999b).
2   The New Deal is part of a much 'broader welfare to work programme' (Ward, 1997: 8) which includes other projects such as the scheme for encouraging lone parents back to work (Bryson *et al.*, 1997). The New Deal schemes for disabled people and other categories of unemployed people (Skills and Enterprise Network, 1998) are also part of this wider framework.
3   New Deal is a more generalized term for identifying New Labour's overall policies for education and training, including links with the UfI, Individual Learning Accounts (ILAs) and the National Grid for Learning made in *The Learning Age* (DfEE, 1998a: 11) alongside connections between the New Deal and National Traineeships and Modern Apprenticeships (31, 40–1).
4   In addition to the above, all of which might be described as aspects of the New Deal for individuals, there is also the link with the new admininstration's wider policies to attack social exclusion in the form of the New Deal for Communities (Social Exclusion Unit, 1998). Launched in September 1998 with a budget of £800 million over three years, this community-oriented version of the New Deal is designed to 'give some of our worst-off local communities the resources to tackle their problems in an intensive and co-ordinated way' (7).

Against the background of this broad New Deal policy framework, the WtW scheme for 18- to 24-year-olds clearly has a central and seminal role to play and—if the evaluation of the first phase of the scheme was based on the volume of activity (and related literature) created by this project—then New Deal might already be judged to be an overwhelming success. Indeed, both independent and official DfEE evaluations of the first year of WtW operations (DfEE, 1999b,c,d) have recorded some creditable successes of the scheme, particularly in finding unsubsidized employment (obviously a policy priority) for unemployed young people. However, it remains to be seen whether these welcome 'relief' and 'recovery' functions of the New Deal can be extended and transformed—perhaps by the proposed Learning and Skills Council outlined in *Learning To Succeed* (DfEE, 1999a)—into the necessary 'reform' measures which will address the perennial problems of our PCET system.

Values and visions in New Labour policy

In a recent collection of articles on contemporary VET in the UK, Esland *et al.* (1999)—commenting on the 'main parameters of policy for the Labour government after it took office in May 1997'—observe that:

> Although there have been changes of emphasis and priority, and some alleviation of the more extreme right-wing elements of employment policy, the neo-liberal promotion of free market economic globalization has continued to provide the overarching framework for Britain's political economy as it enters the new millennium. (1–2).

I would broadly endorse this analysis, though I would need to allow for more substantive and potentially far-reaching policy shifts in terms of VET and *lifelong learning programmes*— as opposed to overall *economic policy*—than Esland and his co-writers seem to want to permit. Certainly, as mentioned earlier, there is a fairly high degree of continuity between

New Labour PCET policy and the former Conservative administration's commitment to individualism and an economistic perspective on VET. In the *UfI Pathfinder Prospectus*, for example, the Secretary of State tells us that 'learning is the key to individual employability and business competitiveness' (DfEE, 1998b: 1). This neatly encapsulates all aspects of official policy, as does the reference in *The Learning Age* to 'learning as the key to prosperity—for each of us as individuals, as well as for the nation as a whole' (DfEE, 1998a: 7).

Thus far, at the level of avowed policy, this fairly straightforward account might be classified—in terms of the typologies oulined earlier—in terms of Edwards' 1b (learning for economic competitiveness), Young's 2b (a credentialist model concerned essentially with employability qualifications) or Ranson's 3b (learning in order to keep pace with technological change). At this level there is little evidence of the broader concern with education implied in the educated society based on learning networks (favoured by Edwards), nor is there much reference to the access model of extending educational opportunities for all types of learning (not just employment-related kinds) which Young's account advocates. Ranson's radical vision based on a learning democracy—and incorporating the recognition that a learning society needs to rethink the fundamental social, political and moral conditions which contextualize all our learnings—is also difficult to locate within this official policy perspective.

On further inspection, however—and especially on examining the practical implementation and wider implications of New Labour policies—other features of the key models concerned with educational and social objectives tend to achieve greater prominence. It is worth noting here that a key difference between the former Conservative and the current Labour perspectives on the ultimate purposes of the learning society is that the former saw learning for economic competitiveness as an end in itself (see, for instance, DTI, 1994, 1995)—justified in terms of a self-sustaining and successful market—whereas the latter (though accepting that a key objective of learning is to achieve economic success) almost always makes connections between economic aims and the further (sometimes overriding) end of fostering the personal development of individuals and wider social cohesion.

This difference is nicely illustrated in a recent report by the National Advisory Council for Education and Training Targets (NACETT) which, in identifying revised education and training targets, argues that:

> The primary purpose of the new targets should be to *make Britain more competitive internationally*. But they will also play a vital role in *promoting social cohesion*. Those two goals need not be in conflict with each other; sustained economic success, for example, is essential is we are to reduce dependency on the State and make work pay.
>
> (NACETT, 1998: 5, emphasis in original)

The implied notion of 'social cohesion' here is, to be sure, rather limited and utilitarian—as well as being absolutely in keeping with the 'third way values' (Giddens, 1998: 66) which underpin current welfare reform strategies—but a wider and more elaborate value position can be discerned in the general DfEE documents on lifelong learning. Alongside the (admittedly, more visible) emphasis on economic competitiveness and employability skills in *The Learning Age*, for example, there are unequivocal references to the development of a culture of learning which:

> will help to build a united society, assist in the creation of personal independence, and encourage our creativity and innovation . . . Learning offers excitement and the opportunity for discovery. It Likes us in directions never expected, sometimes changing our lives. Learning helps create and sustain our culture.
>
> (DfEE, 1998a: 10)

Elsewhere in the document there are allusions to the ways in which learning 'contributes to social cohesion and fosters a sense of belonging, responsibility and identity in communities' (11).

All of this indicates an extension of the basic minimum individualistic functions of education and training to include broader educational and social purposes. Thus, other aspects of the learning society conceptions—particularly Young's access model (2c above) aimed at ensuring a more equitable distribution of educational and life chances, and Ranson's (3a,b) idea of a society which recognizes the need to change dominant modes of learning—begin to enter the picture. At this stage we are still within Edwards' learning market (1b) approach and still concerned mainly with employability but, in New Labour plans for funding lifelong learning, glimpses of the more elaborate visions of the learning society begin to reveal themselves.

The key priorities of current lifelong learning policies—particularly in the flagship UfI and WtW schemes—are unequivocally directed towards those who have benefited least from the system. The principal *Learning Age* document again establishes the main parameters in declaring the overriding intention to:

> bridge the 'learning divide'—between those who have benefited from education and training and those who have not—which blights so many communities and widens income inequality.

(DfEE, 1998a: 11)

To this end, the UfI, for example, will target those organizations (mainly SMEs; see Matlay and Hyland, 1999) which have been most disadvantaged by current provision, and will focus specifically on those people, 'over a fifth of the working population—around 8 million people', with 'either poor basic literacy or poor basic numeracy skills, or both; (DfEE, 1998b: 16). Similarly, the WtW scheme claims to be 'committed to ensuring that the New Deal will actively promote equality of opportunity and outcome for young people of all ethnic and racial groups' (DfEE, 1997: 37). Goals relating to equality of outcome—according to the most recent analyses of statistics (DfEE, 1999b,c,d; Hyland, 1999)—have still to be achieved, but, at the level of avowed policy, the implementation of the scheme offers some potential for the achievement of a system of VET informed by values of social justice.

Policy and practice in the further education (FE) sector—which has traditionally been concerned with accommodating those learners who have been most disadvantaged by schooling—also provides some evidence that current policies might be characterized in terms of the broader access model identified by Young (2c above). The agenda for this post-school sector was firmly established in the Kennedy report which was informed by the ideal of 'developing the capacity of everyone to contribute to and benefit from the economic, personal, social and cultural dimensions of their lives' (1997: 22). In order to achieve this:

> public policy for post-compulsory learning must be dramatically, systematically and consistently directed towards widening rather than simply increasing participation and achievement. A much wider cross-section of the population needs to be involved than now.

In the DfEE response to Kennedy there is a clear endorsement of this key principle of widening participation in the declaration that the:

> Government is committed to the establishment of a learning society in which all people have opportunities to succeed. Increasing access to learning and providing opportunities for success and progression are fundamental to the Government's strategy.

(DfEE, 1998c: 7)

In terms of policy implementation there is also a clear intention to use 'funding as a lever of change' in order to 'widen participation in post-16 learning' (12). The original expansion target of an extra 500,000 places in post-school education—bolstered by an additional £725 million (Nash *et al.*, 1998) has subsequently been increased to take in 700,000 learners in the sector by 2002. The additional funding includes £183 million specifically for student support in FE—with maintenance allowances of £40 a week being piloted for disadvantaged students—linked with a pledge to review the whole system of student support in this important sphere of VET (Crequer, 1998).

These developments point towards not just a general commitment to widening access and opportunities, but a determination to remove the traditional barriers (see McGivney, 1996) by prioritizing schemes for those who have historically been excluded. This seems to be fully in line with Young's access model (2c above) and also begins to address the features of Ranson's conceptions of the learning society (3c,d above) in terms of mounting a campaign to include all members of society in the project of lifelong learning. Moreover, in terms of particular strategies—the range of public/private partnerships (Hillman, 1997), and exploitation of the National Grid for Learning and Learning Direct helpline (DfEE, 1998d) to tap into as broad a range of existing resources as possible—there are also characteristics in the overall policy which match Edwards' 'learning networks' (1c above) perspective through which 'learners adopt a learning approach to life, drawing on a wide range of resources to enable them to support their lifestyle practices' (1997: 184).

A social theory of lifelong learning

The values underpinning the policy changes outlined above signify a reassertion (revival?) of the notion of education as a public good—incorporating moral principles of trust and benevolence matched by social justice aims (Hyland, 1998)—which can provide a foundation for the extension of current policies to work towards the establishment of a social theory of lifelong learning. Such a theory—following trends in the continuum outlined in Figure 10.1—would incorporate reforms and developments in the following areas:

Individual autonomy within a community context

Individualistic conceptions of education and training divorced from the public and community went hand in hand with the neo-liberal economic individualism of the enterprise culture (Heelas and Morris, 1992) and, in a different form, are still evident in certain aspects of New Labour policies (Hyland, 1999). As against this technicist, atomistic conception, the cultural revolution needed to achieve current lifelong learning objectives will need to concentrate more on 'social capital' (Schuller and Field, 1998) so as to reinforce the idea that 'learning is quintessentially social' (Coffield, 1998: 26). Moreover, although a balanced conception of individual effort and autonomy is integral to all learning and development, it will also be important to show how such autonomy needs to be located within wider notions of citizenship which require a 'public dimension' (Smith, 1997) and that sense of shared values which are a prerequisite of induction into any form of genuinely social practice such as learning (Lawson, 1998).

Studentship and learning careers

In spite of the rhetoric on independent and student-centred learning appropriated from the progressive and andragogic tradition (Edwards, 1997), the current 'McDonaldised' (Hyland, 1999) PCET system is informed by a stultifying technicism which militates against genuine choice and creative engagement on the part of learners. If the key objective of *The Learning Age* requiring 'putting learners first' and helping them to 'take charge of their own learning' (DfEE, 1998a: para. 1.1) is to be achieved, some conception of 'careership' (Hodkinson, 1996) which stresses learner empowerment needs to be built into the system. Central to this process is the idea of 'studentship' which, in its broadest sense, is used by Bloomer (1996) to refer to the 'variety of ways in which students can exert influence over the curriculum in the creation and confirmation of their own personal careers' (140). In order to combat the narrow occupational-ism of the technicized model of VET criticised earlier, we need to foreground this notion of a learning career which, for Bloomer (1997), functions as an 'interpretive schema, linked not purely to a single domain of human activity but to *life* and to whatever impinges significantly upon that life in the experience of the interpreter' (147, original italics).

Vocational studies, work and community

The 'new vocationalism' of the 1970s continues to distort and frustrate contemporary VET policy and practice. The approach is founded on a large number of mistaken assumptions and misunderstandings, though the following are centrally implicated:

a)   the false premise that the main problems of VET rest exclusively with the skills deficiencies of school leavers and employees;

b)   a distortion of the needs of industry which has resulted in the reductionist and narrowly focused NVQ occupationalism (Rikowski, 1998, Hyland, 1994, 1999) instead of the broad-based VET common in European systems (Skilbeck *et al.*, 1994);

c)   stemming from a) and b), there has been a marginalization and neutralization of the values dimension of VET which has generated an uncritical and ethically vacuous approach by which something called 'moral competence' (Wright, 1989) is recommended largely as a means of ensuring that youngsters develop 'employability' qualities desired by employers (IIE, 1996).

In order to remedy all these shortcomings a positive conception of VET needs to build on Dewey's broad conception of vocationalism as a conception which bridges the vocational/academic divide and 'stresses the full intellectual and social meaning of a vocation' (1966: 316). Underpinned by a common core of knowledge and skills delivered through a unified post-school curriculum (Young, 1998), such a conception is, above all, one which:

> acknowledges social and personal aims, values and needs, and locates education and training goals in relation to the kind of society we wish to see develop and the qualities in people that are to be fostered and nourished.
>
> (Skilbeck *et al.*, 1994: 46)

Conclusion: New Deal—new educational settlement?

The 'new educational settlement' for the PCET sector called for by Gleeson (1996) is one which embraces:

> an active view of citizenship which links partnership and empowerment in personal education and economic relations, beyond market, qualification and employer-led considerations... It also involves realisation that education, learning, society and work are synonymous, not separate entities. Principles of democracy and social justice are involved here, in terms of how education and training helps to shape, rather than passively reflect on, the future of industrial society. (15)

Can lifelong learning policy and its practical implementation through the various New Deal projects solve the problems of our VET system and lead to this new settlement?

Like lifelong learning and the learning society, 'New Deal' is clearly a concept which possesses too much valuable sloganizing potential to be restricted to any one particular project. Its political origins are, of course, to be found in post-Depression America in the 1930s when, after his inauguration as President in 1933, Franklin Delano Roosevelt (FDR) pledged himself to a 'new deal for the American people' (Johnson, 1966: 570) and went on to ask Congress for the:

> one remaining instrument to meet the crisis—broad executive power to wage a war against the emergency as great as the power that would be given me if we were in fact invaded by a foreign foe.
>
> (Commager, 1963: 242)

Under the slogan 'Relief, Recovery, Reform' the next decade witnessed an unprecedented spate of legislation and reform measures—including massive public work programmes, national work-relief schemes and major reforms of banking, industry, agriculture and labour relations—which gradually brought the country out of the Depression and which made the New Deal 'different from anything that had yet happened in the United States' (Hofstadter, 1959: 302).

Although there are some superficial similarities between FDR's New Deal and the New Labour version, it would be just too much of an exaggeration to describe the present state of the British economy—or even our problematic VET system—in terms of a crisis or an emergency. However, the persuasiveness of the slogan is clearly rooted in the idea of a sharp break with the past and can, with some degree of legitimacy, be applied to WtW and related lifelong learning schemes. Indeed, a previous job creation scheme launched by the Manpower Services Commission in 1985 was described at the time as a 'mini-New Deal' (Ainley and Corney, 1990: 33), and the term was also applied to the Youth Opportunities Programme established by the last Labour government in 1978 (Finn, 1997).

If New Deal and lifelong learning projects are examined against the 'Relief, Recovery Reform' slogan which informed FDR's original New Deal, it seems fair to say that, thus far, policy and practice has been characterized more by relief and recovery than by reform. Certainly, the WtW scheme and related skills and training programmes are explicitly defined by short-term objectives with relief and recovery (from unemployment, skills deficits, underachievement) primarily in mind. The original American New Deal also incorporated such objectives and, if New Labour's educational reforms fall short of the spate of ground-breaking legislation enacted by FDR in the 1930s, it is still possible to agree with McNair's assessment that, in terms of implications for adult learning, the 'last few years have been astonishing' (1999: 3). What is now required is for such reforms to be embedded in a restructured PCET framework in which a social theory of lifelong learning informs VET at all levels.

By way of a conclusion I would highlight the following areas for special attention.

Apprenticeships

There is some evidence of progression from the WtW options to Modern Apprenticeship (Ma) schemes. This movement needs to be positively encouraged so that, as suggested in the LSE Centre for Economic Performance study (Hart, 1998), the current 10 per cent participation in the relevant age groups is expanded to 30 to 40 per cent. The de-skilling of vocational studies and the downgrading of VET has gone hand in hand with the decline of the apprenticeship system. Although Ma schemes have many faults (largely caused by doctrinaire connections with narrow NVQ occupationalism), upgraded Ma schemes may, as Gospel (1998) argues, just provide 'the last opportunity to get work-based training in Britain on the right lines' (23).

Common core, general diploma and unified curriculum

The three-track qualifications framework has failed to bridge the vocational/academic divide and upgrade VET. Most post-school commentators (NCE, 1993; Hodgson and Spours, 1997; Young 1998) now agree that the only way forward is to move towards a unified curriculum and to replace A-levels, NVQs and GNVQs with some form of general education diploma which combines academic and vocational elements and is underpinned by a 'core of common, fundamental learnings for working life' (Skilbeck *et al.*, 1994: 60).

Learning, work and community

As a foundational framework for all post-16 reforms there is an urgent need to reassert the importance of the values dimension of VET and to replace the overly economistic and individualistic policies of the past with a social theory of lifelong learning in which, as suggested earlier, social justice and community needs and interests are given pride of place. There is a need to move from the neo-liberalism of the past (still far too influential in New Labour policy) to a communitarian ethics. As Arthur (1998) explains, whereas liberalism is the 'politics of rights ... communitarianism is the politics of the common good', he goes on to argue that:

> Neither human existence nor individual liberty can be sustained for long outside the inter-dependent and overlapping communities to which we all belong. Nor can any community long survive unless its members dedicate some of their attention, energy and resources to shared projects. (358)

In a similar vein, with vocational learning specifically in mind, economistic, technicist and individualistic strategies need to be replaced by approaches which foreground experience, learning style, studentship and the importance of the social/moral aspects of all learning activity. As Ranson (1998) rightly observes:

> There is no solitary learning: we can only create our worlds together. The unfolding agency of the self always grows out of the interaction with others. It is *inescapably a social creation.*

(20; original italics)

The success of New Labour's lifelong learning policy and the future of VET in particular and the PCET sector in general outlined in the policy framework contained in the *Learning To Succeed* White Paper may ultimately depend upon how closely the practical application of policy accords with such a social vision of learning and development.

References

Ainley, P. and Corney, M. (1990): *Training for the Future: The Rise and Fall of the Manpower Services Commission* (London, Cassell)

Armitage, A., Bryant, R., Dunnill, R., Hammersley, M., Hayes, D., Hudson, A. and Lawes, S. (1999): *Teaching and Training in Post-Compulsory Education* (Buckingham, Open University Press)

Arthur, J. (1998): Communitarianism: what are the implications for education?; *Educational Studies*, 24(3), 352–68

Avis, J., Bloomer, M., Esland, G., Gleeson, D. and Hodkinson, P. (1996): *Knowledge and Nationhood* (London, Cassell)

Barnett, R. (1998): 'In' or 'For' the Learning Society; *Higher Education Quarterly*, 52(1), 7–21

Bloomer, M. (1996): Education for Studentship; in Avis *et al.* (Eds)

Bloomer, M. (1997): *Curriculum-Making in Post-16 Education* (London, Routledge)

Blunkett, D. (1998): Opportunities to live and learn; *Times Educational Supplement*, 27 February

Bryson, A., Ford, R. and White, M. (1997): *Making Work Pay: Lone Mothers, Employment and Well-Being* (York, Joseph Rowntree Foundation)

Coffield, F. (1998): Going into Labour, But Giving Birth to a Tory Child?; *Parliamentary Brief*, May, 25–6

Commager, H.S. (1963): *Documents of American History* (New York, Meredith)

Crequer, N. (1998): Squeezed in the trap of debt and hardship; *Times Educational Supplement*, 4 December

Dearing, Sir Ron (1996): *Review of Qualifications for 16–19 Year Olds* (Hayes, School Curriculum and Assessment Authority)

Dearing, Sir Ron (1997): *Higher Education in the Learning Society* (London, HMSO)

DES (1973): *Adult Education: A Plan for Development* (Russell Report) (London, HMSO)

Dewey, J. (1966): *Democracy and Education* (New York, Free Press)

DfEE (1997): *Design of the New Deal for 18–24 Year Olds* (London, Department for Education and Employment)

DfEE (1998a): *The Learning Age: A Renaissance for a New Britain* (London, Department for Education and Employment)

DfEE (1998b): *University for Industry: Pathfinder Prospectus* (London, Department for Education and Employment)

DfEE (1998c): *Further Education for the New Millennium* (London, Department for Education and Employment)

DfEE (1998d): *Learning Direct: A Guide* (London, Department for Education and Employment)

DfEE (1999a): *Learning To Succeed: A New Framework for Post-16 Learning* (London, Department for Education and Employment)

DfEE (1999b): *New Deal for Young People and Long-Term Unemployed People Aged 25+* (London, Department for Education and Employment) 38/99

DfEE (1999c): *First Independent Report Gives Thumbs Up To New Deal* (London, Department for Education and Employment) 82/99

DfEE (1999d): *Employment Minister Stresses Values of Independent Research on New Deal* (London, Department for Education and Employment) 217/99

DTI (1994): *Competitiveness: Helping Business to Win* (London, HMSO)

DTI (1995): *Competitiveness: Forging Ahead* (London, HMSO)

Edwards, R. (1997): *Changing Places? Flexibility, Lifelong Learning and a Learning Society* (London, Routledge)

Esland, G., Flude, M. and Sieminski, S. (1999): Introduction; in Flude, M. and Sieminski, S. (Eds): *Education, Training and the Future of Work II: Developments in Vocational Education and Training* (London, Routledge/Open University)

Finn, D. (1997): Labour's New Deal for the Unemployed; *Local Economy*, November, 247–58

Fryer, R.H. (1997): *Learning for the Twenty-First Century* (London, National Advisory Group for Continuing Education and Lifelong Learning)

Giddens, A. (1998): *The Third Way: The Renewal of Social Democracy* (London, Polity Press)

Gleeson, D. (1996): Continuity and Change in Post-Compulsory Education and Training; in Halsall, R. and Cockett, M. (Eds); op.cit.

Gospel, H. (1998): The Revival of Apprenticeship Training in Britain; *Industrial Relations Journal*, 26(1), 32–44

Halsall, R. and Cockett, M. (Eds) (1996): *Education and Training 14–19: Chaos or Coherence?* (London, David Fulton)

Hart, J. (1998): Report urges training overhaul; *Times Educational Supplement*, 30 October

Heelas, P. and Morris, P. (Eds)(1992): *The Values of the Enterprise Culture* (London, Routledge)

Hillman, J. (1997): *University for Industry: Creating a National Learning Network* (London, Institute for Public Policy Research)

Hodgson, A. and Spours, K. (Eds) (1997): *Dearing and Beyond: 14–19 Qualifications: Frameworks and Systems* (London, Kogan Page)

Hodkinson, P. (1996): Careership, the Individual, Choices and Markets in the Transition into Work; in Avis, J. *et al.* (Eds) (1996); op.cit.

Hofstadter, R. (1959): *The Age Reform* (New York, Knopf Books)

Hughes, C. and Tight, M. (1998): The Myth of the Learning Society; in Ranson, S. (Ed); op.cit.

Hyland, T. (1991): Taking Care of Business; Vocationalism, Competence and the Enterprise Culture; *Educational Studies*, 17(1), 77–87

Hyland, T. (1994): *Competence, Education and NVQs: Dissenting Perspectives* (London, Cassell)

Hyland, T. (1998): Morality and Further Education: towards a critical values foundation for the post-compulsory sector in Britain; *Journal of Moral Education*, 27(3), 333–44

Hyland, T. (1999): *Vocational Studies, Lifelong Learning and Social Values* (Aldershot, Ashgate)

Hyland, T. and Matlay, H. (1998): Lifelong Learning and New Deal Vocationalism; *British Journal of Educational Studies*, 46(4), 399–414

IJLE (1998): Editorial; *International Journal of Lifelong Education*, 17(2), 69

IIE (1996): *Towards Employability* (London, Industry in Education)

Johnson, T.H. (1966): *The Oxford Companion to American History* (Oxford, Oxford University Press)

Kellner, P. (1998): Our mutual friends; *Times Educational Supplement*, 19 June

Kennedy, H. (1997): *Learning Works: Widening Participation in Further Education* (Coventry, Further Education Funding Council)

Lawson, K.H. (1998): *Philosophical Issues in the Education of Adults* (Nottingham, University of Nottingham Continuing Education Press)

Legge, D. (1982): *The Education of Adults in Britain* (Milton Keynes, Open University Press)

Maclure, S. (1998): Through the Revolution and Out the Other Side; *Oxford Review of Education*, 24(1), 5–24

McGivney, V. (1996): *Staying or Leaving the Course: Non-completion and Retention of Mature Students in Further and Higher Education* (Leicester, National Institute of Adult Continuing Education)

McNair, S. (1999): From Worthy Margin to Lively Mainstream; *Adults Learning*, 10(5), 3

Matlay, H. and Hyland, T. (1999): Small Firms and the University for Industry: An Appraisal; *Educational Studies*, 25(3), 253–67

Milner, H. (1998): The Broker and the Catalyst; *Adults Learning*, 9(5), 15–17

NACETT (1998): *Fast Forward for Skills* (London, National Advisory Council for Education and Training Targets)

Nash, I., Crequer, N. and Slater, J. (1998): Door Open for Excluded Groups; *Times Educational Supplement*, 4 December

NCE (1993): *Learning To Succeed: Report of the National Commission on Education* (London, Heinemann)

Ranson, S. (Ed) (1998): *Inside the Learning Society* (London, Cassell)

Rikowski, G. (1998): Only Charybdis: The Learning Society Through Idealism: in Ranson, S. (Ed): op. cit.

Robbins, L. (1963): *Higher Education: Report of the Committee* (London, HMSO)

Schuller, T. and Field, J. (1998): Social Capital, Human Capital and the Learning Society; *International Journal of Lifelong Education*, 17(4), 226–35

Skilbeck, M., Connell, H., Lowe, N. and Tait, K. (1994): *The Vocational Quest* (London, Routledge)

Skills and Enterprise Network (1998): *Labour Market and Skill Trends 1998/1999* (London, Department for Education and Employment)

Smith, R. (1997): The Education of Autonomous Citizens; in Bridges, D. (Ed): *Education, Autonomy and Democratic Citizenship* (London, Routledge)

Social Exclusion Unit (1998): *Bringing Britain Together: A National Strategy for Neighbourhood Renewal* (London, The Stationery Office)

Stephens, M.D. (1990): *Adult Education* (London, Cassell)

Tight, M. (1998a): Lifelong Learning: Opportunity or Compulsion?; *British Journal of Educational Studies*, 46(3), 251–63

Tight, M. (1998b): Education, Education, Education! The Vision of Lifelong Learning in the Kennedy, Fryer and Dearing Reports; *Oxford Review of Education*, 24(4), 473–85

Training and Employment Network (1997): *Target 2000 Briefing and Consultation* (London, Training & Employment Network)

Ward, C. (1997): More about the New Deal; *Educa*, No.177, 8–9

Wright, D. (1989): *Moral Competence* (London, Further Education Unit)

Young, M. (1998): Post-Compulsory Education for a Learning Society: in Ranson, S. (Ed); op.cit.

11 Life politics and popular learning

Jane Thompson

At the G8 Economic Summit held in Cologne in 1999 the heads of state of eight major democracies issued a joint charter of aims and ambitions for lifelong learning.[1] The charter catches precisely the dominant orthodoxy in prevailing definitions of lifelong learning, whilst laying bare the usual assumptions and preoccupations which have encouraged an all-to-easy political and professional consensus to be achieved. According to the Cologne Charter, the challenge every country faces is

> how to become 'a Learning Society' and to ensure its citizens are equipped with the knowledge, skills and qualifications they will need for the next century. Economies and societies are increasingly knowledge based. Education and skills are indispensable to achieving economic success, civic responsibility and social cohesion.

In fact, this strategic vision of 'the learning society', linked to lifelong learning, and created by governments in partnership with the private sector, in relation to individuals, represents a late capitalist solution to 'investing in people'—in their human, cultural and social capital— as the key to future employment, economic growth, mobility and cohesion.

Richard Edwards[2] points to the advantages of simplicity and conceptual clarity in definitions of the learning society—and in this case lifelong learning—as a way of enabling different (contested) notions to collect beneath the same banner. He identifies three main tendencies. The first is based on liberal democratic notions of a free and democratic society in which everyone is offered the same opportunities to use formal education facilities. This idea is picked up in the Cologne Charter as a declaration about equal access to knowledge, education and training, in which basic education should remain free of charge and 'special attention' should be paid to 'the needs of the disadvantaged' and to 'combating illiteracy'.

The second relies on the idea of a free education market, in which various providers offer vocational training and enhanced qualifications to improve the economy's competitive strength. The Cologne Charter makes much of the 'entrepreneurial role' of education—in terms of forming partnerships with business and the private sector—to ensure 'ready opportunities' for adult 'reskilling throughout life' as a 'passport to mobility', increased flexibility and change in the modern economy. It also recommends the 'continued development and improvement of internationally recognised tests to benchmark achievement... to establish clear targets in terms of higher standards and levels of achievement... and to enhance mobility in a globalised world'.

Edwards' third tendency relies on the postmodern commitment to open learning networks, able to respond to the requirements of different learners, and used creatively by them in increasingly self-directed ways. The Cologne Charter is very clear that whilst governments should expand their investment in education and training—especially in collaboration with business and the private sector—it is the responsibility of individuals to develop 'their own abilities and careers' on the basis of 'self generated learning' and by means of 'modern and effective ICT networks' and 'distance learning'.

As with the range of British and Irish Government and European Commission discussion papers on the subject, intent on preparing the ground for economic prosperity in the twenty-first century, the Cologne Charter mentions three other superficially simple concepts; 'quality of life', 'civic responsibility' and 'social cohesion'. The implications of these notions are not elaborated or dwelt upon but their mention—in passing—adds to the illusion of consensus, which masks the considerable possibility of ideological and actual disagreement about the meanings and values underpinning their realization.

Richards does not detect in the prevailing language of the learning society and lifelong learning any recognition of an otherwise historic tension in adult education—the tension which has existed between adult education's concern to serve the interests of political and social movements committed to social justice and progressive social change and its role in ser-vicing the state and the economy. For obvious reasons, the Cologne Charter does not spell out the arguments of the more radical option either, although the thrust of its preoccupations with employability and technicist considerations immediately invites the criticism of radicals about the absence of any reference to collective as distinct from individual learning, to the democratization of education, to what counts as knowledge and skills, to the role critical intelligence and empowerment might be expected to play in the creation of real choices, demo-cratic renewal and progressive social change; and how a radical, democratizing education needs to reach beyond government and business interests to articulate urgent problems and pressing concerns with people other than professional politicians, employers and educational providers.

Platitudes revealed in the charter about 'the needs of the disadvantaged' on the one hand and globalization on the other have next to nothing to say about the extent, the consequences and the range of structural inequalities which currently exist *within* G8 democracies and *between* countries of the rich north and the much poorer—and less powerful—south. Similarly, the recourse to 'self help' and 'individual responsibility' minimizes the impact of structural con-straints and overlooks the huge disparity in the resources available to different social groups—both of which affect their capacity to change the circumstances of their lives on an individual basis.

In the absence of much radical discussion about values and purpose, the emerging discourse of lifelong learning remains boxed in by the alleged synergy between economic and educa-tional interests, and by functional definitions of learning which reduce the complexity of intellectual, emotional, practical, pleasurable and political possibilities to the language of targets, standards and skills. But it is not the main purpose of this chapter to interrogate the language of lifelong learning which signals the arrival of a new professional discourse in adult education. The possibilities and opportunities that might be provided by stretching the discourse[3] in order to recapture and revision the more radical tradition in adult learning will not be achieved by theoretical writing that simply deconstructs the language and epistemology of a developing discourse without more constructive and democratic engagement with adult learners in ways that make a material, practical, pleasurable and political difference to their lives.

As an example of what I mean I want to draw into the discussion some reference to the Rosemount Resources Centre in Derry, and to include the experience of some women whose lives I have recently come to recognize as emblematic of the struggle to connect relevant and useful learning to big ideas and collective action in pursuit of personal and political change. This is the sort of popular learning that is characterized by social purpose, the development of 'really useful' knowledge and the concern of social movements—like the women's movement and community politics—to move people from where they are to where they want to be as the realities of their lives are changed.

Derry is an old and beautiful city dating back to the sixth century, situated along the banks of the River Foyle in surroundings of enormous natural beauty. It is a working-class city, divided geographically along religious lines into Catholic and Protestant areas, from which the middle class have moved out to safer and more desirable suburbs. Working-class communities in Derry have grown used to poverty. Eleanor Marx made a visit here in 1891 to encourage the growth of 'organisation and combination' among unskilled workers in the shirt factories. The recession of the 1930s cut deeper and lasted longer than elsewhere in the UK. The post-war boom was shorter lived. By 1970 consumption per inhabitant was only three-quarters the UK average.[4] In the period between Partition and the resumption of Direct Rule from Westminster, Protestants used their influence as capitalists, property owners and administrators in the public sector to make sure the opportunities which did exist went to Protestants. These days both communities face similar problems. The manufacturing industry and jobs in the public sector—which once provided steady employment for men—have been devastated by economic recession and by Conservative policies. Women, as everywhere else, shoulder the main responsibility for unpaid domestic work, take most responsibility for managing family poverty and have the worst choice of low paid, part time and 'unskilled' jobs.[5]

Derry has also been the site of some of the most serious repercussions of 'the troubles' outside Belfast. Bloody Sunday happened here in 1972. The local cemetery holds the bodies of those from the Derry Brigade killed in the armed struggle and of hunger strikers who died in custody during the period of Internment and Direct Rule. Republican and Nationalist street murals painted onto gable ends mark the entrance to the Bogside and Free Derry Corner. A hoarding expresses 342 days of solidarity with those still under siege in Drumcree as tension mounts towards another marching season. In the Waterside area of the city, Loyalist street murals depict Loyalist paramilitaries invading the Bogside carrying a Union Jack, whilst an IRA man lies on the ground with a stake through his heart. On the corner of Queen Street and Asylum Road the police barracks are fortified with metal sheeting, barbed wire and security cameras—still looking like a bunker in a war zone despite the paramilitary cease fire and the precarious optimism of the peace process. In the world of Irish politics, it has usually been the middle and more affluent classes, with financial and ideological interests to defend, who have acted as professional politicians, but it is the working class who have done the fighting and sacrificed their lives.

On the domestic front—across both communities—gender battles are still being negotiated and decided. Culture, religion, sectarianism and 'the troubles' have all contributed to a traditional form of gender division in which men have retained predominance, authority and control, although women are seen as strong and central to sustaining family and community life in terrible and traumatic times. The strength of sexual stereotyping is reinforced by other factors—all of which are inter-related. These include the psychological and material consequences of poor employment opportunities for women; poverty, and what is sometimes called 'time poverty' caused by the prevalence of women's multiple roles; the absence of women in influential positions; and the absence—until very recently—of a platform for the expression of women's interests.[6] In addition the fear and experience of sectarian, police and military violence on the streets—which is widely associated with active masculinity, heroism and martyrdom—has compounded the difficulties of discussing domestic violence in the home. In conditions of 'armed patriarchy'[7] personal violence also erupts easily but is rarely related to oppressive patriarchal relations, women's economic dependency or men's traditional attitudes to the exercise of power.

Debates about gender politics and feminism have received less attention in Northern Ireland than in the rest of the UK in the face of more pressing and historical definitions of politics and priorities. A small, embryonic women's movement struggled throughout the 1970s and 1980s but was split by religious and political divisions. It was isolated from the larger, more confident movement in the south, largely because Irish feminism closed its eyes to the situation in the north, wary of inward looking and church dominated tendencies in Irish politics and introverted nationalism. At the same time, British feminism was notoriously indifferent and deeply ignorant about the conditions facing women in Ireland. As second wave feminism was gathering momentum in Britain, the big issue facing Northern Irish women was the war. Some might have wanted a women's movement and feminist social change, but they also had the war to live with. In Northern Ireland, on top of poverty, discrimination, British imperialism and patriarchy, the gendered nature of the war blighted and restricted women's choices even more.[8]

It would be wrong to regard women as bystanders in 'the troubles', however, or to underestimate women's involvement in sectarian conflicts. Eilish Rooney argues that 'those who see the state of Northern Ireland as reformable, see 'the troubles' as an avoidable additional burden on women's lives. They generally applaud how women cope with and confront violence'.[9] And yet women throughout the period of 'the troubles' have been active in protests, in organizing demonstrations, in establishing support groups for prisoners and their families and in becoming political prisoners themselves. In some respects women have been active 'in the background', carrying goods from place to place, hiding guns and other weapons and smuggling letters in and out of prison. But they have also played a more visible and prominent role in the Civil Rights marches and have lent support to those on hunger strike. They have attended military funerals and gathered together in large numbers during peace rallies. They have campaigned on behalf of the peace process and voted for peace in massive numbers in the wake of the Good Friday Agreement. Whilst working-class women in Britain have been portrayed (inaccurately, in many respects) as apathetic about politics and about political participation, those in Northern Ireland have become widely involved in the struggle to defend their communities and to extend the democratic rights of ordinary people—but in ways that do not fit the usual definition of what counts as politics.

The concept of 'life politics' used by Anthony Giddens[10] captures the essence of what I mean—although the radical feminist conviction that 'the personal is political' made the same point a quarter of a century earlier. Life politics refers to the range of circumstances, conditions, struggles and commitments which affect people's everyday existence at home, at work, in their communities. In Derry this has meant getting up in the morning, raising children, doing the business of everyday life in a war zone. But it also includes making ends meet, holding down a job, experiencing the effects of discrimination, taking part in education, negotiating changes in personal and social relationships, dealing with statutory authorities, feeling involved or excluded from what is happening in the wider world. These are typically the concerns which acquire significance and meaning in the private sphere, which may be experienced as 'individual problems', and which are often constructed as the consequence of 'personal failure' or 'the way life is'. They involve issues which are so 'ordinary' they become accepted and taken for granted—especially if people feel they do not have much control over their own lives or much room for manoeuvre. They are certainly not the kind of issues which are conventionally viewed as 'political' in discussions about party politics, representative democracy and constitutional reform. However, they are the issues and concerns which shape the lives of ordinary people on a personal and everyday basis in ways that may give rise to anger and frustration but also to demoralization and fear. They are closely related to conditions of power, inequality and structure and are the reasons why more people currently join self-help groups, community groups, voluntary organizations and social movements than political parties.[11]

This is especially true in Northern Ireland where political neglect has characterized the relationship between Britain and the province for many years. In the period before the Good Friday Agreement, Direct Rule created an anomalous arrangement in which the six counties were regarded as being neither inside nor fully separate from the mainland. Leadership was exercised through a senior minister with cabinet responsibility, a job that, until the appointment of Mo Mowlam, had acquired the status of a penalty or banishment among British politicians. Day to day administration was carried out by non-elected civil servants from the Northern Ireland Office, supplemented by ad hoc quangos. Local government enjoyed fewer powers than in the rest of the UK. Decision-making was neither accountable nor transparent and there was considerable scope for patronage and the abuse of discretion—especially in support of Unionist and Protestant self interests. For many years Sinn Fein and the Social Democratic and Labour Party undertook a boycott of electoral politics—for reasons of partiality, nepotism and discrimination in the system—but the effect was to further diminish the democratic credibility of political structures.

If the working class have been deprived of democracy in Northern Ireland, women have been additionally excluded. In the research carried out by the Women and Citizenship Research Group into political participation in 1995[12] it was found that all the Northern Irish representatives in the British and European Parliaments were men, and men held 88 per cent of local council seats. According to Cynthia Cockburn, men in Northern Ireland are firmly in charge of all the major institutions of power—church, state and quango.[13]

In the absence of political structures and a strong feminist movement to reflect women's immediate concerns, working-class women in Northern Ireland began to get organized on their own account. The form their movement took was distinctive and was organized around the development of locally based community centres. It is well known that women are more likely to be involved in community groups than men, and more involved in community based activities than in conventionally defined politics.[14] However, the extent of women's participation in Northern Ireland is more noticeable than in many other working class communities in the UK, and has been rising.[15]

In Derry, as elsewhere, local community initiatives and organizations spring into existence like flowers after rain, born out of common needs and collective energy. Developing the resources for a journey of hope[16] in circumstances of extreme poverty, violence and political exclusion is monumental, and yet the business of getting on with what needs to be done is also a strong component of everyday existence. In this capacity women play an impressive and frequently unrecognized role, characterized by what Mary Robinson once described as 'shared leadership, and a quiet, radical, continuing dialogue between the individual women and the collective women'.[17]

The significance of women's involvement in community groups has also been recognized by others as central to the well being of their communities.[18] The effectiveness of women's community action in challenging women's secondary status is equally well known. 'The values underlying ways of organizing emphasize local control and autonomy, local social and cultural activities, relating theory to practice, encouraging procedures and leadership styles which make participants feel confident and involved, and recognizing that different views about tactics and strategy may be rooted in real experience and are worth listening to and discussing'.[19] In difficult times the participation of women confirms the critical significance of receiving support from others; in being the means of helping other women to speak out; in being an expression of pride in self-sufficiency during many years of conflict; and in engendering the solidarity necessary for public campaigning.

The activities which characteristically emerge are concerned with tackling inequality, and about countering prescriptions of deficiency and pathology with an alternative ideology based on empowering the poor. Women who do not readily regard themselves as political—when politics means the Ulster Unionist Party or Sinn Fein, a power sharing Assembly or the Northern Ireland Office—can find in community activities solutions to their problems and a platform for their immediate interests. These usually include making ends meet, tackling the effects of drug dealing in the neighbourhood, the shame of domestic violence and alcohol abuse, the legacy of police and army raids, the loss of loved ones to sectarian violence, the responsibilities involved in caring for elderly relatives, the closure of another factory and the scarcity of decent jobs. In all of these circumstances it is not surprising that women seek out other, similar people, with whom to build community and to become involved in support groups, campaigns, life-saving and life-enhancing responses.

The Women's Group which meets in the Rosemount Resource Centre in Derry was formed in 1997 and started when a small group of women got together to provide support and social contact for women in the area. The group members are all women from working-class, mostly Catholic, backgrounds; the majority are unwaged and many of them are in receipt of state bene-fits. From small beginnings the number of women attending the group has grown substantially and they now meet three times a week. Initially the emphasis was on issues related to bringing up children and women's isolation but they now organize a number of activities dealing with social, leisure, health and general educational issues. As well as providing a safe and friendly place to meet, the centre is also a place to get welfare advice and to formulate action on perso-nal and local issues including drugs, alcohol abuse, vandalism and domestic violence. It is a place to make contact with other women facing similar issues in an effort to find individual and common solutions.

Increasing enthusiasm and a growing membership have stepped up the demand for educa-tion. For women growing up in serious material poverty and in the middle of 'the troubles', the usual disjunction between gendered, working-class existence and the culture of schooling, is even more pronounced. All the women I met in Derry had their schooling seriously dis-rupted by the war. Bernadette remembers

> heading down William Street and the Roseville Flats to watch the men and young fellas throwing stones and petrol bombs at the much-hated police. We even helped to gather the stones and empty milk bottles to make effective bombs. I remember walking to school every morning and collecting empty CS gas canisters which had been fired at the men who were defending the Bogside from the police.

Her family were strong Nationalists and her home became the place were Civil Rights leaders met from time to time, among them Bernadette McAlisky. Police and army raids on her house in the early hours of the morning were commonplace. 'All my schooldays were over-shadowed by army jeeps and army personnel crawling over the whole area where I still live. I remember the way they intimidated even the school children, sitting in their Saracens outside the school gates, taunting them. Stones and bottles would be thrown and another riot would begin'.

At sixteen Cathy watched in horror whilst the police smashed down the door into her front room with a battering ram and beat her father senseless before kicking her to the ground as well. When he died three months later from the effects of his injuries, her mother was left with nine children to bring up on her own. Expecting trouble during the annual Apprentice Boys march in August, she removed herself and the children to the Republic for the weekend where they watched on television as their house in William Street—including all their posses-sions—was burned to the ground in what was later to be known as the Battle of the Bogside.

Like Cathy, most women in the group left school at the first possible opportunity. Usually they went to work in one of the local shirt factories where it was common to stitch three hundred dozen pairs of cuffs with stiffeners onto as many shirt sleeves in a day, in a regime which charged workers for their materials and docked their pay if they did not meet their targets.

Thirty years later most of the biggest factories have closed down in the face of competition from third world labour markets, where low wages and lack of union recognition have made them more attractive to multinational capitalism operating in a global economy. Women's and men's unemployment is now as high as 80 per cent in parts of Rosemount and other working class estates in Derry.

For all these reasons women are not immensely confident about their educational abilities but they are determined and enthusiastic about pursuing courses and qualifications. Thirty women signed up to do the autobiography project I was able to arrange, producing writing about their lives which is powerful, complex and exceptional by any standards, and which draws on their own experiences to reveal tough lives lived in the spaces between poverty and hard work, family loyalties and family responsibilities, sexual desire and sexual oppression; and between men's considerable capacity for violence, institutionalized by 'the troubles' in the wider society and by patriarchy in intimate relationships.[20] The women's stories liberate important voices whilst their meetings have become subversive spaces in which feminist and alternative explanations can be developed. These are places which Henri Lefebvre[21] refers to as 'spaces of ennunciation' and where Chantelle Mouffe finds, in the 'hegemonic gap', more than a little room for political manoeuvre.[22] They are the spaces within which women still have the chance to make their own history and can begin to renegotiate the terms and conditions of their relationships and their lives, especially when they have spoken 'out loud' about their feelings, their concerns and their priorities in the company of others with whom they share experiences, solidarities and understandings.

In conversation with me, the women talk about what they know as being 'common sense'. They laugh and shrug their shoulders and say 'but everyone knows about things like this—it's life'. They do not regard their writing as being particularly political, but they could have chosen to write about something totally innocuous—about a favourite pet or an outing to the seaside. Instead they describe women who are definitely not victims. Women who have battled through distressing and appalling circumstances, looking for solutions to their problems, finding friendship, solidarity and some pleasure along the way; who are strong enough and sufficiently eloquent to give meaning and significance to the moments of being that have shaped their lives. And who are still learning from their continuing struggles.

They do not regard themselves as 'educated' either. Reading some of the accounts of their childhood it is hard to imagine how school could possibly have been taken seriously. A lot of learning was going on informally about family, poverty, history, violence, religion and injustice, but formal education, for the most part, was something that circumstances and schooling persuaded them they were not very good at long ago. This 'having another go' has only come about because they are members of what is now a strong women's group whose enthusiasm is contagious for doing things together that would previously have been thought impossible.

For the record, all but a handful of women completed the course. They worked partly on their own from resource packs and partly as a group in weekly sessions with a locally based tutor. They also met informally to give each other encouragement and to talk through some of the issues they were writing about. All of them made use of the new computer installed in the centre to produce their work 'in the best possible light' for assessment. 'Going for assessment' was not an obligatory part of the arrangement but, in the end, everyone decided to have a go. It was no surprise to me, having met the women on various occasions, that the quality and range of writing they produced far outclassed the OCN requirements for accreditation. All of the women who handed in work achieved credits and twenty did so at the equivalent of A level standard.

The workshop which was arranged to discuss some of the learning that went on, and to decide what to do next, was attended by all of the women who had taken part in the autobiography project, plus a number of volunteers and centre workers. Jacqueline came on her way to a frightening court appearance concerning allegations of child abuse against her former partner. Bernadette brought her mother in a wheelchair—who is recovering from a stroke—both of whom are half way through writing their autobiographies and did not want to miss the session. Eilish was in the middle of arranging a wedding party, Ann and Frances were on their way to work. Almost all the women inhabit difficult and busy lives but still made space for 'education' when it mattered to them and in a context which seemed relevant.

The workshop was informal, personal, irreverent, thoughtful—and deadly serious. Brid had not talked before about her illegitimate child. Cathy had not talked about her father's death or spoken about how it felt to be kept at home as a girl whilst 25,000 people took part in his funeral. She had not, until this project, attempted any kind of political analysis of what happened to her family in 'the troubles'.

Writing and listening to each other's stories is very powerful and helps women to take another look at where they stand—not only in their own lives but also in each others battles—to begin to examine what is going on underneath. It is a process that can be painful and can be wonderful. In terms of consciousness and change it is something that has to be gone through, and gone through as collectively as possible. Education will only empower women if it enables them to act collectively on their own reality in order to understand it. Theory cannot be separated from practice and personal experience cannot be related to the wider social context without some reference to theory. This is not an argument for similarity—although I do believe that as women, we have at least as many things in common as things which make us different. In writing about women's identity in situations of conflict, like Northern Ireland, Cynthia Cockburn makes use of the term 'mixity' to denote an intermingling of elements that retain their uniqueness. The democratic space between women must involve bridge building but also allow for difference. The point is to steer a way collectively through the mixity and the difference towards 'a careful and caring struggle in a well lit space'.[23] In the end, women have to make sense of the world together, in order to change it for the better.

Centres like Rosemount are not unusual in Northern Ireland and illustrate what can happen when the local state—and government—loses the confidence of local people and is unable—or unwilling—to deliver the kinds of services and support they need to survive. In general Centres like Rosemount confront three main problems. They have to establish democratic structures and ways of working that are capable of reconciling conflicting interests and internal differences. Most have originated in the religious and physical circumstances of separatist communities but the majority now operate across the sectarian divide. As they become more established, they need to chart a skilful course between the requirements of those who give them money, their responsibilities to the communities they serve, and their declared intention to retain their autonomy. Powerful external forces inevitably have an interest in trying to control them. In the 1980s political vetting operated as a way of restricting the funding of community organizations seen to be engaged in 'political' activities. At different times central and local government, churches, quangos, parties, and paramilitaries have all exercised 'a pervasive and at times threatening surveillance'.[24] Since funding has become more lucrative—via the European Social Fund and Peace and Reconciliation money—educational providers and NGOs have also become more entrepreneurial about partnership agreements, developing just the kind of links which Government and the

Cologne Charter are keen to encourage. It has to be said, however, pragmatic cooperation between organizations and agencies with different degrees of status and power—sometimes with objectives relating to organizational agendas that are not always fully transparent—are not automatically 'a good thing' for community organizations concerned about advancing the interests of their members and maintaining their autonomy.

The third problem facing community centres is the problem of funding. Sustaining development and survival depends on securing project money and core funding from sources that keep different groups in competition with each other for scarce resources. Of course the bidding culture and the promotion of competitive self-help suits the interests of a government concerned to control public spending and reluctant to redistribute economic resources through taxation, but local competition also acts to frustrate attempts to build solidarity across disparate communities which just might get organized in more united—and potentially more powerful—ways.

What is interesting in these circumstances—and very inspiring—about the Rosemount Centre is the way in which its members have responded 'from below' to the perception of problems and solutions in ways that are transformational in character. In my brief association with the centre I have seen the increasing influence of women in decision-making structures and participatory roles, which has had the effect of increasing women's visibility in the community and begun to shift the balance of power in gender relations. I have seen a prominent local educational figure—with something of an international reputation in community development—having his entrée into the centre terminated once it became clear that he was more interested in acquiring control of development money raised by the centre for educational projects—to enhance his own reputation and career prospects in the academic organization which employed him—rather than become a genuine ally and resource for those seeking knowledge and educational qualifications.

I have also been present at a meeting of community and cross-border representatives, reflecting the entire spectrum of working-class political organizations in Northern Ireland. Groups with paramilitary connections and with long and painful histories of mutual antagonism and hostility which remain unresolved, at a time when professional politicians trying to set up a power-sharing Assembly in Northern Ireland were in deadlock. The purpose of the meeting was to put political differences on one side and to establish an inclusive network to advance the common interests of impoverished communities—to access funds from the private sector, to create jobs, and to build a learning framework capable of delivering training in ICT, qualifications in community development, and educational opportunities tailored to the needs and interests of local people—based on the model used in the women's autobiography project. And all this in the context of ideas and energy coming directly 'from below', based on experience and local knowledge, with very little 'professional' input, and totally outside the remit and control of 'official' institutions. In fact, very nearly the kind of partnership New Labour would love to take credit for and try to monitor in terms of 'targets', 'standards' and 'skills', but which is rooted in dissenting politics, emancipatory learning and local control in ways that do not fit easily into the ideology of 'helping the disadvantaged' or functional training for labour market flexibility.

The development of the Rosemount Resource Centre and the Women's Group illustrates a number of issues which those concerned with adult education should want to have recognized in any discussions about 'the way forward' for lifelong learning. 'Top down' solutions, framed within a glib, economistic consensus about the kinds of skills governments and employers think their citizens should have in the future, do not pay sufficient attention to where different communities of people are coming from and what their perceptions of the issues might be. Debates about active citizenship, democratic renewal, participation and life politics are all part of the life world in which ordinary people already have lots of experiential knowledge and a whole range of different skills which they use to survive, negotiate and challenge the circumstances in which they find themselves. For the last 30 years—at least—the working class women of Rosemount have negotiated class politics, poverty, exploited labour in the local factories and stereotypical gender relations on the home front. Their lives have also been inextricably tied up in 'the troubles' in ways that have left no one untouched by the politics of poverty, sectarianism, imperialism and war. These are the starting points from which their interests have to be understood and their educational needs considered.

Becoming enthusiastic and serious about education—against all the odds—has been inspired by mutual support and collective solidarity in a strong women's group. A group in which differences are negotiated and 'doing things together' has achieved the kinds of results that individuals could not achieve on their own. Individuals are making individual changes to their lives, but in the context of life politics, popular learning and change has to be conducted within—as well as against—the very real constraints of structure. Changes to 'the structures' will only come about if people act collectively on their own realities to recognize, challenge and begin to change the structural constraints which restrain them.

In my view, they are giving voice to what Anthony Giddens[25] calls 'life politics', revealing disputes and struggles about how, as individuals and groups of people, we should live in a world that used to be fixed by nature or tradition but which is now subject to human decisions involving power and, hopefully, dialogue and participation. In pursuit of what Giddens calls 'generative politics' and the 'democratising of democracy', it is critical that individuals and groups of individuals are involved in making things happen rather than being told what to do by 'experts' or have things happen to them. It is also vital that this be achieved through dialogue rather than through pre-established and arbitrary forms of power. Finding a voice to do this—and in the Derry women's case, a collective voice—is clearly gathering momentum through the social, mutually supportive, and educational activities of their group. This should be regarded not only as popular learning but also as political activity, in which spaces are being opened up for public discussion about the issues with which they are concerned. They are forcing into the public domain aspects of social conduct that previously went undiscussed or were settled by traditional practices. And as such, their voices help to contest the traditional, the official, the patriarchal, the privileged and the academic view of things.

In addition, these are working-class women who keep families and communities together, despite the disasters provoked by wider social and political circumstances and by individuals (men, mostly) over whom they have very little control. It is a world in which those who are supposed to help—the politicians, the army, the police and social workers, for example—have become part of the problem. It is impossible to read the women's stories without hearing the voices and something of the character and the spirit of the women coming through. These are not the same voices which are heard in the speeches of career politicians and academics talking about working-class and women's lives or lifelong learning. They tell a different story about poverty, oppression, resistance and resilience that is not statistical, pathological or conventionally political, but which is grounded in the democratic and reflexive authority of lived experience. An experience which is understood as accurately and passionately as any of us ever manage to do as we sort through the realities and contradictions of complicated and shifting uncertainties.

When voices such as these make knowledge, narrow definitions of what is thought to be 'educated knowledge'—and who makes it—are thrown into question. The accounts written by the Derry women reveal 'that people can develop better understandings of their social world through more democratic knowledge-making practices and structures than are current at present; and they can work to transform it'.[26] They serve to illustrate and enact part of what Susan Bordo refers to as 'the messy, slippery practical struggle' to 'create institutions and communities that will not permit some groups of people to make determinations about reality for all'.[27] They demonstrate—quite vividly—the significance of what Michele le Doeuff has called one of the 'major contradictions of our times', by which she means the loss of language amongst the learned—fossilized in professional discourse—and the urgent need to discuss problems with people other than academics.[28] They enable the articulation of what Sandra Harding[29] and Jean Barr refer to as 'voices from below', which are not 'truer and more accurate accounts of the world' by virtue of being from below 'but because, in identifying and making available spaces where alternative ways of thinking and being can be worked up, such practices increase the possibilities of knowledge—that is, knowledge which is useful to those who generate it'.[30] In this respect a radical, democratizing lifelong learning needs to reach beyond the academy, the Government, the boardroom and Cologne to demonstrate its commitment and its relevance to the urgent problems and real concerns of ordinary people. Freire's insight that education either functions to conform people to the logic of the present system, or else it enables them to deal critically and creatively with their world in order to change it, remains a useful reminder about the tension between 'really useful knowledge' and 'merely useful knowledge'[31] in the history—and the future—of educational struggle.

Notes

1 *Cologne Charter—Aims and Ambitions for Lifelong Learning* (1999) adopted by the Heads of State of eight major democracies (G8) in their 25th Economic Summit held in Cologne, 18–20 June.
2 Richard Edwards (1995) 'Behind the Banner: Whither the Learning Society?' in *Adults Learning*, 187–9, Leicester: NIACE.
3 Ian Martin (1999) 'Lifelong Learning: Stretching the Discourse', in P. Oliver (ed) *Lifelong Learning and Continuing Education: What Is a Learning Society?*, Ashgate.
4 Bob Rowthorne and Naomi Wayne (1998) *Northern Ireland: The Political Economy of Conflict*, Cambridge: Polity.
5 Cynthia Cockburn (1998) *The Space Between Us: Negotiating Gender and National Identities in Conflict*, London: Zed.
6 Women and Citizen Research Group (1995) *Power, Participation and Choice*, Belfast: EOCNI.
7 Lynda Edgerton (1986) 'Public Protest, Domestic Acquiescence: Women in Northern Ireland' in Rosemary Ridd and Helen Callaway (eds) *Caught Up in Conflict: Women's Responses to Political Strife*, London: MacMillan.
8 Marie Mulholland and Ailbhe Smyth (1999) 'A North South Dialogue' in *Movement*, Feminist Magazine 3 University College Dublin: WERRC.
9 Eilish Rooney (1997) 'Women in Party Politics and Local Groups: Findings From Belfast' in Anne Byrne and Madeleine Leonard (eds) *Women in Irish Society*, Belfast: Beyond The Pale Publications.
10 Anthony Giddens (1994) *Beyond Left and Right: The Future of Radical Politics*, Cambridge: Polity.
11 Giddens, ibid.
12 Women and Citizenship Research Group, op. cit.
13 Cockburn, op. cit.
14 Anna Coote and Polly Pattullo (1990) *Power and Prejudice*, London: Wiedenfelt and Nicholson.
15 E. Evason (1991) *Against the Grain: The Contemporary Women's Movement in Northern Ireland*, Dublin: Attic Press; M McWilliams (1991) 'Women in Northern Ireland: An Overview', in Hughes (ed) *Culture and Politics in Northern Ireland 1960–90*, Mylton Keynes: OUPress; Taillon (1992) *Grant Aided... Or Taken for Granted? A Study of Women's Voluntary Organisations in Northern Ireland*, Belfast: Women's Support Network.
16 Raymond Williams (1989) *Resources of Hope*, London: Verso.
17 Mary Robinson, cited in Cathleen O'Neill 'Reclaiming and Transforming the Irish Women's Movement: Notes for a Debate', in *Movement*, op. cit.
18 Veronica McGivney (1990) *The Women's Education Project—Northern Ireland*, Belfast: WRDA.
19 Pauline Murphy (1997) 'Personal, Political and Professional Development for Women' in Shirley Walters (ed) *Globalisation, Adult Education and Training: Impacts and Issues*, London: Zed.
20 Jane Thompson (2000) 'Derry Days' in *Women, Class and Education*, London: Routledge.

21 Henri Lefebvre, cited in Jean Barr (1999) *Liberating Knowledge: Research, Feminism and Adult Education,* Leicester: NIACE.
22 Chantelle Mouffe (1992) *Dimensions of Radical Democracy,* London: Verso.
23 Cynthia Cockburn, op. cit.
24 Cynthia Cockburn, op. cit.
25 Anthony Giddens, op. cit.
26 Jean Barr, op. cit.
27 Susan Bordo (1990) 'Feminism, Postmodernism and Gender Scepticism' in L. Nicholson (ed) *Feminism and Postmodernism,* London: Routledge.
28 Michelle le Doeuff (1991) *Hipparchia's Choice: An Essay Concerning Women, Philosophy etc.,* Oxford: Blackwell.
29 Sandra Harding (1994) 'Subjectivity, Experience and Knowledge: An Epistemology from/for Rainbow Coalition Politics' in Roof and Weigand (eds) *Who Can Speak: Questions of Authority and Cultural Identity,* Urbana: University of Illinois Press.
30 Jean Barr, op. cit.
31 Richard Johnson (1979) 'Really Useful Knowledge: Radical Education and Working Class Culture', in Clarke, Critcher and Johnson (eds) *Working Class Culture,* London: Hutchinson.

Part 3

International perspectives

12 Lifelong learning for a new society

The South African case

Shirley Pendlebury and Penny Enslin

Concept and context

Lifelong learning is a contested concept. In the context of recent debates about the so-called learning society, it has been conceptualized as having three interdependent aims: democratic citizenship, economic progress and personal development (Chapman, 1996). On this triadic conception, a policy of lifelong learning provision is regarded as crucial for achieving and sustaining a democratic polity and institutions that practise and promote social inclusiveness, justice and equity. At the same time, it is regarded as crucial for achieving and sustaining a strong, adaptable economy and a rich range of activities for the personal reward of individuals who choose to participate in them. The triadic conception brings together extrinsic and intrinsic justifications for lifelong learning; it also cuts across the boundaries between schooling and continuing education, between formal and non-formal education; between institution-based education and workplace learning. Perhaps the range and reach of this conception is best captured in the slogan 'Lifelong learning for all'. Judith Chapman argues that lifelong learning has to be seen as:

> ... a complex and multifaceted process, that begins in pre-school times, is carried through compulsory and post-compulsory periods of formal education and training, and then continued throughout life, through provision of learning experiences, activities and enjoyment in the work-place, in universities and colleges, and in other educational and cultural agencies and institutions—of both a formal and informal kind—within the community.
>
> (Chapman, 1996, p. 30)

On the face of it, there is a neat fit between the triadic conception and South Africa's most urgent project, which is to achieve a democratic polity, a just, equitable and inclusive society, and a strong, globally competitive economy. Post-apartheid policy-makers have recognized the importance of lifelong learning for this project. In this chapter we analyse and evaluate the ways in which the elements of the triad have been taken up in post-apartheid education policy. We also comment on some of the complexities and internal contradictions in the application of the triad in current South African policy and practice. At the same time, we evaluate the policy itself. Three criteria guide us in these tasks. First, are all three elements of the triad present in new South African policy for lifelong learning? Second, is the treatment of lifelong learning consistent with the vision of the good society expressed in South Africa's new Constitution? Third, how far does policy make provision for addressing conflicting imperatives, dilemmas of distributive justice and the pragmatics of implementation?

A prior assumption in our pursuit of these aims is that policies of lifelong learning cannot be judged without consideration of their implementation context. Two features are crucial to a consideration of South Africa as a context for lifelong learning. One is that, for all its mineral wealth and pockets of affluence, South Africa is a developing African country with limited resources; the other is that South Africa is a country that has only recently emerged from a long history of inequality and oppression. Apartheid systemically neglected and obstructed lifelong learning not only through separate and unequal education but also through a severely restricted set of working conditions and opportunities for the vast majority of the population. The contextual demands of these socioeconomic features set up a tension between two imperatives. On the one hand, there is an imperative to ensure that all South African children are able to attend properly functioning schools; on the other, there is an imperative to provide education for those youths and adults who sacrificed their already limited educational opportunities as a consequence of apartheid. If lifelong learning involves education across the life-span, then both imperatives must be met. Yet under conditions of fiscal constraint and severely limited human resources, there remains a question about how to meet both imperatives justly and effectively. To complicate matters, South Africa is not just a developing country and a new democracy, but also one driven by the exigencies of globalization, as is evident in the ANC government's current market-oriented macroeconomic policy.

In our view, a principled response to conflicting imperatives must acknowledge and, if possible, resolve several dilemmas of justice. There is more than one conception of justice at work in calls for lifelong learning in South Africa. The first is a notion of transitional justice which must ensure recognition and recompense for those who suffered under apartheid and made sacrifices in the struggle to overthrow it. The second is a notion of distributive justice, creating equal access to educational goods. Some may be eligible under both conceptions of justice, but these conceptions make conflicting demands on priorities and resources.

'Lifelong learning', we assume, refers to learning across the human life-span from cradle to grave. This is not entirely in keeping with dominant current uses of the term, some of which appear to exclude primary and secondary schooling as well as the education of adults who have dropped out of school or who have had no schooling whatsoever. Such informal learning as might occur through watching television, doing a job with a more experienced fellow worker, or participating in the institutions of civil society also seems to be ignored. Much current international discussion of lifelong learning focuses on post-compulsory education, which in developed countries means accredited post-secondary or higher education. In recent policy in the UK, pride of place has been given to lifelong learning, especially in the agenda for higher education in the so-called learning society. Here it is assumed that lifelong learning will meet the needs 'of an increasingly sophisticated economy for a skilled and educated workforce' and fulfil the desire for wider participation (Taylor, 1998, p. 301). Despite fairly strong support, such policies are controversial from an educational perspective. Instead of broadening participation in education, they have tended to be concerned with a single dimension of the triad, economic competitiveness, narrowly concerned with vocational skills and certification.

Outside of the developed Western world, there is an additional difficulty with these conceptions of lifelong learning—one of scope rather than focus. Whatever the formal commitment to compulsory primary education, in much of the developing world a substantial proportion of the adult population will not have completed primary school. In any case, post-compulsory education is more likely to be post-primary than post-secondary. South Africa is a case in point, despite being one of the more developed countries in Africa. Under these circumstances, to limit lifelong learning programmes to post-secondary and higher education or to a programme of vocational skills enhancement is a betrayal of the educational needs of the country and its people. In countries hitherto ravaged by war and poverty or, in South Africa's case, protean policies of exclusion, disempowerment and inequality, the moral and political imperative is to ensure that educational provision does not further disempower the already disempowered. Uncritical policy borrowing runs the risk of ignoring this imperative. But even if the imperative is taken as a guiding principle, it does not on its own make for a neat deductive line of incontestable policy and implementation decisions.

The chapter has two main sections. The first, 'Policy for a new society', provides an account of lifelong learning in recent South African policy and examines how far and in what ways the elements of the triad are reflected. Here we also address the question of whether the policy treatment of lifelong learning is consistent with the vision of the good society expressed in the Constitution. The second section, 'Just dilemmas', assesses South Africa's lifelong learning policy. Here we take dilemmas of gender justice and inter-generational justice as test cases for the policy's feasibility and desirability. Although our arguments focus on South Africa, several of the conclusions may apply to Africa more generally.

Policy for a new society

In its preamble, South Africa's Constitution of 1996 recognizes past injustice and those who suffered in the long struggle against it. The Constitution sets out to establish a democratic, open and just society in which citizens will be able to fulfil their potential and in which their fundamental rights will be protected. To this end, it includes, for the first time in South Africa's history, a Bill of Rights which establishes a range of individual, socioeconomic and cultural rights, including the right to education. The Bill of Rights may be regarded as a statement of the public good for a new society. As the opening move in formulating post-apartheid education policy, the White Paper on Education and Training (1995) casts the Bill of Rights in the Interim Constitution, under which the transitional election of 1994 took place, as its moral framework:

> In a democratically governed society, the education system taken as a whole embodies and promotes the collective moral perspective of its citizens, that is the code of values by which society wishes to live and consents to be judged. From one point of view, South Africans have had all too little experience in defining their collective values. From another, our entire history can be read as a saga of contending moralities, which in our era has culminated in a historic agreement based on the recognition of the inalienable worth, dignity and equality of each person under the law, mutual tolerance, and respect for diversity. In the Charter of Fundamental Rights and the Schedule of Constitutional Principles, the 1993 Constitution expresses a moral view of human beings and the social order which will guide policy and law in education, as in all other sectors.
>
> (Department of Education, 1995, p. 17)

A variety of processes and documents predated and contributed to the development of this vision. For the purposes of this chapter, the Reconstruction and Development Programme (RDP) (African National Congress, 1994) is especially significant as an early, extended vision statement. The RDP not only helped to shape the vision of the public good, but was also the policy framework for government after the 1994 election. It identified the development of human resources as a key to reconstruction and, to this end, advocated provision of education and training from cradle to grave. The RDP captured forcefully several of the problems that would face education after apartheid, for example vast disparities in educational provision and little or no access for large numbers of adults, women, out-of-school youth and pre-school children, and a consequent lack of career paths for workers.

As a first move towards alleviating these problems, the RDP provided for the establishment of an integrated qualifications framework which would enable 'learners to progress to higher levels from any stating point' and 'to obtain recognition and credits towards qualifications from any point of the system towards another' (ANC, 1994, section 3.3.7). The National

Qualifications Framework (NQF) has since been legislated in the South African Qualifications Act of 1995. The RDP also acknowledged assessment and recognition of prior learning from experience as crucial to an effective system and placed a premium on educare or early childhood education as 'an important step toward lifelong learning and the emancipation of women' (ANC, 1994, section 3.3.8). So, from its very beginnings, South Africa's vision for a new society has taken cradle-to-grave educational and training provision as crucial. But vision is not all. Neither educare nor adult basic education have yet received either the attention or the injection of funding implied by the slogan 'Lifelong learning for all'.

The RDP served as a manifesto for the government-in-waiting. After the first democratic election of 1994, the White Paper on Education and Training (DoE, 1995) set out in detail the new government's programme for transforming education and training to 'enable all individuals to value, have access to, and succeed in *lifelong education and training of good quality*' (DoE, 1995, p. 22; original emphasis). Enhanced possibilities for lifelong learning are seen to require increased access, quality and mobility for all learners. It is argued that the basis of policy should be the satisfaction of the constitutional guarantee of equal access to learning for all. This guarantee goes well beyond schooling. Through an increasing range of learning possibilities, the system should offer learners 'greater flexibility in choosing what, when, where, how and at what pace they learn' (DoE, 1995, p. 22). This is not a matter of simple distributive justice, where each individual is to get the same as every other. Equal education, given the legacy of apartheid, requires special emphasis on the redress of past inequalities among those people 'who have suffered particular disadvantages, or who are especially vulnerable, including street children, out-of-school youth, the disabled and citizens with special educational needs, illiterate women, rural communities, squatter communities, and communities damaged by violence' (DoE, 1995, p. 22).

Like the RDP, the White Paper attends to all three elements in the triad. Its concern with historically disadvantaged groups and with redress for this injustice reflects the personal and democratic elements of the triad. While lifelong learning is commonly regarded as a necessary condition for a flourishing democracy, parts of the White Paper suggest a more dialectical relationship between lifelong learning and democracy. A particularly telling claim is that the 'realisation of *democracy, liberty, equality, justice and peace* are necessary conditions for the full pursuit and enjoyment of lifelong learning. . .' (DoE, 1995, p. 22; original emphasis). Human resource development, the economic arm of the triad, features prominently in the White Paper.

Since the publication of the White Paper, much work has been accomplished in developing a range of policy instruments and passing related legislation pertaining to different aspects of lifelong learning. As we will show, some policy focuses more strongly on human resource development than on other elements of the triad, sometimes to their detriment. Most, if not all, of the new policy instruments operate within a National Qualifications Framework (NQF). A brief sketch of the NQF is thus necessary for understanding the proposed approach to providing, promoting and recognizing lifelong learning in South Africa.

The NQF consists of three bands: the compulsory band of General Education and Training; the Further Education and Training band; and the Higher Education band. No band is tied solely to a particular provider. General Education and Training includes both school-going children for the first nine years of formal education and adults who have not yet received basic education. Further Education and Training includes workplace training programmes, as well as education provided by community and technical colleges, and the more usual secondary schooling. Post-compulsory school-going youth and a wide range of adults are catered for in this qualification band. Higher Education and Training may be provided by several types of institutions. This is a uniform qualification framework, allowing for both vertical and horizontal articulation. For example, an adult who has had no formal schooling but has completed general education may enter a college for further training and subsequently may proceed to higher education. In practice this requires recognition of prior learning, flexible credit accumulation and portability of credentials.

Further Education and Training has already received a fair degree of attention at the intersection of initiatives by the Departments of Education and Labour. In establishing goals for Further Education and Training to promote lifelong learning within the framework of the NQF, the National Committee on Further Education attends to all three elements of the lifelong learning triad in arguing that:

> ... FET must be broadly constituted to contribute to personal development as well as social cohesion and the development of modern society. If it is too narrowly associated with work, there is a real danger of further education and training becoming purely instrumental and vocational. People must be enabled to develop the skills, to understand and integrate all aspects of life, the economic, the social, the political, the psychological so as to create a better future.
>
> (DoE, 1997a, p. 1)

In arguing that the pre-employed, the employed and the unemployed should all have access to Further Education and Training, the committee endorses the core principles of equity and redress. Redress is supposed to address the legacy of apartheid by providing opportunities to learners who were excluded or disadvantaged by previous policy and practice. Among the learners noted in the report are: women, particularly those in rural areas and informal settlements; unemployed youth and adults; and homeless and imprisoned youth and those militarized at a young age through the struggle against apartheid.

Unusually, the category of youth in South Africa is taken as falling between the ages of 14 and 35 years. Since the 1976 uprising the youth have played a key role in the struggle against apartheid. Schools became a site of resistance. Under these conditions, order and authority broke down, some youth left school to become activists or freedom fighters, others drifted out of school into high rates of unemployment and crime. Many of these conditions still persist, despite the demise of apartheid. Reversing these conditions has proved very difficult. Early experiences of violent and shattered communities, imprisonment for some, and the habits and ways of life of militarization all mitigate against both the commitment to and the capacities for systematic learning. While it may be an exaggeration to call these youth a lost generation, their involvement in the struggle came at a heavy price. Transitional justice seems to require both recognition of their sacrifices and recompense in the form of special provision to enable them to gain lost ground in their education.

Transitional justice also requires recognition and recompense for the less visible sacrifices and deprivation of the rural poor, especially rural women. Access not only to basic education but also to social services and work opportunities continues to be severely limited for women in rural areas (DoE, 1997a). Most spend the equivalent of a day a week collecting firewood and carrying water. They are farmers and homemakers in a teetering subsistence economy where survival is dependent on the remittance of salaries earned by migrant family members. Customary ideas about the role and place of women are partly responsible not only for the domestic burdens of rural women but also for their high rate of illiteracy. Against this grim portrait, the committee urges that facilities and services be provided to enable women to become 'agents of change' and 'marketable members of the labour force' (DoE, 1997a). While they are not ignored, women's personal needs and development are not adequately dealt with in this scenario.

In the ensuing Green Paper on Further Education and Training (1998) two world-wide criteria for judging FET systems are identified: one is how effectively they articulate with work, the other whether they grant genuine access to higher education and lifelong learning. To date, South Africa's system has failed on both counts.

The Skills Development Act (1998, p. 501) addresses the first of these criteria. It sets out:

> To provide an institutional framework to devise and implement national, sector and work-place strategies to develop and improve the skills of the South African workforce; to inte-grate those strategies within the National Qualifications Framework . . . to provide for learnerships that lead to recognized occupational qualifications; to provide for the finan-cing of skills development by means of a levy-grant scheme and a National Skills Fund; to provide and regulate employment services . . .

In doing so the Act declares that the purposes of these measures are, first, to develop skills among the workforce in order to improve workers' quality of life, work prospects and mobility, to improve both workplace productivity and employers' competitiveness, to encourage self-employment and to improve social services. Secondly, the Act aims to make investment in quality education and training worthwhile by encouraging employers to create a learning environment in the workplace; providing employees with opportunities to acquire new skills; giving new entrants to the labour market opportunities to gain work experience and to make employment possible for those who have difficulty in finding work; encouraging workers to participate in training programmes; improving employment prospects for those disadvan-taged by unfair discrimination; and regulating the provision of employment services. Thirdly, the structures to be set in place to promote these goals include a National Skills Authority, a National Skills Fund, a levy-grant scheme on employers' personnel costs to fund skills development, labour centres and a Skills Development Policy Unit.

While the emerging vision for FET and provisions for skills development both set out to cater for the pre-employed and unemployed as well as the employed, little has been done so far for the unemployed. Among other things, the National Skills Fund is intended to support pre-employment training and learnership programmes, some of which will include basic adult education and improve employment possibilities for youth, the disabled, the rural poor and workers in the informal sector. Nonetheless, it is doubtful whether these proposals will yield any benefits for the most disadvantaged groups in our society (Education Policy Unit, 1997). Furthermore, they indicate that the economic arm of the triad is ultimately given prior-ity over democratization and personal development as the interests of the unemployed give way to skills development for those in the formal sector.

The dominance of the economic arm of lifelong learning policy and doubts about the effi-cacy of the Skills Act in improving the lot of the most disadvantaged groups are confirmed by controversy concerning progress in adult basic education and training (ABET) since 1994. A recent initiative to assess the state of ABET involving various stakeholders produced an acri-monious debate. Whatever the merits of the arguments, there are grounds for believing that little if any progress has been made to provide inclusive and readily available adult basic edu-cation and training to South Africa's large population of illiterate adults, who according to one estimate comprise 11 per cent of the adult population. What is more, 45 per cent of the adult population have not received a full general education. While a number of NGOs worked with a minority of illiterate adults before the 1994 transition, funding to the non-governmental sector has shrunk since then. Evidence suggests that the state has not yet been able to have a sig-nificant impact in reaching what were probably unrealistic expectations (Aitchison, 1998).

This does not augur well for lifelong learning, for two reasons. First, it can be argued that adult basic education and training is crucial to the successful development of lifelong learning for those excluded from basic and general education. Without literacy, any policy of lifelong learning is doomed to failure. In his recent call to action, South Africa's new Minister of

Education, Kadar Asmal has identified illiteracy among adults and youths as one of the nine priorities for an education and training system for the twenty-first century (Ministry of Education, 1999). At the same time, he acknowledges severe budgetary and organizational constraints on achieving a literate population within five years and calls for 'the civic virtue of voluntary service in support of our illiterate compatriots' (Ministry of Education, 1999, p. 9). This leads to the second reason for pessimism regarding the provision of lifelong learning for all. The development challenges of ABET and lifelong learning are similar. If the NGOs who previously provided adult basic education on a patchy basis have now declined because of lack of donor funds and if the state has, by its own acknowledgement, neither the organizational capacity nor the budget required for extensive systematic delivery, especially in remote rural areas and among the unemployed or informally self-employed, is the rhetoric of lifelong learning no more than an empty and irresponsible promise? Empty and irresponsible though it may be, we concede that the call for lifelong learning has played an inspirational role for lifelong learners and NGOs, especially in poor communities.

Just dilemmas

All three elements of the triad are present in lifelong learning policy for South Africa and are present in a way that is consistent with the country's vision of the good society. As principled and compelling as the policy is, the pragmatics of implementation throw up profound dilemmas of justice which require principled but painful decisions about priorities. On its own, the triad offers little help in these hard cases and is probably not intended to do so.

The human resources dimension of South Africa's vision has been more adequately addressed in policy than the personal and the democratic. Human resource development is indeed crucial to the accomplishment of democracy. The democratic project will run aground if there is no economic progress and this is dependent on human resource development. However, will too myopic a concern with human resource development, mainly within the formal sector, serve to realize 'necessary conditions for the full pursuit and enjoyment of lifelong learning', namely, *'democracy, liberty, equality, justice and peace'*? (DoE, 1995, p. 22; original emphasis).

The hard case in the pragmatics of implementing lifelong learning policy in South Africa is to reconcile two demands of justice. On the one hand is a demand of transitional justice, a backward-looking demand that calls for recognition and recompense for those who sacrificed, or were never offered, educational goods under apartheid; on the other is a demand of distributive justice, which can be interpreted as a demand for fair distribution in the present or as a forward-looking demand. This raises the question of justice between the generations. While this is a problem in any society, it is especially pressing in those societies whose schooling system is largely dysfunctional and where universal basic education cannot be taken for granted. Lifelong learning is often paraded as a way of making up for opportunities never enjoyed. The paradox is that lifelong learning is more feasible only if people have started right (Ball, quoted in Chapman, 1996, p. 33). Starting right involves not just the basics, but learning how to learn and 'how to want to learn' (Smethhurst, quoted in Aspin, 1996, p. 28). In South Africa, the past policy and practice of Bantu Education has given people a distorted sense of how to learn. Bantu Education entrenched a highly authoritarian approach to teaching coupled with rote learning, regurgitation and an unquestioning acceptance of so-called 'facts'. The move towards an outcomes-based curriculum, which stresses such capacities as relational and critical thinking, problem-solving and collaborative learning, is intended to help people learn how to learn. While undoubtedly necessary, this move on its own will not redress the long-term effects of Bantu Education unless it is accompanied by a fully functioning schooling system. Currently, many South African schools are seriously dysfunctional (see Christie, 1998).

In our view, the first duty of the state is to get the schooling system right for learners at school now and for future generations. A possible objection is that there are other more morally compelling priorities. For example, what are the state's obligations to illiterate adults, rural women, marginalized youth and pre-school children? With respect to rural women, it could be argued on both moral and pragmatic grounds that abandoning their educational needs will make it harder to get schooling right in rural areas. The problems are inextricably inter-woven and this makes hard choices even harder. Providing lifelong learning for rural women requires far more than providing some learning facilities in the neighbourhood. Such are their life circumstances and the expectations that others have of them that many will be unable to exercise the opportunity for education. Educational uptake among rural women depends not only on the alleviation of their poverty but also on confronting the ideologies of gender and cultural practices that underpin their oppression. Confronting such deep-seated ideology is an educational matter and one for the whole school, involving the broad community (DoE, 1997b). Whatever their limitations, and these are severe, schools offer the best hope for getting lifelong learning going. A feasible and practicable policy of lifelong learning requires both get-ting the basics right and ensuring an infrastructure of schools as community resources for the delivery of a range of educational programmes and opportunities for the full spectrum of the community. The priority, then, is to accomplish a system of properly functioning schools. This would be the courageous and forward-looking choice in which the long-term view prevails.

Our argument has questioned the feasibility of cradle-to-grave educational provision in South Africa. On the one hand, lifelong learning is entrenched as a constitutional right; on the other, the Minister of Education himself has acknowledged the state's incapacity to provide for all without the support of voluntary groups.

Even in societies such as the United States of America and Sweden, with well resourced mass education systems and high participation rates, a substantial proportion of the population remains either under-involved or excluded. Hughes and Tight (1995) emphasize the utopian nature of lifelong learning. In the South African case is it not, perhaps, cruelly utopian?

Acknowledgements

We thank David Beckett, Paul Hager and participants in the Wits School of Education Research Seminar for their suggestions.

References

African National Congress (1994) *Reconstruction and Development Programme*, Johannesburg, Umanyano Publications.

Aitchison, J. (1998) 'Naught for Your Comfort: Critique and its Denial in South African Adult Basic Education and Training', unpublished paper, Pietermaritzburg.

Aspin, D. (1996) 'Lifelong Learning for All: Concept and Conceptions', Fifth Biennial Meeting of the International Network of Philosophers of Education, Johannesburg.

Chapman, J. (1996) 'A New Agenda for a New Society' in LETHWOOD, K. *et al.* (Eds.) *International Handbook of Educational Leadership and Administration*, Dordrecht, Kluwer, pp. 27–39.

Christie, P. (1998) 'Schools as (Dis)organisations: The "Breakdown of the Culture of Learning and Teaching" in South African Schools' *Cambridge Journal of Education*, 28, 3, pp. 283–300.

Department of Education (1997a) *Report of the National Committee on Further Education: A Framework for the Transformation of Further Education and Training in South Africa*, Pretoria, August.

Department of Education (1997b) *Gender Equity in Education: Report of the Gender Equity Task Team*, Pretoria, October.

Department of Education (1998) *Green Paper on Further Education and Training: Preparing for the Twenty-First Century Through Education, Training and Work*, Pretoria, April.

Department of Education (1995) *White Paper on Education and Training*, Pretoria.

Education Policy Unit (1997) *Quarterly Review of Education and Training in South Africa*, Johannesburg, University of the Witwatersrand, 5, 1, 22 September.

Hughes, C. and Tight, M. (1995) 'The Myth of the Learning Society' *British Journal of Educational Studies*, 43, 3, pp. 290–304.

Ministry of Education (1999) 'Call to Action: Mobilizing Citizens to Build a South African Education and Training System for the 21st Century', Statement by the Minister of Education, Pretoria, 27 July.

Republic of South Africa (1996) *The Constitution*, Pretoria, Government Printer.

Republic of South Africa (1998) *Skills Development Act* (No 97) Pretoria, Government Gazette.

Republic of South Africa (1995) *South African Qualifications Authority Act* (No 58), Pretoria, Government Gazette.

Taylor, R. (1998) 'Lifelong Learning in the "Liberal Tradition"' *Journal of Moral Education* 27, 3, pp. 301–12.

13 Confucianism, cultural revolution and corporate classrooms

China's attempts at 'a Learning Society'

John Morgan

Go to people, live among them, learn from them, love them, serve them, plan with them, start with what they have, build on what they have.

(Chinese proverb)

The purpose of this chapter is to consider what the concept of 'a Learning Society' might mean within the context of contemporary China and to give some examples. Given the complexity of China's history during this period, this is an ambitious proposal within the space available, while there are a number of other difficulties—conceptual, contextual and in terms of accurate information. Nevertheless, it is believed to be worth attempting, as it is commonly accepted that China will exert increasing influence over world affairs during the twenty-first century, as a polity, as an economy and as a culture already many centuries old. Again, it may be argued that existing definitions of 'a Learning Society' are based on Occidental and democratic capitalist values and are presented as part of the trend towards globalization. Such a society is seen as one which premises equality of opportunity, individual and social justice, cultural development, tolerance and a civil society, as well as economic progress. It is a society in which the acquisition of knowledge and understanding of the world is promoted actively, with the results disseminated for the benefit and improvement of all. The understanding of China's potential as 'a Learning Society', the distinctive cultural and social characteristics it would add from its own historical experience and the obstacles to its achievement, would be a contribution to the building of such a society internationally.

China's path is towards modernization with the need to build an infrastructure capable of sustaining a market economy, the development of education and training being seen as the key to this. It is true that if China achieves only some of its growth targets, the volume of demand will put enormous pressures on international markets; absorbing China into the global economy and polity is a challenge. But a poor China would be no less so and with a desperate population and internal unrest she might become dangerously volatile.[1] So it is vital that China is supported in its efforts to develop and is reassured about access to resources. Relations with China depend on whether the challenge represented is seen as a threat or as an opportunity.

The realization of China's enormous potential as 'a Learning Society' is fundamental to the success of this process. But what does it mean in practice? It is over 90 years since the formation of Republican China and 50 years since Liberation in 1949 created a 'New China' under the rule of the Communist Party. The country has undergone political, social and economic upheaval as it has moved from the traditional patterns of culture and education laid down by centuries of Imperial rule, through the war-torn Republican period, socialist modernization and Cultural Revolution, to the present drive for a social market economy within an authoritarian political structure. China's experience should be regarded as a dramatic, socialist exception to the analytical paradigm which explains how traditional societies achieve modernity. China is most obviously comparable in terms of scale and longevity with the former Soviet Union, a state socialist and multicultural experiment which emerged from the Russian Empire.[2] The Soviets also experienced a version of Cultural Revolution during the *Proletkult* of the 1920s.[3] China, like the Soviet Union, experimented with alternative modernities at different stages in its contemporary history, during which colonial and capitalist models appeared to be rejected decisively, though in practice certain cultural and social norms, such as Han and Russian domination or bureaucratic élitism, survived even the most determined attempts to eliminate them. Soviet state socialism has now imploded. China, though remaining divergent in theory, is in turn being pressed towards the dominant global model by factors such as the massively uneven development of its economy and the need to participate in world trade. China's willingness to adhere to the World Trade Organization is probably decisive of this.[4]

China is attempting to cope with two transitions: from a command to a market economy and from a predominantly rural to an increasingly urban and industrial society.[5] These would allow it to achieve economic modernization, which is not the same thing as industrialization, as well as social modernization, which require an educated and urbanized population. Political modernization and the emergence of a civil society in place of the Party's authoritarian rule could follow. The demands of an increasingly knowledge based economy, together with the need to ensure social stability amongst China's vast and diverse population present a crucial dilemma for the ruling élite. How can it generate and utilize knowledge in a way that will contribute simultaneously to sustained economic growth and yet might open the way to a third transition, to an open, civil society, capable of developing mature political institutions which, and this aspiration is becoming increasingly evident, also bear the stamp of Chinese cultural identity?

China's experiments en route from tradition to modernity, while they have had an economic and class-based core, have also been culturally normative attempts to reconstruct the country fundamentally as 'a Learning Society' in the interest of the immense majority. This chapter is based on a reading of materials translated from the Chinese, on commentaries and analyses available in English, with material in French and Russian also consulted, and on several visits to China over the last decade. It presents an historical and comparative view of the concept of 'a Learning Society' in China, focusing on some key examples such as the legacy of Confucianism, the Christian and social service inspired Mass Education Movement of the 1920s, the Chinese Communist Party's programme of political education, including the significant Yan'an Forum on Literature and Art of 1942 and, most dramatically, the Great Proletarian Cultural Revolution of the 1960s. The final section provides an analysis of current trends which asks whether 'a Learning Society' is a necessary and achievable objective if China is to complete its transition from a traditional and authoritarian to a democratic and civil society?

The legacy of Confucianism

Classical China was a society where 'Lifelong Learning' was regarded as both an individual and a societal ideal. Confucius (551–479), the most influential educator in Chinese history, was said to have gathered over 3000 disciples propagating his teaching and code of conduct; other famous educators of the classical period include Mo Zi, Mencius and Xun Zi. By the time of the Western Han (206 BC–24 AD) China had a coherent dual educational system, private and public, as the basic cultural intellectual foundation of a feudal economic and social system, following a virtually unchanging classical curriculum. The most popular textbooks for novices were *The Three Character Classics, One Hundred Surnames, One Thousand Characters*, while advanced scholars were expected to master *The Four Books* (*Analects of Confucius, Mencius, Great Learning* and *The Doctrine of the Mean*) and *The Five Classics* (*Book of Odes, Book of Documents, Book of Rites, Book of Change* and *The Spring and Autumn Annals*).

The introduction of competitive civil service examinations based on the classics during the Tang dynasty in the seventh century had a fundamental impact on the structure of formal education and on public and private attitudes towards it. Success in the Imperial Examinations was essential if a candidate was to gain entry to the governing élite, which was regarded as a meritocracy, and thence to the possibility of promotion to the highest office. This system which persisted in its essentials until the abolition of the traditional Imperial Civil Service examinations in 1905, left a deep imprint on Chinese consciousness and explains the high, if uncritical, regard with which scholarship and learning have been held traditionally.[6] It is an attitude shared by other Asian societies influenced by Confucianism, such as Korea, Japan, Singapore and Vietnam. It also emphasized the élitist nature of education in its selection and training of the governing class, regarding abstract theory as superior to mere application and scorning physical work as beneath the dignity of an educated, cultivated person.

Has this legacy persisted? The cultural context for the Chinese learner has been examined recently by Lee Wing-On, who discusses the Confucian conceptions of learning in relation to such beliefs as human perfectability and educability, and the emphasis on effort and will power in demonstrating learning and achievement motivations. Lee points out that in the Confucian tradition education '. . . is perceived as not only for personal improvement but also for societal development'.[7] It rests on the Confucian assumption that everyone is educable, that education should be free of class distinctions, with society and the example of others providing the climate and inspiration for learning. Ultimately, however, scholarship and wisdom were the rewards of individual diligence and effort. Lee also points out that after the founding of the Ming dynasty (1368–1644), when the examination and academic degree system became more elaborate and the school system truly nationwide, there was a real possibility of upward mobility through educational success. Even if the immense majority did not benefit directly, the possibility provided an ideological incentive 'for many ordinary people to study hard for a better future'.[8] As Lee concludes, the Confucian concept of education '. . . is strongly coloured by a sense of égalitarianism—you can achieve it if you want to'.[9] This is an attitude that is encountered regularly in the societies of East Asia and increasingly so amongst the young of contemporary China. It is reminiscent of the persuasiveness of the 'The American Dream'— egalitarian in that it rejects élitist exclusivity and individualistic in that it is inspired by personal ambition.

There have certainly been attempts in recent years, inspired by human capital performance and significant economic development, to present the region as cohesive, with common values and identity.[10] Advocates identify 'characteristic Asian values', though it is the Confucian countries of East Asia that they have in mind. These are a respect for learning, diligence, a powerful work ethic, a sense of propriety and moral norms, frugality with a high propensity to save and to invest, discipline with a strong sense of family and group, all rooted in a common Confucian educational and cultural heritage. The argument for this is obviously most powerful among the Chinese diaspora. Such self-discovery in Asia, whichever direction it takes in the aftermath of financial crisis and economic slowdown, has occurred historically in the process of meeting an Occidental challenge. It would obviously be of benefit to all the peoples of the region, Chinese and others, if a common cultural and value system arising from what Joseph Needham called 'the nucleus of crystallization' could be identified as a unifying factor and developed educationally.[11] However, as an explanation for dramatic and recent economic growth it has been criticized, notably by the economist, Bela Belassa.[12] He points out that as recently as the 1950s and 1960s, the Confucian ethic was being given as a reason for the economic sluggishness of the same countries. He argued further that the differing economic performance of countries with common cultural traits but different policies, shows the import-ance of the latter over the former. His argument is persuasive, but does not close discussion on the role of cultural factors in development.

The Mass Education Movement

The Chinese classical scholars had taught: 'People are the foundation of the nation: if the foun-dation is firm, then the nation enjoys tranquility.'[13] However, the reality of Imperial and of early Republican China was that the mass of the Chinese people were excluded effectively from formal education and its benefits which continued to produce, inefficiently, a stratified semi-feudal governing élite. China was not in any meaningful sense 'a Learning Society'. This fact was recognized by the manifesto of the Mass Education Movement founded in 1923. That China had one-fourth of the world's population was, it said, a fact familiar to all; but nearly 80 per cent of them did not read or write. 'Democracy and illiteracy cannot stand side by side. One of the two must go. Which shall it be?' China's illiterate masses must, it argued, be educated and educated soon if the democratic republic was to succeed. Hence the Mass Education Movement.[14]

Although interest in *pingmin* or popular education was not new, the social and intellectual climate of the 1920s made possible the rapid growth of the new initiative. It owed its origins to the influence of American-educated Chinese, particularly those who had studied under the supervision of John Dewey at Teachers' College, Columbia University and who were now responsible for teacher education at various American Christian sponsored normal colleges and universities in China. Dewey's own extended visit to China between 1919 and 1921 was part of their campaign for a 'new education' which paralleled their aspirations for 'a new cul-ture', based on democracy and individualism. A Society for the Promotion of New Education was formed in early 1919 to achieve these objectives.[15]

The key figures in extending the 'New Education' and the 'New Culture' to the masses were Tao Xingzhi and Yan Yangchu (James Yen) who in 1923 together founded the National Association of the Mass Education Movement. Tao, who was head of the Department of Education at the National South Eastern University, became increasingly committed to non-formal learning, as the Mass Education Movement extended its activities from the urban to the rural areas as, reportedly, it 'swept through China like wildfire'.[16] Tao was a pioneer of basic literacy education, with peasant literacy his chief concern. It was he who developed 'the relay method', where semi-literates or even those who had learned only a few characters taught them to others. This led to the 'little teacher' scheme, with children learning first and then teaching characters to adults. James Yen, who became the Movement's General Director, had also been educated in the United States, but was not part of the Columbia University group. His inspiration came from his experience in organizing literacy training programmes for the Young Men's Christian Association (YMCA), a project which developed from his earlier social service among Chinese labourers recruited by the Allies to work in France during the First World War.

The basic programmes organized by the Mass Education Movement drew upon young stu-dent volunteers, who attempted to teach part-time over a cycle of months, a syllabus known as The People's Thousand Character Lessons. The Movement argued that one of the chief rea-sons for the high rate of illiteracy in China was the intricacy of the classical language, which '. . . to learn to use with any degree of proficiency means a lifetime of study'.[17] The illiterate masses cannot spare the time or the money, having to struggle for their rice. Finally, '. . . the vocabulary acquired must be practical and useful for him in his daily life as a man and citizen of a Republic.'[18] Following the Literary Revolution of 1917–1919,[19] *Pai-hua* or the standard spoken language had replaced the classical language for all general literary purposes, with public notices, magazines, newspapers and novels and even modern academic texts being published in it. As it was also 'the most widely spoken language in the country',[20] a matter of some importance given China's diversity, it was adopted by the Movement as '. . . the most effective tool in the education of the masses'.[21]

The Mass Education Movement claims significance as the first organized attempt on a large scale to educate the Chinese masses. There had been in reality an 'aristocracy of learning'. The Movement championed the cause of 'education for all' and worked systematically and persistently to bring education within people's reach. In so doing it raised the cultural aspirations of the masses, stimulating a demand for more and better education generally and for a literature that would meet the needs of the growing reading population. It commented in its manifesto that hitherto '. . . almost anything worth while done in literature had been done for the scholar and practically nothing for the common people',[22] but now envisaged '. . . a people's literature in the making'.[23] The Movement also claimed to be a popular movement which unified the Chinese people and provided a much needed training for citizenship through which the well to do and well educated recognized '. . . that the welfare of the community depends upon the development and the intelligence of the masses',[24] while the illiterate develop a sense of worth and responsibility, both as individuals and as citizens of the Chinese nation. The manifesto concludes: 'The world can ill afford to see China's millions kept ignorant and ignored . . . she must have something to contribute to the peace and progress of the world.'[25]

This is a vision of 'a Learning Society' and one in which the examples of American Protestant missions and Rotary Club social service have a powerful influence. John Dewey, though critical of religion, was a representative of this type of middle-class progressive social movement. It is reminiscent also of the early Workers' Educational Association in Britain, in which the English historian R. H. Tawney was to play such a leading part. Tawney was a member of the four person League of Nations Mission of Educational Experts to China which reported in 1932.[26] He had a direct interest in the work of the Mass Education Movement and was to remain in correspondence with Y. C. James Yen. The Mass Education Movement, in a clear allusion to Abraham Lincoln's Gettysburg Address, claimed that it was: 'A Movement of the People, by the People, and for the People.' It was supported voluntarily and financially 'by the public spirited members of the community, such as business men, gentry, pastors, teachers and students of the schools and college'. There was also something Tolstoyan, of the nineteenth century Russian *narodniki*,[27] in the original inspiration of Tao Xingzhi who describes 1923 as a period of personal awakening during which he decided to buy a set of cotton peasant clothes and go 'back to the way of the common people'.[28] Y. C. James Yen's awakening had come in France where, as he told the American novelist Pearl S. Buck, he had suddenly become aware that: 'Those who have learning keep it for themselves . . . they do not think of it as something which ought to be shared with all.'[29]

As Suzanne Pepper has pointed out, such views brought Tao Xingzhi, and to a lesser extent Y. C. James Yen, into the debate over the social role of Chinese intellectuals. The status of the classical scholar was based on an obsolete technical mastery of dead knowledge, with the purpose of personal advancement. In Tao's opinion 'real knowledge could only derive from experience, and anyone could acquire it'.[30] This was very close to John Dewey's philosophy of pragmatism, though Tao also argued that many of those modernizers who sought inspiration from abroad, the so-called national self strengtheners, were logically on the same path as the classical scholars. They 'copied the entire foreign education system', importing its ideas, its products, even its personnel, whilst neglecting or disparaging China's own characteristics. Tao's aim was to break the cycle. Books were to be used, not learned, and everyone, not just scholars, should have access to them.[31] Tao's direct influence ended with the coming to power of the rightwing *Guomindang* (*GMD*) after 1927 and he fled temporarily to Japan. Indirectly, however, the aims that he espoused were taken up by others, while the Mass Education Movement itself continued in a much more limited way under Y. C. James Yen.

Mao Zedong's *Talks at the Yan'an Forum on Literature and Art*

Drawing on the revolutionary experience of the Soviet Union and under the guidance of the Communist (Third) International, the Chinese Communist Party recognized the importance of political and ideological education from the outset. For example, in 1923, Mao Zedong established an 'open entry, self study university' at Changsha in Hunan Province, which contributed a few years later to his well known *Report of an Investigation of the Hunan Peasant Movement*.[32] The experiment at Changsha reflected Mao's criticisms of the formalistic nature of conventional university studies and took as its motto : 'Read by oneself; ponder by oneself; mutually discuss and study.'[33] After the Long March between 1934 and 1935, the Chinese Communist Party (CCP) established itself in the stronghold of Yan'an in north-west China, where it proceeded to carry out its own programme of mass education as reported by the American journalist Edgar Snow in the Left Book Club's *Red Star over China*.[34] There was an effort to integrate mass adult education, through general literacy classes, with social and economic programmes such as cooperatives, designed to raise collective consciousness amongst workers and peasants in the liberated areas. The general education policy at that time was determined by the pressing needs of the war against Japanese aggression so that 'cadre education was more important than mass education and adult education was more important than children's education.'[35] This explains the priority given to the work of the Anti-Japanese Military and Political College.

   Another crucial question was that of the Party's relationship with intellectuals and their role in educational and cultural work. The CCP was suspicious of the class origins of intellectuals inside the Party and regarded progressive intellectuals ouside the Party, such as those in the Mass Education Movement, as exploitative bourgeois idealists. However, once a formal anti-Japanese united front with the GMD went into effect in 1936, Mao Zedong reminded the Party that 'The proletariat cannot produce its own intellectuals without the help of intellectuals already existing in society.'[36] Mao had regained a place within the leadership of the CCP during the Long March and continued to emphasize to the Party the lessons of that 'historic punishment'.[37] He was conscious of the dangers inherent in the pact with the GMD and of the fact that, while Party membership was increasing under the pressure of the Japanese invasion, the clarity of its class position was in danger of being obscured. As early as 1938 he advocated that the Party should itself go back to school, through a mass programme of political education and ideological rectification. It began on an all-Party basis early in 1942 and lasted for two years.

   Mao's own *Talks at the Yan'an Forum on Literature and Art* was a key study document used in this campaign and is a clear statement of his ideological position on this issue.[38] In two sessions, at the beginning and the end of the forum, Mao spelled out the relationship between Marxist–Leninist goals and the contribution to be made by China's intellectuals, including its professional educators. He pointed out that the liberation of the Chinese people will take place on 'various fronts, among which are the fronts of the pen and of the gun, the cultural and the military fronts'.[39] The military are the primary force, but the cultural army 'is absolutely indispensable for uniting our own ranks and defeating the enemy'.[40] He identifies the problems facing intellectuals in building this cultural army. First, there is the problem of class stand: 'Our stand is that of the proletariat and the masses'.[41] Then there are the problems of attitude and of audience. He recalls that when he was a student, 'I felt that intellectuals were the only clean people in the world, while in comparison workers and peasants were dirty'.[42] It was only after his long and painful experience as a revolutionary, that he had come to realize that 'in the last analysis, the workers and peasants were the cleanest people and even though their hands were soiled and their feet smeared with cow dung, they were really cleaner than the bourgeois and petty bourgeois intellectuals'. This in turn meant that 'prior to the task of educating the workers, peasants and soldiers, there is the task of learning from them'.[43] This is a theme which he emphasized and re-emphasized: the need of intellectuals to change fundamentally, as he had done, 'the feelings implanted in me in the bourgeois schools'.[44] It was essential for the intellectual to understand that: 'Only by speaking for the masses can he educate them and only by being their pupil can he be their teacher'; otherwise, '. . . no matter how talented he may be he will not be needed by the masses and his work will have no future'.[45]

The study and rectification campaign between 1942 and 1944 has been described as perhaps Mao Zedong's 'greatest political triumph'.[46] He had learned from the masses and was now their teacher, the undisputed leader and ideological spokesman of the Chinese Communist Party. Moreover, Mao insisted that the the lessons learned be applied, with each Party member's political record and revolutionary potential re-examined. This often painful process was concluded by the senior cadres' conference between October 1942 and January 1943, during which the participants rigorously analyzed and criticized their personal and collective records, current work and plans. The campaign as a whole may be seen as a pioneering and totalizing Maoist effort to shape the CCP as 'a Learning Organization' model for the emerging communist version of 'a Learning Society'. The campaign also foreshadowed the future political objectives and pattern of the Great Proletarian Cultural Revolution which Mao Zedong was to launch in 1966.

The Great Proletarian Cultural Revolution 1966–1976

Many Westerners, liberals and conservatives alike, regarded the Great Proletarian Cultural Revolution simply as an outbreak of fanatic philistinism and it remains one of the best known and least understood episodes in the history of modern China. For instance, a British adult educator writing in 1992 said: 'The effects on the people of the Cultural Revolution were devastating, notably in respect of education. Education effectively came to a halt and millions of people were therefore denied access to education. The reasons for this are complex, and now almost irrelevant, except that they underline the present need for recovering from that situation through adult education.'[47] Yet at the Cultural Revolution's core was the need to ensure that millions of people, workers and peasants, not only had access to education, but were able to define its meaning and purpose. After the military and political victory of Liberation on 1 October 1949, there followed a period of ideological consolidation through the mass literacy programmes of the early 1950s. The emphasis then shifted, under Soviet influence, to the development of formal education structures, combined with skills oriented 'spare time' education in the factories and agricultural communes.

Mao Zedong believed, however, that ideological direction was being lost and tried to launch another rectification campaign on the lines of Yan'an in 1942, through the Socialist Education Movement launched in 1962, which became the precursor of the Cultural Revolution. As he emphasized to students: 'The class struggle is a principal subject for you. Your college should go to the countryside . . . and to the factories . . . [if] you know nothing about the class struggle, how can you be considered as university graduates?'[48] The aim of the Cultural Revolution which followed was 'to prevent revisionism from usurping the leadership of the Party and State [and also] to prevent the comeback of Capitalism'.[49] In the circumstances of Liberated China, this meant a revolution in the superstructure which rose above the economic base, something which Mao had referred to theoretically in his essay *On contradiction*, of August 1937, when he had written:

> When the superstructure [politics, culture, etc.] obstructs the economic base, political and cultural changes become principal and decisive. Are we going against materialism when we say this ? No. The reason is that while we recognize that in the general development of history the material determines the mental and social being determines social consciousness, we also—and indeed must—recognize the reaction of mental on material things, of social consciousness on social being and of the superstructure on the economic base. This does not go against materialism; on the contrary, it avoids mechanical materialism and firmly upholds dialectical materialism.[50]

Mao believed that the social structure, intellectual climate and academic forms and curricula would continue to promote traditional, hierarchical and capitalistic ideology and that socialism's opponents would justify this on Confucian grounds of intellectual achievement and personal endeavour. As Jean Esmein comments: 'If there was any chance of reaction this would be the source of counter revolution. If, on the other hand, the whole superstructure became the focus of the proletarian ideology that would in its turn affect the whole society.'[51]

This was the ideological thrust of the Great Proletarian Cultural Revolution, a radically different educational development model. Mao Zedong's aim was to produce a new type of intelligentsia and the May 7th Cadre Schools, which he initiated, had the task of uniting education in the army, the factories, the communes and amongst the bureaucracy, with that of formal education. The same motive lay behind the July 21st Workers' Universities. In the *Peking Review*, he stated:

> It is still necessary to have universities; here I refer mainly to colleges of science and engineering. However, it is essential to shorten the length of schooling, revolutionize education, put proletarian politics in command and take the road of the Shanghai Machine Tools plant in training technicians from among the workers. Students should be selected from among workers and peasants with practical experience and they should return to production after a few years study.[52]

The experimental educational programmes of earlier years—adult literacy and spare time education—were also integrated with the formal educational pattern. John N. Hawkins, an American commentator on Mao Zedong's educational thought said, in 1974, that: 'By breaking down traditional barriers between school and society' Mao Tse-tung [*sic*] has succeeded in creating a 'learning' society whereby education becomes the task of virtually all institutions instead of being restricted to the more formal educational institutions.'[53] Hawkins concludes by saying that: 'This attempt to balance the pace of economic development so that eventually the entire society will become a great 'commune' as well as a great 'school' is perhaps one of the most ambitious national development programs currently underway.'[54]

He was not alone in this assessment. Indeed, economist John Simmons, writing in 1980, ironically described China's education system as the one that 'comes closest to the World Bank's model program for a developing country'.[55] Again, the British development sociologist Ronald Dore described China's education policies as the first nationwide antidote for the 'diploma disease' which he had identified as responsible for many of the troubles with education generally.[56] In fact, the educated élite had become the 'target for transformation and status reversal rather than a source of political power and support'.[57] The Great Proletarian Cultural Revolution had been chaotic and often brutal; it had also been an unremitting ideological class struggle. The foreign observers had noted the ends, without commenting on the means.

Careers and corporate class rooms

The Cultural Revolution was not, however, to be a permanent one. Mao Zedong died in 1976 and by 1980 the official line of Party and State was that the period had been one of unremitting turmoil, about which 'not one good thing' could be said. Educators throughout the country declared themselves incredulous that the outside world could derive positive lessons from China's experience.[58] The country was now described as struggling to overcome 'three lows and one lack'—low cultural level, low technical standards, low management ability and a lack of qualified technicians.[59] This reflected the new policy of economic liberalization led by Deng Xiaoping. China's educational system has since followed much the same model as that of other developing countries in the region, with a strong emphasis on human capital formation.[60] This is how the concept of 'a Learning Society' has evolved over the past 20 years of movement towards a market economy and of the Open Door. It has seen the widespread revival of interest in education as the means to build individual careers. This is coupled with an evolving official strategy to build China as a modern nation, free of the burdens of a command economy and participating responsibly in global politics and trade.

It is important to note that the supply of skilled labour has not kept pace with China's expanding economy and market potential. This problem is aggravated by a fundamental lack of knowledge or experience of international business and management, not least in the development of human resources. Many foreign businesses active in the country now carry out their own workforce training, which would have been unthinkable two decades ago. The scarcity of highly skilled, qualified and experienced Chinese, who are paid differentially, may be the initial reason for developing training programmes, but foreign businesses and their governments are also aware of the long-term benefits to them of such schemes. For example, the Confederation of British Industries' Overseas Scholarship Scheme has provided bursaries which enable Chinese graduate engineers to study in the United Kingdom for periods of between six and twelve months. The CBI's view is that although it is difficult to quantify the benefits to British business, the scheme is 'an excellent mechanism to promote British technology and management techniques in China'.[61] There are many other such programmes now operating at the corporate, governmental and academic level between China and the countries of the developed world. Becoming part of China's development process in such a direct way provides opportunities to influence its direction and to penetrate further the country's vast market potential.

The evidence also suggests that in such a climate, the 'privatization' of Chinese education will continue, with supplementary tutors, voluntary community schools, fee-paying schools and private vocational training agencies emerging rapidly. This has aggravated inequalities. The system of decentralized financing announced in the 1990s brought particular pressure to bear on rural areas with meagre resources. Private tutorial classes have revived after 40 years, acknowledged as the only means of providing low-cost elementary instruction for poor rural children whose parents cannot afford the fees charged in the state schools. By contrast, in the relatively prosperous urban areas there are the well advertised élite schools, charging deposits, tuition and boarding fees. In deference to public sensibilities the government has renamed all private schooling as *minban* or 'people managed'.[62] The same trends are seen in tertiary education. The World Bank's view now is that 'Destroyed by the Cultural Revolution

(1966–1976), China's higher education was rebuilt only in the later 1970s as one element of a strategy to modernize the country.[63]

This strategy requires Chinese higher education to play two key roles in sustaining economic growth and in achieving socially and environmentally responsible development in the country. These will be achieved through educating a graduate leadership with a 'strong, broad based education and problem solving skills', who will 'fill high level scientific, technical, professional and managerial positions in the public and private sectors'.[64] It will also generate and utilize knowledge for China's development effort, though it is important to note the development of patent firms in China and the growing legal, commercial and academic interest in intellectual property rights. It is important to note that this focus on the human resource aspects of modernization has also been applied to that fundamentally inportant political organization, the People's Liberation Army. Under Deng Xaioping's direction after 1978, the command structure of the army was reorganized and its educational base reformed, improving its capacity to absorb advanced technology. By 1987, it was concluded that 'the reformation of the PLA officer education system is basically complete'.[65] This may have been significant during the political upheaval two years later.

Enrolments in higher education have grown, a trend which should continue in response to student demand. In addition to the 1080 regular public universities and colleges, there are 1172 public adult education institutions at post-secondary levels, including radio and television universities, independent correspondence colleges, and continuing education courses run by the regular universities. In the mid 1990s, these institutions enrolled 2.35 million students on a part-time basis and employed 250,000 staff. About 90 per cent of students were in short-cycle programmes and only 10 per cent were in regular undergraduate studies.[66] It is a widespread view among Chinese academics and policy-makers that this sector has grown rapidly over the past five years and will continue to do so, both in size and in importance, with distance education and various types of open learning likely to be significant.[67] Such programmes are seen as necessary to China's economic development plans, providing both initial training and continuing education for middle grade managers and technicians who are currently both poorly qualified and in short supply, a legacy of a technical and vocational education and training system designed to serve the state-owned enterprises of a command economy.[68]

It is anticipated also that higher education institutions will be expected by government to allocate an agreed part of their budgets to community projects, as well as developing partnerships with the growing private sector of the economy.[69] Furthermore, over 800 private post-secondary institutions are now in operation, although relatively few have, as yet, been accredited by the State.[70] Fees for higher education were introduced in 1997 and the proportion of self-financing students should grow significantly. Such trends are reinforced by the keen competition for entry to 'key' secondary schools and to the prestigious universities. The numbers studying abroad are also likely to increase as the market economy creates a fresh class of relatively prosperous families.

Traditionally in China, formal education was the high road to personal advancement and, with the rejection of the deschooling experiment of the Cultural Revolution and the individual ambition stimulated by the market economy, the Chinese 'Learning Society' is losing its socialist orientation. A *People's Daily* editorial of 24 August 1989 blamed the events at Tiananmen Square, of May and June that year, on bourgeois liberal ideas that had flooded in to fill an ideological vacuum.[71] Yet it was the Chinese Communist Party and State which, in its dash for economic growth, re-established an élitist and competitive system of education, together with an Open Door for trade and study, in an effort to produce quickly the scientists, engineers, managers and, for that matter, *entrepreneurs*, who would lead economic development. It is a policy fraught with ideological danger, as the Chinese leadership's strongest critics emanated from the most privileged and best funded sectors of the education system.

The Chinese are now struggling with the tensions that have resulted: the growing urban–rural disparities, the question of national minorities, the élite–mass distinctions and the return of class and inequality to Chinese education and to Chinese society, with the increasing need to resort to foreign models and guidance.[72] There is also the prospect of a genuine civil society emerging in the wake of the market economy and its instrumental restructuring of the education system. Civil society may be defined 'by its refusal of the authoritarian or totalitarian propensity to meld party, state and people. Citizens in a civil society, therefore are critical—they exhibit a propensity to discriminate among levels of the political system'.[73] This capacity is enhanced by their participation in 'a Learning Society', which, in China, could eventually be of a democratic capitalist type. The genie is out of the bottle and will not now be replaced.

Notes

1 Jenner, W. J. F. (1994), *The tyranny of history: The roots of China's crisis*, Penguin, London.
2 See for instance Price, R. (1987), 'Convergence or copying: China and the Soviet Union', and Orleans, Leo, A. (1987), 'Soviet influence on China's higher education', in Hayhoe, R. and Bastid, M., *China's education and the industrialized world: Studies in cultural transfer*, M. E. Sharpe Inc., Armonk, New York and London, pp. 158–83 and pp. 184–98.
3 Morgan, W. J. (2001), 'Proletarian education and culture in Bolshevik Russia', in Jones, D. (ed.) *Censorship: An international encyclopaedia*, Fitzroy Dearborn Press, London.
4 *Financial Times*, October 1, 1999, 'China Survey'; see also Lloyd, J. (2000), 'The China syndrome', *Financial Times*, January 8/9.
5 Minxin Pei. (1994), *From reform to revolution: The demise of Communism in China and the Soviet Union*, Harvard University Press, Cambridge, Mass. and London; Liu Weiling (1999), 'Hinterland beckons: Vital new thinking needed to assist western economies', *China Daily Business Weekly*, Hong Kong edition, December 5–11.
6 Wu Ching-Tzu (1957), *The scholars*, Foreign Languages Press, Beijing, China.; this provides a brilliant and entertaining satire of the Imperial Examination System.
7 Lee Wing On (1996), 'The cultural context for Chinese learners: Conceptions of learning in the Confucian tradition.', in Watkins, David A. and Biggs, John H. (eds.), *The Chinese learner: Cultural, psychological and contextual influences*, Comparative Education Research Centre, Hong Kong, and the Australian Council for Educational Research Ltd, Melbourne, Australia, p. 26.
8 *Ibid.*, p. 38.
9 *Ibid.*, p. 39.
10 Morris, P. and Sweeting, A. (eds.), (1995), *Education and development in East Asia*, Garland Publishing Inc., New York and London.
11 Needham, J. (1970), 'China and the West', in Various Contributors, *China and the West: Mankind evolving*, Humanities Press, New York, p. 20.
12 Belassa, B. (1988), 'The lessons of East Asian development: An overview.', in *Economic development and cultural change*, Vol. 36, No. 3, pp. 5273–90.
13 Quoted in Yen, James Y. C. (1925), *The mass education movement in China*, The Commercial Press Ltd., Shanghai, China, p. 1.
14 *Ibid.*
15 Dewey, J. (1973), *Lectures in China, 1919–1920*, translated by Clopton, R. W. and Ou Tsuinchen, University Press of Hawaii, Honolulu; See also Keenan, B. C. (1977), *The Dewey experiment in China: Educational reform and political power in the early Republic*, Harvard University Press, Cambridge, Mass.
16 Quoted in Pepper, S (1996), *Radicalism and education reform in 20th Century China: The search for an ideal development model*, Cambridge University Press, Cambridge, England, New York and Melbourne, p. 93. Suzanne Pepper's work is an essential source of information and analysis, comparable with Sheila Fitzpatrick's work on education, politics and society in the early Soviet Union.
17 Yen, op. cit. (1925), p. 1.
18 *Ibid.*, p. 3.

19 Yen, Y. C. James (1923), *How to educate China's illiterate millions for democracy in a decade*, Chinese National Association for the Advancement of Education, Vol. 11, Bulletin 15.
20 Yen, op. cit. (1925), p. 1.
21 *Ibid.*,
22 *Ibid.*, p. 23.
23 *Ibid.*, pp. 23–4.
24 *Ibid.*, p. 25.
25 *Ibid.*
26 League of Nations Mission of Educational Experts (1932), *The re-organization of education in China*, The League of Nations Institute of Intellectual Co-operation, Paris; see also Tawney, R. H. (1932), *Land and labour in China*, Allen and Unwin, London, Chapter 6.
27 See for instance the essays on 'Russian populism' and on 'Tolstoy and enlightenment' in Berlin, I. (1979), *Russian thinkers*, Pelican Books, Harmandsworth.
28 Pepper, op. cit., p. 92.
29 *Ibid.*, p. 105.
30 *Ibid.*, p. 93.
31 *Ibid.*; See also Buck, P. S. (1959), *Tell the people: Talks with James Yen about the Mass Education Movement*, International Institute of Rural Reconstruction, New York and also Hayford, C. W. (1990), *To the people: James Yen and village China*, Columbia University Press, New York.
32 Mao Zedong, (1927), *Selected Works*, Vol 1, Foreign Languages Press, Peking, pp. 23–59.
33 Coletta, N. J. (1982), (Guest Editor), 'Worker and peasant adult education', *Chinese Education*, Vol. 15, Nos. 1–2, Spring–Summer. p. 6.
34 Snow, E (1937), *Red star over China*, Victor Gollancz Left Book Club edition, London. There is a memorial stone to Snow in the grounds of Peking University.
35 Yao Zhongda, (1981), comments at Beijing Symposium on Adult Education, quoted by Coletta, op. cit., p. 8.
36 Pepper, op. cit., p. 129.
37 *Ibid.*, p. 138.
38 Mao Tse-Tung (1956), *Talks at the Yenan forum on literature and art*, Foreign Languages Press, Peking.
39 *Ibid.*, p. 1.
40 *Ibid.*, p. xiii.
41 *Ibid.*, p. 2.
42 *Ibid.*, p. 7.
43 *Ibid.*, p. 17.
44 *Ibid.*, p. 7.
45 *Ibid.*, p. 23.
46 Pepper, op. cit., p. 140.
47 Thomas, J. E. (1992), 'Afterword', in Zhang Xiang Dong and Stephens, Michael D., *University adult education in China*, The Department of Adult Education, University of Nottingham, Nottingham, England, p. 238.
48 Hawkins, John N. (1974), *Mao Tse-Tung and education: His thoughts and teachings*, Linnet Books, Hamden, Conn, p. 114.
49 Decision of the Central Committee of the Chinese Communist Party Concerning the Great Proletarian Cultural Revolution, No. 181, 10th August, 1966; Chin, Steve S. K. (1979), *The thought of Mao Tse-Tung: Form and content*, Centre of Asian Studies, University of Hong Kong, p. 105.
50 Mao Tse-tung. (1967), *On contradiction*, Foreign Languages Press, Peking.
51 Esmein, J. (1975), *The Chinese cultural revolution*, Andre Deutsch, London, p. 22.
52 *The Peking Review*, August 2nd, 1968; cited in Robinson, J. (1969), *The cultural revolution in China*, Pelican, Harmandsworth, p. 150.
53 Hawkins, op. cit., p. 15.
54 *Ibid.*, p. 159.
55 Simmons, J. (ed.), (1980), *The education dilemma: Policy issues for developing countries in the 1980s*, Pergamon Press, New York, pp. 9–10; quoted in Pepper, op. cit., p. 1.
56 Dore, R. P. (1976), *The diploma disease: Education, qualification and development*, Allen and Unwin, London, Chapter 14; cited in Pepper, op. cit., p. 2.
57 Pepper, ibid., p. 19.
58 *Ibid.*, p. 2.
59 Coletta, op. cit., p. 15.

60 Morris and Sweeting, op. cit.
61 'Training to succeed: With the Chinese market place becoming more sophisticated and competitive, foreign investors are increasingly aware of the importance of offering career development and training to local staff', *China Economic Review*, January, 1996, pp. 23–5; see also Siu, Wai-sum and Chan, Allan K. K. (1991), 'International business education in China: Present needs and future challenges', *Journal of Teaching in International Business*, Vol. 2, Nos. 3 and 4, pp. 83–95.
62 Mok, Ka-ho and Wat, King-yee, 'Merging of the public and private boundary: Education and the market place in China.', *International Journal of Educational Development*, Vol. 18, No. 3, pp. 255–67.
63 The World Bank (1997), *China: higher education reform*, The World Bank, Washington, D.C., p. xi.
64 *Ibid.*, pp. vii and xi.
65 Henley, L. D. (1987), 'Officer education in the Chinese PLA.', *Problems of Communism*, May–June, pp. 55–71.
66 *Ibid.*, p.
67 This has been confirmed during several interviews conducted by the author during an extended visit to China in December, 1999; See also Xiao, Jin. (1998), 'Higher adult education: Redefining its roles', in Agelasto, M. and Adamson, R. (eds.), *Higher education in post Mao China*, Hong Kong University Press, Hong Kong, pp. 189–210.
68 Yang Jin (1993), 'Technical and vocational education in the People's Republic of China: Current status and prospects.', *The Vocational Aspect of Education*, Vol. 45, No. 2, pp. 135–43.
69 Min Wei-fang (1995), 'Higher education institutions and community development in China', in Postiglione, G. A. and Lee Wing-on (eds.), *Social change and educational development: Mainland China, Taiwan and Hong Kong*, Centre for Asian Studies, University of Hong Kong, Hong Kong, pp. 106–19.
70 World Bank, op. cit., p.
71 *The People's Daily*, 24 August 1989, Beijing, China.
72 Epstein, I. (1993), 'Class and inequality in Chinese education', *Compare*, Vol. 23, No. 2, pp. 131–47.
73 Chan, A. L. and Nesbitt-Larking, P. (1995), 'Critical citizenship and civil society in contemporary China.', *Canadian Journal of Political Science*, Vol. 28, No. 2, June, pp. 293–309; see also Wakeman, P. (1993), 'The civil society and public sphere debate', *Modern China*, Vol. 19, pp. 103–38 and He Baogang, (1993), *The dual roles of semi civil society in Chinese democracy*, Institute of Development Studies, Discussion Paper 327, University of Sussex, Brighton, England.

14 Lifelong learning in Australia

David Aspin, John Collard and Judith Chapman

Australia is a highly urbanized, multi-cultural country with a middle-sized economy that is strongly influenced by and subject to international economic conditions. The nation has a political system that has its antecedents in English political and legal traditions. While its population and culture are predominantly European in origin, in recent years the migration of peoples from the nations of Asia, the South Pacific and Indian Ocean has considerably altered the ethnic composition of the population and diversified its culture.

Considerations arising from Australia's economic position, the changing nature of its society, and its geopolitical situation have been among the major factors driving educational reform during the course of the 1990s. In particular, a major restructuring of the labour market, a shift from reliance on raw materials export towards more value-added exports, and a greater emphasis on developing a highly skilled, flexible and productive workforce have exerted strong pressure on government to bring about change in education and training.

In this chapter we will analyse the part played by considerations of 'lifelong learning' in the reform effort in education and training in Australia. We shall point to developments in 1999 which suggest that lifelong learning is an idea that is now beginning to be taken more seriously and to find overt expression in policy pronouncements, planning, and institutional developments and initiatives across Australia. These include: better co-ordination and rationalization of educational provision; establishment of qualifications frameworks; encouraging competition among providers; reducing costs and increasing flexibility through information and communication technology. All of these have been implemented in Australia in recent years.

Australia's consideration of lifelong learning in international perspective

Consideration of lifelong learning in Australia has taken place within an international context in which the notion of lifelong learning has assumed immense importance. An increasing number of countries and international agencies, with which Australia has strong links, have concluded that a lifelong approach to learning should be instituted and deployed as one of the main lines of attack on some of the major problems needing to be addressed as we enter the twenty-first century. The deliberations of OECD, UNESCO, and the Asia-Pacific Economic Co-operation Forum [APEC] have revealed a strong commitment to policies of learning across the lifespan. Continued access to education and training for all a country's citizens is seen as an investment in the future: a pre-condition for economic advance, democracy and social cohesion, and a significant factor in increasing personal development and growth.

A number of themes can be seen to run through the work of international agencies: the emergence of an awareness of the importance of the notions of the knowledge economy and the learning society; an acceptance of the need for a new philosophy of education and training, with institutions of all kinds—formal and informal, traditional and alternative, public and private—having new roles and responsibilities for learning; the necessity of ensuring that the foundations for lifelong learning are set in place for all citizens during the compulsory years of schooling; the need to promote a multiple and coherent set of links, pathways and articulations between schooling, work, further education and other agencies offering opportunities for learning across the lifespan; the importance of governments providing incentives for individuals, employers, and the range of social partners with a commitment to learning, to invest in lifelong learning; and the need to ensure that emphasis upon lifelong learning does not reinforce existing patterns of privilege and widen the existing gap between the advantaged and the disadvantaged, simply on the basis of access to education (Chapman and Aspin 1997).

In this chapter we shall consider how Australia has addressed such themes. We will argue that, while in Australia there has been, on the part of many policy-makers, educators and community members, a strong commitment to the idea of lifelong learning, until recently there has been much less clarity about the ways in which the term itself is understood and even less about ways in which it may be and should be applied. Thus, although the concept of 'life-long learning' has been used in a wide variety of contexts in Australia and has a wide currency, its meaning has often been unclear and its operationalization and implementation has not been hitherto widely achieved.

Part of the problem is conceptual in nature. One approach to conceptualizing life-long learning lays it down that life-long learning is concerned with the promotion of skills and competences necessary for the development of general capabilities and specific performance in given tasks. Skills and competences developed through programmes of lifelong learning will, on this approach, have a bearing on questions of how workers perform in their tackling of specific job responsibilities and tasks and how well they can adapt their general and specific knowledge and competences to new tasks (OECD 1994). This approach presents us with a very narrow and limited understanding of the nature, aims and purpose of 'lifelong education'. Nevertheless it is this 'instrumental' view that has hitherto dominated approaches to lifelong learning in the Australian educational arena.

We have seen from the recent work of OECD, UNESCO, the European Parliament and the Nordic Council of Ministers, however, that there are much broader and more multi-faceted ways of approaching the conceptualization of lifelong learning. Instead of seeing education as instrumental to the achievement of an extrinsic goal, education may also be perceived as an intrinsically valuable activity, something that is good in and for itself. From this perspective the aim is to enable those engaging in learning, not merely to arrive at a new place but 'to travel with a different view' (Peters 1965). The point here is that those engaging in educational activities would be enriched by having their view of the world continually expanded and transformed by the increasing varieties of educational experience and cognitive achievements that education would offer them for their illumination and enrichment throughout their lives.

This kind of argument reaches its full flowering in the realization that, for those engaging in lifelong learning, there is continually being made available and expanded a rich range of additional options, from which people may construct a satisfying and enriching pattern of activities and life-enhancing choices for themselves (see White 1982). Lifelong learning offers people the opportunity to bring up to date their knowledge of and enjoyment in activities which they may have either long since laid aside or always wanted to do but were previously unable; to try their hands at activities and pursuits that they had previously imagined were outside their available time or competence; or to work consciously at extending their intellectual, vocational and personal horizons by seeking to understand and grasp some of the more significant advances of recent times, that have done so much to affect and transform their worlds.

From this viewpoint, the expansion of cognitive repertoire and the increasing of skills and competences is an undertaking that can—and indeed, must—continue throughout one's life, as an essential part of one's growth and development as a human being, as a citizen in a participative democracy, and as a productive and efficiently operating agent in a process of economic change and advance.

In 1996 OECD ministers argued (OECD 1996) that none of these aims of lifelong learning can really be separated from the others: all three elements interact with and cross-fertilize each other. There is a complex inter-play between all three, that makes education for a more highly skilled work force at the same time an education for a better democracy and an inclusive society and a more rewarding life. For this reason, OECD ministers argued that the whole notion and value of 'lifelong learning for all' has to be seen as a complex and multi-faceted process, that begins in pre-school times, is carried on through basic, compulsory and post-compulsory periods of formal education and training, and is then continued throughout life, through provision of such learning experiences, activities and enjoyment in the workplace, in universities and colleges, and in other educational, social and cultural agencies and institutions—of both a formal and informal kind—within the community.

From this position lifelong learning is seen as fundamental to bringing about a more democratic polity and set of social institutions, in which the principles and ideals of social inclusiveness, justice and equity are present, practised and promoted; an economy which is strong, adaptable and competitive; and a richer range of provision of those activities on which individual members of society are able to choose to spend their time and energy, for the personal rewards and satisfactions that they confer. To bring this about nothing less than a substantial re-appraisal of the provision, resourcing and goals of education and training, and a major reorientation of its direction towards the concept and value of the idea of the learning society, will be required.

Until recently, there has been little evidence in Australia of the overall or widespread adoption of this more integrated, multi-faceted approach towards lifelong learning. As things stand currently, a sophisticated and multi-dimensional conception of the idea of lifelong learning is only beginning to emerge and be put into effect. There is, however, some evidence that change is taking place and that reforms are being implemented across the Commonwealth and in many of the states to bring about the realization of lifelong learning for all. These developments are evident in the school sector, higher and further education, and adult and community education.

Lifelong learning and the school

Goals of schooling

Australia has more than 9000 schools attended by over three million students. Constitutionally, in each state the government system must provide educational opportunity for all children regardless of physical or intellectual ability, social and economic circumstances, cultural background and religious beliefs. Parents, however, have the right to choose to send their children to non-government schools for religious or other reasons. Within the non-government sector in each state there is usually a Catholic school system, other non-government systems, and independent schools. Parents electing to send their children to the non-government sector are usually called upon to provide additional financial input to the school of their choice.

Schooling is compulsory for all young people aged six to fifteen years. Constitutionally, state and territory Ministers of Education have responsibility for all school education in their respective states and territories. The states and territories bear the administrative and major financial responsibility for government school education in Australia; however, the Commonwealth plays an important role in considering the broad purposes and structures of schooling and in promoting national consistency and coherence in the provision of schooling. In cooperation with the individual states the Commonwealth addresses resource equity and quality issues through its recurrent, capital and specific purpose programmes. Through the agency of the Ministerial Council on Education, Employment, Training and Youth Affairs [MCEETYA] the Commonwealth Government also contributes to the articulation of National Goals for Schooling.

In 1999 the Commonwealth Government's MCEETYA Taskforce released a document, *Australia's Common and Agreed National Goals for Schooling in the Twenty-first Century*. This document constitutes a major step towards the conceptualization and articulation of the goals of Australian schooling framed from a lifelong perspective. Mr Geoff Spring, Chair of the MCEETYA Taskforce, speaking to education leaders on the topic of 'Education for the Twenty-first Century' (1998), revealed how the consideration, development and articulation of Australia's *Goals for Schooling in the Twenty-first Century* have been influenced by international developments, and in particular the conceptualizations of lifelong learning as contained in the UNESCO Report *Learning: The Treasure Within* (UNESCO 1996), especially as it pertains to the 'Four Pillars for Learning' set up in that report: Learning to Know, Learning to Do, Learning to Live Together, and Learning to Be.

At the same time as public policy documents in Australia are beginning explicitly to declare a new philosophy of school education framed around the concept of lifelong learning, specific policies are being put in place that are underpinned by lifelong learning concerns. This is particularly the case in the area of literacy and numeracy. The current Commonwealth Minister for Education, Training and Youth Affairs in Australia, Dr David Kemp, believes that literacy and numeracy are key requirements for lifelong learning: in his view, competence in the skills of literacy and numeracy provides the foundation for all subsequent learning. Major initiatives with strong financial support from Commonwealth and state governments are now being put in place to enable schools and school systems to ensure that all young people get 'the right start' (Sir Christopher Ball 1994) to their lifelong learning endeavours through the development of literacy and numeracy skills in the compulsory years of schooling.

Articulated pathways between schools and universities

Progress is also being made in the development of articulated pathways between schools and higher education. In particular progress has been made in the ways universities cooperate with schools, as they seek to cater for students of above average ability and learning achievement. Various ways are being explored to achieve this end. There is one approach, which maintains that schools can teach some university subjects. A second approach is one in which universities accept the school students as *bona fide* students who may join university classes. In this case the university does not provide any special programmes for such students. A third approach is to find a half-way house between these two positions. In such cases it is assumed that about half of the learning should come from school-based resources, and half from university-based resources. This can be delivered in two ways. One way involves setting up a cluster of schools that can bring together a group of students outside school hours; in this arrangement the class is jointly taught by teachers and university staff. There are many benefits accruing from such an arrangement. The school staff become quite deeply involved with the appropriate departments in the university, and the advantages of the development of such collegial relationships for both institutions are clear. The limitation is that one has to get viable groups together. To address this, mutually complementary relationships are being set up, often operating by distance education schemes and programmes. Students, particularly in more isolated locations, can benefit from these arrangements, that are based on multi-media utilizing a range of distance delivery resources. Contact by telephone or e-mail is used to keep students in constant contact with the university staff and a mentor among the teaching staff in the school.

Such arrangements to promote articulated pathways between schools and universities have also enhanced the lifelong learning opportunities for members of school teaching staff. As a result of such enhancement programmes, for example, Monash University in Melbourne has created a number of Teaching Fellows where a schoolteacher is brought in to work in a university department for a year to assist with transition arrangements and become better acquainted with the first year course. When such teachers return to the schools they are effectively fully qualified first year university teachers. The advantages of having such people at Monash University with knowledge of both schools and universities is clear.

At Monash University too programmes have also been set up for helping school students make the transition to university study easier and more enjoyable. Videos have been prepared and distributed to all schools in the state of Victoria, giving school students information about university, showing how life in one is different from the other, and providing helpful guidance on how students can better prepare for it. The same university organizes visits to schools by its Student Theatre Department, in which the university students enact performances based on stories from students about their experiences in the first year at university. Following these performances, discussions are then conducted between students from both institutions, designed to help the school students prepare for their own first year in the university. Such discussions lead to ongoing dialogue between schools and the university about transition issues.

Another university has arranged for some of their medical and engineering students to go out into schools, helping school students learn about important matters in their domain of intellectual and professional interest and so extending school students' understanding of and interest in issues that are at the leading edge of intellectual enquiry and professional development. In the case of at least one university this has become a formal course unit offered by the Faculty of Education to the Faculty of Medicine, in which the university students undertake a school-based project concerned to help future professionals to develop an understanding of children's learning about health issues and of the values which children bring to their view of themselves and the world, and to learn how to work with professionals from another field. The university students, some of whom elect to work with students in primary classes, are able to take these activities in schools as 'options' that count as credit in their courses and that can be sources of ongoing professional and academic interest to them.

Unfortunately this kind of partnership approach tends currently to be only in operation with students of accelerated learning potential. The question is whether such partnerships could apply in the case of would-be students who are disadvantaged or challenged in some way, perhaps by non-English speaking background groups, people with learning difficulties, and so on. Some universities, such as Australian Catholic University, are aware of the needs of such groups and are beginning to respond positively to their need for access and participation in tertiary study. One area where some universities are beginning to do this well is with Aboriginal students. Some universities have arranged for students to have a special year of preparation, and during at least their first year in the institution they are given some special help so that they can work at the level of those students coming from different backgrounds.

Universities agree that there are groups of students who potentially could benefit from admission to their courses of study, though that depends not just on the issue of selecting or putting them in but on providing ongoing support and counselling systems. There are such schemes in place in some institutions but this whole area still needs considerable development. It is an area in which there could be much greater cooperation between universities and schools than perhaps exists at present with respect to the levels of support and the pathways institutions provide to prepare such students realistically for further study, to secure them entry, and then to monitor and assist with their progress once they are in.

Articulated pathways between school and work

In Australia the decade of the 1990s has been one of economic turbulence in the nation and one aspect of this has been the escalation of unemployment rates. Youth unemployment has been particularly problematic (Wooden 1997, 1998). In such a context, young people's transition to the world of work has been of considerable concern.

Reforms designed to facilitate the transition between school and work have been far-reaching. One of the most radical manifestations has been in the expansion of vocational provision in the senior secondary school curriculum. In Australia senior secondary schools have been traditionally oriented to serving students who have wished to pursue a pathway to further academic study. The high rates of youth unemployment in the 1990s, however, have meant that the cohort continuing at school to the age of 18 has become more diverse than traditional academic provision could accommodate. In 1999 the Liberal Government limited youth employment benefits by changing income support rules. Since 1 January young people under 18 years of age are generally no longer entitled to income support in their own right unless engaged in recognized education and/or training. The consequence of this has been that approximately 8500 16- and 17-year-olds, who would normally have exited the school systems before the final years of schooling, are expected to be retained or returned to schools in 1999. Senior secondary schools in Australia have been challenged to diversify their programmes to cater for a much broader range of students and to move towards the provision of multiple pathways from school to work and further education.

The extent to which lifelong learning and the need to facilitate the transition between school and work have helped to reshape policy in Australian senior secondary education is clearly reflected in Australia's *Common and Agreed Goals for Schooling in the Twenty-First Century*. Whereas there was only incidental reference to such goals in the *Hobart Declaration* of the *Goals for Schooling in Australia* promulgated by the Australian Education Council in April 1989, there are a number of explicit clauses in the new document. These include references to developing 'understanding of the world of work' and enabling students to 'make informed decisions about pathways from school to work, vocational education and training and higher education in the context of lifelong learning'. The document also reflects a shift in understanding of the nature, type and range of education provision at the senior secondary level. The school is no longer envisaged as a solitary agency of educational provision but is encouraged to 'promote productive learning partnerships among students, parents, educators, business, industry and the wider community'. This is a radical departure from the 'fortress tradition' of many Australian secondary schools in the past and indicates that the shift in programme focus has implications for school structures and exerts pressure to dissolve boundaries between schools and their communities to enable learning to occur in a variety of settings including the workplace.

The seeds of such changes in senior secondary provision in Australia were sown in the early 1990s and found expression in the Finn, Mayer and Carmichael Reports (1991, 1992, 1992). These reports advocated reform of the compulsory years of schooling and the introduction of vocational initiatives. Early implementation occurred through the Australian Vocational Training System pilot project whereby small amounts of seed funding were made available to selected schools who wished to explore vocational provision for their students. This frequently took the form of trialing the delivery of TAFE modules with targeted groups of students and then negotiating 'advanced standing' for students who wished to enrol for TAFE courses upon completion of their schooling. Another initiative was the Key Competencies Project (1994–96), which sought to identify the extent to which generic competencies, which the Finn Report had identified as essential for young people in the workforce, were embedded in school curricula throughout Australia. The competencies were: collecting, analysing and organizing information; communicating ideas and information; planning and organizing activities; working with others and in teams; using mathematical ideas and techniques; solving problems and using technology. There was considerable debate about the merits of an eighth competency, cultural understanding, which was attributed different status in particular states and territories.

Despite these initiatives, in the years 1991 to 1996 the development of vocational initiatives in Australian schools was a relatively slow and piecemeal process. Policy and funding initiatives came mostly from the Commonwealth Government with the state and sectoral authorities cooperating to implement specific projects. These projects were limited in reach in that they only targeted limited numbers of schools and resulted in uneven provision across states and systems. They were complemented by local initiatives in some areas but these were dependent upon local leadership and support.

However, the last months of 1996 saw major changes in policy and funding. The newly elected Liberal Government placed vocational initiatives high on its educational agenda and devoted 56 million dollars of Commonwealth funding to promote school-based implementation for the years 1997 to 2000. Some state governments also made it a priority and devoted substantial funding to it for the first time. These factors contributed to a new wave of activity as states and sectors developed funding models and strategic plans to implement vocational programmes in their schools. Funding was utilized to assist schools to purchase delivery from TAFE colleges and industry providers, for professional development of teachers, for strategic and business planning at school and regional levels, for the development of industry partnerships, for provision in remote areas, and for the development of curriculum resources and quality assurance mechanisms.

One can argue thus that 1997 was the start of a new era. Policy and funding initiatives were coming from both levels of government. Local and regional partnerships between schools, TAFE colleges, group training companies, industries and employer groups were being forged with differing levels of success in various locations. The fact that the Commonwealth funding was only committed to the end of 2000 meant that schools and related organizations had to begin planning for sustainability from within school budgets beyond that time. This resulted in system authorities, such as the Catholic Education Commission of Victoria, urging its principals to begin regarding vocational programmes as part of their mainstream provision at senior secondary level, to diversify and rationalize programme offerings to ensure a range of post-school pathways, and to budget for vocational provision in the same way as they would for other curriculum areas. In the years 1997 and 1998 there was a 150 per cent increase in student enrolments in vocational programmes in Catholic secondary schools in Victoria.

It is important to note that school-based initiatives in vocational provision have been dependent upon the development of national frameworks such as the Australian Qualifications Framework and the National Training Framework. The latter is based upon identified workplace requirements and pays particular attention to the structured learnings and assessments required to achieve competencies in particular industries. This interface between schools and the workplace is reflected in a clause from a Victorian report which emphasizes that satisfactory completion of the vocational education and training (VET) units must be 'based on assessment of national industry competency standards using assessment criteria contained in nationally recognized qualifications and, where appropriate, state registered curriculum and training packages' (VCE Review, Clause 18, 1998).

The National Training Framework has also provided the structure for the development of a New Apprenticeship System in Australia since 1998. This is an entry level training programme leading to a nationally recognized qualification in a particular industry area through a combination of productive work and structured training which may be both on and off the job. It requires both the employer and the apprentice to enter into a registered training agreement with a State Training Authority. For the first time in 1998 school students were able to enter 'contracts' as part-time New Apprenticeships and combine senior secondary schooling with employment and training. This means that for the first time some school students are concurrently fulfilling two 'contracts' simultaneously: one with a school, another with an employer. The most common combination is for the student to spend approximately half the week at school, the other half in the workplace or off-the-job training. At the end of 1998, 1400 students had signed such agreements throughout Australia (MCEETYA Taskforce, 1999). Such arrangements again challenge secondary schools to become more open and flexible institutions and to enter into partnerships with local employers and other training providers.

Mount St Joseph's Girls College in the Melbourne suburb of Altona provides an illuminating case study of how the adoption of vocational initiatives can diversify senior school curricula. The school has an enrolment of 700 girls from Years Seven to Twelve and draws from working-class suburbs where a large proportion of the families come from non-English-speaking backgrounds. Until 1997 it offered a traditional academic curriculum for senior students and 60 to 70 per cent of these continued on to further education. In 1997 the College decided it needed to provide a broader range of pathways. Two years later over 150 of the senior students include vocational programmes in their school certificate programme. Courses are offered in Hospitality, Small Business Practice, Sports and Recreation, Information Technology, Multimedia, Music Industry Skills, and Laboratory Technology. The majority of these courses are conducted on the school site but there is a significant partnership with a nearby TAFE college and all students do extended periods of work placement in local industries. Some students are also combining school studies and part-time work with a fast food chain and the training they receive in the restaurant contributes towards their school certificate. Mount St. Joseph's is no longer a school behind walls. Its teaching and learning programmes encompass partnerships and dialogue with a broader environment. As such it exemplifies the learning from diverse environments and individual responsibility which are hallmarks of lifelong learning.

An important further development has been a growing recognition of the potential for vocational learning in the middle years of secondary schooling. This has been stimulated by a series of reports over the past two years, the most notable of which is entitled *Australia's Youth: Reality and Risk* (Dusseldorp 1998) which examines the increasingly marginalized position of 15- to 19-year-olds in the labour market. An outcome of these reports has been a belief that all students in the middle secondary years, regardless of their preferred immediate and post-school destinations, should be offered opportunities to engage in vocational learnings. It has been argued that such learnings should be linked to vocational programmes in the senior years and that student proficiencies achieved in Years Nine and Ten should be recognized in an appropriate manner. A draft policy is currently before state and Commonwealth ministers on this matter. It defines 'vocational learning' as the development of 'a general knowledge and understanding of the world of work, including the workplace and related further education and training'. It is seen to have the potential to 'extend and reinforce learning in the classroom and contribute to the development of particular skills and competencies'. Rather than being conceived as a specific programme, vocational learning is seen as a dimension of general education at these levels. It seeks to enrich the traditional curriculum through community-based programmes, school-industry partnerships, the development of competencies and enterprise skills, the encouragement of experiential learning in real life settings and the use of adult mentors other than teachers. A particular goal is to assist students to develop 'transition plans' for their movement from compulsory to post-compulsory levels of schooling. Such themes reiterate those put forward by advocates of lifelong learning and suggest a particular way in which schooling in the compulsory years can lay foundations for active learning across the lifespan.

The developments in vocational education in the past few years in Australia can therefore be seen as a dimension of an emerging consciousness about the need to develop broader and more flexible learning and teaching programmes which equip individuals for diverse life and lifelong learning pathways. These have been predominantly limited to learning for economic purposes to enhance the well-being of individuals and that of society in general. There has been limited attention paid to some other core themes of lifelong learning in the discourse but it is possible in some of the initiatives to see the potential for developing greater civic consciousness and participation.

It should be noted that, despite the amazing growth in school-to-work transition programmes, Australian provision still falls far short of the more coherent structures of nations like Germany, Norway and Sweden. Perhaps the key explanation for this is that federal structures can work against cohesion. The Commonwealth may initiate visionary programmes but their implementation still lies clearly within the jurisdictions of states, territories and sectors. Even at the Commonwealth level itself there are multiple agencies charged with developing policy and distributing funding for vocational initiatives. Such diffusion can result in contradictory agendas and accountabilities, and subsequent frustration for those charged with implementation. That is probably why the current Report to Ministers calls for a 'co-ordinated strategy'. Another dimension, which is under-developed in Australia at present, is the role of local government authorities in planning and implementation at appropriate levels. These issues will continue to be challenging in subsequent years.

Lifelong learning: further and higher education

Vocational and technical education

The Vocational Education and Training (VET) sector in Australia has been well placed to offer leadership in important aspects of lifelong learning. Adult students in Australian vocational education and training already comprise a high proportion of the total. Eighty per cent of all students undertaking vocational programmes are aged 20 or over; and 62 per cent are aged 25 or over. The average age of students undertaking personal enrichment programmes of one kind or another is 40.

VET institutions have long experience and have developed considerable expertise in working with local industry, business and commerce; they have learned to be responsive and efficient in identifying training needs for industry. Working with employers they have provided courses on the clear premise that people should be taught relevant and up-to-date knowledge and skills that will advance their workplace adaptability.

The concern of VET institutions that their courses should be skill acquisitive has provided a strong foundation for their leadership in opening up opportunities to their students. The staff of VET institutions are very much aware of the need to point the way forward from what they do for their students: they put in a great deal of work to ensure that the ethos of their courses and the culture of the college is consistent with lifelong learning, providing recognition of prior learning, new vocational opportunities, and increased knowledge of further pathways of personal development.

Sometimes these opportunities are constrained by the times at which students can get access to them: usually VET students, for example, work during the day and have to attend courses at night or at the weekend. To offset this many VET institutions try to take education to the community by offering access in many ways and at different times and places to suit the convenience and the needs of their students. VET institutions now bring their courses to people in all kinds of settings: at college, in the workplace, at the community centre and in the home, through television, work off-campus and on-site, during the evenings and weekends.

Many VET institutions are also doing all they can to provide for the interests of particular groups whose learning needs merit special consideration. Special entry provisions are made for single parents, students from non-English speaking backgrounds, women, Aboriginal students, physically disabled, mentally disabled and socially disadvantaged. Pastoral care is provided and guidance and counselling offered by specially appointed people. Such people also offer assistance in solving problems of transport for students both younger and older, looking to their security and safety and helping oversee their activities while their relatives or friends are occupied elsewhere in work or their own learning.

VET institutions have a vital role to play and a critical job to do in helping in providing leadership to members of the learning community, taking lifelong learning as a concept, a value and a set of opportunities to people from schools and other institutions and sectors, orienting them into the awareness of the ways in which they can augment and increase their skills, while at the same time helping them to gain high levels of self esteem.

Universities

Universities also have a strong part to play in promoting lifelong learning. The initiatives that universities can take in this enterprise spring from the nature and purpose of universities and their traditional role as educating institutions. Thus, an important contribution of universities to lifelong learning is the inculcation in their graduates of the attributes that both enable and encourage them to become lifelong learners. Philip Candy conducted a study (Candy 1994) which raised the question as to whether and if so how this was occurring. Universities such as RMIT University in Melbourne and the Australian Technology Network universities are working on the study of graduate attributes, which is linked to this. This would certainly appear to be one of the key areas in any discussion of the role of universities in providing for an introduction to and promoting lifelong learning.

But just as other educational providers are changing in response to changing social and economic circumstances, changes in conceptions of knowledge and styles and technologies of learning, so too universities are having to adapt to similar new challenges confronting them. In the case of the universities, the need for this kind of adaptability and flexibility are reinforced by two major factors—the globalization of knowledge and the move to mass higher education.

In the current context, the concern for extending the provision of lifelong learning opportunities offers a great opportunity to reassess the academic and professional beliefs, values and attitudes that have traditionally been embodied in the operations of universities in Australia. Many universities, particularly those that have been formed in the more recent past, are coming to the view that universities can no longer be seen as some people have traditionally represented them—as repositories of traditional knowledge, as elite institutions of learning. The benefits of university education, including the development of intellectual and personal maturity through university education, are best achieved, they argue, in the light of the principle of continuous learning. Universities must be flexible and creative in offering life-long learning opportunities from which all members of the community can derive benefit.

The Australian Vice-Chancellors' Committee (AVCC) has noted the burgeoning interest in lifelong learning but as yet has not formulated anything that might seem to commit them to this notion as a definitive policy. Universities are undertaking a number of activities conducive to lifelong learning. Universities are forming strategic alliances with partners in the business, industry and commerce sector, and in this way are increasing their provision of industry-specific training in areas such as engineering, computing and recruitment, as well as increasing their offerings of post-graduate and professional courses for professionals wishing to specialize or upgrade their skills. Some universities are also starting to form strategic alliances with VET institutions, which cover credit pathways, course development, joint research and staff development, and alliances with industry to provide pathways from education to employment. The AVCC and ANTA (the Australian National Training Authority) have jointly undertaken a study into the credit transfer and articulation implications of training packages which have been developed by government and industry to establish national competency standards, assessment guidelines and national qualifications.

One of the most important developments is that universities in several states have established or are starting to try to set up Learning Communities or Learning Cities, that integrate educational institutions, high technology industry, residential areas, commercial and retail services, accommodation and recreational facilities. Universities and state governments have also established community-based Learning Centres to improve access to education and training. These centres are located in universities, council buildings, schools, government offices, TAFE colleges and industrial sites of all kinds. This means that, as regards increasing the range of opportunities open to individuals and groups with various interests, the choices available to learners of beyond the school age have increased and proliferated with the establishment of learning centres, learning cities, improved distance education provision and increased on-line access to educational services.

The Commonwealth Government is very keen that as many people as possible have contact with and benefit from the higher education sector at some point in their lives—perhaps even at many points. But the question here is how are these contacts to be funded?

In the current context in Australia, there has been a diversification of the student population. This has led to a considerable broadening of emphases in the aims and activities of many institutions. This is reflected in the current agenda of the AVCC Committee on Students. But universities are increasingly looking into the demographic questions for lifelong learning students. For example, the school participation rates in Australia have now settled at around 72 to 73 per cent, yet both major political parties want to see significant increases in this figure—the Labor Party (ALP) to over 90 per cent. Clearly there are implications for higher education institutions (HEIs) here: if additional numbers of students move on from school to HEI study, the questions of costs, infrastructure and the rest will have to be addressed. What will be the costs of people returning to HEIs for further study; or of those people who 'missed out' first time coming to HEIs as mature-age students? And for such students, not needing access to other facilities available for younger undergraduate students on campus—union buildings, crèches, sports facilities and the like—the bulk of the increased funding will have to be devoted to the major cost items of teaching, library and other infrastructure resources, etc.

Some of these costs may be amortized. For example, in terms of resource implications for HEIs because of people returning several times to further study, it is worth noting that the government has deregulated the post-graduate market, in the main. While there is greater demand on institutional resources, HEIs can now charge post-graduate students fees which are not regulated (with the exception of minimum fees for overseas students).

For those returning to HEIs for further professional studies, however, the question is what kind of 'topping up' or additional study do they need? How many additional awards or credentials are going to suffice? Yet, given that, on some estimates, a large proportion of people in the workplace will need to go back and do professional up-grading work every five years or so—which, in a working lifetime of 30 or 40 years, could number some six to eight further periods of study—the questions of the frequency and duration of such courses and whether they must be award- or non-award-bearing, whether such courses are available by multi-media or distance study or have to involve face-to-face interaction such as supervised practica of various kinds, merit considerable further reflection. For here too the questions of the provision of the available resources and the optimizing of access, participation and success rates become very pressing, when HEIs are already facing additional demand from first-time students of all ages.

But this is only to raise one set of issues—those relating to resources, provision and funding. There are also major questions of principle to be tackled. Within and across institutions there is now a philosophical divide and this has led to a situation where institutions have not moved uniformly or quickly to develop their own policies for lifelong learning. This divide is seen in the differences between the missions of some institutions to be comprehensive and in others to be research intensive. Another difference is in the clear commitment of some institutions to the notion of the provision of educational opportunity as a definite public good, whereas other institutions see themselves as leading, or making offerings to, a consumer/client market, in which people pick and choose from the offerings provided, to develop their interests and career paths—very much as some kind of supermarket of knowledge. For some institutions it could be argued that the rhetoric of lifelong learning provides them with a soft human face to cover the reality of what would otherwise be the more crass features of marketing according to clients' needs and wishes. This is set against the role some other institutions set for themselves—that of giving leadership in providing learning, culture and values to the wide community which is their host.

In this last model, however—the role of institutions (and/or the individuals in them) seeing themselves as some kind of public intellectual—there is some danger of paternalism if not of arrogance. For in these days so much knowledge is now being discovered, developed and promulgated outside the formal settings of tertiary institutions and on the part of commercial, research or communication media undertakings of all kinds. This leaves the vital question to be asked: what is the role of universities in these times of lifelong learning provision, where 'a hundred flowers bloom and a hundred schools of thought contend'? It is true that many universities are now developing partnerships with professional associations, and the business, commerce and industry sector. But, in the case of the most sophisticated of these agencies and instrumentalities, some of which are international in character and remit, the question about the ability of the university to be a competitor is increasingly being raised.

One way in which universities could be more proactive in lifelong learning provision is by extending their schemes of community outreach, of taking lifelong education programmes out to the community. Some universities institute and strongly support such initiatives. There are of course some questions to be addressed: how are such initiatives to be funded and resourced? In the case of the enhancement approaches, one generally finds that there is a willingness on the part of students to make some payment. In the case of the professional programmes that are now being offered in the workplace, employers are paying or individuals are paying.

Thus many universities feel that, provided there can be some scheme in place whereby there is some willingness on the part of the community, the individual or the employer, to make a contribution to having such initiatives adequately resourced, then the provision of such outreach undertakings is part of their mission.

It is here where use of the new technologies will play a key role in assisting an appropriate level of resources and materials to be made available to interested groups and target audiences. There will be increasing use of the Internet as online services grow in universities. It is already used for overseas delivery; many universities connect to their external students through learning centres to the home. Lecturers, instead of having to go out to distant locations each week, can appear on a large screen, or talk to the students in a computer tutorial and in these ways costs associated with general provision can be reduced. Also, in linking into the Internet, the government has invested 29 million dollars in the establishment of OLA (Open Learning Australia—a consortium of universities providing undergraduate and post-graduate education by distance and offering single subject bachelor's degrees and a range of post-graduate qualifications); while OLA student numbers have never been very large, it is an important vehicle for life-long learning in a range of ways. The government is also assisting in promoting on-line flexible delivery systems such as those being developed by Charles Sturt University and the University of Southern Queensland. There are also Telecentre Networks developing to improve access to learning (such as the Queensland Learning Network). All this is being helped by the Commonwealth Department of Communications, Information Technology and the Arts.

The new technologies have made all these forms of the delivery of learning-teaching packages and other kinds of interaction much more possible. As new technologies become ubiquitous, teaching and learning and lifelong learning will increasingly use these technologies and the importance of such developments in facilitating and making it possible for all kinds of people to add further increments to their learning cannot be over-stated.

What is crucial in all this is that institutions cooperate with each other. This is not only crucial in respect to the problems of reducing costs, securing appropriate accreditation and cross-crediting arrangements, and in providing appropriately qualified staff. It is also a normative feature of and an imperative for the productivity of such partnerships operating at this level in education that there be a sense of equality and equal commitment to the educational purposes of such enterprises. For example, a vitally important part of lifelong learning is the involvement and engagement of universities and VET institutions in local and regional business and industry, identifying needs, meeting those learning needs, promoting learning, and cooperating with each other and employers in making further and more advanced forms of education, training and qualification possible. Thus the more that VET staff and university staff work together, the greater the likelihood of the development of a willingness to agree that certain materials could count in the others' courses.

This is more likely to be achieved if there can be a sense of contribution, ownership and monitoring by the crediting institution, and jointly supportive and mutually complementary arrangements for delivery. It is vital that universities have confidence about the work being carried out in the schools. The one question here is that of teachers and lecturers being able to have an involvement, to play a part in the kind of programmes, where this cross-boundary and cross-institutional course linkage is occurring, on the part of all parties. Such partnerships will only prosper and flourish when there is more of an involvement and more interaction between the staff, and the students and staff, across their different institutional boundaries. Then we may hope to see greater progress in providing a wider range of articulated pathways in which all institutions in partnership can achieve better outcomes for their students.

It is, however, going to be very hard to achieve the full potential such partnerships have, unless there is genuine movement in—possibly even some levelling of—the boundaries between institutions, together with an emphasis on securing a sense of involvement and a real sense of ownership by all the parties involved. That is what real partnership in promoting lifelong learning for all requires and entails—and it is to building such real partnerships that all such institutions must now turn, if the aims of lifelong learning for all are to be realized.

Lifelong learning: adult and community education and education for seniors

Adult and community education

The notion of partnership has been particularly important in the provision of lifelong learning in the adult and community education sector. In 1993 the Ministerial Council on Employment, Education, Training and Youth Affairs endorsed a national policy on Adult and Community Education (ACE). The policy had six main objectives: to realize the potential of ACE, to achieve access and equity, to provide diverse opportunities and outcomes for lifelong learning, to provide learning pathways and to ensure quality, and to strengthen partnerships of community with government, industry and other educational sectors (*Developing Adult and Community Education in the ACT* 1996, pp. 18–19). The Council itself is an advisory body to Commonwealth and state ministers and it did not necessarily lead to a binding national policy or co-ordination of adult and community education throughout Australia. Adult and community education has continued to be very much within the jurisdiction of state and territory authorities and its shape therefore varies considerably throughout the country. One of the leading commentators on lifelong learning in Australia has noted this lack of coordination describing it as a 'fragmented part of the educational domain' where much of the learning is hidden and difficult to quantify because of the voluntary nature of much of the activity (Candy and Crebert 1997, p. 79).

However, two peak bodies are promoting the development of a more cohesive approach. The Australian Association of Adult and Community Education, recently renamed Adult Learning Australia, developed a policy statement in 1997 that all states and jurisdictions are now using as a reporting framework. The first report will be published later in 1999. A ministerial taskforce is coordinating this effort. Key players from each of the states meet regularly through this taskforce and are becoming increasingly involved in developing consistent policy and practice throughout the nation. They play a particularly important advisory role to the Australian National Training Authority and promote activities such as Adult Learners Week.

The fact that adult and community education is largely a state responsibility and that the Commonwealth has not initiated major policy and funding interventions on the same scale as in the vocational field means that patterns of provision are uneven throughout the nation. Some Commonwealth funding has been made available in recent years through the Australian National Training Authority but this is limited. Two factors seem to be central to the strength of provision in individual states and territories: the extent of the commitment of particular governments and the vitality of community organizations that sponsor adult learning. The former determines the funding available for the field and, in this respect, New South Wales and Victoria are the best resourced. The latter influences the shape of the provision and its vigour and robust condition in the Australian Capital Territory reflects the strength of such organizations in that location.

Victoria promulgated its Adult, Community and Further Education Act in 1991 and in 1999 has devoted over 39 million dollars to such endeavours. As early as 1995 references to a multi-dimensional concept of lifelong learning appeared in the Annual Report to the Victorian Department of Education (Candy and Crebert 1997, p. 83). In 1997 the Victorian Adult, Community and Further Education Board published a curriculum policy explicitly informed by concepts of lifelong learning. The goals it articulated reflected the influence of the Delors Report (Delors 1996) in that they went beyond a vocational agenda to incorporate 'all aspects of living meaningfully in today's world' by incorporating 'understanding, knowledge, ethics as well as observable behavior, skills and performance' (*Transforming Lives, Transforming Communities* 1997, p. 11). The goals in turn reflected a number of recurrent themes, which were summarized as multiplicity, connectedness, critical intelligence and transformation. The document is inspiring in its recognition that adult learners are in a process of personal transformation and that this has a flow-on effect to their interpersonal relationships and to the multiple communities in which they move. As such it has influenced subsequent documents throughout the country, particularly the national statement of the peak body.

The following year (1998) the same Board published a vision statement *Taking ACE To The Year 2000*. In Victoria, the ACE Board administers funds and develops plans and policies through a network of nine regional councils. As such the sector is composed of community-owned and managed adult education agencies. It comprises general adult education, adult literacy and basic education, access and preparatory education, the senior school certificate for adults, English as a second language, and vocational programmes delivered within the ACE sector. The published vision statement reflects a conception of lifelong education as community based and civically inspired: 'Lifelong learning opportunities in Adult and Community Education generate educated, empowered citizens, and a stronger Victorian community.'

The subsequent mission statement also recognizes the multiple roles individuals play within the community by seeking to develop their potential as 'individuals, citizens and workers'. (*Taking ACE To The Year 2000*, p. 3). In 1997–98 over 500 community-based providers conducted programmes for 9 per cent of the Victorian population. Significantly more women than men participated in these activities (Adult, Community and Further Education Board, *Annual Report* 1997–98, p. 3).

The Australian Capital Territory also developed legislation for the field of adult and community education in 1995 and published a major discussion paper the following year. Like the Victorian documents it places a strong emphasis upon community agencies.

However, the rhetoric about democratic citizenship is more pronounced in the ACT paper and suggests that a different local context has resulted in a somewhat different policy framework. There is a strong emphasis upon linking funding to the achievement of participation targets which 'reflect the demographic profiles and needs of communities' (*Developing Adult and Community Education in the ACT* 1996, p. 6). The administrative structures are also different from those in Victoria. The Vocational Education and Training Authority is responsible for ACE in the ACT and the training discourse of the vocational sector is more evident in its documents. Nevertheless, the policy document which was released in 1997 emphasizes 'maximising lifelong learning opportunities' as its first goal and elaborates upon this point by stating 'the Government believes that all adults, regardless of background and circumstance, should have access to a range of diverse and affordable learning opportunities to meet their needs to become lifelong learners and help them participate fully in society' (*ACT Policy on Adult and Community Education* 1997).

The scale of the provision is also very different in the ACT. A recent press release indicates funding of $244,000 for 1999 to be distributed amongst 28 community-based providers who will deliver programmes to over 1200 students. A review of the actual programmes also reveals different emphases, with particular initiatives for indigenous and older age groups.

Not all states and territories have legislative provision for adult and community education. In such cases ACE most frequently comes under the jurisdiction of vocational legislation and agencies. In Queensland this is the VET division and similar arrangements exist in Tasmania and the Northern Territory. South Australia has recently created an Adult Community Education Council. Its *Strategic Plan* for 1998–89 also emphasizes the community basis of the provision but with a stronger emphasis upon issues of access and equity than that evident in documents from other jurisdictions. It is made explicit that the 'ACE Council has a specific brief to improve access to education and training for disadvantaged members of the community'. Particular target groups include the unemployed, indigenous populations, those with physical and intellectual disabilities, those with limited literacy and numeracy skills, those from non-English speaking backgrounds, the geographically and socially isolated, and the socioeconomically disadvantaged (South Australian Adult Community Education Council *Strategic Plan* 1998–99, p. 5).

In 1997, 87 organizations delivered over 130 non-accredited programmes in South Australia. Sixty-one per cent of the students enrolled through the Workers' Educational Association of South Australia and this possibly reflects the heritage of craft and worker guilds in that state. It is therefore not surprising to note that the rhetoric from the training sector is more pronounced in the South Australian documentation than elsewhere. The *Strategic Plan* voices an 'acute awareness' of the need 'for people to be able to re-skill for multiple career changes throughout life'.

In Tasmania an Institute of Adult Education has been established within the Office of Vocational Education and Training. The structural arrangements mean that these state vocational aspects are the main focus, although there are some community house programmes funded from State resources. However, in reality most of the provision of ACE in Tasmania is through TAFE Tasmania. There is a strong emphasis upon accredited training, especially in information technology.

Extended lifelong learning for adults in the latter years

One of the institutions that has done a great deal to develop and deliver a range of learning activities for seniors in the community has been the University of the Third Age, branches of which are now in existence and flourishing widely across Australia. Councils of Adult Education and other agencies are active in offering similar opportunities in seniors' centres and retirement villages. No one who has seen the enthusiasm exhibited by seniors and their readiness for hard work, often at the most demanding and sophisticated levels of operation, in subjects such as advanced mathematics, philosophy and literature, can be in any doubt as to the major difference that engagement in such work can make to the quality of people's lives and their enhanced sense of personal autonomy, dignity and worth. Such enhancement is the stuff of all learning and educational endeavour—for the welfare of individuals and the communities in which they live.

Seniors find that access to new pursuits and pastimes increases substantially their quality of life. Such people then become additional resources for the community's cultural and educational milieux and for its commercial undertakings; employers have seen the benefits of drawing on the knowledge, skills and mature judgment such people offer them and using them to support their firms' endeavours. Once people see that their wisdom and further learning is valued, they increase their enjoyment in advancing their intellectual horizons and developing their interests by enthusiastically engaging in further learning of this kind.

The International Year of the Older Person Project presents lifelong learning policy-makers in Australia with issues of an ageing population in Australia, and the ways in which their continuing learning needs and interests can be met. Currently Commonwealth government research is under way in three areas: barriers to training for older workers (those between 45 and 65); mentoring, in which older people are used as mentors for children in schools to enhance student learning; and Universities of the Third Age coming 'on-line'.

Conclusion: issues to be resolved in the provision of learning across the lifespan

Financing

The question must now be raised as to the approaches that might be best adopted towards the funding of lifelong learning initiatives across all sectors and levels of provision. Indeed it has already been raised at government level by the OECD in a request addressed to all its member countries seeking information on recent developments in the financing of lifelong learning.

There will also be many employers who will argue that they are already playing a key role in funding or providing opportunities for lifelong learning, both formal and informal. The question to be asked of them, however, is whether they are doing enough in this regard.

There is evidence to suggest that individuals' participation in lifelong learning, both formal and informal, declines rapidly after the age of 30. Some might ask, therefore, what is the point of providing further opportunities after that point? The problem here is that only those people in work and to a considerable extent already enjoying the fruits of education are participating in lifelong learning. This raises the question: what are the appropriate levels that employees need in their thirties to give them continuing employability in their forties and fifties? And what of those people not participating in education at all: what can/should be done about the unemployed and under-employed and the still under-educated who are not participating at all?

Achieving coherence

In the evolution of policies and programmes for lifelong learning, certainly at the 'official level', these are early days for Australia, though a number of interesting and important developments are occurring. There is in fact a great deal going on in the way of promoting, developing and assisting the expansion of opportunities for, and programmes of, lifelong learning, both from an official government point of view, from that of the business, industry and commercial sectors, from the standpoint of the education service, and from community initiatives generally. However, to date, advances have been taking place piecemeal and on a number of different fronts and it would be right to say that there has been no single, unitary, coherent, and across the board policy in place. There is no over-arching framework, no comprehensive and overall policy. What we have, rather, is a set of fairly pragmatic approaches and advances on a number of fronts. Nevertheless, what is clearly the case is that many agencies, official and unofficial, formal and informal, convertional and alternative, are not only addressing issues in the area of lifelong learning, but are actually getting many things done.

In particular, through a variety of initiatives the Commonwealth government is currently doing much to build sound foundations for lifelong learning. For example, it is seeking to lay such bases by encouraging the development of increased and augmented credit transfer and articulation arrangements and has set up an Australian Qualifications Framework which provides a comprehensive, nationally consistent yet flexible framework for all qualifications in post-compulsory education and training. Further, secondary teachers, schools and some academics are very much working together in many places to enhance such developments and goals. There are also important developments in University-Industry linkages, increasing. R&D in this area, and in funding Chairs of Information Technology. EDNA (Education Network Australia) is supported by all sectors and stake-holders. Some Universities offer programmes in this way. The University of Queensland, for example, has booklets showing courses and opportunities in professional fields of study and these are listed on the appropriate web sites.

Indeed the DETYA *Corporate Plan* has identified lifelong learning as one of the Minister's strategic priorities. In state governments (such as Tasmania and Victoria) lifelong learning is part of state government policy, with a concern to develop the requisite skills and predispositions for engaging in lifelong learning throughout the lifespan. Governments are keen to see social divisions eliminated or at any rate diminished by lifelong learning schemes, programmes and courses. An emphasis on Healthy Ageing is one way of doing this: helping people stay as active citizens, social participants, and personal growers. The Commonwealth government is undertaking research on issues pertaining to groups that might be missing out on lifelong learning opportunities. They have several study projects relating to issues on 'Youth Falling through the Cracks', the performance of indigenous students, issues of learning advance as between boys and girls, the learning needs of people and groups of non-English speaking background, rural dwellers, and so on. Funds for lifelong learning initiatives are also being provided through social income-support systems of various kinds. Youth Allowances, for example, now permit young people (for good reason) to drop in and out of study and come back again as and when they feel able. Similarly, government funded programmes for homelessness; youth suicide; job placement; employment for education and training—are all further examples of such social support schemes.

Research and policy development

What is now needed is to add a research dimension to all these activities and initiatives. A number of topics need to be tackled urgently: soundly-based research work is needed on topics such as the realities and options for government in providing lifelong learning; demographic and sociological factors influencing participation in Education and Training; the econometric factors influencing provision of entry-level training by employers; the factors influencing employers' provision of continuing education and training; the informal factors influencing lifelong learning, and education and training in the work-place.

All the above considerations and a thorough-going programme of research and development could contribute to the articulation, development and institution of policies for lifelong learning. Perhaps one of the chief of these is: How will all this feed into the growth of the 'knowledge economy' and the 'learning society' where for a long time still there will continue to be non-expert jobs and lower-level skills? The changing nature of the job market, both now and into the future, will increasingly require much better and higher levels of education and training than now, especially when there are the obvious facts of an ageing population and increasing unemployment to be added into and to complicate all our thinking, policy-making and community educational endeavour, if we are all to benefit from the opportunities of and requirements for learning throughout life.

The development of our nation

One thing needs to be made clear in all this. In Australia there is an increasing awareness of the obligation for educators and policy-makers to take into account the social dimension of the need for learning across the lifespan. Australians are extremely conscious of the need for social cohesion, and the imperative of trying to diminish the socially dysfunctional gap between the haves and the have-nots. The impetus here can perhaps begin with our attention to the education and training needs of the young unemployed and the needs of older workers.

But of course it must go much further than this, extending to the need for social inclusion and democratic participation for all. There is a strong need for engagement on the part of every member of our polity and community in programmes of civics and citizenship education, and education for democracy. This is especially critical in a time in which we shall all be required to reconsider the optimum form for our constitutional and political arrangements in our consideration of the case for a republic.

In this and in many other initiatives currently underway or being developed in Australia there are clear opportunities for learning across the lifespan: our commitment to democracy, tolerance, justice, equity and 'a fair go' for all demands nothing less of us. It is heartening to reflect that many of the conditions for this kind of engagement are already in place or are now being established by the various initiatives, schemes and programmes of lifelong learning currently to be found in Australia.

Note

This chapter extends consideration of some themes identified in our book *The School, the Community and Lifelong Learning* (London: Cassell 1998), with particular reference to the Australian context.

References

Australian Bureau of Statistics (1996) *Australian Social Trends 1996* ABS Catalogue No. 4102.0 Canberra, Australian Bureau of Statistics

Australia's Common and Agreed National Goals for Schooling in the Twenty-First Century, Commonwealth amendments using Victorian redraft, January 1999. Canberra: Australian Government Publishing Service (AGPS)

Ball, C. (1994) Summation of the Conference at the Conclusion of the *First Global Conference on 'Lifelong Learning'*. Rome

Candy, P. J. (1994) *Developing Lifelong Learners through Undergraduate Education* National Board of Employment, Education and Training. Canberra: AGPS

Candy, P. J. and Crebert, R. J. (1997) 'Australia's Progress Towards Lifelong Learning, in *Comparative Studies on Lifelong Learning Policies* Report of a NIER/UIE Joint Research Project, edited by National Institute for Educational Research of Japan and UNESCO Institute for Education, Tokyo, Babel International

Carmichael, L. (1992) *The Australian Vocational Certificate Training System* Report to the National Board for Employment Education and Training of the Committee chaired by Mr Laurie Carmichael, Canberra: AGPS

Chapman, J. D. and Aspin, D. N. (1997) *The School, the Community and Lifelong Learning* London: Cassell

Collard, J. L. (1998) *School-Industry Programs in Norway and Sweden* A research report to the Australian Student Traineeship Foundation, Sydney, Australian Student Traineeship Foundation

Dusseldorp, J. (1998) Address to the Annual Conference of the Victorian Association of Secondary School Principals, 18 August

Delors, J. (Ed.) (1996) *Learning: The Treasure Within* Report to UNESCO, General Conference, Paris: UNESCO

Finn, B. (1991) *Young People's Participation in Post-Compulsory Education and Training* Report of the Australian Education Council Review Committee (Chair Mr Brian Finn) Canberra: AGPS July

Mayer, E. (1992) *Employment-related Key Competences: A Proposal for Consultation* Report of the Mayer Committee, Melbourne 1992; Canberra: AGPS

MCEETYA Taskforce on Vocational Education and Training (VET) in Schools (1998) *Vocational Learning for Students in Years 9 & 10* Discussion Paper, September 1998. (1999) Progress Report to CESCEO. March 1999

OECD (1994) *Jobs Study: Facts, Analysis, Strategies* Paris: OECD

OECD (1996) *Lifelong Learning for All* Meeting of the Education Committee at the Ministerial Meeting, 16–17 January. Paris: OECD

Peters, R. S. (1965) 'Education as Initiation' in Archambault, R. D. (Ed.) *Philosophical Analysis and Education* London: Routledge & Kegan Paul

Spring, G. (1998) *Education for the 21st Century; A South Australian Perspective* Keynote Address to Forum of South Australian Education Leaders, Flinders University, 17 November

Teese, R. and Polesel, J. (1998) *VET In Schools; A Study of Post-School Destinations* Education Outcomes Research Unit, University of Melbourne

White, J. P. (1982) *The Aims of Education Re-Stated* London: Routledge

Wooden, M. (1998) The Labour Market for Young Australians in *Australia's Youth: Reality and Risk* Dusseldorp Skills Forum (A revised version of an earlier paper Learning and Work: The Situation of Young Australians, In *Learning and Work: The Situation of Young Australians* Parliament House Forum, Canberra, 11 November 1997)

15 Lifelong learning

A North American perspective

Robin Barrow and Patrick Keeney

As every schoolboy knows, North America is a continent comprising three major countries—Canada, the United States, and Mexico, three major language groups—English, French, and Spanish, and a myriad of regional ethnicities, religions, cultural traditions and races. Additionally, in Canada and the US, the constitutional division of powers cedes authority over education to provincial and state legislatures. Unsurprisingly, provinces and states tend to guard their jurisdiction tenaciously, thereby frustrating the ability of Ottawa or Washington to form coherent educational policies at the national level. Add to this a population which is increasingly litigious when it comes to educational matters, coupled with a judiciary which is more and more willing to intrude into matters of education and schooling, and we have an intricate set of circumstances which defies any simple generalizations about North American educational issues. It also somewhat confounds commentators who seek to address national or international educational trends in North America.

Yet, as in other parts of the world, the slogan 'lifelong learning' has gained prominence in North American educational rhetoric in recent years, usurping such phrases as 'adult education' or 'continuing education'. And while Israel Scheffler long ago warned against taking educational slogans literally, he did remind us that they nevertheless serve a function: they act as rallying-cries, as devices for drawing our attention to some significant feature (or features) of the educational engagement which has either been overlooked or underplayed, and so needs to be emphasized and stressed (Scheffler 1960, 40–6). How, then, does the rhetoric surrounding 'lifelong learning' function in the North American context? What are the social, political, and educational circumstances surrounding this emphasis on 'lifelong learning'? In what follows, we examine two major aspects of the lifelong learning phenomenon.

The first is straightforwardly economic. A variety of economic trends and indicators suggest why 'lifelong learning' is the motto of choice for business and industry, and why a great deal of the current emphasis on lifelong learning can be directly attributed to a certain economic nervousness in both government and industry. Given the rapid pace of technological change, the new information age and the globalization of trade, how can we be assured that we are producing competent and qualified workers who are prepared to meet the reality of a new economic order? In this context, the cries for lifelong learning are the contemporary version of the ever-present demand for schools and post-secondary institutions to produce more efficient, better trained, and more highly skilled workers. As we argue below, lifelong learning can be an enormously helpful and liberating slogan, provided that we mean by it something more than mere skill-based training sessions. Yet despite the normative and soothing overtones which the phrase evokes, it too frequently masks an unacknowledged and less reputable ideology: namely a newly sophisticated industrial utilitarianism in which 'practical' and 'relevant' skills are emphasized at the expense of broader sorts of understanding typified by a liberal education. We argue that educational policy-makers need to keep their eye on the educational prize and avoid short-sighted attempts to substitute narrow and technicist abilities for educational aims.

In the second part of the paper we turn to what is arguably a more authentically North American sense of the phrase, for, in many ways, lifelong learning is the American motto par excellence. V.S. Pritchett, on travelling in America, commented:

> My opinion is that there is a deep, even defensive dislike of definition among Americans because it would limit and work against the American sense of possibility and becoming. It is profoundly part of the energetic and moralistic American tradition that a man may, indeed must, become something else and that he not only has the right but must have the resilience necessary to the heartrending pursuit of life, liberty and happiness.
>
> (Pritchett 1990, 205)

To speak of lifelong learning in a North American context is to some extent to evoke that 'energetic and moralistic' tradition of which Pritchett writes. Indeed, it might plausibly be argued that the intellectual habits of North America are, in some sense, a continuous, on-going and radical exercise in remaking oneself. Americans—and to a lesser extent those who exist within the umbrella of the American imperium—see the creation of the self as an ethical enterprise of the highest order, such that the idea of lifelong learning is more than merely an opportunity for training and job advancement. Rather, 'lifelong learning' is construed primarily as an egocentric enterprise, all learning being ultimately 'learning about oneself'.

The economic imperative

The increased complexity of the workplace poses considerable challenges to educational policy-makers. The globalization of trade, technological advances and intensifying international competition for markets mean greater uncertainty in the job market. Given the dynamism and unpredictability of the new economic reality, students, parents, employers and governments alike are increasingly demanding courses and programmes which translate into readily marketable skills and training. For example, in 1995 British Columbia launched the 'Skills Now' initiative, which takes as its slogan 'Real skills for the real world'. Its emphasis is on technology and practical training, aiming to ensure that British Columbians 'get the new skills for the new jobs in our changing economy' (B.C. Ministry of Education 1995). Similar initiatives can be found throughout the industrialized world. Thus, there seems to be a widely held, if seldom well articulated view, that, due to the shift in our economic base, colleges, universities and post-secondary institutions need to become more practically oriented and 'relevant' to the needs of both the economy and students. By and large, the tendency is to make educational institutions more responsive to the demands of today's marketplace, by emphasizing practical skills and abilities, while correspondingly devaluing understandings and abilities which seemingly have no immediate or obvious application.

However, it is not as easy as it might first appear to state categorically what is or isn't relevant or practical. While no one would argue for educational 'irrelevance' or 'impracticality', reasonable people can and do hold radically different ideas of what constitutes practicality and relevance in any given endeavour. So while we might agree that students should be adequately prepared for employment in their chosen field by taking courses which are relevant and practical, we still need to fill out what we understand by these terms. Furthermore, we need to be cautious about placing too much emphasis on the practical and relevant, even when we agree on instances of either.

It may prove very short-sighted to focus on skills and practical training at the expense of broader and deeper sorts of understanding which allow students to think for themselves and hence become 'life-long learners' in a wider sense. When both technical expertise and adaptability on the part of workers are the order of the day, the challenge is to graduate students who are also able to appreciate the underlying concepts and principles in their chosen field; who are capable of making connections, detecting patterns, and analysing emerging trends; who can speak and write with accuracy and precision; who are, in a word, educated.

In short, what are most needed in this rapidly evolving economy are precisely intellectual abilities that do not have an obvious or immediate utility; what is required is not so much technical know-how, as those various qualities of mind which we subsume under the label of understanding. We should be seeking to develop in students conceptual understandings which revolve around the ability to think critically, creatively and with analytical acumen. Educated workers provide the key to adding value to the economy. If vocational programmes are to meet the challenges of the global economy, then they need more emphasis on their educative, as opposed to their training, component.

In order to consolidate and advance this view, we shall expand on the following four claims:

1   Time and again, the message that business and industry sends to post-secondary institutions is that they are interested in something more than narrowly focused, if highly trained, graduates.
2   From the vantage point of cost effectiveness, it makes little sense to use valuable institutional resources to teach competencies and abilities which are best learned either on the job, or by students on their own.
3   Institutions have a moral responsibility to ensure that students possess something more than skills which grow obsolete as technology advances.
4   Comparing and contrasting 'training' with 'education' brings out the critical need for vocational programmes to emphasize the latter.

From training to education

What does industry want?

It is one of the great ironies of our age that at the same time as industry has come to understand the futility of trying to retool the educational system to meet the perceived needs of the business community, governments are increasingly directing our institutions to provide students with practical, 'hands-on' skills. So while there is a growing consensus among business leaders that business should not try to co-opt the education system into teaching business-specific skills, government increasingly focuses on ensuring that technical ability and know-how remain uppermost on the educational agenda. As the former Chairman of the Bank of Montreal, Matthew Barrett, recently observed, 'A student who can divine the patterns of imagery in Chaucer's Canterbury Tales can surely be taught the principles of double-entry accounting' (Galt 1996, A13), implying that the former, while being more educationally worthwhile, is also of greater utility.

If Barrett is right, as we believe he is, then we need to rethink the current emphasis on skills and training, particularly in those programmes which require from our students considerable commitments of time. Of course, no one disputes that there will always be a need for short-term programmes which aim at training students for specific skills and trades. There is a continuous need for cooks, mechanics, hairdressers, carpenters, plumbers, and so forth, and, by and large, our institutions do an admirable job of preparing individuals for the trades.

But while trades programs will doubtless continue to be a staple offering of our vocational institutions, they will surely become increasingly de-emphasized as we see a decline in resource-based industries and a move to service and information-based industries. As the B.C. Ministry of Education suggests, 'Projections for new and replacement jobs over the next ten years show a general increase in education and training requirements' (B.C. Ministry of Education 1995). In America, the Hudson Institute, in a report to the US Department of Labour, reported that 'between now and the year 2000, for the first time in history, a majority of all new jobs will require post-secondary education'. The report further states that 'technology will introduce change and turbulence into every industry and every job. In particular, the necessity for constant learning and constant adaptation by workers will be a certain outgrowth of technological innovation' (Johnston *et al.* 1987, xxvii). In short, if workers are to keep pace in their chosen field (let alone advance in their profession), they will need to be flexible, lifelong learners.

Similarly, business repeatedly states that what it is most in need of are graduates who have strong, analytic interpersonal and communication abilities. It recognizes that graduates from our colleges and universities are often highly competent technically, but narrowly focused and equipped with skills which may not be relevant to their specific environment.

Study after study has shown that those who excel in the business world are not those who are narrow and specialized, but those who are adaptable, flexible and able to master new information. The complexity of the marketplace demands that students become adept at analytic reasoning, critical thinking and problem-solving, which will enable them to acquire both further understanding and new skills.

> In the information age ... flexibility will be the critical foundation of success. Future generations will need more than just mastery of subject matter, but mastery of learning. Education will not be just a prelude for a career, but a lifelong endeavor. Some of the important elements that will promote this new paradigm for lifelong learning are: (1) the development of conceptual skills, and the ability to test reality against multiple points of view; (2) the nourishment of individual creativity and the encouragement of exploration; (3) the encouragement of collaboration, and an emphasis on clear communication.
>
> (Sculley, 1988)

Thus, it is the view of the business community itself that 'schools and universities should teach students how to think, and inculcate in them a love of learning', rather than equip them with specific practical skills.

Instructional and institutional resources

It makes little sense to spend valuable and expensive instructional time teaching those skills and abilities which students can either pick up themselves, or which are best learned on the job. For example, keyboarding skills, essential as they are to computer literacy, are easily mastered by students on their own. They require only time and practice, and not the costly overhead of institutions and the waste of faculty expertise.

Furthermore, if we understand that the specific skills needed for particular business environments are constantly changing, then surely we must concede that it is business and industry—rather than colleges and universities—which are best placed to provide the customized training needed. Business and industry must take more responsibility for imparting those skills and abilities which are specific to a particular working environment. After all, they are in the best position to know exactly what their needs are, and the precise sorts of skill they require of their employees.

There is a natural division of labour here, one which has too often been overlooked. Industry must realize that, given the realities of teaching institutions and the necessary bureaucratization of higher education, schools cannot shift gears overnight to accommodate the perceived needs of the business community. (One study concludes that in the 3 to 4 years it typically takes for a college to respond to a perceived economic challenge, the challenge has passed, and the college is stuck with a curriculum which is every bit as irrelevant as that which it started with (Spring 1989)). For their part, colleges and post-secondary institutions should cease to promise the sun and moon and take honest stock of what can and cannot be well accomplished by an educational institution. What colleges can ensure is that they produce flexible and adaptable graduates, individuals who are able to thrive and prosper in various environments, and who can readily adapt to the changes which will confront them throughout their careers. The employer should be responsible for imparting the specific skills required in a particular working environment.

Our responsibility to students

Institutions have a moral responsibility to ensure that their students possess something more than skills which grow obsolete as technology advances. Skills per se are remarkably unstable commodities on the job market. One need only remember the siren calls for 'keypunch operators' in the 1970s, and the great promise of a secure career to those who were enticed into this particular field. Technology advanced, and it turns out that keypunch operators are now as redundant as buggy-whip manufacturers.

If we are serious about preparing our students for the future, then we must look to their education—a concept which implies that we are concerned with something more than a narrowly defined set of skills. It suggests as well that we concern ourselves with the whole person and not just their viability as a commodity on the job market. This means that if instructors (in every field) understand themselves as educators first and foremost, and not merely as providers of a service, then a certain sort of moral contract with our students emerges. Here is not the place to pursue this line of thought; suffice to point out that the relationship which holds between educators and their students is qualitatively different than that between 'service-providers' and 'clients'. The metaphors we use to conceptualize our task are crucial, and we must keep on constant guard against those metaphors which—however apt they may be for the business world—can only be imported into the educational setting at the cost of doing both our students and our institutions a grave disservice. To think of students as 'clients', or to conceive of our institutions as 'service providers', distorts and undermines the educative dimension of the task at hand.

Education vs. training

As we have indicated, the distinction between education and training is crucial. Education is about developing the mind, which is to say developing intellectual knowledge and understandings. Training, on the other hand, is about developing contextually-bound skills. Let us illustrate this distinction with an example drawn from teacher education.

Faculties of education are given a mandate to prepare students for the professional responsibilities of classroom teachers in state schools. One of the perennial problems facing faculties of education is deciding on what, exactly, this means. Should we prepare our students to teach the currently prescribed local curriculum? Or should we ensure that they are equipped with those understandings which will enable them to perform competently in whatever jurisdiction they work? In British Columbia, this question was brought forcibly home to faculties of education during the time of Year 2000, a provincial initiative which promised radical changes to the way in which public education was to be delivered. The pressure was applied to faculties of education to 'train' teachers to be adept at the new Year 2000 teaching techniques and teaching methods, all of which were said to be child-centered. But Year 2000 is no more, and the government is now putting the economy, not the child, at the centre of the curriculum. (All this within the space of a few short years.) The lesson here is that faculties of education must be wary of responding to the latest government initiatives, and ensure that students are equipped with those competencies and abilities which transcend the flavour of the month, or any particular ideology. In short, teachers need to be educated, not trained.

Similarly, how we decide to conceptualize education has important consequences for how we choose to conceive of vocational education. Insofar as we are willing to accept vocational courses as mere training grounds for industry, then it is perfectly legitimate to speak of drilling and instructing students in rather low-level skills and competencies. However, if we are to put the concept of education front and centre, then it behoves us to ensure that certain understandings are in place. Clearly, educators must emphasize principles which organize and transcend particulars. By putting cognitive and conceptual understandings first, and by looking to principles and understandings which transcend the particular, we expand and develop the mind. 'The learning of many things,' said Heraclitus, 'does not teach insight' (Stokes 1967, 480). What develops the mind is *understanding*, a concept which implies bringing students to acquire knowledge in an active and vital way, and coming to grips with particular subject matter in a creative and critical manner. When we sift through the prevailing rhetoric concerning skills and training, it is these sorts of cognitive ability which are most in demand in the emerging workplace.

Lifelong learning and the loss of teleology

There is another sense in which the phrase 'lifelong learning' has a peculiarly North American flavour. In English-speaking Canada, as in the United States, there is an increasing disaffection with state schools and a growing perception that they are in a state of extended crisis. It is easy, of course, to overplay this hand. As predictable as death and taxes, every age produces its share of educational Cassandras. Yet in an age typified by a trend towards what might be termed a 'hyper cultural pluralism,' we are witnessing a continent-wide breakdown of shared ideals and a concomitant erosion and lessening of institutional and cultural authority. Neil Postman in *The End of Education*, suggests that public schooling in America has lost its 'overarching narratives' and so can no longer successfully provide an answer to the question, 'What is education for?' 'The idea of a public school,' he writes, 'is irrelevant in the absence of a public; that is, Americans are now so different from each other, have so many diverse points of view, and such special group grievances that there can be no common vision or unifying principles' (Postman 1995, 196). On this view, it has become politically untenable to offer anything other than empty truisms and platitudes when publicly discussing educational ends. Divested of teleology, education is increasingly conceptualized as an exercise in personal self-fulfilment, an avenue by which individuals can search for and try on new identities. In this context, the emphasis on lifelong learning masks the failure of North American schooling to posit some common account of various understandings, dispositions and virtues, i.e., bodies of shared impersonal standards to which both the teacher and the learner must give their allegiance.

There may be no quick answers as to why this state of affairs came about. But, in part, it is surely due to 'the long-standing American tendency to try to solve social, political, and economic problems through educational means, and in so doing invest education with all kinds of millennial hopes and expectations' (Cremin 1989, p. 92). North Americans have come to vest educational institutions with romantic optimism, such that schools are expected to be not only practical and relevant to everyday life, but also to ameliorate a host of social problems, such as poverty, racism and the need for economic competitiveness.

Additionally, vast shifts in immigration patterns have created an increasingly multicultural society. Official policy in both Canada and the US is given to the strengthening and perpetuation of ethnicity. The metaphor of the 'melting pot' is now passé, and citizens are encouraged to take pride in their ethnic roots and celebrate their distinctive traditions. Unsurprisingly, in an age of cultural pluralism, there is a cacophony of voices concerning the ends and aims of schooling.

For such and other reasons talk about the ultimate end of education has disappeared from public discourse, and this, we maintain, represents a failure of the first order. But it is important to appreciate the extent to which this state of affairs has long been an almost inevitable by-product of the way in which North America has perceived and thought about education.

Americans and Canadians have a great traditional respect for education and this respect has, at the cost of much material sacrifice, spread education over a vast continent and across an enormously heterogeneous society in a relatively short time. From the time of Thomas Jefferson in the US and Egerton Ryerson in Canada, education has been broadly understood as the democratization of liberal culture. It would not have occurred to either man that the point of literacy might be to increase the nation's economic competitiveness. Democratic equality demanded that 'the best education for some is the best education for all.' However humble and impoverished, the one-room schoolhouse on the prairie was nevertheless understood to be a venue for conveying to pupils the intellectual, cultural, and moral training which represents the best of a long and honourable tradition of Western civilization. In the cities, the common school was a place where immigrant children from all classes, backgrounds and creeds would be socialized into the new society, thus creating friendships and common interests which would ameliorate future social strife.

But, in an increasingly pluralistic and diversified society, the politicization of schooling has taken on a shrill new tenor and tone. And, curiously, this completely new social reality has to some extent come about with support from America's most influential educational philosopher, John Dewey. For, we would argue, there are two aspects of Dewey's work which have in practice worked to undermine rather than support what he intended to achieve, namely, a common school which would join together in harmony an increasingly heterogeneous population.

The first aspect is his explicit insistence on the continuity of the political and educational domains. The second is his account of the concepts of experience and growth, which lies at the heart of his 'experiential' pedagogy.

As the title of his most famous book, *Democracy and Education*, suggests, in Dewey's view education is to be placed squarely in the service of democracy:

> If democracy has a moral and ideal meaning, it is that a social return be demanded from all and that opportunity for development of distinctive capacities be afforded all. The separation of the two aims of education is fatal to democracy.
>
> (Dewey 1966, 122)

Contrasted with the older, traditional notion that schools were a place apart, where a new generation could, in Oakeshott's phrase, 'encounter [their] moral and intellectual inheritance' (Oakeshott 1989, 69). Dewey decried any artificial distinction between school and the social world, seeing rather a continuity of interests between the school and the larger society, and was famous for decrying 'mandarin knowledge,' by which he meant any knowledge which was not socially useful and did not have an immediate and direct social utility. His insistence on the continuity between the school and society—his casting the school as an instrument of social reform—resulted in a radical politicization of schooling. The task of the teacher was to introduce the student to his community life and responsibilities, saturating him with an ethic of service. Intellectual knowledge, unless tied to the service of the state, was dismissed as a 'static, cold-storage ideal of knowledge' (Dewey 1966, 158). Schools were to be 'embryonic communities', suffused with the spirit of civic duty and mimicking the larger society of which they were a part. From the time of Dewey onwards, North American schools have come to be seen not as institutions isolated from the hurly-burly of the social world, where disinterested scholars could come to know their intellectual inheritance, but rather as institutions whose mandate it is to ensure their relevance, utility and connectedness to the larger society. That is, schools were harnessed directly to social responsibilities and particular social ends, and, in the process of becoming instruments of social reform, were politicized to an extent not seen in other liberal democracies.

The politicization of education has deepened significantly in recent years, to the extent that educational institutions are the locus of some of the most embittered and partisan battles of the culture wars. In multiethnic and multiracial nations, it has become politically untenable to offer unifying and ordered visions of culture, history or values. Instead, given the intensification of group identity, the emphasis falls on differences, separatism, the relativity of values, and on such subjective elements as 'self-esteem'. Instead of transmitting unifying principles intended to assimilate and bring together disparate groups, schools are increasingly the site of acrimonious and divisive political battles.

The second element of Dewey's thought that has contributed unintentionally to the peculiarly American connotations of 'lifelong learning' is his experiential philosophy of education. He sought to promote an American educational system which was based on the personal experiences of the students, and which—consistent with democratic egalitarianism—respected all sources of experience. The role of the teachers is to employ their knowledge to arrange and direct the experiences of the students.

The point of all this experience was the 'growth' of the individual. But when asked what one was growing towards, the answer was the tautological, 'more growth'. Dewey notoriously fails to establish criteria of worth by which we can judge the quality of experiences, or by which we can rule out some experiences as non- or mis-educative. Any experience is said to be good, provided it leads to more experience and growth. In a famous (or infamous) passage, Dewey confronts the question of whether a burglar's experiences are to count as educative, presuming that the burglar grows into a more expert one. His answer is both equivocal and illuminating: 'I shall leave you to answer these questions, saying simply that when and only when development in a particular line conduces to continuing growth does it answer the question of education as growing' (Dewey 1937, 36). Most people would surely find this answer stunningly unsatisfactory. What is most tellingly absent from Dewey's philosophy is any clear notion of what an educated person should look like. In particular, the question, 'What sorts of knowledge do we want our students to possess?', is one to which he has no coherent response.

Because of Dewey's enormous influence on American educational thought, and, specifically, partially as a result of his views on the relationship between education and politics and the crucial role of experience, discourse about public education has an other-worldly quality to it; discussion about the means of teaching is ubiquitous, but strangely absent from public debate are those crucial questions concerning what all these means are means to. There is no sustained debate concerning what kind of a mind we are seeking to develop in schools. In turn it has become an article of faith that the government has no business in the realm of intellect or spirit, and 'may take notice only of outer persona, of acts, not thoughts... the privacy of the mind is [one of] our stock of basic notions. Public authority is unlicensed in the private world. It must leave the mind alone' (Tussman 1977, 5). The education of the individual is seen not as something to be achieved in a public world of politics, civic involvement and, above all, shared understandings, but rather as a private, personal achievement, brought about by individuals through their own efforts in a private world of their own making.

The implications of this unteleological ethic, in combination with a public ethos which stresses freedom, individuality, and the essential independence of citizens, are tremendous. It is perhaps necessary to stress here how successful modern notions of selfhood and freedom have been in permeating public discourse in North America. For many North Americans the individual is the whole, and education is conceived not in terms of the attempt to impose an order on our thoughts and feelings by reference to a public world, but in terms of the search for 'inner harmony', 'self-discovery', and 'self-esteem'.

In short, the educational ideal increasingly revolves around the analysis of a unique and mysterious inner self, whose purposes, aims and goals cease to be formed by reference to a public world, but are somehow generated out of itself. This educational ethic emphasizes the legitimacy of inner, private, individual experience in the formation of character, at the expense of the idea of a public world.

Conclusion

In common with many other jurisdictions, but perhaps to a greater degree, North America is experiencing a time marked by the breakdown of shared ideals, a diminishing of belief in common objective understandings, and an economic situation that calls for constantly changing sets of skills. In addition, not least thanks to the paradoxical influence of John Dewey, schooling has come to be seen more and more as a not very successful means of dealing with social, rather than educational, problems.

In such a situation the idea of lifelong learning has instant and obvious appeal. First there is the fairly straightforward notion that the workplace is now such that individuals need to be constantly re-equipping themselves with new skills throughout their lives. While this, which is surely not unique to North America, is, we have argued, reasonable if taken at face value, it is to be treated with great suspicion when vocational training becomes confused with a genuine education. A worthy form of lifelong learning must be based upon the idea of lifelong education.

Secondly there is a more specifically North American nuance to the idea of lifelong learning, which arises out of a pervasive tendency to conceive of the individual as if in a vacuum, divorced from any significant social factors that help to define the individual. To some extent, we have suggested, the thought of John Dewey has been influential here, albeit his intention was probably not to bring about such a solipsistic viewpoint. At any rate, the idea of lifelong learning as a narcissistic voyage of self-discovery is one which we believe needs to be treated with caution.

References

British Columbia Ministry of Education. 1995. *Skills Now!* Queen's Printer, Victoria, B.C.
Cremin, Lawrence A. 1989. *Popular Education and Its Discontents*. Harper & Row, New York.
Dewey, John. 1937. *Experience and Education*. New York, Collier Press.
Dewey, John. 1966. *Democracy and Education*. New York, The Free Press.
Galt, Virginia. 1996. 'Bank Chairman Advocates Teaching Students To Think'. *Globe and Mail*, Toronto, 30 November, p. A13.

Johnston, William B. *et al*. 1987. *Workforce 2000: Work and Workers for the 21st Century*. Hudson Institute for the US Department of Labour.

Oakeshott, Michael. 1989. 'Education: The Engagement and its Frustration'. In Timothy Fuller, (ed.), *The Voice of Liberal Learning: Michael Oakeshott on Education*. Yale University Press, London.

Postman, Neil. 1995. *The End of Education*. Alfred A. Knopf, New York.

Pritchett, V.S. 1990. *At Home and Abroad*. Chatto & Windus, London.

Scheffler, Israel. 1960. *The Language of Education*. Charles C. Thomas, Springfield, Illinois.

Sculley, J. 1988. 'The Journey Continues' (speech excerpts from MacWorld Expo 1988), *HyperMedia Magazine*, Summer, p. 107.

Spring, Joel. 1989. 'Education and the Sony War'. In James Wm. Noll (ed.), *Taking Sides*. pp. 126–32. Dushkin Publishing Group, Guildford, Connecticut.

Stokes, Michaels C. 1967. 'Heraclitus of Ephesus'. In Paul Edwards (ed.), *The Encyclopedia of Philosophy* (vol. 3). pp. 477–81. Macmillan Publishing Co. & The Free Press, London.

Tussman, Joseph. 1977. *Government and the Mind*. Oxford University Press, New York.

16 Europe and lifelong learning

Investigating the political and educational rationale of expansionism

Klaus Künzel

Approaching the issue of lifelong learning from a European angle exactly at this point in time is a formidable yet tempting enterprise. Recent efforts to review and appreciate the Europeanization of educational policy sectors (Field 1996; Künzel 1997) or to formulate strategic guidelines for building 'learning societies' all over the continent (EU Commission 1995) are indicative of the fact that any attempt to do justice to a European perspective is a tough assignment—notably in areas prone to regional idiosyncracies such as culture or education. However, by exploiting the symbolic potential of the millennium divide one feels inclined to seize the opportunity and consider the question as to whether the grand if somewhat loose design of 'lifelong learning' can act as a conceptual catalyst for giving rise to a new era of resolute European commitment in educational policy. There is today a widely shared understanding that any such policy should, in its temporal orientation as well as in its social mandate and operational range, be governed by the overarching principle of 'inclusiveness'. But is this an original, compelling message and does it—for all its overt universalism—contain some discreetly European motif or manifestations of occidental identity? Can the theoretical discourse on 'modern lifeworlds and learning' (Williamson 1998) be construed in any other way than in terms of a 'radical' critique born of and governed by the ubiquitous forces of globalization (Giddens 1999), or would 'a constructivist understanding of learning and action oriented pragmatism' embedded in 'the context of European educational tradition' (Dohmen 1998: 9) offer greater viability and empirical substance? And, finally, what bearing will the imminent extension and further integration of the European Union have on the ability of 'lifelong learning' to be translated into negotiable patterns of meaning and purposeful action?

The questions raised so far may already indicate that a European perspective can hardly result in a set of clear-cut and conclusive facts and points of view. In constructivist terms the following observations could be treated as tentative designs to survey the pedagogical and structural implications of lifelong learning. The chapter does this firstly by treating lifelong learning as a thematic denominator for behavioural changes required throughout the 'knowledge civilisation of Europe', and secondly by exploring its function as a master plan and rationale for European policy actors involved in laying the foundations and expanding the terms of reference for the learning society. As its title suggests, the chapter makes use of the symbolic properties of 'expansionism' as a semantic frame for locating and spelling out the driving forces behind the European movement of lifelong learning.

Starting with a description of the vantage point chosen for a European perspective, the chapter indicates that there is a spatial as well as a temporal component to be considered. As a territory of varying size and constitution, depending on the political criteria applied in its definition, Europe offers access to lifelong learning in a number of ways. One is to report on the progress that has been made in European countries in and outside the EU in making policies of lifelong learning work (Kaiser *et al.* 1994). This could be done only in a passing and exemplary manner. Within the context and purpose of this chapter, a closer look at the supranational state of affairs promises to be a more viable choice. In historical retrospective, stretching roughly over the last three decades, the rise and gradual modification of lifespan approaches to education will briefly be touched upon, suggesting not only that earlier global concepts like *'education permanente'* (Council of Europe 1970) or 'recurrent education' (OECD 1973) reflect in their aims and argumentation different spheres of and corporate interests in Europe, but that in spite of these differences they embody and share many features central to the topical notion of lifelong learning. According to the OECD (1996: 88) the differences 'between the strategies advocated in the early 1970s and those that appear to be more appropriate today ... are less conceptual than contextual', resulting mainly from major changes in the economic and social environments 'in which policies are shaped and implemented'. Due to the political momentum released in its hemispheres by unification and transformation (Wittschorek 1999), Europe's contextual conditions for establishing systems of lifelong learning should become more standardized and more complex at the same time. By casting some light on these issues the article intends to facilitate the appreciation of their influence on the future fate of lifelong learning in Europe.

Against this background, the reader's attention is then directed towards the macro-operational or strategic level of lifelong learning and will be done in two stages. First, policy aspects of lifelong learning will be explored at a supranational level. By reviewing some exemplary actions and current trends in the EU educational policy spectrum the widening scope of its leadership mandate is examined. Secondly, the article discusses the underlying paradigms and ambiguities of an expansionist design of lifelong learning as it is emerging today, leaving its mark on the European discourse on learning 'for life's sake'—arguably the most sweeping and allusive policy formula in the years to come.

Europe: supranational viewpoints and approaches

For the purpose of identifying from a supranational viewpoint the programmatic and operational links between the empirical shape of 'Europe' and the abstract idea of lifelong learning, no less than four 'mediating' organizations must be mentioned:

- the 'Organisation for European Economic Cooperation', founded in 1948 and renamed 'Organisation for Economic Cooperation and Development' (OECD) 1961 after the period of economic reconstruction had come to an end and the United States and Canada gained full membership status;
- the 'Council of Europe', founded in 1949 with the prime aim 'to bring about closer relationships between its partners for the sake of protecting and fostering the ideals and principles which represent their common heritage' (Kohler-Koch *et al.* 1996: 118);
- the 'European Union' with its forerunner, the 'European Economic Community' created by the Treaty of Rome in March 1957. After the Single European Act of 1986 and the Treaties of Maastricht and Amsterdam, the development of the EEC from a supranational body with regional economic aims to an alliance for comprehensive European integration was politically put on its rails;
- the 'Organisation for Security and Cooperation in Europe' (OSCE), the permanent and institutionalised successor to the 'Conference for Security and Cooperation' since 1994; chiefly responsible for the evolution of policies and procedures to solve intra-European and ethnic conflicts by means of mediation and in a spirit of mutual trust.

In their prime objectives these institutional expressions of 'Europeanness' have, of course, different bearings on the establishment of learning rationales and policies. Both the OECD and the EU regard the advancement of economic progress, competitiveness, trade relations and technology as their main *raison d'être* whilst paying increasing attention to matters of welfare policy such as unemployment and social exclusion (Commission of the EU 1994, OECD 1998). In their education and training strategies the development of marketable skills (Crouch *et al.* 1999), human capital investment (OECD 1998), higher levels of literacy (OECD 1997) and lifelong learning (Commission of the EU 1995; OECD 1996) are of paramount interest. Again, uncustomary topics such as education for *sustainability* (Huckle and Sterling 1996) and citizenship are moving up on the agenda. In spite of these noticeable trends one must bear in mind that the OECD and the EU, though not identical in membership, statutory purpose and political creed (and power), are most visible representations of industrial civilization propagating an economic and social concept of Europe which is deeply entrenched in the Western tradition of democratically 'supervised' capitalism. Whether this ideological bondage will necessarily determine the EU's policy of lifelong learning in the years to come is an open question, and one which is attracting more and more attention (Griffin 1999).

If strength of membership and its spread across the European continent are to be taken as a principal criterion, then clearly the 'Council of Europe' with its 41 accredited states would figure as the natural and most representative embodiment of Europe. Indeed it is Europe's supreme moral and cultural authority, and is responsible for numerous conventions and statements particularly in the sphere of human rights and inter-European cooperation in education and cultural affairs. The Council's concept of and political approach to Europe is different from that of the EU, but it increasingly feels inclined to interpret its supranational role in a complementary Euro-strategic fashion. For the Council of Europe, whose metier is not the formulation of executive orders and regulations but the passing of conventions and recommendations, lifelong learning is a human right (Stobart 1994: 29), whereas in the eyes of the European Commission it is a functional catalyst of economic and political integration (Künzel 1997: 52). In one important aspect the role of the Council of Europe has gained impressively in status and weight: by assisting former COMECON states in their efforts towards democracy and liberalization the Council has effectively performed a bridging function for the 'first wave' of eastern European countries to join the EU (Verheugen 1999: 14). On the other hand, it is equally evident that after the fall of Communism and the steady expansion of the European Union, the mandate and special contribution of the Council of Europe within the framework of educational policy have been scaled down considerably—just as the EU's engagement in training and education is being progressively stepped up (Knoll 1996).

Compared to the relatively broad educational policy spectrum covered so far, the mandate of the OSCE is rather narrow though, politically speaking, of growing importance. When the historic Helsinki Conference passed its Final Resolution—the Helsinki II Document—in 1975, it paid tribute to the role of intergovernmental and intercultural cooperation in the field of education and science, with a remarkable emphasis on higher education, language teaching and a multilateral exchange of learning material and pedagogical expertise (Volle and Wagner 1976: 279). Bearing in mind that the OSCE is the only international governmental organization of European making in which Russia enjoys full membership status, its political role in regional conflict management and inter-ethnic mediation—probably the most pressing learning assignment of the new century—can hardly be overestimated. Considering the abundance of regional conflict areas and minority issues, for instance, in the Balkans and within the former Soviet Union, the OSCE's change from being a European agent to promote and improve East–West relations to becoming a facilitator of political mediation and conflict solution should have eminent consequences for the future of pan-European 'learning policies'.

Although for the moment the chances for and the contribution of organizational forms of training and education towards the settlement of ethnopolitical conflicts seems to be minute, there is some evidence that conflict management and mediation by learning will assume increasing significance in the civic foundation of lifelong learning (Baier-Allen 1998). Recent experiences seem to support the view that this task cannot be performed solely by the OSCE but that it needs to be supported by grassroots and civil society approaches of non-governmental organizations (Ropers 1998).

The political landscape of Europe has changed profoundly over the past 25 years. Processes of post-communist nation building and ethnopolitical peacekeeping are as visible and compelling as the pan-European movement towards closer cooperation and multiple structural integration. All this is happening under the influence of the still wider, abstract regimes of modernization and globalization (Brown 1999: 4). Among the effects which can be attributed to the present coexistence of diversifying and unifying political forces, changes in the position and role of Europe's supranational actors are particularly interesting. The previous tidy compartmentalization of policy domains, typical of the period from 1945 well into the 1980s, has given way to more integrated supranational strategies of economic and social progress. New issues for educational interventionism have emerged in the name of change and manifold challenges, underlining the assumption that the instrumental reflexes of learning subjects and organizations are not just taken for granted but are expected to prosper in the present climate of European expansionism. There is reason to believe that removing the boundaries between an organizational, pedagogically ordained model of education and the 'more open "moorland" of Adult Learning' (Edwards 1997; Johnston 1999: 179) will fuel suspicions that if great care is not taken, the enlightened project of lifelong learning could be allowed to expand indiscriminately and might serve as one of the new features of 'obscurantism' (Bourdieu 1999: 46). The semantic and political problem with lifelong learning, one could argue, is that it naturally lends itself to multiple variations in purpose and basic conceptualization. Indeed its international usage seems to rely greatly on its remarkable potential to mean different things to different people. A closer examination of the strategic implementation of the lifelong learning formula should reveal its ideological susceptibility, and endorse the importance of acting on the forces of expansionism by strengthening the issues of 'identity' and pluralism, issues central to the creation of a European civic society.

European expansion and the agenda of lifelong learning

There is something intriguing about the synchronous dramaturgy behind the enlargement and unification of the political territory of Europe on the one hand and the conceptual ambitions to extend the rationale and range of education to the whole life cycle on the other. It can hardly be overlooked that the 'benign' expansionism of the European Union—specified in its Agenda 2000 and politically endorsed by the European Council meetings in Luxemburg (December 1997) and Helsinki (December 1999)—shows striking similarities with the lifting of strict demarcation lines between the institutional practice of education and a universalistic view of human learning freed from formal (over-)determination but also sensitive to manifold forms of instrumentalization. Both European integration and the growth of a societal culture of lifelong learning can be regarded as plausible consequences of the changes which are reshaping the political geography of Europe and its 'lifeworlds' (Welter 1986).

In analytical respect and for the purpose of exploring the nature of its relationship with lifelong learning, the phenomenon of expansionism deserves a little more attention. Broadly speaking, areas which are essentially affected by expansionist tendencies include the macropolitical geography of Europe, the widening mandate of the EU, and the information society.

Macro-political geography

First and foremost, the dynamics of expansion in political and economic terms are owed to the 15 members of the European Communities and the 'organic growth' of the Union 'from common pursuits requiring convergence' (Brock and Tulasiewicz 1994: 5). Since 1989 the EU has effectively seized the principal role of determining and controlling the course of European integration and its administrative management, including, of course, the choice of new members. The impending inclusion of ten Middle and Eastern European countries will not only stretch the political confines of the European Union and further enhance its economic sway, but it may also serve as a manifestation of the unilateral nature of the 'learning and assimilation contract' between the established (core) community and the rank and file of Eastern applicants. In principle, the EU does not negotiate the terms of membership but expects total compliance with the *'acquis communautaire'*—200,000 pages of community laws and regulations. Candidates must satisfy the EU in respect of 'institutional stability' and a democratic order shaped in accordance with (Western) European values and procedural requirements. In addition to that, they must further give proof of a functioning market economy robust enough to withstand the pressures of economic competition and globalization and agree to support and execute the collective political aims of the Community (Wittschorek 1999). In order to fulfil the requirements laid down in EU legislation and reinforced by the political agenda of the Union's constituent bodies (European Parliament, Council of Ministers, Commission), future member states have been submitted to a painstaking, exhaustive learning ordeal ever since 1989, when the fall of state communism initiated the extensive transformation of Eastern Europe, a process which is quite ostentatiously following the premises and patterns of Western European modernization (Beierwaltes 1998).

If one accepts the learning analogy prompted by the pulling power of the EU, this process of assimilation can be characterized, borrowing a phrase from a textbook on learning psychology, as 'an organised reaction to the expectations of an environment which makes demands' (Holzkamp 1995: 12; Künzel 1996). It is tempting to label this 'defensive' learning habit (Holzkamp) as a reactive behavioural result of 'modernisation by colonisation', not forgetting, of course, that the assumed expansionist or colonizing drive is not an explicit motive of EU policy—indeed there are still remarkable strategic and pragmatic reservations against a proliferation of membership status—but can partly be explained by the internalization of the Western leadership role and its effects on the psychology of political action. In its wake collective teaching habits have been formed and built into the mechanism of top-down, or rather West–East instructional procedures employed to prepare the chosen national candidates for life in the European Union (Künzel 1993).

Generally speaking, these procedures are composed of several policy elements. Apart from economic, technical and financial assistance, support programmes for EU membership contenders include operational activities in the field of vocational training, typically in the area of agricultural development and the economic transformation of rural regions. There is mounting evidence that the recent reform of the Structural Fund, with its declared intention to put still greater emphasis on a policy of 'structural alignment' and on the application of more stringent criteria for priority funding, is partly motivated by the prospect of having to cope, within the next few years, with the influx of more regional aspirants falling under that description. As for the educational, employment and political implications of the reformed Structural Fund the explicit reference to a 'policy of lifelong learning' seems noteworthy, though hardly surprising since this policy is closely directed towards the overriding aims of employability, access to the labour market and personal mobility.

Widening mandate of the EU

The gradual acquisition of a leadership role in areas which have hitherto fallen under the terms of reference of other supranational bodies is particularly obvious in PHARE (Polish Hungarian Assistance for Recovering Economies), an OECD program for which the EU has assumed responsibilty in its coordination and financial management (Woyke 1996: 26). From the EU's point of view its widening mandate should be seen as a necessary and therefore legitimate consequence of expansion not only in size but, above all, in terms of political complexity and regional pluralism. It is consistent with its controlled admission policy that the EU makes its new generation of Action Progammes, LEONARDO and SOCRATES (2000–2006), available for no less than 25 European states. It is also most significant that two of the prime action goals are 'employability' and 'European citizenship'. They correspond with two of the most crucial political assignments of the Union—to combat unemployment and social exclusion on the one hand, and to facilitate the development of a European identity as a meaningful, liveable biographic and cultural concept. Their prominent position in the new education and training agenda results from a growing concern that a community fixed primarily on economic objectives and a utilitarian rationale is hardly conducive to creating emotional acceptance and a firm European commitment amongst its members (Brock 1994: 4). The new SOCRATES proposals, finally accepted by the Council of the European Union in November 1999 (Bmb+f 1999), take therefore great care in communicating the programme's 'contribution to the further development of the European Community' as a threefold one, incorporating a sharpened and more streamlined interpretation of aspects such as quality, innovation and management:

- SOCRATES is a cornerstone of the policy to bring the European Community closer to all its citizens … The potential of SOCRATES for encouraging a positive sense of identification with the process of building Europe is manifest.
- SOCRATES has a vital role to play in developing high-quality human resources, a key factor in stimulating employment, promoting competitiveness and achieving greater economic growth.
- SOCRATES is centre-stage in the process of enlarging the Community to embrace the wider Europe through the pre-accession extension of strategically important programmes to the associated countries of Central and Eastern Europe and Cyprus.

While the global aims of SOCRATES II reflect a spatial and functional dimension of expansionism, the description of the single actions which will be launched under the new Programme indicates that COMENIUS, ERASMUS and GRUNDTVIG are positioned as 'vertical measures' aimed at 'the three basic stages of lifelong education: school, university and other' (European Commission 1998: 41). Complementing the two preceding temporal stages, GRUNDTVIG is the most visible community action to follow the conceptual lead of the EU's White Paper on the 'Learning Society'. It takes up the expansionist motif of earlier policy statements, targets its temporal dimension of lifelong learning 'in particular at young people who have left the school system with insufficient basic training and adults wishing to acquire or improve their knowledge for personal reasons' and speaks of 'other educational pathways' which it intends to open up for the sake of lifelong learning. In terms of its operational objectives. GRUNDTVIG is directed to support multilateral partnerships whose purpose is in particular to:

- stimulate adults' individual demand for learning, so that they continue to remain active participants in a society undergoing rapid change;
- develop support services for adult learners and the providers of such education;

- develop teaching material which may be adapted to multimedia methods of learning and to exchange good practice;
- develop accreditation, validation or certification schemes;
- support the training of educational staff working in this sector.

(European Commission 1998: 41)

In addressing these objectives the conceptual design of GRUNDTVIG basically 'preempts' the recommendations passed by the authors of an evaluation study which summarizes the outcomes of the Adult Education Action with SOCRATES I (Nuissl 1999). The financial situation of GRUNDTVIG is such that it receives 7 per cent of the 1.85 billion Euro earmarked for SOCRATES in the period 2000–2006 (Bmb+f 1999).

LEONARDO II, the vocational branch of the EU's educational policy mandate (§127, Treaty on European Union) is starting its operations in 2000 and will have a budget of 1.25 billion Euro for a period stretching to the year 2006. In the Council's decision dating from April 1999 the number of countries participating in the Action Programme was extended to 31. In reference to the White Paper on the 'Learning Society' LEONARDO will be expected to contribute to the operationalization of a Community policy of lifelong learning. In the general outline of LEONARDO's programmatic intentions the Council states that the process of lifelong learning should:

- include, for reasons of demographic and technological changes, all age groups and all levels/forms of employment;
- be induced and supported by measures aimed at raising the innovative potential and quality of the national systems of vocational training and the European dimension therein;
- be understood in the most inclusive way, in as far as all discriminatory tendencies are concerned, above all fighting resolutely against racism and sexism;
- be organised in such a manner that within the 'emerging learning society' the acquisition of new knowledge will be facilitated by all conceivable forms of learning incentives;
- allow the development of a 'European space of education' in which the transnational exchange and recognition of vocational qualifications, linguistic competence and personal mobility will be regular features;
- be reiterated and receive further endorsement by the principle of 'European added value', a formula which stresses the desired synergetic effects of complementarity and coherence.

(Ant 1999: 101, trans. K.K.)

One of the 'spatial' implications of LEONARDO's agenda for lifelong learning has already been put into practice. In December 1998 the Council of the European Union decided to introduce EUROPASS, a transnational document certifying sequences of vocational education (including higher education) organized in collaboration between European training partners (Bmb+f 1999).

It certainly would be premature to pass judgements on the feasibility and prudence of the second generation of LEONARDO and SOCRATES. However, there is ample evidence to suggest that the role of the EU in forging a supra- and transnational training strategy with a policy of lifelong learning has been strengthened still further and its scope of action widened. In its programmatic positioning and wording future actions will be carried out in the spirit of §3b of the Treaty on European Unity requiring that the principle of subsidiarity and proportionality be duly observed (Ant 1999: 105). But since the 'defining power' as to what measures of educational policy constitute a case for the application of subsidiarity, their factual realization should not meet with much resistance—considering too the financial rewards offered to the regional recipients of centralist actions. Furthermore, §128 provides room for an expansive interpretation of the Community's directional and pacemaking powers, not forgetting also that the political and legal obligation to treat subsidiarity as a 'dynamic concept' may turn out to increase the Commission's discretionary powers in delineating its expanding frame of reference (Müller-Brandeck-Bocquet 1997).

The information society

Sociological discourses on what determines and describes the present nature of European societies vary, and so does the nomenclature of the EU's programmatic 'trend scouts'. In differing degrees and contextual usage 'knowledge', 'information' and 'learning' are being enthroned as the heralds and chief denominators of present or emerging societal patterns. As in the case of the 'learning society' the search for a conclusive, widely accepted and empirically valid formula is, as Colin Crouch (1999: 1) notes, 'dispiriting', to say the least. For the purpose of this paper it seems sufficient to register the coexistence of plural conceptualizations of what gives Europe—especially when viewed from a unifying standpoint—a distinctive cultural flavour and structural appearance.

Perhaps one should not overinterpret the fact that in December 1997 the EU, after having paid so much lip service to lifelong learning decided 'to stimulate the establishment of the Information Society in Europe' (Council of the EU 1997) by launching a multiannual programme for the period 1998–2002 and by amending the rationale of expansionism with a dedicated plea for a society prepared for a comprehensive regime of 'knowledge technologies' and information literacy as an indispensable behavioural norm. Observers may, however, feel inclined to suspect that the 'penetration of people's homes by the Internet' has not only raised concerns about 'how the technology can be used to enable learners rather than alienate them' but that the 'plague proportions' reached by this medium (Gray 1999: 125) are a welcome opportunity for the EU to articulate its striving for mental and political leadership in a sphere of obvious and instant public consent and approbation. Maybe 'learning' proves to be a conceptual idea too elusive and abstract for instantaneous administrative conversion?

In its introductory passage the Council's Decision on the information Society emphasizes its 'particular relevance for European countries which are transforming their economy' (Council of EU 1997: 2). As to its general aims and direction, the programme follows three lines of action:

- increasing public awareness and understanding of the potentional impact of the Information Society and its new applications throughout Europe . . .;
- optimizing the socioeconomic benefits of the Information Society in Europe, analysing its technical, economic, social and regulatory aspects, by appraising the challenges raised by the transition to the Information society . . . and by promoting synergy and cooperation between European and national levels;
- enhancing Europe's role and visibility within the global dimension of the Information Society.

(Council of the EU 1997: 2)

Meanwhile, the European Commission has initiated several projects and organizational formats to put the Council's policy framework into practice. A leading role in these efforts is being played by PROMISE (Promoting the Information Society of Europe), a working group of the Commission's Directorate General XXII and responsible for the running of the ISPO, the 'Information Society Promotion Office' in Brussels. The Centre's main objectives and priorities arise, it is claimed, 'from the need to overcome … lack of cohesion in the EU, and increase consistency and synergy of Member States' policies'. It has a 'core position in monitoring the progress of the Information Society in Europe' and intends to produce 'European added value' across the entire spectrum of PROMISE (European Commission 1999: 1). Its operational functions include information and coordination of 'Information Society' policies, networks and 'best practices'.

This article cannot possibly do justice to the massive response which the Commission's operations have produced in the field of laying the foundations of the European Information Society. The introduction of 'Netd@ys', for instance—an initiative to 'promote the effective use of online technology in education and training'—has become, in the Commission's own. estimation, 'the world's largest demonstration of awareness-raising on the use of the Internet and new media for learning'. In 1998 more than 5000 events took place, Netd@ys alone attracting some 35,000 participating organizations (EU Commission 1999). One of the areas where PROMISE will have direct relevance for and access to lifelong learning is the contribution of information technology to provide online resources for self-directed learning—one of the most cherished prospects of future educational environments.

Explored for its educational relevance, the expansive nature of information technologies and of the EU's policy reaction to them brings to mind considerations well endowed with notions of classical modernity. In a world sworn in on modernization, the amassment of knowledge tools is as present as the multiplication of choices. But instead of simplifying the process of orientation it enhances the innateness of uncertainty. Interfaces between virtual and analogue reality require more, not less guiding assistance, just as the expansion of what makes up the much acclaimed 'European space of knowledge' has created a dynamic grid of learning tasks which no life can be long enough to address, no repertoire of self-directed learning sufficiently complete.

Expansionism and learning in Europe: critique and conclusions

One of the central characteristics of the European debate about adult learning and its educational facilitation is its deep involvement in the process of deciphering the scope and direction of modernization. For all their cosmopolitan ambitions the discourses on globalization, postmodernity or new mental regimes are firmly entrenched in the habits and moods of European intellectualism and, above all, in the pioneering role of European civilization in living out the precepts of the Enlightenment—for better and for worse. It is therefore not at all surprising that the European Commission's White Paper on the 'Learning Society' (1995: 45) draws our attention precisely to this dual face of Europe's modern history:

> European civilisation … is today divided between a deep thirst for research and knowledge, the legacy of a tradition which made Europe the first to bring about a technical and industrial revolution and thus change the world, and a deep-seated call for stability and collective security. This is a perfectly understandable aspiration for a continent so long torn apart by wars and divided by political and social conflicts. Unfortunately, it is also one which can engender a reactionary reflex to change.

It is within this historical context that reference is made to 'uncertainties and concerns' by the authors of the White Paper which in their mind appear to be 'without doubt stronger in

Europe than elsewhere' (45). When the Council of Europe (1980: 120) deliberated on the 'Development of adult education' 20 years ago, it too regarded the 'challenge of uncertainty' to be the 'central criterion' of a developmental education policy conceived to combat the negative corollaries of modernity, particularly the 'confusion of values [and the] debasement of democracy'. From here it is only a short and logical step to the rise and proliferation of the sociological discourse on the 'risk society' and the apparent need to guide its unfolding with processes of 'reflexive modernisation' (Beck 1992; Beck *et al.* 1994; Jansen and Van Der Veen 1997). The paradigmatic nature of 'reflexivity' as a focal point of contemporary efforts to reframe the biographic, social and political rationale of educational thinking seem to qualify the discourses held in its name as being universally applicable and manifestations of theoretical megatrends, yet a closer look at the historical and cultural assumptions woven into the argumentative fabric of late- or postmodern literature on lifelong learning reveals the sublime ethnocentricity of European rationalism—and expansionism.

This chapter has attempted to search for a distinct European way of finding access to lifelong learning, not so much as a set of educational principles or ventures but as a dynamic pattern of behavioural changes induced and governed by 'expansion'—viewed as a metaphoric medium to characterize ongoing processes of change in the macropolitical level of Europe, in the scope of EU actions and with reference to the Information Society. The perspective chosen for this attempt was one from the vantage point of supranational European 'players'. One of the observations this paper wants to convey is the rise of the EU into a position where its indisputable gains in strategic and managerial power has had manifold consequences for the development of lifelong learning environments. To the expansion of European 'learning space' due to technological progress, the authors of the EU's White Papers have responded in a similar fashion as did the OECD and the Council of Europe before: with the instalment of lifelong learning as a human commitment 'in time'.

The educational policy grid of the European Union has been reshaped after 1994, when eurosceptics and advocates of subsidiarity prompted a more sensitive balance between unitarian and pluralistic interpretations of Europe. The increasing appreciation of coexisting plural expressions of 'Europeanness' includes not only cultures, regional idiosyncrasies or individual life concepts but also a temporal element which has to be considered. Different speeds of economic transformations and of adjusting to the forces of globalization have caused a number of vertical frictions within the European Union and along the pathway of EU membership. Integration as a common political goal is therefore subjected to a complex process of perceiving, validating and coordinating the individual cultural identities and developmental tempi of the member states. Pluralism as a characteristic feature of 'late modern' societies and of Europe in particular will thus make enormous demands on the steering and negotiating capacity of European authorities in a horizontal dimension (difference in space) as well as in a temporal dimension (difference in speed).

The European Council realized the immense importance of European identity as early as 1973, when it formulated its constituent principle and elements (Pfetsch 1998). There can be little doubt today that expansionism fuels the need and the desire to search for a collective identity composed of differences in creed, race, culture, age, learning aptitudes, etc. It will be the responsibility of communities and people across Europe to fill the elusive formula and policy of lifelong learning as understood and conceptually administered by the European Commission. It will never be a viable construct of social and educational policy if it is left to the planning elites of supranational actors, for whom the longitudinal dimension of human learning is hardly accessible. That is why it seems pointless to fall into the trap of criticizing authors of White Papers and other visionary blueprints for ambitions they either do not pursue (Künzel 1996: 87) or prove unable to fill with life.

Finally, lifelong learning is a challenging and risky issue for European educationists too. The dilemma of our profession seems to be that the subjugation under the regime of indiscriminate expansion and facilitation of whatever comes our way cannot be a desirable behavioural option, nor does it serve any foreseeable purpose to (re)introduce comprehensive manoeuvres of educational theorizing. We should however remind both ourselves and policy-makers of the fact that there is an ethical message in lifelong learning freed from ideological, obscuring properties and reinstated as a critical, reflexive 'praxis'. The message is: the answer to expansionism cannot be found in the propagation of learning as a solitary exercise of self-directedness and informatization. It will, above all, require a committed view of lifelong learning as a corporate project in which State and Union will resist the temptation to delegate the corollaries and biographic effects of change to the 'learning society'.

References

Ant, M. (1999). LEONARDO DA VINCI II. Das neue Aktionsprogramm zur Berufsbildungspolitik der Europäischen Union, Kaiser *et al.* (eds) *Europahandbuch Weiterbildung*, 30.10.15., 1–3; 101–26

Baier-Allen, S. (ed)(1998). *Synergy in Conflict Management. What can be learnt from recent experiences?* Baden-Baden: Nomos Verlagsgesellschaft

Beck, U. (1992). *Risk Society: towards a new modernity*, London: Sage

Beck, U., Giddens, A., Lash, S. (1994). *Reflexive Modernization*, Cambridge: Polity Press

Beierwaltes, A. (ed)(1998). *Lernen für das neue Europa*, Baden-Baden: Nomos Verlagsgesellschaft

Bmb+f (Bundesministerium für Bildung und Forschung) (1999). *Der Europass-Berufsbildung*, Bonn: bmb+f

Bourdieu, P. (1999). 'Alles seitenverkehrt. Zivilisiert endlich den Kapitalismus, Günter Grass und Pierre Bourdieu im *Gespräch, Die Zeit*, 49, 2.12., 45–46

Brock, C. and Tulasiewicz, W. (eds) (1994) *Education in a Single Europe*, London: Routledge

Brown, T. (1999). 'Challenging globalization as discourse and phenomenon', *International Journal of Lifelong Education*, 18, 1, 3–17

Commission of the European Communities (1994). *Growth, Competitiveness, Employment: the challenges and ways forward into the 21st century*, Luxemburg: Office for Official Publications

Commission of the European Communities (1995). *Teaching and Learning: Towards the Learning Society*, Luxemburg: Office for Official Publications

Commission of the European (1998). 'Proposal for a European Parliament and Council Decision Establishing the Second Phase of the Community Action Programme in the Field of Education—SOCRATES'. DIE. *Zeitschrift für Erwachsenenbildung* III/98, 39–41

Commission of the European Communities (1999). *PROMISE Work Programme 1999*, Brussels: European Commission

Commission of the European Communities (1999). *Netd@ysEurope 1999*, http://europe.eu.int/en/comm/dg22/netdays/index.html

Council of Europe (1970). *Permanent Education*, Strasbourg: Council of Europe

Council of Europe (1980). *Development of Adult Education*, Strasbourg: Council of Europe

Council of the European Union (1997). *Council Decision on the Information Society*, http//www.ispo.cebe/promise/12988en.html

Crouch, C. *et al.* (1999). *Are Skills the Answer? The Political Economy of Skill Creation in Advanced Industrial Countries*, Oxford: Oxford University Press

Dohmen, G. (1998). *The Future of Continuing Education in Europe*, Bonn: Federal Ministry of Education and Research

Edwards, R. (1997). *Changing places? flexibility, lifelong learning and a learning society*, London: Routledge

Field, J. (1996). 'Towards the Europeanisation of Continuing Education', *Studies in the Education of Adults*, 28, 1, 14–28

Giddens, A. (1999). 'Globalisation', Reith Lecture, http://news.bbc.co.uk/hi/english/static/events/ reith 99/week1/week1.htm

Griffin, C. (1999). 'Lifelong Learning and welfare reform', *International Journal of Lifelong Education*, 18, 6, 431–52

Gray, D. (1999). 'The Internet in lifelong learning: liberation or alienation?', *International Journal of Lifelong Education*, 18, 2, 119–26

Holzkamp, K. (1995). *Lernen. Subjektwissen schaft liche Grundlagen*, Frankfurt: Campus

Huckle, J. and Sterling, S. (eds)(1996). *Education for Sustainability*, London: Earthscan Publications

Jansen, T. and Van der Veen, R. (1997). 'Individualization, the new political spectrum and the functions of adult education', *International Journal of Lifelong Education*, 16, 4, 264–76

Johnston, R. (1999). 'Adult learning for citizenship: towards a reconstruction of the social purpose tradition', *International Journal of Lifelong Education*, 18, 3, 175–90

Kaiser, A. *et al.* (eds). *Europahandbuch Weiterbildung*, Neuwied: Luchterhand

Knoll, J.H. (1996). *Internationale Weiterbildung und Erwachsenenbildung: Konzepte, Instutionen, Methoden*, Darmstadt: Wissenschaftliche Buchgesellschaft

Kohler-Koch, B. and Woyke, W. (eds). *Die Europäische Union. Lexikon der Politik* Band 5, München: Beck

Künzel, K. (1993). 'Die Grosse Umschulung. Anmerkungen zur Erwachsenenbildung im deutschen Einigungsprozeß', in Knoll, J.H. (ed), *International Yearbook of Adult Education*, 21, 5–19

Künzel, K. (1996). 'Learning as a lifelong process'? Psychological and pedagogical comments on the 'learning society', *Vocational Training European Journal*, 8/9, December 2/3, 86–90

Künzel, K. (1997). 'Europäisierung der Weiterbildungspolitik', in K. Derichs-Kunstmann *et al.* (eds), *Weiterbildung zwischen Grundrecht und Markt*, Opladen: Leske & Budrich, 49–64

Müller-Brandeck-Bocquet, G. (1997). 'Der Ansterdamer Vertrag zur Reform der Europäischen Union, Ergebnisse, Fortschritte, Defizite. Aus Politik und Zeitgeschichte, B47/97, 21–9

Nuissl, E. (ed) (1999). *Adult Education and Learning in Europe—Evaluation of the Adult Education Action within the SOCRATES Programme*, Frankfurt: DIE

Organisation for Economic Cooperation and Development (OECD)(1973). *Recurrent Education. A Strategy for Lifelong Learning*, Paris: OECD

OECD (1996). *Lifelong Learning for All*, Paris: OECD

OECD (1997). *Literacy Skills for the Knowledge Society*, Paris: OECD

OECD (1998). *Human Capital Investment. An International Comparison*, Paris: OECD

Pfetsch, F.R. (1998). 'Die Problematik der europäischen Identität', Aus: *Politik und Zeitgeschichte*, B25-26/98, 3–9

Ropers, N. (1998). 'An important Component: The Need for NGOs', in Baier-Allen, S. (ed), 67–78

Stobart, M. (1994). 'Der Europarat und die Bildungsanforderungen im 'Neuen Europa', in Schleicher, K. and Bos, W. (eds), *Realisierung der Bildung in Europa*, Darmstadt: Wissenschaftliche Buchgesellschaft

Verheugen, G. (1999). 'Von der Menschenrechtsagentur zur Stimme Europas', *Europäische Zeitung*, June 1999, 14

Volle, H. and Wagner, W. (1976). *Konferenz über Sicherheit und Zusammenarbeit in Europa. Beiträge und Dokumente aus dem Europaarchiv*, Bonn: Verlag für Internationale Politik

Welter, R. (1986). *Der Begriff der Lebenswelt: Theorien vortheoretischer Erfahrungswelt*, München:UTB

Williamson, B. (1998). *Lifeworlds and Learning*, Leicester: NIACE

Wittschorek, P. (ed)(1999). *Agenda 2000. Herausforderungen an die Europäische Union und an Deutschland*, Baden-Baden: Nomos Verlagsgesellschaft

Part 4

Widening participation

17 Learning in the Isles

Evolving policies for lifelong learning in
the Republic of Ireland and the
United Kingdom[1]

John Field

Anyone familiar with policy-making in Western Europe will be aware of the visibility and frequency of lifelong learning as a theme. Yet there is a paradox at the heart of this process. On the one hand, there is widespread agreement among governments and others that the continuous updating of skills and knowledge are a prerequisite for survival in the face of intense competitive pressures and sharp threats to social cohesion, brought about by unprecedented economic, technological and social change. On the other, there is considerable scepticism over the capacity of central planning and regulation for achieving radically improved educational standards, combined with a growing recognition that little will happen without actively engaging civil society—individuals, employers, local voluntary and representative bodies—in a vigorous process of cultural change. This chapter describes the evolving policies for lifelong learning in two European nations, not just as a simple exercise in comparative policy analysis, but also in an attempt to illustrate the difficulty for governments that the area of lifelong learning itself presents.

In both Britain and Ireland, as elsewhere in Western Europe, lifelong learning has recently commanded considerable policy attention. Nevertheless, despite broad similarities of discourse and approach, the two contexts differ considerably. Of course, much is shared between Britain and Ireland, including a common language and the one land border in these islands. Historical ties and tensions have also played their part, not least in shaping the education and training systems. As in all members of the European Union (EU), some public education and training programmes are partly financed and governed through the European Commission's Structural Funds. Yet the differences are important ones, and mean that the challenges faced by each society are rather different. With less than four million inhabitants, the Republic of Ireland is one of the EU's smaller members; its economy is considerably more dynamic than the EU average, and its population much younger; and although it retains a strong sense of nationhood, the Republic has been an enthusiastic member of the international community, and was among the first group of nations to join the single European currency. In policy terms, the Republic is distinctive in possessing a formal national mechanism for negotiating macroeconomic policy through dialogue between government, trade unions and employers (O'Dowd 1999). From the Programme for National Recovery in 1987 through to the Programme for Prosperity and Fairness in 2000, the main aims of these agreements have been job creation, wage stability and the priorities for public spending. However, they also encompass a range of further issues, including broad plans for education and training.

With a population approaching 60 million, the UK, by contrast, is among Europe's larger nations. Its somewhat sluggish economic performance is largely typical of the wider EU pattern, as is its steadily aging demographic profile; not only is it a cosmopolitan and indeed multiracial society, but recent trends towards devolution have created a broadly federal structure, in which education and training policy are among the responsibilities of the four separate national systems within the UK. To these broad contextual differences should be added the diversity of approaches to education and training. Without entering into too much detail, it is clear for example, that the adult education system was considerably more deeply embedded and developed in Britain before the 1970s than in either the Republic or Northern Ireland, for reasons that are largely historical in nature (Field 1994b). In developing a policy framework for lifelong learning, then, both countries have identified a series of common challenges, but are required to face them in rather different settings.

Promoting lifelong learning

In both countries, lifelong learning now occupies a leading place in policy discourse. In the Republic and the UK, a series of policy papers were produced around the turn of the century, leading subsequently to what appear to be a series of substantial new policy initiatives. In neither case, though, were policy-makers working to a clean slate. While lifelong learning did not feature strongly in Conservative thinking before 1997 in the UK, neither was it entirely absent; in 1995, for example, the government undertook a public consultation on what it called 'lifetime learning' (DfEE 1995), and launched both the Kennedy committee on further education as well as the Dearing inquiry into higher education; administratively, it created a lifetime learning division within the Department for Education and Employment. Lifelong learning also featured in two of the major policy consultations undertaken by Labour while in opposition (Commission on Social Justice 1994, National Commission on Education 1993).

Parallel debates could be seen in the Republic of Ireland, particularly after an OECD team reported that:

> There has been much reference to the ideal of lifelong learning and the importance of second-chance education ... but, as in nearly all other countries, there is no evidence of any concerted effort to render it a reality.
>
> (OECD 1991, 33)

In particular, the Republic lacked a coherent system for educating and training adults, and had no heritage of treating this as a priority (perhaps not surprising, given that until the 1990s, the labour market was able to draw on a ready supply of freshly-educated youngsters). Evidence of new thinking on the issue was seen both in the national consultative debate led by the Commission on Education (Coolahan 1994), as well as in the labour market policies of the Department for Enterprise and Employment, in its 1997 White Paper on human resources (DEE 1997). When the European Commission subsequently declared 1996 to be the European Year of Lifelong Learning, the idea and the language rapidly entered the mainstream political vocabulary in both countries.

Britain offers an instructive example of the speed with which this process occurred. In 1997, the incoming Labour government appointed Dr Kim Howells as the country's first Minister of Lifelong Learning. Advisory committees on further and higher education, appointed by agreement between government and opposition before 1997, published reports couched in the language of the learning society (Dearing 1997; Kennedy 1997). In the following year, separate Green Papers outlined proposals for Wales, Scotland and England, with a consultative paper along similar lines in Northern Ireland. These were followed by a White Paper (*Learning to Succeed*) for post-16 education and training in England. An Advisory Group for Continuing Education and Lifelong Learning, created in early 1998, produced two wide-ranging reports on future policy developments (Fryer 1998; Fryer 1999).

In the Irish Republic, meanwhile, a Minister of State for Education was in 1997 given special responsibility for adult education. Subsequently, the government issued a Green Paper with the title—significantly different from its British equivalents—of *Adult Education in an Era of Lifelong Learning* (DES 1998), and a public consultation was organized throughout the two years that followed, leading to the drafting of a White Paper in 2000 (Flynn 2000). At the level of public debate, then, the language and idea of lifelong learning had clearly come to the forefront. To what extent was this being translated into corresponding, specific policy measures to effect measurable change on the ground?

In the UK, there is considerable evidence of policy innovation. Among other measures announced since 1998, the most significant new initiatives include:

- Learn-direct (previously the University for Industry, or UfI), a brokerage agency designed to stimulate the market for skills updating by undertaking marketing campaigns, providing information, commissioning distance learning packages, and managing a network of some 1,000 local learning centres in libraries, colleges and elsewhere;
- Individual Learning Accounts (ILAs), intended to provide an incentive to individual saving and spending, by meeting part of the costs of learning programmes; and
- the creation of the Union Learning Fund and the Adult and Community Learning Fund, to pilot innovative approaches to workplace learning, basic skills provision and community-based learning.

In addition, government sponsored the creation of local Learning Partnerships, as a means of bringing providers together at local level to pool information, plan provision and provide advice to policy-makers; it provided funds for a series of local adult guidance networks; it encouraged the funding bodies for further and higher education to adjust funding mechanisms so as to promote wider participation; and developed ambitious targets for growth in participation. DfEE also announced new proposals to support research in this field. As well as creating specialist research centres into such areas as the economic and non-economic benefits of learning, it embarked on a series of large-scale studies of participation in adult learning (Beinart and Smith 1998). Last, and by no means least, Government embarked on a large-scale restructuring of its administrative arrangements for planning and funding in post-16 education and training at local level.

While moving in broadly the same direction, developments in the Republic of Ireland have taken a slightly different track. Government in the Republic has certainly attended to workforce skills development, convening an interdepartmental expert group on future skills needs and creating a national business-education forum, and steadily developing a framework for lifelong learning. Skills issues have also been tackled within the negotiations for the first partnership agreement of the century, the Programme for Prosperity and Fairness. Some of the new initiatives mirror developments in the UK; thus the Excellence through People quality standard for companies is analogous to the Investor in People mark, while the national training programme in information technology is similar to aspects of the Learn-direct project. Another proposal, to create a national adult learning bank, was rapidly dropped after criticism from government economic advisers, though interest remained strong in developing a learning account system of some kind (Walshe 1998). Others, though, are more distinctive, including the National Training Fund, announced as part of Budget 2000, and financed through a levy on the employers' social insurance contribution, to create a dedicated fund for training those already in employment. In the increasingly tight labour market of the first decade of the century, the Republic has adopted a series of measures to upskill the adult workforce. However, the main thrust of reform has been aimed at general adult education, where proposals in the White Paper on Adult Education include:

- a new statutory National Adult Learning Council to build an extensive adult education programme and monitor progress at local level;
- funding to appoint adult education staff and subsidise programmes within the schools system;
- the implementation of a national literacy programme; and
- a £IR30 million investment in mature student programmes in higher education.

(Flynn 2000)

Further, the White Paper confirmed the support and interest shown in early discussions for community-based learning, particularly in respect of disadvantaged groups and women.

As a phrase, then, it might be said that lifelong learning, or the learning society, has—as in several European nations—become a convenient political shorthand for the modernizing of education and training systems. However, even a cursory glance at the policy debate in Britain and Ireland suggests that there is also a desire to translate general aspirations into concrete measures. In the UK, the focus has primarily been upon building workplace skills and knowledge, although with important gestures towards community-based capacity building and citizenship, as well as broad support for the idea of 'learning for its own sake', to quote the Secretary of State's foreword to *The Learning Age* (DfEE 1998, 7). Investment in the two Learning Funds, for instance, is dwarfed by the large scale costs of ILAs and Learn-Direct. While the UK has witnessed real policy innovation under the banner of lifelong learning, it has been conducted across the relatively narrow front of vocationally-oriented education and training. It is also noteworthy that some of the major initiatives—ILAs in particular, but also much of the research effort—are concerned with the question of demand and participation; it is in this sense that the new UK policies focus on 'the learner' rather than the suppliers of learning programmes.

By comparison, the Republic's emphasis has been more evenly divided between investment in general adult education infrastructure on the one hand and workforce skills development on the other. It should be stressed that both are relatively recent concerns for policy-makers in the Republic, and are partly a response to very contemporary developments. One of these is the OECD's twelve-nation survey of adult literacy and numeracy, which appeared to show the Republic's education system in an extremely unfavourable light. Internally, rapid economic growth has outstripped the supply of indigenous labour: the working population in Ireland rose by almost 50 per cent in the 1990s alone, for example, so that policy-makers are increasingly looking towards new types of labour market entrant (primarily women, but also a small number of officially-encouraged immigrants) and continuous upskilling for existing workers.

As in Britain, the new policies therefore demonstrate a relatively conventional focus. At the level of rhetoric, the Republic's government has also embraced more radical ideas, as in the 1998 Green Paper, which noted that:

> The importance of Community Education lies in the way that it extends and deepens the democratic process and can successfully engage those who are most excluded in our society. Community Education at its best is concerned to overcome the constraints that limit the potential to participate. It aims to develop the capacity of the more marginalised sectors in the community to participate both in decision making and in the general social and cultural life of the society.

(DfES 1998, 89)

Again, this is more gesture than substance; relatively little has been done to translate this admirable ambition into practice. Rather, the major thrust has been divided between upskilling and general infrastructure, as might perhaps be expected in a society that has only recently been required to acknowledge the potentially significant deficit that it faces in adult education and training.

Finally, it is worth noting that both countries share some important silences. As well as examining what the policy discourse contains, and where the thrust of specific measures lies, it is important to take stock of what is not mentioned. Outstanding is the question of schools reform. For both countries, lifelong learning policy is broadly coterminous with post-school or post-16 policies on education and training.

The faltering policy drive

Over the past decade, lifelong learning has enjoyed a remarkable rise up the policy agenda in both the Republic and the UK. Both sets of governments have placed lifelong learning at the core of policy, and in so doing have noted explicitly the potentially revolutionary policy implications of this concept. Yet the development of concrete measures, and their actual implementation, have lagged substantially behind the language and ambition of the policy community. Although both governments acknowledge the breadth of the lifelong learning concept, policy has advanced across a relatively narrow and conventional front. According to Kjell Rubenson, a similar caution characterizes national policies for lifelong learning across the OECD (Rubenson 1999). Why should this be so? Was this simply a result of political bad faith or lack of political will, as so many claim? (Examples include Baptiste 1999, 95; Boshier 1998, 9; Collins 1998, 45; West 1998, 555.)

One school of thought argues that policy sterility is inherent in the concept. Bernt Gustavsson, for example, suggests that while the term itself is 'used as a vision', it tends to be 'rather empty of content', with no clue as to how it may be 'transformed into practice' (Gustavsson 1995, 92). And indeed, one difficulty lies in the nature of the issue itself. As already noted, it is not governments that will produce more learning among more people, but citizens. This is an issue which requires citizens to act (Beck and Sopp 1997). For governments, this presents obvious difficulties. Rather than government doing things directly, it is required to persuade citizens to change their ways. Instead of talking simply about standards or the supply of opportunities, policy-makers find themselves speaking in terms of 'a spirit of self-help', 'self-reliance' and 'personal growth' (DfEE 2000, 4, 13–14). And in the process of shifting away from service delivery or legislation to offering guidance and trying to steer citizens' behaviour, government has had to change its own ways of working.

Some degree of distance between policy rhetoric and policy achievement is inevitable. Between conception and delivery lies a series of mediating institutions and actors, and lifelong learning has been no exception to this general rule. This was vividly demonstrated in a thorough empirical study of UK government policies on vocational qualifications in the 1980s and 1990s, which showed that—contrary to conventional wisdom—the new competency-based system was not developed as part of an overarching Conservative strategy to reform further education; on the whole, most Conservative ministers who learned of the new system were inclined to view it with hostility. The national vocational qualifications system was driven through by visionary civil servants, taking advantage of ministerial indifference to vocational education, assisted by the divergent objectives of the different government departments with a stake in the area (Raggatt and Williams 1999). What government got, in this case, was very different from what ministers thought they were promoting.

It is also true that policy-makers are unlikely to identify lifelong earning as the next Big Idea in delivering electoral success. The teaching workforce in post-initial education and training is typically dispersed, often part-time, and poorly organized into lobbying bodies. Representative national associations frequently depend on government largesse for their existence, and are easily co-opted. Adult learners rarely define themselves primarily as students, not least because for many it is a part-time and short-term activity undertaken alongside and in support of other, much more important activities. In so far as learners do have a stake in the field, it is highly partisan and biased towards one particular form of adult learning (evening classes on a Tuesday in genealogy, for instance). A study of press releases over the New Deal in the UK suggests that even when government actively publicizes post-compulsory education and training initiatives, it does so by highlighting what it regards as more salient issues; thus Scottish Office press releases tended to play up the national Scottish dimension, while English press releases were more likely to stress welfare reform (Field 1999). No general political lobby exists for lifelong learning, and it is hard to see how this might change.

Third, no government is likely to tax its voters in order to provide the resources required, given the sheer scale of the deficits. To take one example, in early 2000 the UK government's National Skills Task Force recommended an entitlement of a qualification at Level 2 or above for all adults who do not hold one, estimating that the initial cost would add up to over £400 millions over the first three years (DfEE 2000, 49). Even this marked a retreat from an earlier proposal by the Kennedy Committee, which suggested an entitlement of a qualification at Level 3, usually regarded as the level of a skilled manual worker or an 18-year-old able to enter higher education (Kennedy 1997). Moreover, the Skills Task Force costings were based on an assumption that an additional 150,000 people a year would be achieving their Level 2 qualifications, making a relatively modest dent on the estimated 14 million adults in the UK workforce who are not qualified to this rather modest level.

So at one level, the absence of progress might be easy to explain, were it not for one rather obvious problem. Despite these weaknesses, governments internationally persist in placing lifelong learning at the core of their agenda for education and training. Yet the same governments adopt concrete policy measures that are limited in scope, and relatively conventional in focus. Why? This can only be explained with reference to the type of policy animal that lifelong learning represents. Like many other new policy areas—waste management, environmental improvement, community health, transport, crime reduction—lifelong learning belongs to a new species of policy agenda: those issues where it is citizens, and civil society more generally, that take the most important decisions. Developing in response to the perceived problems of globalization and technological change, as well as the accompanying social changes of the past three or four decades, these new policy objectives often deal with 'soft', intangible and complex issues, notably learning rather than education, for example. Further, they involve a broad and diverse range of actors, including large numbers of individual citizens and a variety of policy agencies rather than a single government department.

Lifelong learning is one of several policy areas where there is a new balance of responsibilities between individuals, employers and state. Of course, unlike schooling or conventional higher education, it has never been the case that adult learning was solely a public responsibility. Apart from anything else, many of the most important providers have always been non-governmental bodies. Indeed, much of the modern adult education system is inherited from nineteenth-century social movements that were created partly to challenge the state of their time, like the Swedish temperance movement or the British trade unions. Similarly, many of the costs have always been paid by individuals or employers; the public contribution has always been relatively small.

Even if adult education and training were widely seen as Cinderella services, by the 1940s they were acknowledged as part of the family of public provision that had been established through the social settlements of the late-nineteenth and mid-twentieth centuries. But private initiative far outstripped the state in financing both the supply of learning opportunities and in meeting the costs of learning. According to official estimates in the UK, employers in the late 1990s spent some £10.4 billion a year training their workforce, while total government spending on further education, higher education and work-based training together amounted to £8.2 billion (Felstead and Unwin 1999, 1). No reliable measure exists of the total contribution of individuals to their own learning, but it is clearly considerable, encompassing as it does a wide variety of spending to support learning in an extraordinary diversity of settings, in all of which adults are pretty much accustomed as consumers to spending their money as they wish (Field 1994a). What role is available for government to play in this emerging system, with its new and potentially unstable balance between what had previously been regarded as the private and the public spheres?

What makes matters even more uncertain is that the nature of government itself is changing, partly in response to electorates who are increasingly affluent, individualistic, and sceptical of authority (Giddens 1991). In tackling such fields as lifelong learning, government is more likely to effect change if it works through influence rather than power. Yet faced with increasingly sceptical electorates, governmental influence may—if ill wielded—either fail, or generate precisely the 'wrong' behaviour. As was argued in a recent European Commission working paper, devoted to the subject of regional social and economic development,

> The key issue here is one common to many institutions: how far an administration can move beyond a simple model of hierarchical control to a more decentralised system without losing the ability to coordinate activities. This balance is difficult to achieve, but rewarding in terms of tapping individual expertise and creating the conditions for policy innovation.
>
> (Mouqué 1999, 66)

In these circumstances, it is not surprising that governments face difficulties in identifying and promoting concrete policies for lifelong learning, and that their preferred solutions involve active attempts to mobilize civil society—including education and training providers. However, this in turn poses remarkably difficult challenges to those who manage and lead the institutions of provision.

The new governance

There have been substantial changes in the philosophy and organization of the public sector in recent years. In a reflexive world, the idea of an all-powerful providing State is attractive neither to politicians, bureaucrats nor citizens. It is not simply that the modern state machinery has become too expensive, although this is frequently a charge levelled by fiscal conservatives. In particular, the principle of state provision has in recent years run up against two broad trends. First, there are increasing numbers who can either supplement or opt out of state-provided benefits. In areas such as housing, pensions, health and even education, citizens who have provided for their own needs (or think they have, which is not always the same thing) are not often happy when it comes to spending their taxes on citizens who have chosen (as they see it) to spend their own money elsewhere. Second, universal and direct state provision can serve as an unintended bureaucratic block on society's capacity for learning and innovation. In the field of welfare provision and labour market regulation, for example, this has encouraged a widespread search for 'active measures' which place responsibility on citizens to plan and develop their capacity for earning a living, in place of 'passive measures' that enable individuals to cope with their present predicament (Rosanvallon 1995). One result of these tendencies is that governments are faced with electorates who no longer believe in the efficacy of universal state provision of services.

Where state action is accepted, though, it is increasingly managed in new ways. During the 1980s, a number of Western governments experimented with new forms of governance. Seeking to introduce private sector management, governments explored privatization, market-testing, purchaser-provider splits, disaggregation of separate activities, and closeness to the customer. At the same time, new methods of public management were developed for those services that remained within the public sector: transparent measurement of performance, hands-on professional management, decentralized authority, service-level standards, and target-related funding. Third, efforts were made not simply to provide services, but to engage with the private and voluntary sectors through catalytic partnerships. Finally, and most recently, there has been a new preoccupation with bringing together the different arms of government (and corporate decision-making) at a number of different levels, including the transnational, to function as a coherent network—variously known as 'multi-level governance' or, more popularly, 'joined-up government' (Benington 1998).

Taken together, this transformation of the public sector has been described as involving '"less government" (or less rowing) but "more governance" (or more steering)' (Rhodes 1996, 655). The new public management is not without its problems, however. With the move towards a contract culture, voluntary organizations are being confronted with a series of control mechanisms as government seeks to ensure accountability for public spending. There is a greater emphasis upon the identification of 'approved providers' and the specification of government-approved quality standards; there has been a shift towards steering by output-related funding. By adopting the language of partnership, policy-makers clearly hope to make this change more palatable. Yet the discourse of partnership frequently cloaks a profound inequality between the so-called partners, with the voluntary sector coming a poor third after government and business (Geddes 1997). Voluntary organizations find themselves competing against one another, and against the private sector, for contracts which can destabilize relations within the voluntary sector and unsettle previously harmonious relationships between voluntary bodies and local government (Commission on the Future of the Voluntary Sector 1996, 53). The language of markets and competition is, moreover, in tension with the trust, interdependence and stability required for effective network building, as is shown by the failure of Training and Enterprise Councils in Britain to steer the training system in ways that overcame existing deficits (Rhodes 1996, 664).

Further, many of the new approaches have been found to generate widespread negative unintended consequences. Thus output-related funding, rather than improving performance of service-delivery agencies such as colleges, has often distorted their behaviour. Rather than pursuing the aims originally envisaged by those who drew up the approved list of eligible outputs, organizational managers often seek to improve their share of resources by focusing on reported achievement against the key indicators, or reclassifying existing activities in order to meet new funding criteria, and downplaying other (unmeasured or less generously rewarded) core activities. Finally, the entire approach risks rejection by public opinion. The respected social scientist and Liberal Democrat thinker Ralf Dahrendorf has ridiculed 'Third Way' social democracy for its belief that government should 'no longer pay for things, but tell people what to do' (Dahrendorf 1999, 27). This has a ready resonance, not just with those who manage public services that are effectively privately financed, but also with those service users who pay an increasingly large share of the bill.

Then there is the problem of 'soft' objectives. In its White Paper on post-16 education and training, the British government proclaimed that 'Our vision of the Learning Age is to build a new culture of learning and aspiration' (DfEE 1999, 13).

Cultural change was also central to the recommendations of the Fryer Committee (Fryer 1998, Fryer 1999). If governments have to win people over by articulating a vision and seeking to change people's culture and values, these are not goals that lend themselves to easy measurement. Building a 'new culture' is at best a rather fuzzy political objective, and it is unlikely to be one where ministers or civil servants will feel confident in their capacity to develop clear criteria for judging success (or failure). Rather more to the point, it is unlikely to win support from the key policy-makers in finance ministries (McMahon 1998).

An illustration of the difficulties emerged when the Government revised the National Targets for Education and Training, which then became the National Learning Targets (DfEE 1999). They now included a target for 'reducing non-participation' among adults; while utterly admirable in itself, the difficulties in reaching an agreed definition of 'non-participation' are likely to prove formidable, as are the prospects of deciding who is responsible if this target is not achieved (Tight 1998). Similar complexity characterizes the question of informal learning, yet increasingly economic policy as well as education policy focuses on the role of networks and trust in facilitating the informal transmission of skills and knowledge (OECD 1999; Mouqué 1999, 63). More broadly, intangible factors invariably present policy-makers with measurement problems, as was recently acknowledged during an OECD seminar on knowledge management:

> In particular, knowledge is extremely heterogeneous in nature, and its value is not intrinsic but depends on its relationship to the user, so it cannot be quantified in the same terms as physical objects such as land or industrial capital.
>
> (OECD 1999)

Of course, lack of measurability does not make an objective any the less worthwhile, but it does present problems of political management that may make for a degree of volatility and exposure to criticism. In the absence of agreed and standardized outcome measures, though, the only alternative to high-trust governance appears to be restrictive and heavy-handed regulation, stifling the very process of change that policies have been designed to foster.

Pursuing soft objectives through partnerships with non-governmental actors also lays government open to the charge of throwing money away. Unpleasant it may be to say so, but partnership-based initiatives occasionally show a tendency to fall victim to fraud and abuse. Examples include not only some of the more questionable activities of Training and Enterprise Councils in England, or further and higher education institutions' sometimes relaxed approaches to franchising, but also strategies for community development (for example, see FEFC 1999, NI Audit Office 1995, NI Audit Office 1996). In recent years, such abuses have in turn attracted the attention of government watchdogs, including the influential House of Commons Public Accounts Committee, and of an ever less deferential educational press. Professionals responsible for learning programmes therefore find their actions increasingly exposed to public scrutiny, while at the same time being encouraged to be entrepreneurial and to take risks.

In addition, the new policy challenges cut across existing departmental boundaries. Conventional service delivery models of government usually fit well with government departments organized along classic civil service lines. Schools policy, for example, belongs in most countries to the ministry of education or its equivalent body, as does higher education policy. Lifelong learning, though, crosses these boundaries and involves a wide range of government departments and agencies. In *Learning to Succeed*, it is noted that the new national system of local Learning and Skills Councils for post-16 training and education will need to relate systematically to the Department of Trade and Industry's structures for small firms development, the Regional Development Agencies of the Department of Transport, the Environment and Regions, and the benefits offices of the Department of Social Security, as well as to local government (DfEE 1999). Developing coordinated measures that cross departmental boundaries is an ambitious project, given the extent to which civil service careers and cultures tend to follow well-established vertical tramlines. Pursuing policy objectives that transcend boundaries is therefore likely to provoke turf wars, to the point of intensifying inter-ministerial rivalries at the highest levels.

Yet the new public management holds particular relevance for lifelong learning. Lifelong learning is precisely the sort of problem that persuaded governments that the old ways of working were not enough. It also forms an important component in strategies for public sector reform, such as those that stress 'evidence-based policy-making' (Blunkett 2000). A number of governments have shown interest in the relevance of

> the concept of the 'learning organisation' with systematic improvement of policy from one cycle to the next, rather than a simple repetition of existing programmes. . . . Related challenges include those of establishing 'intelligent' organisational routines and of building a culture of trust and cooperation.
>
> (Mouqué 1999, 66)

Transforming organizational behaviour and attitudes lie at the heart of the new approach to governance.

Conclusions

Lifelong learning is, then, inherently a difficult area for government. Perhaps these intrinsic obstacles help explain why it is that general policy so rarely leads to innovative measures. It may also explain why it is that, when governments do act, as in the Irish Republic and the UK, they restrict themselves to the area of vocational training. First, it has considerable legitimacy, and is therefore politically 'safe' territory. Particularly in respect of training for unemployed people, this is a long-established area of direct intervention; it is associated with wealth-creation and living standards; and state training subsidies are usually welcomed by employers. Second, it represents a relatively easy field for non-regulatory types of intervention. Much responsibility for implementation and delivery rests with relatively low status and local actors (FE colleges, employment offices, local education and training agencies, and so on); partners can be won over through incentive funding; and the prospect exists of hard short term targets (such as jobs found, qualifications gained, or people trained). Third, finance ministries are usually favourable to this type of public spending (this is an extremely important quality for policy-makers). Investments and returns are priced in a way that seems largely impossible for such new, intangible areas as social capital, cultural change, or citizenship. Vocational training is, then, one area where governments feel impelled to act; and even here, they choose relatively familiar and uncontroversial measures, if tweaked in the fine detail.

The general policy banner of lifelong learning also cloaks a second arena for action where governments appear to feel comfortable: expanding third-level education. In the UK, for example, the New Labour government's Green Paper on lifelong learning was used to launch a substantial expansion in initial higher education, aimed at drawing in new types of younger student following two-year vocational programmes (DfEE 1998). The Republic of Ireland's White Paper has been used to promote an expansion of mature entry to the third-level sector, at a time when demographic trends have started to reduce the size of school-leaver cohorts

(Flynn 2000). Otherwise, lifelong learning suffers not so much from policy neglect as bafflement and uncertainty in the face of complexity, immeasurability and risk.

Does all this matter? It could be argued that the general expansion of participation in adult learning, undertaken largely at the behest of individuals and employers, is already driving progress towards a learning society. If so, perhaps it is best that government's role is uncertain and faltering? The financial costs of tackling the very problems that have caused governments to become interested in this area are considerable, yet electoral support for increasing public spending on supporting adult learning is likely to be limited. Interdepartmental boundaries and rivalries mean that many of the most serious weaknesses can only be tackled in a piecemeal manner. Many of the desirable characteristics of a learning society turn out to be fuzzy and unsusceptible to ready measurement. And all of this leaves unanswered the essentially ethical question of whether state or individual is best-placed to decide how, and indeed whether, to invest in the continual acquisition of new knowledge and skills. There are, then, sizeable barriers to sustained and coherent policy intervention to promote lifelong learning.

The prospect of continued faltering of policy intervention, though, also has its costs. Many of these will fall upon those who manage and deliver public programmes of learning opportunities. Ironically, the renewed focus of attention upon the learner has meant that the vicissitudes and predicaments of institutions are frequently neglected. There is remarkably little research, for example, into the impact upon teachers in further and higher education of sharp changes in the organization of the curriculum and the nature of teaching and learning, arising from the influx of adult returners into institutions that were originally designed for young initial entrants. Policies in relation to this phenomenon appear to consist largely in an increased emphasis on quality enhancement and performance measurement, both understood in somewhat narrow, managerialist terms. Continued policy neglect and inconsistency also increase the likelihood that unintended consequences will exact a substantial price. One obvious example is the way that a general push towards lifelong learning is likely to impact upon social inequality and marginalization.

Promoting lifelong learning does not simply require new government measures, but rather a new approach to government. This requires the development of a broad range of new capabilities not only on the part of the wider population 'out there', but also of policy-makers and providers, and of the institutions of government themselves. Experience of government modernization in Britain suggests that, at least in a relatively large nation-state, such reforms can easily fall victim to the insider culture and departmental boundaries of the civil service (Rana 2000). In an era of lifelong learning, wrought by deep underlying processes of change, it may be that smaller nation-states, particularly when deploying partnership-based models of policy-making, are better placed to survive and adapt. This is, inevitably, rather speculative. What is beyond doubt is that neither pathway offers an easy option. What is required appears to be a new concept of government that is rooted in a recognition of inter-dependence and inter-relationships between state (and its different arms), market and civil society, where values are made explicit and contested openly and widely through democratic processes across an expanded public space.

Note

1 Terminologically, describing the constituent parts of these islands represents a linguistic challenge. In this paper, I use 'Ireland' to refer to the island that comprises both the Irish Republic and Northern Ireland; 'Britain' refers to the island comprising Wales, Scotland and England. In addition, I have to thank a number of friends and colleagues for sharing ideas and information on policy issues, including Tom Collins, Ned Costello, Paul Nolan and Tom Schuller. None of these is, of course, to blame for my misunderstandings, errors and misinterpretations.

References

Baptiste, I. (1999) Beyond Lifelong Learning: a call to civically responsible change, *International Journal of Lifelong Education*, 18, 2, 94–102

Beck, U. and Sopp, P. (1997) Individualisierung und Integration: eine Problemskizze, pp. 9–19 in U. Beck and P. Sopp (eds.), *Individualisierung und Integration: Neue Konfliktlinien und neuer Integrationsmodus*, Leske and Budrich, Opladen

Beinart, S. and Smith, P. (1998) *National Adult Learning Survey 1997*, DfEE, Sheffield

Bélanger, P. (1999) The Threat and the Promise of a 'Reflexive' Society: the new policy environment of adult learning, *Adult Education and Development*, 52, 179–95

Benington, J. (1998) Risk, Reciprocity and Civil Society, in A. Coulson (ed.), *Trust and Contracts*, Policy Press, Bristol

Blunkett, D. (2000) Influence or Irrelevance: can social science improve government? *Research Intelligence*, 71, 12–21

Boshier, R. (1998) Edgar Faure after 25 Years: down but not out, pp. 3–20 in J. Holford, P. Jarvis and C. Griffin (eds.), *International Perspectives on Lifelong Learning*, Kogan Page, London

Collins, M. (1998) Critical Perspectives and New Beginnings: reforming the discourse on lifelong learning, pp. 44–55 in J. Holford, P. Jarvis and C. Griffin (eds.), *International Perspectives on Lifelong Learning*, Kogan Page, London

Commission on the Future of the Voluntary Sector (1996) *Meeting the Challenge of Change: voluntary action into the 21st century*, National Council for Voluntary Organisations, London

Commission on Social Justice (1994) *Social Justice: strategies for national renewal*, Vintage, London

Coolahan, J. (1994) *Report on the National Education Convention*, National Education Convention, Dublin

Dahrendorf, R. (1999) Whatever happened to liberty? *New Statesman*, 6 September 1999, 25–7

Dearing, R. (1997) *Higher Education in the Learning Society: Report of the National Committee of Inquiry into Higher Education*, NCIHE, London

Department for Education and Employment (1995) *Lifetime Learning: a consultation document*, DfEE, Sheffield

Department for Education and Employment (1998) *The Learning Age: a renaissance for a new Britain*, DfEE, Sheffield

Department for Education and Employment (1999) *Learning to Succeed: a new framework for post-16 learning*, Stationery Office, London

Department for Education and Employment (2000) *Tackling the Adult Skills Gap: upskilling adults and the role of workplace training: third report of the National Skills Task Force*, DfEE, Sheffield

Department of Education and Science (1998) *Adult Education in an Era of Lifelong Learning*, Stationery Office, Dublin

Department of Enterprise and Employment (1997) *Human Resource Development*, Stationery Office, Dublin

European Commission (1994) *Growth, Competitiveness, Employment*, Office for Official Publications, Luxembourg

European Commission (1996) *Teaching and Learning: towards the learning society*, Office for Official Publications, Luxembourg

Felstead, A. and Unwin, L. (1999) *Funding Systems and their Impact on Skills*, Skills Task Force Research Paper 11, DfEE, Sheffield

Field, J. (1994a) Open Learning and Consumer Culture, *Open Learning*, 9, 2, 3–11

Field, J. (1994b) Policy-borrowing and adaptation in the development of continuing education in Northern Ireland 1921–50, pp. 134–52 in *Cultural and Intercultural Experiences in European Adult Education*, ed. S. Marriott and B. J. Hake., University of Leeds Studies in Continuing Education, Leeds

Field, J. (1999) Skills and Employability in the Spotlight: exploring official discourses of training, pp. 101–6 in B. Merrill (ed.), *The Final Frontier: exploring spaces in the education of adults*, Standing Conference on University Teaching and Research in the Education of Adults, University of Warwick, Coventry

Flynn, S. (2000) White Paper Recommends £30m for Mature Students, *Irish Times*, 28 February

Fryer, R.H. (1998) *Learning for the Twenty-first Century*, First Report of the National Advisory Group for Continuing Education and Lifelong Learning, Department for Education and Employment, Sheffield

Fryer, R.H. (1999) *Creating Learning Cultures: next steps in achieving the Learning Age*, Second Report of the National Advisory Group for Continuing Education and Lifelong Learning, Department for Education and Employment, Sheffield

Further Education Funding Council (1999) *Bilston Community College Inspection Report*, FEFC, Coventry

Geddes, M. (1997) *Partnership Against Poverty and Exclusion? Local regeneration strategies and excluded communities in the UK*, Policy Press, Bristol

Giddens, A. (1991) *Modernity and Self-identity*, Polity, Cambridge

Gustavsson, B. (1995) Lifelong Learning Reconsidered, pp. 89–110 in M. Klasson, J. Manninen, S. Tøsse and B. Wahlgren (eds.), *Social Change and Adult Education Research*, Linköping University, Linköping

Kennedy, H. (1997) *Learning Works: widening participation in further education*, Further Education Funding Council, Coventry

McMahon, V. (1998) A Conceptual Framework for the Analysis of the Social Benefits of Lifelong Learning, *Education Economics*, 6, 3, 309–46

Mouqué, D. (1999) *Sixth Periodic Report on the Social and Economic Situation and Development of the Regions of the European Union*, European Commission, Brussels

National Commission on Education (1993) *Learning to Succeed: the way ahead*, National Commission on Education, London

Northern Ireland Audit Office (1995) *Community Economic Regeneration Scheme and Community Regeneration and Improvement Special Scheme*, Stationery Office, Belfast

Northern Ireland Audit Office (1996) *Department of the Environment: control of Belfast Action Teams' expenditure*, Stationery Office, Belfast

O'Dowd, J. (1999) Three-way Stretch, *People Management*, 16 September 1999, 50–4

OECD (1991) *Reviews of National Policies for Education: Ireland*, Organisation for Economic Co-operation and Development, Paris

OECD (1999) *Measuring knowledge in learning economies and societies: Report on Washington Forum on 17–18 May 1999 organised jointly by the National Science Foundation and the Centre for Educational Research and Innovation*, Organisation for Economic Co-operation and Development, Paris

Raggatt, P. and Williams, S. (1999) *Governments, Markets and Vocational Qualifications: an anatomy of policy*, Falmer, London

Rana, E. (2000) Open-plan Government, *People Management*, 6, 5, 34–42

Rhodes, R. A. W. (1996) The New Governance: governing without government, *Political Studies*, 44, 4, 652–67

Rosanvallon, P. (1995) *La nouvelle question sociale: repenser l'État-providence*, Editions du Seuil, Paris

Rubenson, K. (1999) Adult Education and Training: the poor cousin. An analysis of OECD reviews of national policies for education, *Scottish Journal of Adult Continuing Education*, 5, 2, 5–32

Tight, M. (1998) Bridging the 'Learning Divide': the nature and politics of participation, *Studies in the Education of Adults*, 30, 2, 110–19

Walshe, J. (1998) Plea for Funds to Help Adult Students, *Irish Independent*, 29 July 1998

West, L. (1998) Intimate Cultures of Lifelong Learning: on gender and managing change, pp. 555–83 in P. Alheit and E. Kammler (eds.), *Lifelong Learning and its Impact on Social and Regional Development*, Donat Verlag, Bremen

18 Inclusive learning for 'active citizenship'

Disability, learning difficulties and lifelong learning

Mary Stuart

> I do not know why I was not allowed to fulfil my potential then. Perhaps it was thought then
> that people who were seen as slow learners should not show what they could do with their
> lives. We, like children, should be seen and not heard. We were labelled as people with a men-
> tal handicap, and were not to be seen to be mixing with normal people.
>
> (Adams, 1995: 40)

Mary Adams who wrote these comments in her autobiography died in 1995 at the age of 65.
She had lived most of her life, from when she was 18 till she was 63, in a convent home for people
labelled as having learning difficulties.[1] Segregation from mainstream society into long-stay
institutions was the experience of many people labelled with learning difficulties throughout
the twentieth century. Cooper who was also institutionalized for over twenty years says in
her autobiography:

> In them days if you had learning difficulties or anything that's where they used to put
> you . . . They would just say, 'You, you've gotta go into a big hospital' and that's it.
>
> (Cooper, 1997: 29)

While our education services were being developed and expanded through the twentieth century, people who were at the time called 'mentally deficient' and later 'mentally handicapped',
were denied not only the right to learn but were being segregated, often forcibly, from the
mainstream of our society. At the same time people with physical disabilities were also denied
mainstream education and segregated in institutions. The 1944 Education Act, which was
seen at the time as a triumph for the provision of education for all, created barriers for people
with disabilities and learning difficulties and did not remove the notion of some people being
'ineducable'.

> Whatever may have been the intentions of those passing the Education Act, 1944, the
> effect was to define special educational needs as springing from physical or mental disabil-
> ity. The formal process that was required in order that a local education authority could
> 'ascertain' the need for special education often entailed resort to compulsory medical
> examination or the use of intelligence testing and invariably meant assigning the child to
> one of the statutory categories of handicap.
>
> (Tomlinson, 1996: 2)

Hence at the heart of our education system is a virulent form of exclusion based on a medical
model of social value which itself was rooted in a capitalist perspective of people's worth
(Oliver, 1990, 1993).

Watson and Taylor (1998) identify that the lifelong learning discourse is framed within a
tension between an economic or democratic imperative. However the social purpose

movement, which informs those who look to develop lifelong learning as a form of democratic learning have seldom taken account of the thousands[2] of people who were denied the right to education, both initial schooling and further and adult education, until 1970 (Tomlinson, 1996).

As the lifelong learning debate develops and is critiqued by advocates of a social purpose perspective, the rights of people with learning difficulties and disabilities need to be highlighted to develop a more inclusive form of radicalism. Riddell *et al.* (1999: 49) point out that 'adult education has yet to develop theoretical frameworks which can inform practice by articulating an understanding of the status 'adult with learning difficulties' and how educational action can address it'.

This chapter explores some of the issues relevant to an inclusive perspective on lifelong learning, drawing on debates on difference and different knowledges, policy developments, particularly in relation to widening participation and inclusion, and notions of active citizenship and I use the biography of Mary Adams as a case study to examine some of these theoretical questions. I suggest that creating learning environments that enable people with learning difficulties to participate more equally in the wider society is one of the greatest challenges facing the development of lifelong learning.

The issues raised by this challenge make us face quite starkly the realities of inclusion and exclusion, not just for people with learning difficulties, but for any group in society that has been labelled as different.

To facilitate an understanding of these issues I begin by outlining the history of the experience of education of people with learning difficulties during the twentieth century.

Certified to exclusion

As far back as the mid-nineteenth century, specialist 'idiot' asylums developed to provide education and to 'improve' the behaviour of 'idiots' (Wright, 1997) based on a developing 'scientific' classification system of 'types' of people (Foucault, 1978; Digby, 1997; Gladstone, 1997). These were, like much of the educational services at the time, largely voluntary or private. Later, after 1870, a broad-based formal education system was developed. The new schools began to identify 'children who could not learn' (Gladstone, 1997) and while earlier attempts at educating 'idiots' had some success, the new education system deemed some children as 'ineducable'. For some children this process happened before they started schooling, for others it was during their years at school that they were labelled as 'deficient'. The 1913 Mental Deficiency Act, that implemented large-scale institutionalization, grew out of these educational and moral debates along with a scientific desire to categorize degeneracy and mental deficiency (Jones, 1986; Alaszewski and Nio Ong, 1991; Williams, 1996). Young women, often between the ages of 14 and 18, were at particular risk of being certified as 'mentally deficient' and therefore institutionalized if they were sexually active (Williams, 1992; Cox, 1997; Gladstone, 1997). Jones notes that the majority of people placed in institutions were working-class and while women were at particular risk of institutionalization, boys were also segregated, often for petty theft or rowdy behaviour. Care provision for women was given priority in institutions[3] during the 1930s (Potts and Fido, 1991), because of fears of hereditary transmission of degeneracy and feeble-mindedness, fanned by the eugenics movement (Jones, 1986). Care in this sense was used as a method of control, and with the loss of rights through institutionalization these people lost their right to adult status (Walmsley, 1993). The definition of 'ineducable' which these young people attracted was 'imprecise' (Wright, 1997: 126), and medical practitioners who were charged with certifying a person's 'deficiency' often relied on the hearsay of family or friends. The connection between rowdy behaviour, sexual interest and intelligence may seem ridiculous to us now, but the increase in exclusions from school are perhaps an indication that behaviour and ability are still being connected in our education system today. During the first half of the twentieth century, for people with learning difficulties and for people with disabilities, education became a series of tests and limitations and for many their lives were constrained within institutions. Exclusion for these people was not only real, but it was permanent.

During the review of mental deficiency, in the early 1950s it was recommended that categories should be changed and certification ended, but until 1971 their right to an education was not enshrined in law. In looking at modernity's history of formal education from the perspective of people with disabilities, it becomes clear that many of the claims of ordinary people gaining rights to learn are contradictory. The 'scientific' developments of the early twentieth century including IQ tests and medical advances, rather than enabling people with disabilities limited their potential. Any debate of new policy, such as lifelong learning and inclusion, must not ignore the contradictory nature of the history of our current education system. The notion of lifelong learning is not as yet a 'taken-for-granted' concept as some policy-makers would have us believe, but is a contested 'idea' within the field. Before I go on to discuss the challenge posed by people with learning difficulties and disabilities to debates on lifelong learning, I will outline some of the key concepts that are needed to explore what lifelong learning may mean.

Lifelong learning: self reflective and participatory or learning for the economy?

Edwards (1997) highlights the shifting sands of adult learning in this context which is no longer 'bounded' by an enclosed 'field' (1997: 148). Johnston argues that 'lifelong learning is now centre-stage and adult educators should welcome it for the emphasis it places on adult learning' (1999: 175). However the concept cannot be simply equated with adult learning as Field and Schuller (1999) have pointed out. Lifelong learning is more about a different role for education and the development of different players in the definition of learning in society. Alheit (1999:) makes this point clearly. He says:

> We are observing a paradigm shift away from the concepts of education and training towards the concept of learning, in other words from a 'system-controlled' to a 'learner-controlled' notion of education and training.

Traditional adult education, whether liberal or radical, has focused on an education discourse which, although it may have included a negotiated curriculum, was still centred on a notion of a curriculum and a 'tutor'. These concepts are now more blurred and ill-defined in a world which is controlled by 'learners'. Other definitions of lifelong learning have highlighted learning in different environments such as the workplace (DfEE, 1998) which provides a challenge to the established learning institutions such as schools, colleges and universities. It will not only be determined by specific educational episodes in particular environments but will focus on a continuum of learning experience located within individuals and groups and engendered through a variety of encounters with others. Usher *et al.* (1997) highlight many of these themes in their discussions on adult education in the postmodern era where lifestyles play a significant part in the consumption of learning.

More recently Johnston (1999) has argued for a reconstruction of the social purpose model of adult education. He suggests that there are needs to recognize learning for different aspects of citizenship in the lifelong learning debate: inclusive citizenship, pluralistic citizenship, reflexive citizenship and active citizenship. He argues that citizenship encompasses both rights and inclusion and that learning across the lifespan would be a vital part of active citizenship. Some adult education theorists have begun exploring the role of social network and social capital (Coleman, 1988) and its relationship to learning (Schuller and Field, 1998) which raises some interesting questions about the possibilities of citizenship through particular networks. These debates are rooted in broader sociological debates about the nature of globalization, modernity and postmodernity (Giddens, 1991; Jameson, 1991; Beck, 1992) which continues to be unresolved.

Within the field of learning difficulties study, these debates are also raging. Having been excluded from society as people with learning difficulties were, theorists have attempted to suggest a range of solutions to develop inclusion, including the development of traditional social networks. As Riddell *et al.* (1995: 54) note:

> In the field of learning difficulties, normalisation theory, developed by Americans such as Wolfensberger (1972) and O'Brien (1987) has had an . . . impact. In its normative function-alism it also implicitly draws on social capital theory.

Normalization was developed as a result of the work of sociologists such as Goffman (1961) who pointed out that institutional services for people with mental health difficulties created more dysfunctional behaviour than the so-called 'medical' conditions with which patients were labelled. Normalization suggested that services needed to be more 'ordinary' to enable people to participate more 'naturally' within society and was a driving force in challenging the notion of ineducability. The 1971 *Better Services for the Mentally Handicapped* offered people with learning difficulties opportunities to learn a number of leisure pursuits such as drama and horse-riding. This was the first example of traditional adult educational opportunities being made available for adults with learning difficulties. At the same time special schools were developed in local authorities to offer children who were 'statemented' a chance to learn. By the 1980s a number of policy documents such as the Fish report (1985) and later the Griffith report (1988) called for integration of 'special education' into main-stream schools and colleges. Atkinson (1997) has pointed out that social policy and practice for people with learning difficulties has undergone several revolutions since the 1960s. She notes:

> Normalisation heralded the demise of modernity. . . it challenged the old certainties about institutional care. Ironically, though, it instituted new certainties of its own to do with integration and conformity and helped establish a new set of experts.
>
> (Atkinson, 1997: 140)

What Atkinson is particularly highlighting can be rephrased within the larger lifelong learn-ing debate. In other words, although from the early 1970s people with learning difficulties were given the right to education, they had no control over their learning environment, whether segregated or integrated. Nor was there any acknowledgement of the extent of learn-ing which people with learning difficulties and disabilities experienced throughout their lives. As with other areas of the debate on lifelong learning, the focus of educationalists, policy-makers and practitioners has been on service provision and not on individual or group learning experience. To examine some of the reality of this history and its implications for an inclusive learning citizenship, I will discuss the biography of Mary Adams. Mary, who was labelled as having learning difficulties came, by the time she was 62, to co-facilitate a series of reminiscence workshops with me and to teach word processing at her local adult education centre.

The power of informal lifelong learning

Biographical research into learners experiences have become popular in recent years (Stuart, 1995, Thomson, 1995, West, 1996, Alheit, 1999). It provides examples of specific experience of learning. It both challenges the grand theories of education and also reveals the reality of policy and practice on individuals (Atkinson, 1997).

The experience of Mary Adams highlights some of the key examples of the 'problem' with modernist formal education in Britain during the twentieth century. Her life also provides testimony to the significance of informal learning as both a positive and a negative socialiser. Most of all her life story highlights the value of continued learning opportunities which can enable people to develop and grow through extensive change.

Mary Adams's experience of schooling provides a first-hand account of the process of limiting people's learning potential. She recounts her first experience of school at the age of four when she was left by her parents. She notes that her experience of school was dominated by issues of class prejudice as well as ablism. She says:

> At school I was made to feel a dunce in a lot of subjects because the school I was at was really for daughters of posh people and my parents were rather poor, but they took me because mother could not find the right school for me ... The children were snobs and of course I had a bad time with their bullying.

> (Adams, 1995: 11)

In researching the experience of disabled children in schools, Leicester also highlights that prejudicial attitudes were also a factor:

> Some of the adult respondents had been educated in special schools and some in main-stream schools. When they were asked what they remembered about their schooling, interestingly they mainly commented on incidents reflecting prejudicial attitudes.

> (Leicester, 1999: 61)

However Mary's autobiography which she completed just before she died, highlights that there were significant learning experiences which arose from her family leaving her at the school which affected her sense of self-worth. She wrote:

> I was sent to a pre-prep school at four years old attached to the main prep school, as a boarder. I was brought there by my parents ... My parents thought it was a good idea to leave then, but I clung to mother screaming my head off and would not leave them ... I was devastated and very unhappy. It was then I started to feel that I was not wanted by people.

> (Adams, 1995: 11)

Clearly Mary was learning, about herself and about her relations with others. It was not only the process of formal learning that created her negative self-image, but also this sense of not being wanted was reinforced by other incidences of shaming at school. She went on to say:

> There were two girls in our form who used to torment the life out of me, and when the teacher left the room they made me, by pinching me, stand on the table and pull my knickers down so that the children would jeer at me. I trembled often with fright and burst into tears.

> (Adams, 1995: 16)

This process of shaming children is common in many stories and arguably affects the sense of self-esteem that an individual has (Simons, 1992). Although Mary indicates that she 'enjoyed and was good at English and History', when it came to exams, Mary had 'difficulty remembering things' (Adams, 1995: 16). Mary had two IQ tests, one at 14 and one at 17, just before her parents took her to live in an institution. These tests like many of the processes in formal modernist education were significant moments which shaped the future of the individual's learning opportunities. For someone like Mary who was labelled as a 'slow learner', these moments were important in defining her exclusion from the mainstream of society. She told me she had:

> . . . *quite a low IQ, mind you it's only since I've come here at the convent* [the institution where she was placed] *that my brain has woken up and I've realised I have potential.*
>
> (Mary, 1992)[4]

As well as her 'brain waking up', Mary describes how over the years the Sisters gave her tasks and roles. Mary told me she knew she could learn because she had proved it at the convent where she had become active in theatre productions where she would take the female lead; *'like the plays here, I learnt all my lines, I can't be stupid if I can learn lines'* (1993). Being successful was rewarded and she became the chief ticket seller for the convent's bazaars.

The formal education system, which clearly delineated between able learners and 'mentally handicapped' people, did affect Mary's parent's decision to place her in the convent for the rest of her life. However, during her early life at school informal learning experiences played a significant role in limiting her potential. Mary told me that her parents had told her she needed to live in the convent because she *'cried a lot'* (Mary, 1993). On examining Mary's accounts of being bullied and her sense of shame which developed, crying may seem an understandable response. Adult education theorists have argued for many years (Rogers, 1987, 1992) that informal learning is a significant part of the learning process. In Mary's case as with many people with disabilities and other excluded groups, informal learning was important (Leicester, 1993, 1999). Her ability to learn continued as she took up word processing in the 1990s when she was in her sixties. Her tutor was impressed with her development. When I told her this, she anxiously asked if he thought she *'was being forward'* (Mary, 1993). This sense of insecurity, born out of the shaming of her early life lessened during her last years (Stuart, 1993). As she took on new roles, including being invited to teach in several adult education classes and to act as a child minder for families in her local parish, her self-esteem grew. Having her manuscript accepted for publication gave her a great sense of pride and achievement. In her family history, Mary wrote, 'I have become intellectually better, and have become very independent' (Adams, 1991).

Mary had been originally 'named' as a 'slow learner', who was *'timid'* and *'would be taken advantage of'* (Mary, 1992, 1993). However this changed as her years in the convent progressed and she was recognized as successful. She wrote in her autobiography:

> It was in the 1970s that a nun came who showed me a lot of affection and trust. She started me on the road to independence, which I had been fighting for years (and had been held down by my parents). Everything changed then and I was looked up to and respected.
>
> (Adams, 1995: 45)

Mary needed the social recognition to build her esteem and to counteract the earlier shaming she had received. What we learn here is that learning is an integral process of both formal and informal experience. Being shamed or offered esteem (Scheff, 1991, 1996) impacts on our intellectual development and can affect the way our ability to learn is perceived by professionals. Equally Mary's positive learning experiences occurred in the convent before she encountered formal adult education. It is unlikely that she would have been as successful in her adult education classes if she had not been 'started on the road to independence' (1995: 45) as she says. In other words for people who had been denied maturity and devalued as learners the need for recognition and valuing of their abilities as adults is vital. This area is exactly what Leicester found to be lacking in many colleges. She notes:

> Another respondent... experienced ... [a] lack of recognition of her adult status: 'I liked the college but my only negative feeling towards it was... the way we were treated by the staff... we were told before we actually went there we would be treated like adults'.
>
> (Leicester, 1999: 77)

Equally much of the current curriculum in colleges does not take account of broader personal experience as Riddell *et al.* (1999: 63) point out:

> Current educational practice with adults with learning difficulties has a heavy emphasis on the transmission of social capital in the form of 'social skills'. Such provision is generally constructed within functionalist assumptions, seeking to minimise the deviance of the person with a learning difficulty.

Unlike this experience, Mary Adams took on a range of learning opportunities. When I first met Mary in 1992, she was already being 'trained' to move out. In 1993, Mary moved from the main convent building to a flat owned by the movement, down the road from the main convent site. She was very happy. She blossomed. She had been the first woman from the convent to go out and sell raffle tickets for the bazaars in the 1970s and was an active member of the women's group in the parish. In 1993 she was elevated to being a 'Eucharist Minister' (Adams, 1995: 48) in the church. Mary's attitude to living in the community was positive: '*I really do like being independent*' (Mary, 1994). The independence which Mary developed was supported by a number of different opportunities. The convent gave her a part-time job as a receptionist for the day centre they had developed, which she found '*interesting*' (Mary, 1994) and her work in the church helped her find a valued place within her community.

In September 1994 she moved into a bedsit of her own in an unsupported home. She became assistant tutor on adult education courses in local history and computing and co-led a reminiscence group with me till December 1994 when she fell ill. As Mary said in her developing autobiography in October, 1994, 'I go up to the convent every day from Monday to Fridays to do my charges so you see I am not lonely and it suits me fine' (Adams, 1995: 48). She had a range of support networks and shifted between friends and contacts in the parish community and the convent. Mary's involvement in planning the workshops for the reminiscence sessions was vital to the success of the project. It was an important learning experience for me as it helped me ensure that the process of planning sessions was clear. Involving people with learning difficulties and disabilities in course design is a relatively new concept but experience from the Open University course, *Equal People*, shows that such 'participation can be invaluable' (1993: 11). Unfortunately my partnership in learning with Mary was short-lived.

Mary visited her brother for Christmas holidays in December 1994. After staying a few days, she complained of stomach pains.

Mary was taken to hospital in the middle of January 1995. She was diagnosed as having cancer with a maximum of a year to live and she died in March 1995. Her funeral was held in the local Catholic Church. Despite holding over two hundred seats, the priest had to squeeze in extra chairs. At the service people spoke of Mary's dedication to the parish and her work for the convent. It was an emotional service and she was later buried in the grounds of the convent.

Mary's story is a sad reminder of the effects of the certainties of modernist discourses. Although there were many factors which 'caused' Mary's lack of success in her IQ tests, not least our current belief in the unreliability of the tests (Bogdan and Taylor, 1982), the certainty of scientific definitions of learning ability confirmed her parents' anxiety about her ability to live within society. It was not until she received encouragement and support that she was able to flourish although this was short-lived. Mary's learning experiences are a mix of formal and informal learning, both of which proved to be significant in the shaping of her life. Modernist traditions have emphasized formal education for all, but as I have argued, the 'all' was only those who were considered able to learn. The knowledge which educational establishments offered during the twentieth century is currently being fragmented and a growing recognition of difference is emerging. It is within this debate that a democratic vision of lifelong learning emerges and it is here that the idea of real inclusion becomes imperative. As with any biography, Mary's life was unique but it was also typical of several generations of young people with learning difficulties and disabilities. By using biographical material, issues and difficulties with theory are thrown into sharp relief. In the final section of this chapter I will explore how lifelong learning could offer a more enabling learning environment for people with learning difficulties and disabilities, and highlight some of the potential dangers for the future of lifelong learning if people with learning difficulties and disabilities are not included in future practice.

Conclusions: an agenda for change?

While within Johnston's typology of learning for citizenship, discussed above, 'active citizenship' is seen to encompass all the elements of learning for citizenship, the inclusion of people with learning difficulties and disabilities in learning agendas would require a particular emphasis on what he calls 'pluralistic citizenship'. He argues that pluralistic citizenship:

> can build on but extend beyond inclusive citizenship . . . Pluralistic citizenship recognises the existence of basic universal human rights but also leaves room for negotiation and variability, so taking account of the postmodern emphasis on heterogeneity, fragmentation and de-centring. It is a citizenship that is no longer based on sameness that, on the contrary, embraces diversity and cultural pluralism.
>
> (Johnston, 1999: 183)

This proposal seems like a useful agenda for enabling disabled people to participate in learning in their own right, which at present seldom occurs. As Leicester argues in her agenda for lifelong learning that is inclusive of the rights of people with disabilities:

> This emphasis on rights goes hand in hand with respect—respect for each individual as a unique centre of consciousness and a full citizen; such respect seems not to be encouraged in a culture of conformity which devalues legitimate differences between individuals.
>
> (Leicester, 1999: 114)

This is not to argue that learning for active citizenship should not be the goal for learning with people with disabilities but simply to emphasize the reality of their invisibility in most lifelong learning discourse. The Tomlinson report highlighted that provision for people with learning difficulties was not only patchy in colleges but that in most colleges the quality of provision was considerably lower than other areas of equality work, such as literacy programmes (1996: 6). Tomlinson did talk to Kennedy while she was working on her recommendations for widening participation and suggested in his report that there was a need for 'a general strategy to widen access and participation [giving] benefit to those with learning difficulties' (Tomlinson, 1996: 6). However, *Learning Works*, the Kennedy report (1997), does not highlight the needs of people with disabilities and in practice in colleges her agenda is being seen as focusing on other areas of inequality (Mercer, 1998). The contribution of people labelled as having learning difficulties or people with disabilities to a learning culture is not recognized. As highlighted in Mary Adams's biography this contribution can be invaluable. Her ability to point out difficult areas for our reminiscence workshops during the planning stage avoided unnecessary pain for the participants. Her sensitivity to people's learning needs enabled the curriculum of the word processing course to be adapted to the needs of people with learning difficulties.

Field and Schuller (1999) note that with the emergence of lifelong learning a new research agenda is required. They highlight the recommendations from a symposium on lifelong learning, which suggested that certain aspects of lifelong learning require on-going research. These included continued debate about the field of lifelong learning, how participation in learning is changing and developing, the environments in which learning occurs, the biographies of learners and the relationship between formal and informal learning, as well as how difference and knowledges impact on learning as well as the impact of finances and time on learning. They also point out that the research agenda has so far been rather limited:

> The focus of much research is still on a relatively narrow front. It is strongly geared towards formal education, and particularly towards the study of adult learning within the higher education system.
>
> (Field and Schuller, 1999: 6)

Certainly their agenda accords with key issues in developing an inclusive learning agenda for people with disabilities as discussed in this chapter. In undertaking this broader research agenda the contradictory nature of the debate on lifelong learning is thrown into sharp focus in examining the possibilities for 'widening participation'. The emphasis on assessment, rather than recognition, of learners and educationalists, often seems contrary to the more fluid and inclusive learning for citizenship which is advocated here. This chapter sounds a note of caution in attempting to develop new certainties in assessment. It is clear that historically our society not only created unnecessary suffering for many people through definitions of people's ability to learn, but also limited the wider society's ability to learn from difference. That is what the biography of Mary Adams teaches us and it is this recognition of difference that lifelong learning and learning for active citizenship will hopefully begin to facilitate.

Notes

1 I use the term learning difficulties throughout this chapter influenced by the self-advocacy movement who prefer this terminology and in line with Bogdan and Taylor's (1982) assertion that definition is socially constructed. During the period covered in this study, 1913–1996, legal definitions have included idiot, imbecile, moral defective and feeble-minded (1913, 1927 Mental Deficiency Acts). In 1959 the Mental Health Act ended certification and redefined definitions to include subnormality, severe subnormality and mental disorder. Moral Defectives as a category was removed. Mental Handicap was used in 1971. Learning disability was first used by the Department of Health in 1990.
2 The National Council for Civil Liberties ran a major campaign in the 1950s that identified about 100,000 people who lived in institutions.
3 I use the term 'institution' as a broad term to cover a range of residential segregated provision including, from the nineteenth century, asylums, colonies, established after the 1913 Mental Deficiency Act, hospitals that replaced them in 1959, and voluntary sector religious homes, a thread of residential provision that ran throughout the period.
4 I use italics to denote Mary Adams' speech taken from interview material gathered between 1991 and 1995.

References

Adams M (1991) 'The Atkinson Family Tree in words', unpublished hand-written work

Adams M (1995) *Those Lost Years*, QueenSpark Books: Brighton

Alaszewski A and Nio Ong B (1991) 'From Consensus to Conflict: the impact of sociological ideas on policy for people with a mental handicap' in Baldwin S and Hattersley J (eds)(1991) *Mental Handicap: Social Science Perspectives*, Routledge: London

Alheit P (1999) On a contradictory way to the Learning Society: A critical approach in *Studies in the Education of Adults*, Vol. 31 No 1 (April) 66–83.

Atkinson D (1997) *An Autobiographical Approach to Learning Disability Research*, Ashgate: Aldershot

Beck U (1992) *The Risk Society*, Sage: London

Bogdan R and Taylor S (1982) *Inside Out*, University of Toronto Press: Toronto

Coleman J (1988) Social Capital in the Creation of Human Capital, *American Journal of Sociology*, 94, 95–120

Cooper M (1997) 'Mabel's Life Story' in Atkinson D, Jackson M and Walmsley J (eds)(1997) *Forgotten Lives: Exploring the History of Learning Disability*, BILD: Plymouth

Cox P (1997) 'Girls Deficiency and Delinquency' in Wright D and Digby A (eds)(1997) *From Idiocy to Mental Deficiency: Historical Perspectives of People with Learning Disabilities*, Routledge: London

DfEE (1998) *The Learning Age: A Renaissance for a New Britain* (DfEE: London)

DHSS (1971) *Better Services for the Mentally Handicapped*, Cmnd 4683 HMSO

Digby A (1997) 'Contexts and Perspectives' in Wright D and Digby A (eds)(1997) *From Idiocy to Mental Deficiency: Historical Perspectives of People with Learning Disabilities*, Routledge: London

Field J and Schuller T (1999) Investigating the Learning Society, Studies in the *Education of Adults*, Vol. 31 No 1 (April) 1–10

Foucault M (1978) *The History of Sexuality: An Introduction*, Penguin: Middlesex

Giddens A (1991) *Modernity and Self Identity: Self and Society in the Late Modern Age*, Polity Press: Cambridge

Gladstone D (1997) 'The Changing Dynamic of Institutional Care: The Western Counties Idiot Asylum 1864–1914' in Wright D and Digby A (eds)(1997) *From Idiocy to Mental Deficiency: Historical Perspectives of People with Learning Disabilities*, Routledge: London

Goffman E (1961) *Asylums: Essays on the Social Situation of Mental Patients and Other Inmates*, Doubleday: New York

Griffith R (1988) *Community Care: Agenda for Action*, HMSO: London

ILEA (1985) *Educational Opportunities for All: Report of an Independent Review Committee (Fish Report)* Inner London Education Authority

Jameson F (1991) *Postmodernism, or, The Cultural Logic of Late Capitalism*, Verso: London

Johnston R (1999) Adult Learning for Citizenship: Towards a Reconstruction of the Social Purpose Tradition, *International Journal of Lifelong Learning*, Vol. 18, No 3 (May–June) 175–90

Jones G (1986) *Social Hygiene in Twentieth Century Britain*, Croom Helm: London

Kennedy H (1997) *Learning Works: Widening Participation in Further Education*, FEFC: Coventry

Leicester M (1993) *Race for Change in Continuing and Higher Education*, Open University Press Buckingham

Leicester M (1999) *Disability Voice: Towards An Enabling Education*, Jessica Kingsley: London

Mercer J (1998) Widening Participation in FE (Seminar presentation at the University of Sussex Continuing Education Forum)

Open University (1993) *Working Together as Equal People*, Open University K503

Oliver M (1990) *The Politics of Disablement*, Macmillan: Basingstoke

Oliver M (1993) 'Re-defining Disability' in Swain J, Finkelstein V, French S and Oliver M, *Disabling Barriers, Enabling Environments*, Sage: London

Potts M and Fido R (1991) *A Fit Person to Be Removed: Personal Accounts of Life in a Mental Deficiency Institution*, Northcote Press: Plymouth

Riddell S, Baron S and Wilson A (1999) Social Capital and People with Learning Difficulties, *Studies in the education of Adults*, Vol. 31, No 1 (April) 49–66

Rogers A (1987) *Teaching Adults*, Open University Press: Buckingham

Rogers A (1992) *Adults Learning for Development*, Cassel: London

Schuller T and Field J (1998) Social Capital, Human Capital and the Learning Society, *International Journal of Lifelong Education*, Vol. 17, 4, 226–35

Simons K (1992) *Sticking Up for Yourself: Self Advocacy and People with Learning Difficulties*, Joseph Rowntree Foundation: York

Stuart M (1993) Speaking Personally: The Self in Educational Oral History Work in N Miller and D Jones (eds) *Research: Reflecting Practice* (Manchester: SCRUTREA Conference Proceedings) 95–7

Thomson A (1995) Starting with Self: Life History Approaches to Training Adult Educators, in I Bryant (ed) *Vision, Intervention, Intervention* (Southampton: SCRUTREA Conference Proceedings) 171–7

Tomlinson J (1996) *Inclusive Learning: Report of The Learning Difficulties and/or Disabilities Committee* FEFC

Usher R, Bryant I and Johnston R (1997) *Adult Education and the Postmodern Challenge: Learning Beyond the Limits*, Routledge: London

Walmsley J (1993) 'Citizenship and Learning Difficulties' in Swain J, Finkelstein V, French S and Oliver M (1993) *Disabling Barriers, Enabling Environments*, Sage: London

Watson D and Taylor R (1998) *Lifelong Learning and the University. A Post Dearing Agenda*, Falmer: London

West L (1996) *Beyond Fragments: Adults, Motivation and Higher Education*, Taylor and Francis: London

Williams F (1992) 'Women with Learning Difficulties Are Women Too' in Day L and Langam M (eds) *Women, Oppression and Social Work*, Unwin Hyman: London.

Williams F (1996) 'Race Welfare and Community Care: A Historical Perspective' in Ahmad W and Atkin K (eds) *Race and Community Care*, Open University Press: Buckingham

Wright D (1997) 'Childlike in His Innocence: Lay Attitudes to Idiots and Imbeciles in Victorian England' in Wright D and Digby A (eds)(1997) *From Idiocy to Mental Deficiency: Historical Perspectives of People With Learning Disabilities*, Routledge: London

19 Black and other ethnic minority communities' learning needs

Alyson Malach

In recent years the globalization of the economy and changes in the labour market and organizational structures have pushed lifelong learning high on the political agenda. It is now widely recognized that in order to maintain and improve the country's competitiveness, skills and knowledge must be developed and up-dated throughout people's working lives. There is also a growing emphasis on the role of learning in helping the regeneration of local communities and encouraging active citizenship as well as combating social exclusion (Fryer, 1997; Edwards, 1997). This chapter has been written in the light of the current weight and attention being given to education and training, and specific government efforts to improve lifelong learning opportunities and widen participation for those who are disadvantaged, socially excluded and difficult to engage in learning. Its particular focus is on the place of black and other minority ethnic communities in the learning society.

Lifelong learning involves people learning throughout their lives, both formally and informally, in a range of different settings: in the home, in the workplace, in the community and in non-formal as well as formal educational settings. It involves learning across the spectrum from training in basic numeracy and literacy to training in the latest computer software packages. At the heart of lifelong learning lies the important principle of inclusiveness. It is essential that all members of society have access to real, relevant and appropriate learning opportunities: 'This country needs to develop a new learning culture of lifelong learning for all' (Fryer, 1997).

Black and minority ethnic people, however, are often those most marginalized in education and training, as in many areas they can be excluded by overt and covert discriminatory practices. Traditionally, further and higher education has predominantly served white, academically able learners. There are a substantial number of black and minority ethnic people who have been defined as failures by the education system and who remain outside the lifelong learning agenda. These include young black men—a group disproportionately likely to be excluded from school—and women of Bangladeshi origin. Nevertheless, some ethnic groups are participating at higher levels than expected, indeed rather higher than the average, for example men of African origin in further and higher education programmes (Sargant, 1991).

Participation patterns

Although the participation of black and minority adults in education is increasing it is uneven. There are evident imbalances in learner profiles within further and higher education. This can include significant variations within the black and minority ethnic communities. A study of the participation patterns of different ethnic groups (Sargant, 1991) showed that although overall around one in three adults (32 per cent) were engaged in recent or current study, there were significant differences between and within different ethnic groups. For example, 60 per cent of the African sample were studying currently or recently compared with 20 per cent of the Pakistani group. Other trends revealed by the study were that: more African and Chinese women were involved in current learning than men; a higher proportion of women than men were learning across all groups (although slightly more men from the Caribbean and Indian sub-continent were involved in learning than women from those communities); many respondents were studying full time as their main activity (including 21 per cent of African respondents and 10 per cent of Chinese); and high proportions of people from the African, Chinese and Indian communities were staying on in post-18 education. (The proportions from Pakistan, the Caribbean and Bangladesh were much lower.)

The differences between ethnic groups can also be seen within different education sectors. For example, although participation by black and ethnic minorities in higher education has increased steadily in the past decade—they now represent almost one in eight of all UK-domiciled students—they are more likely to be found in 'new' than old universities and their representation is uneven across the sector as a whole.

Looking at post-compulsory education as a whole, however, it is clear that a high proportion of members of black and other ethnic minority communities still do not engage in any form of organized education or training. One recent national survey of participation, *Pathways in Learning* (La Valle and Finch, 1999), confirms the findings of previous studies in showing that those least likely to have participated in learning after leaving continuous full time education include:

- those who left full time education without qualifications;
- those not in full time employment;
- manual workers.

Adults from black and other minority communities are disproportionately found in all three categories, and are highly unlikely to return to learning after leaving full-time education.

Reasons for non-participation

A range of reasons has been suggested for non-participation for these groups—lack of time or money, inappropriate locations, negative past learning experiences and lack of information. The latter issue is of particular significance at a time when the system itself is changing, and when so many of the new initiatives (such as Individual Learning Accounts) require individuals themselves to take action. A recent survey conducted by DfEE (La Valle and Finch 1999) found that although black and other ethnic minorities are highly motivated and keen to learn, 11 per cent of respondents said that they did not enjoy learning; 30 per cent had problems with fees; 30 per cent did not know what was available to them and 25 per cent felt unqualified to follow a course. A common finding is that people in the ethnic communities are unaware of the opportunities available: 'There is likely to be an inter-relationship between people's interest in learning, the style of learning they say they prefer, and their awareness of local opportunities for learning' (Sargant, 1991). There is also widespread evidence that black and minority ethnic individuals feel alienated in white middle-class learning environments where the curriculum is essentially Eurocentric (McGivney, 1990). Another finding is that racism plays a major part in the learning experience and subsequent learning intentions of black people. As the school exclusion rate of African–Caribbean young men is between four to six times higher than that of their white counterparts, it is not surprising that this group are significantly under-represented in forms of post-compulsory learning. While the Prime Minister's commitment to *'education, education, education!'* may appear to complement the ambition of parents of black children, the reality is somewhat different. There can be no doubt that the education system continues to fail black children, in some cases failing to provide them with any education at all (Hyatt, 1999). It is important that when considering the needs of black and other minority learners, we do not ignore the impact of their school experience on their attitudes to participating in learning.'Exclusion not only impacts on the academic achievements and future employment prospects of young black people but also leaves them open to (continuing social exclusion within society' (Audit Commission, 1996).

Geographical factors also enter the equation. It is often found that disadvantaged communities experience exclusion based on prejudice about the areas in which they are resident. For black and other minorities living in these areas, this experience is exacerbated by additional factors linked to racial discrimination.

Thus the reluctance of black and other minorities to engage in post-compulsory education may have more to do with attitudes, perceptions and expectations arising from their past experiences than with any practical barriers (McGivney, 1990). This does not mean that the black and ethnic communities do not want education and training. On the contrary, the black communities traditionally set great store by the well-being of their children and the establishment of Saturday supplementary schools for black children indicates that such communities value education very highly, and not only for children. The NIACE survey (Sargant, 1991) found strong evidence of unmet demand for provision of accessible English-language teaching and for appropriate learning opportunities across a wide area of (mainly vocational) subjects. However, the survey also indicated a need to raise awareness, among the different groups, of the opportunities available. There is little doubt that these learning needs could be easily met by education providers with careful strategic planning and, overall, education institutions could do far more that they are currently doing to integrate black and other minority adults into learning.

Improving participation among black and ethnic communities

If we genuinely wish to encourage lifelong learning then measures should be taken to widen participation in further and higher education by targeting black and other minority communities and by tackling racism within educational institutions. Education and Employment Minister Malcolm Wicks recently urged universities to step up their efforts to engage learners from black and other minorities in learning activities. Speaking at the conference, *Learning Through Diversity* (November 1999) he noted that 'In many ways ethnic minorities are succeeding in higher education. Entry rates are high and the number of well qualified graduates from ethnic backgrounds is increasing.' Robin Landman, Chair of the Black Managers Network, has also reminded colleges that 12 per cent of further education students are black and that colleges rely on black students for their business survival (*Times Education Supplement*, 3 December 1999).

Since so many of the barriers to education and learning are socially constructed, a key element in reconceptualizing provision for black and minority ethnic communities is the recognition that their needs are cognate with those of all learners. However, to maximize learners' opportunities to achieve and progress, the education system also needs to address the issue of diversity in participation by differentiating learning programmes as well as teaching and learning approaches according to learners' previous experiences, curriculum needs and preferred learning styles. In short, the concept of lifelong learning needs to be conducted with particular reference to black and minority ethnic communities' requirements and in close consultation with local communities.

Challenges for further and higher education institutions

Colleges and universities face a range of challenges in increasing participation of members of black and other minority communities. They need to review their provision to address the lifelong learning needs of these groups focusing on the educational entitlement that all adult learners should have. If we are to achieve the widening of participation in lifelong learning, the chronic under-representation and under achievement of black and minority ethnic communities should be a priority for all educational organizations. Many have not yet begun to seriously implement equal opportunities policy issues such as the recruitment of black and minority learners, discrimination and harassment, staff development and training, curriculum development and review. These should all be major considerations for discussion.

If there are institutional factors that inhibit the access and achievements of black learners, it is important that institutions find out what these are and deal with them openly. The Macpherson enquiry following the death of the black teenager Stephen Lawrence has highlighted the fact that unintentional racism can and does affect the way organizations operate, as well as the way people treat each other. The report described the way organizations condone 'institutional racism' which it defined in the following terms:

> the collective failure of an organisation to provide an appropriate and professional service to people because of their colour, culture or ethnic origin. Institutional racism can be seen or detected in processes, attitudes and behaviour which amounts to discrimination through unwitting prejudice, ignorance, thoughtlessness and racist stereotyping which disadvantages minority ethnic people.
>
> (Macpherson Report, 1999)

It is important that organizations are seen to address the issue of institutional racism whether it is intentional or not. There is a need to change any attitudes and practices that exclude or disadvantage individuals and/or groups of people from black and other minority backgrounds from actively participating in mainstream education or gaining access to resources and information on the basis of their racial or ethnic background.

It is no longer acceptable for organizations to ignore institutional racism because of lack of knowledge or apathy. Too many organizations have 'colour blind' policies and practices, which clearly ignore diversity of need, experiences and views of black and other minority people. Colleges and universities need to take the issue of race equality seriously if they genuinely wish to widen learning opportunities and participation for all. The experience of those organizations that are well advanced in tackling these issues is that they reap the benefits from implementing race equality policies and practices, e.g. terms of improved retention and achievement and better community understanding and relationships.

Race equality issues are not only relevant to colleges and universities in areas with a large number of people from black and other minority backgrounds; they also need to be tackled in rural areas where there are fewer numbers. It is a mistake to link race equality with the numerical or proportional size of the black and ethnic minority population in an area. To someone experiencing racial discrimination, it is irrelevant whether they live in an area where black and other minority groups are a small or large proportion of the population. Racism and racial disadvantage should be challenged in any area or institution.

Anti-racist strategies

The first step in any anti-racist strategy is an internal audit to remove the obstacles to access and stamp out racism. Organizations should:

- Value the contributions that black and minority people make to their organizations and society as a whole.
- Scrutinize and review the curriculum offered to ensure that all subjects and content are relevant to a multi-racial society.
- Offer curricula that value personal experiences and validate knowledge, culture and the experiences of black and minority ethnic people.
- Ensure that mechanisms that deal with student access, retention and progression are of a high quality and are fair and equitable.
- Ensure that anti-racist strategies in relation to curriculum delivery, student support, recruitment of staff and learners are firmly in place and implemented.

It is also important that education and learning institutions address issues and gaps within provision with rigour. Effective and equitable access to an institution means having in place procedures which ensure that black and minority learners have appropriate advice and guidance and are placed on suitable programmes of study with the appropriate level of learning and personal support to meet their individual learning needs. All this is particularly important given the policy commitments to substantial expansion in third-level education. For example, in Britain the Labour government has set itself the target of recruiting an additional 500,000 young people into further and higher education.

Institutions need to be sure about what they mean by access for black and other minority ethnic learners. They need to ensure that access is holistic and includes:

- equal access to institutions (pre-course);
- equal access to provision and progression (on course);
- equal access to cultural representation;
- equal access to the labour market (post-course).

Community consultation

In order to ensure that different groups gain real rather than token access to learning opportunities, institutions need to work in partnership with their local black and other minority ethnic communities, seeking their views and generally consulting them about their needs. This is particularly important given the role of lifelong learning in local and urban regeneration strategies, such as the New Deal for Communities in Britain which disproportionately affects the lives of black people and other inner-city populations.

Consultation with black and other minority ethnic communities involves developing provision with (not for) those it is intended to benefit. Organizations need to be conscious of the real meaning of capacity-building and of the dangers of disenfranchising the communities they work with by always presuming that they know best and acting and speaking on behalf of the communities. It is time that institutions recognized that consultation is an important factor in developing provision and engaging and retaining black and minority ethnic learners. Dialogue with community groups enables an organization to learn about their educational needs and aspirations. Seeking the communities' views and working collaboratively with them in real partnerships will gain trust and respect.

Although colleges and universities are skilled at working in partnerships with local people, local businesses and so on, disadvantaged groups like black and other minorities are often left out of any partnerships. Future efforts to widen participation by colleges, universities, local education authorities, lifelong learning partnerships and the new local learning and skills councils must therefore include black and other minority groups and associations.

Information, advice and guidance

Information, advice and guidance to assist learners to make appropriate choices about programmes of learning is not always available or in accessible language or format for black and minority ethnic communities. If people are not aware of what opportunities are available it is difficult, if not impossible, for them to take advantage of them. It is also the case that people with less previous educational experience and confidence find it more difficult to identify what it is they might want or what might help them unless they can see the nature of the provision and others like them successfully using it (Sargant, 1991).

If black and minority ethnic people are to be attracted to learning, provision of accessible advice and guidance must be made more widely available in a range of formats to meet the needs of these groups. Government policies for lifelong learning in Britain have included the creation of a national free-phone helpline and the allocation of resources to local adult guidance networks across the country. Good and impartial information, advice and guidance can help people to identify and explore all available options and point them towards institutions that offer good learning and language support. Effective guidance is not about erecting hurdles or sapping confidence, it is about identifying needs and aspirations, assisting people to make appropriate choices and ensuring that they have all the relevant information they need to form realistic and realizable goals (Dadzie, 1993). A recent discussion I had with a number of black learners revealed that those who had received no advice or guidance ended up studying at institutions where the level and provision of learning and language support were not appropriate, as a result of which they felt dissatisfied with their educational progress. Those who had made decisions and choices on the basis of good professional advice and guidance were satisfied with the learning and language support offered and felt that they were making good progress with their programmes of study and education as a whole.

Guidance staff require a deep understanding of the educational implications of racism, discrimination, social exclusion and disadvantage affecting black and other ethnic minority learners. Information and advice systems and referral networks should therefore be staffed by people with the awareness and sensitivity to respond to the needs of black and minority ethnic learners, especially asylum-seekers and refugees who have very specific needs based on their past life experiences.

Curriculum issues

In the interest of black and minority ethnic learners, learning institutions need to look more holistically at curriculum content, planning and delivery. Too many programmes for black and minority learners are stand-alone or bolted onto general institution provision. The nature of curriculum content and delivery is important to all learners but in particular to black and minority learners. Often the ethos and nature of the curriculum deter some sections of the black and minority ethnic community from entering or staying on programmes of study. Issues concerned with the experience and lives of black people should feature wherever possible in curriculum development. Too often the curriculum is Eurocentric and fails to take account of the specific experiences of black learners. As a minimum, the curriculum should acknowledge the major contributions of prominent black people such as Marcus Garvey,

Martin Luther King, Mahatma Gandhi and others. Books and written work by black authors can be easily introduced into the curriculum.

Staff recruitment and development

In order to make education and training more attractive to black and minority ethnic adults, educational institutions need as a priority to concern themselves with staff recruitment and retention. At present, only 6 per cent of teaching staff in colleges are from minority ethnic background and only 2 per cent of college managers and just two principals are black or Asian (*Times Education Supplement*, 1999).

A conference on diversity in post-16 education held in November 1999 heard delegates call for new league tables to reveal the extent of race discrimination in further education. There is no current data on the pay and status of black lecturers in FE. As NATFHE General Secretary Paul Mackney said at the conference: 'it is disgraceful that no figures are available to reveal the status and pay of black lecturers in FE'. Irrespective of the absence of detailed statistical data about the recruitment and selection of black and minority ethnic teachers, it is clear that there are disproportionately low numbers of teachers from these groups. The under-representation of black and minority ethnic teachers is a matter of great concern, which requires immediate attention and strategies for action. Institutions that are staffed by an all-white workforce or confine black staff to temporary roles give potential and incoming black students clear messages that public declarations about black access and equality should not be taken seriously (Dadzie, 1993). Many more black managers, teaching and support staff are required within educational and learning institutions as a whole. The absence of these staff speaks volumes about an institution's commitment to racial equality.

Education institutions need also to address inequalities in their selection and recruitment processes by recognizing that they may unwittingly construct institutional barriers that work against black and minority ethnic people for teaching support and management jobs. (For example, building into the specification, characteristics that are not a necessary requirement for the job and which can negatively impact on black and other minority applicants.)

There have been some welcome developments in addressing these issues. In England, the Secretary for Education and Employment, David Blunkett recently required all higher education institutions to introduce and implement policies on equal opportunities. Part of this would be an attempt by institutions to reflect on the composition of their communities by employing black and minority ethnic teachers. There has also been the establishment of a new commission on black staff in further education, to be chaired by the Director of Education for York, Michael Peters. Let us hope that these changes will make a difference.

However there also need to be changes in staff development practices. All staff should be offered training in equal opportunities and diversity. Initial and on-going continuing professional development does not fully equip teachers to address the issues and problems raised by racism, harassment and stereotypes. No teacher training institution appears to have succeeded in providing a satisfactory grounding in multicultural education or in managing diversity in the classroom/workshop for all its students. The majority of teacher training students are entering teaching having received little or no guidance on how to adopt a broad-based approach to teaching and learning which will take account of the presence and needs of black and minority ethnic learners. Teachers should be trained to examine their own attitudes and actions in an effort to ensure that their expectations of, and behaviour towards, black and minority ethnic learners are not influenced by stereotypes, misconceptions or negative views of these learners. Quality staff training can take place in a range of different forums, including course team meetings and working parties. It is necessary so that sceptics can be won over to more student-centred styles of interviewing, teaching and tutoring; and so that the converted can have sufficient time to think through and embed their efforts (Dadzie, 1996).

Language and learning support

Tutors frequently assume that black and minority ethnic learners who lack English communication skills require basic education. This is, of course, not always the case. Many black and minority ethnic people who lack English skills are highly qualified and multilingual. Often the deficit is not with the learners but with the institutions and the problem maybe that the quality and level of language and learning support provided by some institutions are insufficient. Staff in some learning institutions are often unaware of the needs of black and minority ethnic learners and in particular, refugees. For such students educational institutions need to ensure that they develop language policies if these are not already in place.

Functional language teaching requires close cooperation and planning between subject and language tutors. To improve language provision, staff should audit the learning needs of students. This will involve:

- identification of individual language needs;
- analysis of programme/course language requirements;
- identification of individual learners and their learning support needs.

A meaningful assessment of individual needs will involve thorough investigation of what learners can do in their first language, their previous educational experiences and a diagnostic assessment of the language needs of their chosen course and their ability to meet these successfully. It is also important that teachers monitor their own use of language to ensure that the subject matter is clear. This means identifying the language demands of the course and planning appropriate teaching and learning strategies.

Language support should be combined with the provision of appropriate information and guidance so that learners can take responsibility and control of their own learning. It should be flexible and wide-ranging, be an integral part of the curriculum offer and be written into an individual learning agreement where required. Of course not everyone needs help in improving English; however, a prerequisite for those who do is the knowledge that accessible programmes are available.

Mentoring

To assist and support new groups of learners, some institutions have established mentoring schemes. Mentoring as a support structure has supported black and minority ethnic learners well over time. For example, a further education college in Manchester has established an excellent mentoring programme for black access students. However, this service is funded externally and is therefore dependent on funding being maintained. I see mentoring as a tried and tested interventionist strategy whereby individuals are charged with supporting and guiding learners by using their own skills, knowledge and experiences. Mentoring can be and is used to produce, among other outcomes, role models, higher aspirations, increased motivation, improved attainment and the reduction of angst at transition phases. David Blunkett, Secretary of State, quoted in the *Times Educational Supplement* (13 March 1997), endorsed the principle of mentoring when he outlined the Government's plans for the role of industry in education.

Mentoring has proved beneficial in a number of ways and could be usefully supported in the future by learning institutions to benefit all learners, in particular those who have been the hardest to engage in learning because of previous negative educational experiences or exclusion

An agenda for change

This brief consideration of ways to bring more members of different ethnic communities into learning suggests the need for several key areas of action:

- A reduction of the rate of exclusion of young black boys from school. We need to explore and agree strategies for reducing the exclusion rates for this group, removing constructed barriers to learning and education and offering a wider range of activities and programmes that meet their identified interests and needs.
- Action on the lack of tutors and managers from black and minority ethnic communities. There is a clear need for positive action initiatives on staffing as an integral part of strategic planning and operational development. Now is a good time to do this. At a conference held at Lewisham College (15 March 1998) David Melville, Chief Executive of the Further Education Funding Council, was quoted as saying: 'The projected increase in student numbers by 80,000 over the next three years, requiring 23,000 new staff, is a real opportunity to bring about better representation in the workforce.' Black and minority ethnic teachers are role models for their communities and should be more visible at different levels in the workforce.

In addition:

- Adequate funding is required to meet the educational, training and support needs of black and minority ethnic learners.
- There should be a coordinated system for the provision of information.
- Guidance and support for black and minority ethnic learners. Information and guidance needs to be more readily available both inside and outside institutions.
- Guidance staff should be recruited from the black and ethnic minority communities.
- Information should be provided in different languages where necessary.
- More flexible and responsive forms of induction and assessment are needed to enhance black and minority ethnic learner access to the curriculum in educational and learning institutions. Such learners would also benefit from employment of teachers, managers and support staff who have an understanding the needs of black and other minority ethnic learners.
- Provision of continuing staff development and training to raise staff awareness of intercultural issues.
- Establishment of mentoring and peer support systems.
- Tutorial support.
- A wider range of programmes and content for black and minority ethnic learners.
- Curriculum content which addresses black and other minority adults' history and culture.
- Provision (where necessary) of flexibly available learning and language support on entry, on programme, and on exit.
- Dissemination of effective and good practice across the sector with regard to meeting and supporting the needs of black and minority ethnic learners.

- Development of an institutional ethos and environment in which all learners, cultures and contributions are welcomed, valued and treated with respect.
- Institutional commitment to creating a learning environment where racism, discrimination and harassment are not tolerated.
- Consultation with black and minority ethnic communities about the planning and design and support of educational programme and materials.
- Written publicity that actively assists and empowers black minority ethnic learners.
- Marketing and publicity strategies designed to reach black minority ethnic communities using language that can be clearly understood by everyone who may not be familiar with educational jargon or the British educational culture.

This will require a concerted effort by policy-makers and institutional leaders to build a climate that is truly inclusive, and promotes partipation by adults from a variety of backgrounds.

In addition, the government's lifelong learning strategy needs to ensure that the requirements of underrepresented groups are addressed by:

- Securing the representation of different community groups in emerging strategies for lifelong learning and the proposed Learning and Skill Councils.
- Raising awareness among teachers, managers and governors of colleges and learning institutions about the lifelong learning needs of black and ethnic minority communities.
- Promoting debate on the issues facing black and minority ethnic communities in their quest for lifelong learning.
- Encouraging long-term dialogue between organizations providing learning opportunities specifically targeted at black and minority ethnic communities.

Conclusions

If we are serious about widening participation in education and training among disadvantaged groups (in particular black and minority ethnic people) and promoting lifelong learning, then we must urgently consider the implications of the issues raised in this chapter and incorporate the principles and strategies advocated into our institutions' strategic and operational plans for widening participation and tackling lifelong learning.

If higher levels of participation and achievement of black and minority ethnic people are to become a reality, then the needs and entitlements of these learners must be addressed as a matter of urgency. Institutions have to listen to what the black and minority ethnic communities have to say. Black people have a lifetime of living with these issues. Talking to them and listening to what they have to say is the starting point for action to redress the balance. If the government is serious about lifelong learning they need to address the issues highlighted here and to support and encourage the black communities to learn.

Strategies to consult with the local black and minority ethnic communities, good practice in curriculum development and planning, fair and equitable staff recruitment and selection, which are all designed to improve the quality of teaching and learning for black and minority ethnic learners, are likely to enhance the prospects not only for black and minority ethnic learners, but for all learners whose needs have not previously been sufficiently recognized.

Improving access for black and minority ethnic communities requires substantial intervention by education providers and government, and the development of innovative approaches to teaching and learning. It appears that the government is genuine in its commitment to improving learning opportunities and widening participation. But good intentions need to be backed by practical anti-racist measures. As long as institutions still have equal opportunities policies that are paper-based only and black people from all walks of life continue to be discriminated against in education systems and the labour market, it will take more than just commitment to address the issue of inequality in education and learning.

References

Dadzie S (1990) *Educational Guidance with Black Communities*, National Institute for Adult Continuing Education, Leicester

Dadzie S (1993) *Working with Black Adult Learners*, National Institute for Adult Continuing Education, Leicester

Dadzie S (1996) *Older and Wiser: A Study of Educational Provision for Black and Ethnic Minority Adult Elders*, National Institute for Adult Continuing Education, Leicester

Fryer R H (1997) *Learning for the 21st Century: First Report of the National Advisory Group for Continuing Education and Lifelong Learning*, DfEE, Sheffield

La Valle I and Finch D (1999) *Pathways in Adult Learning Survey: Summary Report*, Department for Education and Employment, Sheffield

Leicester M (1993) *Race for Change in Continuing and Higher Education*, Open University Press, Buckingham

Macpherson W (1999) *The Stephen Lawrence Inquiry*, The Stationery Office, London

McGivney V (1990) *Education's for Other People: Access to Education for Non-Participant Adults*, National Institute for Adult Continuing Education, Leicester

McGivney V (1990) *Excluded Men: Men Who are Missing from Education and Training*, National Institute for Adult Continuing Education, Leicester

Sargant N (1991) *Learning for Purpose*, National Institute for Adult Continuing Education, Leicester

Skillington R and Morris P (1996) *Race in Britain Today*, Sage, London

20 Lifelong learning and voluntary organizations

Konrad Elsdon

A feast of languages and the cook's intentions

Once upon a time there used to be something called adult education, which included any form of learning engaged in by adults, whatever its aims, content or organization; it took cognizance of all their roles and ages. But we 'have been at a great feast of languages and stolen the scraps'. Since then we have belaboured each other with recurrent, permanent, continuing, community education, Freire, andra-and all the little-gogies, and now we are sentenced to lifelong learning. Like all these terms it is wonderfully flexible and means precisely what each user says it means or, more often, implies without saying.

Moreover, a term's meaning is greatly affected by whatever the government of the day understands by it. Few countries can have enjoyed such long continuity of educational policy as Britain has under Callaghan, Thatcher, Major and Blair. Governing a country where a 'down' is a hill, by 'lifelong' they naturally mean 'strictly limited'. As in its other connotation, lifelong is subject to a tariff. For all general purposes government intends it to mean 'for the term of paid employment or potential employability'. In the same way learning equals 'any formal course of instruction however provided which bears a clear, immediate and tested relation to the supposed requirements of the market and directly improves the marketable and tested qualifications of individuals.' Education has its own Newspeak forged in the fires of prejudice and political expediency.

This is not a new approach to education in Britain or at any rate England and Wales. It was well known to Matthew Arnold and the would-be reforming but ignored Royal Commissions of the nineteenth century. The difference is that it has come to be regarded as respectable; theoretical assumptions and practices which differ are scorned as strictly anti-educational. The idea of a wide educational spectrum which granted the propriety and indeed necessity of short-term utilitarianism at one end but also looked to broader understandings and long-term goals, which would be truly adult, truly lifelong, and relate to all of an individual's interacting economic, personal and social roles, used to be defended on the grounds of creativity, flexibility, learning capacity, transferability and consequent effects on employability and health; civilization and citizenship; sheer fun.

As wise employers such as the postal service and the chocolate barons knew earlier in the twentieth century, and as tough managers like Ford and British Telecom in our greedier age, it also worked. Yet what was, for a time, the world's leading educational provision for adults has now been reduced to a rump of vocational competencies with frills attached for the few who are able to afford them, and the even fewer who are conspicuously deprived and can't be choosers.

Government conceptions of educational purpose

Whatever their principles, in practice governments, especially in Britain, have almost always been opposed to education, especially for adults, which is strategically conceived, or to any kind of learning chosen by individuals for themselves, to any which is not subject to an apparatus of examinations, and which cannot be shown to subserve some marketable short-term objective. There have been some obvious exceptions. Tax income is still being forgone to maintain the privilege of broad education which survived in the best of the public schools until the examination system was tightened and university admission universally tied to it. More positively, there was a period during which British primary education in particular was encouraged to develop wide and intelligent reading, fluent but precise imaginative writing and an understanding of number, rather than sacrificing the education of children to a scramble for a school's position on a meaningless league table. Moreover, there was a time when the duty to provide the whole range of lifelong learning, including even provision for leisure time education, was enshrined in law. True—as papers beginning to become available show only too clearly—provision of the latter kind began to be resisted by the ministry soon after the passing of the 1944 Education Act and nothing as positive as even the vague treatment in its *Further Education* pamphlet of 1948 ever emerged again. Yet there was an astonishing development of the whole informal and non-formal field of work with adults, which did not begin to be reversed until the middle and late 1970s. It was achieved in the teeth of government and administration resistance by sheer demand, the marshalling of developmental pressures, and the improvement of curricular, organizational and professional standards from below, all discreetly aided and channelled by the small group of HMI who specialized in this field. Work with young people fared better. The Chief Inspector who presided over the field, Salter Davies, explained: 'The Albemarle Report was accepted in full and overnight because society is afraid of the young. Nothing will be done for adult education until old men start heaving half bricks through shop windows, (cf. Elsdon and others, 2001, *passim*).

Alas, old men mostly remained well-behaved and, despite some large protests, the last generation has witnessed the systematic destruction of what had briefly been the world's best adult provision, first of all by simple starvation accompanied by raising costs to learners at the rate of multiples of inflation, then by legislation which reduced the democratic legitimacy of local government in education. Government then priced non-school activities out of school buildings, and finally removed the ability of all providers (including higher education) to offer non-examinable and leisure learning to any but the affluent.

Government lacks power to interfere with independent learning

The impact of these changes on lifelong informal learning was gradual but nevertheless dire. Professional organizers and teachers, specialist institutions, large programmes of work diminished and were lost. Many of them attempted to continue in private ventures, but even if they were content with diminished earnings, costs remained prohibitive for anyone less than well-to-do.

However, none of the measures which began to be introduced by the Callaghan government, were exacerbated under those of Thatcher and Major, and continued under Blair, could directly affect any educational or learning bodies, organizations or activities which were independent of government. The innumerable voluntary organizations in which lifelong learning is not often a very conscious process, but takes place invariably and powerfully, continued on their way. True, a brass band could no longer affiliate to a local adult centre and have its conductor paid by it as a tutor. The cost to members of paying for his services might be high, but they would manage. More difficult for an operatic society which had the same arrangement but needed a school hall for its rehearsals; the new policy of Local Management of Schools meant that this public building suddenly became school property. Here charges for the evening use of its hall rose to the point where the operatic society had to charge literally prohibitive fees to its members.

Organizations which depended on grant aid found it harder and harder to extract it from their indigent local authorities. Many of the large social service organizations could only keep going by becoming contract-bound to public services desperate to shed their duties on others who could claim to fulfil them more cheaply, and often ceased to carry out their own aims in the search for contracts to help them pay their staffs. Yet despite all these problems, the voluntary sector survived and was the one and only area where lifelong learning could continue on a broad basis.

Significant exceptions

The statement about successive governments' opposition to strategically conceived education was qualified by an 'almost always'. Adult learning without utilitarian or age restrictions has, in fact, been encouraged or even provided by British government—sometimes on a spectacular scale. Army education during and for some years after the 1939–45 war involved literally millions in regular weekly non-vocational learning. Penal education, on a substantial scale, continues to do so. It is not only at the Home Office and Defence that educational values for adults seem to be understood; the Departments of the Environment, Agriculture and Fisheries, Health, and Culture and Heritage have unbroken records of such support. In fostering community centres and community development, Women's Institutes, Young Farmers' Clubs, self-help groups of every kind, and in providing local government (however modestly) with the means of aiding voluntary learning, effort and organization, they are to-day the main source of public support for informal lifelong learning by young people out of school and the whole adult population.

When it was near its peak, adult education expenditure in England and Wales was found by the Russell Committee to amount to 'barely 1 per cent' of all educational expenditure (Education and Science 1973, p. x), and it was this which the Ministry and the Department feared so greatly and sought continually to depress further. Yet recently available public information shows that when adult work was able to draw upon other parts of the education budget no hairs were turned. Perhaps lifelong learning would have fared better in Britain if it had been the responsibility of any department as long as it was not Education or if, within Education, it had hidden behind the skirts of some other branches (cf. Elsdon and others, 2001, *passim*).

Where is public support for informal activity directed?

Today, thus, public support from the education system to informal lifelong learning is negligible. However, there is relatively substantial support from other sectors of the government apparatus. This goes mainly to voluntary organizations, though largely to a tiny proportion of them. At the same time the present Labour government is showing a degree of interest in this field which is new, and will require consideration in its own right. What needs attention first is just what this universe of VOs is, on whose behalf this paper makes its claims, and what kind of lifelong learning it fosters.

The VO universe

For reasons too complex for brevity, but fully argued in Elsdon *et al.* (1998, Part 1), it has long been assumed that the voluntary sector consists of those large, usually well-staffed and old-established philanthropic and charitable organizations which employ large numbers of volunteers under professional control, which are well known to the public and, mainly, represented by the NCVS. It was assumed that there were approximately three or four VOs per 1,000 in the population, and perhaps 200,000 plus in the country. This assumption lies behind all the major reports on the subject, most recently that of the Deakin Committee (Deakin 1996); it also informed the Labour Party's pre-election (1997) document on the subject, *Building the Future Together.*

Occasional doubt was thrown on this mainly by community developers and adult educators in touch with VOs (Elsey 1974, 1975; Percy K. 1983, 1988; Chanan 1991, 1992), but the real situation only emerged from the case studies and locality studies of the Nottingham University project (Elsdon *et al.* 1991, 1992, 1993, 1994, 1995, 1998). This was set up to study adult learning in VOs, on the initial assumption that this could be done by means of a sample of intensive case studies of individual organizations and their members. In the process it found itself forced to develop a reliable typology of the sector as a whole in order to develop its sample, and to conduct reliably complete local surveys of it in order to study inter-relationships, effects, and incidence. A radically new picture of the voluntary sector emerged from this:

> The voluntary sector is incomparably bigger because most of it is the rich and free and infinitely varied expression of an active, lively and irrepressible populace. The voluntary sector includes not just those organisations which provide services to people who need help, advice or care; it embraces all those, formal or informal, large or small, which people set up and join because they like to play football or sing, perform plays or garden, watch birds, study the heavens or dig up the past, engage in politics, worship or Morris dancing. Even the care sector includes far more small, local, unstaffed and unsung informal groups and the rapidly growing brigade of self-help groups, than the well-known major organisations which government can colonise into its contract culture. The voluntary sector is infinitely richer and more varied than we have cared to assume, and a far more convincing and encouraging mirror of what our communities are about.
>
> (Elsdon *et al.* 1998, p. 9)

What all this means quantitatively can only be summarized in crude numbers here (Elsdon *et al.* 1995, 1998). In reality the incidence of VOs per 1,000 population ranges between 20 and 25. Nationally they total not less than between 1.3 and 1.5 millions. Just over 50 per cent have less than 30 members and some 30 per cent have between 30 and 99. Only 15 per cent have more than 100. Only 15 per cent of organizations employ any paid staff, and the great majority of these are concentrated in a much smaller proportion of large organizations. As many as 92 per cent of VOs are either formally or informally democratic. This percentage does not include those very large, mostly national, organizations which are governed by committees over whose composition and policies ordinary members have little or no control. However, the average percentage of individual members who take some form of active and responsible part in the running of their group or organization may be as high as 30 per cent, although a figure some points lower (perhaps 20 per cent), is possible.

The distribution of group aims is no less surprising. The large welfare-oriented, usually oligarchic, organizations which deploy volunteers under the control of paid staff in order to provide services to passive clients or users—i.e. what had been thought of as the essential 'voluntary sector'—represent less than 8 per cent of all VOs and of their individual memberships. The rest consists of organizations which are based neither on 'users and providers', nor on 'volunteering' and 'volunteers'. Far from being concerned with forms of patronage, these are organizations based upon the principle of responsible membership: they exist because individuals come together to pursue an interest or activity of their choice, making their own policy and controlling their own organization, including any paid staff they may employ. In that process they see themselves as independent persons who own their group. The high activism rates show that much work is involved in this, but like the process of defining objectives and making policies, this is controlled from within the group, not externally by staff or a remote headquarters, nor by a statutory service which uses volunteers to do part of its work and supplement its finances.

The approximately 92 per cent of VOs whose members pursue their own interests include a considerable proportion (probably some 18 per cent) concerned with health and caring, but these are usually small, self-governing, membership-based and local. They include both small carers' groups and self-help groups—two kinds of organizations which are growing rapidly in number and importance. A further 18 per cent are devoted to public service and environmental issues, while at least 54 per cent are devoted to the pursuit of strictly personal interests of all kinds. Among these, sport of all kinds seems to fluctuate between 35 and 40 per cent. Finally: at least 85 per cent (the same as those with less than 100 members and no paid staff) are entirely financed by their own efforts, and at a level which means their finances are of no interest to the authorities.

The distribution of both ages and sexes varies to some extent according to group objectives. Overall, however, women and men are equally represented both in membership and in rate of activism, and so are the age groups, from youth service and playgroups up to organizations devoted to service to, and activities by, the old. Financial accessibility, measured on the basis of national average wages, places just over 80 per cent of VOs in the low cost bracket; 12 per cent require some financial sacrifice; and 7 per cent (e.g. golf clubs, Rotary) are high-cost. The voluntary sector is inclusive as well as lifelong.

What learning and how much of it?

The learning which, it is claimed, takes place in the voluntary sector, is lifelong in that it escapes any 'tariff' and is (mostly) socially accessible. It is non-formal in not being tied into any external institutional structures, and informal in the sense that it is mostly contextual to chosen activities rather than externally imposed curricula. Moreover, much of it, and probably its most important aspects, are unpremeditated and often unconscious in the sense that it was only the interviews which made respondents aware of it. Few people, after all, make conscious resolutions to engage in a piece of informal learning. In this sense the concepts, and the experience, of learning and of change are not clearly distinguishable in this context, 'each turning into the other, being interchangeably cause and effect'.

But what is being learned, and how far-reaching, how penetrating are these learning activities? The field of enquiry opened up by these questions is too wide for general treatment, and the Nottingham research decided on an a priori division into five kinds of learning: social and group-related, content, occupational, political and personal, while realizing that there would be inevitable overlaps between these or any other conceivable categories. Their meanings and their distribution, will emerge in the following sections. The information rests upon a body of 31 intensive case studies of individual VOs and their members, and two locality studies, yielding a total of more than 1,100 interviews, and its interpretation in the project's publications. The project's subsequent, more recent studies and replications elsewhere (by the Community

Development Foundation in the UK and by a number of projects in Germany and in a current SOCRATES project) confirm the findings.

Social and group learning

As a term this was intended to capture social and interpersonal benefits and learning, both individual and arising from group membership. There were some instances of initial reluctance to acknowledge what might seem extraneous to an organization's aim. Yet social learning both as a personal bonus and as social education delivered to a membership, figured more prominently than any other kind in the responses. At 92 per cent it was second only to one other category. Even where its direct utility to the work of an organization was denied, it was claimed as essential to the process of group formation, group maintenance and cooperation. Respondents claimed to have gained in personal confidence, to have made contact with and learned to understand and appreciate people from a wider range of social backgrounds than their own, to share interests, cooperate. Mutual tolerance, accepting and being accepted, undertaking commitments, acquiring a sense of mutual support and being valued, of being a constructive member of a social network and many other aspects emerged, as did interesting variations related to group size, sex, objectives and other factors.

Content learning

Most members claimed that the content of whatever group they belonged to had been their main reason for joining it in the first instance; they were concerned with whatever activity, skill or knowledge were involved in the particular set of aims. As a result this kind of learning was mentioned more frequently than any other (98 per cent), but at the same high value in the context of social and group learning. Respondents felt that social learning and mutual support had enabled their content learning, while successful content learning (by which they understood the acquisition of competence regardless of subject or skill) bred confidence and all its related social learnings.

Clearly a vast variety is involved here, from specific subject (physical, craft or academic content) which might be offered by VOs such as community centres, women's organizations or specialist groups engaged in sporting or cultural activities. Some of these—say pigeon fancying—in their turn might involve ramifications in surprising directions such as genetics and meteorology as well as cost-benefit accounting and risk management. In addition to sometimes impressive specialization of learning there is also widespread evidence of its extension, as when proximity (for instance in a community or arts centre) or the inherent variety of some interest leads to the broadening of an individual's learning commitments.

Occupational learning

Occupational learning, as a term, was chosen in recognition of the fact that not everyone happens to be paid for whatever may be their vocational commitment. Because VOs are (like general as opposed to occupational AE) by definition a leisure-time occupation, it is not surprising to find that a high proportion of VO members treat them, almost aggressively, as a deliberate contrast totally unconnected with work. Nevertheless, interviews revealed unexpected connections in many instances, and the total of occupational learning effects amounted to as much as 57 per cent. Indeed, as many as 23 per cent of respondents gave instances of skills and knowledge acquired in a VO being transferred directly to their daily work. They ranged right across the gamut of practical, intellectual and social demands of the labour market, but also included deliberate organizational support of individuals engaged in training courses and the provision, for example, of adult basic education.

As many as 29 per cent of respondents gave evidence of generic skills acquired in VO membership which were transferable and valued in their occupations. They include competence, confidence, interpersonal and negotiating skills, ability to organize, manage, frame and execute policies, all of which were recognized in their jobs, improved their performance and raised their standing or led to promotion. Learned more particularly in committee and other responsible service (bearing in mind the almost one third of members thus involved at any one time), all these also benefited them in all forms of paid work and frequently in elected office.

Finally there was evidence of the effects in occupational performance and standing of maintaining the habit of learning and personal development, and the confidence to embrace new knowledge and responsibility. This, too, respondents claimed, was a capacity which, being transferable, was as it were ready to hand and gave them an edge over others at work. Moreover, transfer was found very frequently to extend to VO members serving not just as role models, but becoming quickly and strongly involved in formal training activity at work. Parallels, and important additions referring more particularly to the long-term unemployed, appear in the case studies of Aulerich (1998).

It needs to be borne in mind that 57 per cent of this national sample, in whom informal adult learning produces these occupational benefits, scale up to at least 15 million members of the adult population: the myopic contempt with which informal and leisure time adult learning has been, and continues to be treated by government in general and education ministries over the years in particular, baffles the mind.

Political learning

This was broadly defined to include 'all forms of learning and change which relate to understanding and responsible participation in group activity at *all levels* from the particular organization to the local community and to national and international issues'. The definition mirrors the very process by which individuals and, indeed, VOs as organized bodies contribute to the development of effective democratic civil society, a process which has been more fully described and argued in Elsdon (1997). Here it is possible to distinguish four developmental levels of responsibility, skill, knowledge and action, namely within the particular VO, on its behalf vis-à-vis others, within broader patterns, and at national and international levels.

We have already pointed out that 92 per cent of VOs are democratic and member-based. Since most are small, and the few larger ones usually create sub-structures, a sense of belonging and of ownership was found to be almost universal. Whatever the initial motives for joining, a habit of responsible service to the group quickly became no less important, and with this the political skills of discussion, tolerance, listening, ability to tolerate disagreement, as well as the ability to develop one's own opinion and stand up for it in public. Taking on responsible office within the organization usually follows, and this in turn involves representation vis-à-vis other organizations and the public sector. Even members of such small and informal bodies as most self-help groups are, find themselves advocating and negotiating on behalf of their members with elected and, especially, professional officials who may have a poor opinion of lay people wishing to paddle their own canoe.

As part of these processes members acquire a knowledge of the public sector and its needs and constraints, and it is hardly surprising to find that a high proportion of elected councillors in local government and a notable one of Members of Parliament received their initial experience of and training in political responsibility in the voluntary sector. Throughout the sample there was evidence both of all these levels of political learning, and of individuals graduating up the scale of interests. It was interesting to find that even among so small a number as the 31 case study organizations, two produced evidence of political learning and involvement having reached the highest, international, level. More generally, 76 per cent of respondents claimed to have become more aware of public policy issues as a result of VO membership and mainly in relation to this. Fewer, but still 59 per cent, had become aware and were learning about broader social issues and 49 per cent had become more aware politically in consequence. Thirty per cent had become more aware of specific political implications at a local, national or supra-national level, and as many as 25 per cent had translated this into overt action.

In respect of this particular kind of learning it may be permissible to take up space for a little of the more detailed analysis. Interestingly enough personal characteristics did not seem to relate to it except in one respect: women benefited significantly more than men in learning to speak, to advocate a point of view and to take action at all four levels. On the other hand there are strong correlations, both positive and negative, with organizational characteristics. Purely sociable organizations scored least on political learning, while women's organizations scored highest all round. The larger the organization, the better off financially, the less political learning and awareness. These are highest where there is no paid staff and numbers are small; learning diminishes as staff are introduced and numbers rise. In general, then, the more VO members depend on their own efforts and responsibility, the greater their political awareness and learning.

Personal learning and development

This is defined as that 'which seemed *to the respondents concerned* to have affected, or changed them *personally* in ways that seemed significant to them'. Almost all of them provided evidence of this at one level or another. A basic sense of security breeding confidence and the ability to give and take was the first outcome for as many as 81 per cent. A sense of achievement and competence, and therefore ability to cooperate, followed almost universally. Greater self-reliance and a sense of one's own worth were referred to again and again especially but by no means only by women branching out after years of domesticity. From this followed a readiness to trust and to stand up for one's own opinion, a readiness and ability to commit oneself not just in speech but in relationships. This in turn led to a sense of mutual respect and caring, of solidarity. All these made it easier for people to accept and discharge responsibility, to allow themselves to be stretched and in that process to discover and begin to exploit new and greater potential in themselves than they had been aware of. This in turn meant growing flexibility as a result of adopting new roles and new tasks, of continuous learning demanded by these. In effect there is, almost invariably if in different measure, a record of self-discovery and thereby of personal growth: people become more like what it is in them to become.

What all the responses under this heading had in common was a sense that this was learning and change which were so deep-seated that they became permanent and changed people's behaviour and attitudes for good. This was true regardless of individual characteristics, but the incidence of such learning did correlate to a significant extent with the organizational characteristics of the groups to which people belonged. As with political learning, it was the small groups without paid staff, and also those which demanded most activity from their members, that were most likely to precipitate personal learning and change at a high level.

Transmission, influence, co-operation and need

Extremely high values were obtained for transmission of all five kinds of learning. Interests and skills were found to be shared widely with friends and family, neighbours and colleagues at work, but it was invariably the more deep-seated forms of learning—changes in values, attitudes and behaviour—which also produced the most convincing evidence of transmission from observers. Moreover, individual learning and, to some extent, change, pass into the collective personality of the organization, and this itself learns, grows and develops over the years. We need to bear in mind that these members of VOs are also themselves the great majority of the country's adult population. Their influence is not confined to providing the community at large with a wide range of facilities and activities without which the fabric of civil life would be poverty-stricken. Because VO members are also members of the public and economic sectors, they also transmit their learning and change to these.

In British conditions, interaction between lifelong learning in the informal and voluntary sector and that which is more institutionally based is now less common and active than it could be at a time when a large and expanding system of general adult education was interacting with it. This could happen in a wide variety of ways, including teaching of content that supported the VO's activities and raised standards, or training in skills required for its conduct, as in the massive, demanding and, above all, appropriate training efforts which have long supported youth work or pre-school playgroups. On the other hand the voluntary sector could and did provide many of the organizational contexts which made more formal learning practicable, as for instance in youth organizations and voluntary adult education centres, community centres and village halls, but also under a wide variety of often ad hoc arrangements.

With the severe reduction in general adult education which has been discussed, lifelong learning in leisure-time interests ranging over the whole field and its wider impact, may now depend far more on voluntary organizations—and especially on the small local interest-based organizations—than on the institutional or public sector. They bear this responsibility without the recourse available to them in the past, to resources of organizing, teaching and subject expertise, the awareness of standards of every kind, and the training of tutors, all of which general adult education was able to contribute to them. There are exceptions, of which the internal training activity of the National Federation of Women's Institutes and, especially, the work of its Denman College are impressive examples. Exceptions alone cannot make up for the losses in both quantity and quality of opportunity suffered by what the 1944 Act nobly referred to as *the people of England and Wales*, as opposed to those affluent citizens and work-oriented students to whom services are now limited. The voluntary sector bears a huge responsibility as the organism in which memories of what was, its skills and interests and practices, survive. It must also act as a seed bank for future revival. None of this is possible if a sense of standards does not survive somewhere within it.

In present conditions the voluntary sector is therefore no less in need of training than it has always been. However, training by the formal education system is driven by funding rather than external need or the internal logic of real skill and expertise. Thus the finance of the system makes its institutions all the more anxious to discover opportunities to provide, and funding policy drives them into award and subject frameworks which are rarely relevant to any but professional workers in the voluntary sector—by definition a very small number of social work, health and administrative staff in the large organizations which can afford to pay the high-cost course fees involved. Neither is it possible, as it was for some years over much of the country, for adult learners to advance in subjects of their choice to full qualification, and then to rise by stages to fully qualified teacher status—all of it by part-time courses and at a cost which ordinary people could afford. With reduced opportunities the development of high standards of expertise and teaching skill appropriate to work with adults is still needed, and ways of securing it need to be developed. In the meantime, what the majority of VOs require is more often managerial and organizing skills at levels which do not call for qualifying courses at high fees they cannot afford. Short, informal, on the spot conferences and training, the sharing of experience and expertise among those who possess them in varying measure as a result of current practical involvement, are more likely to be useful and to attract participants. They can be easily arranged on a cooperative basis, or by umbrella bodies on the ground, such as local councils of voluntary services, where these are sufficiently in touch with the whole gamut of organizations, do not confine themselves to those dealing with health and welfare, and resist the blandishments of a growing army of self-styled training consultants which feeds on current funding arrangements.

Government policy and the future

The kind of preservation and development of high standards, and generally the process of enabling VOs to carry the lantern of adult lifelong learning into some brighter future, depends not only on their own efforts, crucial as these are. It also requires recognition, support and resources.

Government is showing signs of taking these needs more seriously with its new *Compact on Relations between Government and the Voluntary and Community Sector in England* (Home Office 1998). It is still heavily coloured by the needs and preferences of the large philanthropic bodies, whom the Government follows in their assumption that they *are* the voluntary sector, reserving the term *community* sector for its ill-informed estimate of the size of the great majority. However, the *Compact* is right in recognizing for the first time that the activities of a considerable number of government departments impinge on voluntary activity. Yet, it vitiates that recognition by leaving responsibility for it with a single department and, moreover, the one which has a history of paying sole attention to the vocal minority, ignoring the real composition of the voluntary universe, and paying no attention to the ways in which other departments' activities (e.g. the DfEE's Further Education finance arrangements and Local Management of Schools) affect a vast swathe of VOs. To become effective, responsibility for the *Compact* ought to be centrally located. The principles of the document are, however, sound as far as they go. So is the decision to flesh it out in greater detail, and above all, to encourage local authorities to implement its spirit in their own practice. Since the vast majority of VOs depend on, or are affected by the policies of local government, this is an essential condition of the new policy having any meaning in practice.

What, then do VOs need from local government if they are to be the lantern bearers of lifelong learning through the dark days of current policy on the education of adults? Recognition, first of all, of their importance and the worth of what they are doing, because this, in our society, is the most important reward of voluntary effort. The great majority of VOs do not need financial aid because their costs are low. However, accommodation is becoming an increasing problem since local management of schools has priced so much post-school activity out of these public buildings. Local government should devise ways in which organizations may be helped to retain or find premises suitable for doing their work in civilized conditions at a cost which does not exclude ordinary people. It should also seize all possible opportunities of obtaining or creating buildings which can become the homes of adult socio-cultural activities, and to give them an appropriate professional staff. Having lost the impact of a professional service of adult education, there remains the problem of how VOs may be enabled to aim at the highest possible standards in their activities. However this problem is addressed, it requires great sensitivity, but it may be less difficult in contexts such as community centres and broad-based councils of voluntary services, with professional staff used to facilitating and enabling rather than instructional roles. Finally, insofar as VOs do need financial aid or aid in kind from the public sector, it is essential to devise a new basis for its allocation. The current one—admittedly caused by short-term budgeting—is destructive. This is especially true of short-term contracts long enough to set up work only to let it go to waste again, but also because annual financing prevents organizations from engaging in rational development. Early notification, as advocated in the *Compact*, is a slight help but cannot touch the root of the problem. Ways of developing longer term, perhaps rolling funding, coupled with some simple form of evaluation, need to be developed.

Lifelong informal learning in VOs is almost certainly the most massive non-domestic pursuit in British society, though very many of those who engage in it see it as anything but 'learning' and might drop it like a hot brick if they were asked to acquire competencies or NVQs in it. It contributes not just to individual health and happiness but to the quality of life and the health of our civil society. It also takes much of the strain created by almost 25 years of destructive educational policy, and carries the promise of future potential. It succeeds in all this because it is democratic and based on the principles of responsible membership. It flourishes despite the fact that society and government concentrate help and attention on the tiny oligarchic segment which is capable of being colonized into the contract culture with the help of its supporting unpaid labour. Simply recognizing the whole voluntary sector for what it is and does would begin to establish its position. Giving it the very modest and sensitive help it needs would transform it to the benefit of all.

Abroad, and home

In other countries very little is known as yet about the link between VOs and lifelong learning, though it is reasonable to assume it exists. Up to now no comparable national, and few comparable locality studies seem to have been carried out. Several very substantial efforts are, however, in progress in a number of countries. Among those which have reached publication stage, Buggenhagen (1997) is of special interest. In making international comparisons it appears there may be some reason to suppose that, given legal arrangements and social patterns conditioned by the Common Law, it is easier for a wide variety of small, interest-based and fully autonomous VOs to flourish as it does in Britain. Conditions shaped by derivatives of Roman Law seem to favour large and formal, often barely semi-independent philanthropic bodies.

Nevertheless it is in certain Continental countries rather than in Britain that UK findings have been taken on board and exploited. Replications, adaptations and, above all, applications to policy and practice, are being pursued on a substantial scale in Germany and, through a European Union SOCRATES project, there and in Austria, the Netherlands, Hungary and Italy as well as the UK.

Most significant in the present context is the work of a large action research project set up as an independent programme by the German government to engage in the socioeconomic regeneration of the Eastern part of that country. As one would expect, both its practice and its theoretical foundations have been worked out and commented upon in generous detail; many and substantial publications have ensued. Among so many, perhaps Kirchhöfer (?1998) may illustrate the quality of conceptual thinking; the monthly journal *Berufliche Kompetenzentwicklung Bulletin* and especially the occasional policy-oriented articles by Johannes Sauer are important and informative. Readers looking for a brief and heavily practice-oriented description drawing on British experience with the concept may wish to consult Elsdon's 'Lernen im sozialen Umfeld' in Kossack (1997).

Accepting the need to create a democratic civil society, a sense of active citizenship and a spirit of enterprise, it was eventually realized that neither preaching these virtues nor the provision of training courses for non-existent jobs could deliver more than very limited success. The LisU programme (Lernen in der sozialen Umwelt—Learning in social Contexts) was the result. Its local projects set out to discover grassroots activities and societies in deprived communities, and found (as in the UK) that there were far more of these, and far more experience and civic responsibility on the ground than anyone had realized. They proceeded to build on this through encouragement, training, advice, injection of modest human and material resources. The results are the re-building on a new democratic foundation of individual and social confidence, the creation of new resources of independent and active citizenship, and of communities which are beginning to develop a capacity for autonomy, enterprise and self-government. The interesting point is that these economic, political and morale developments are being fostered in and through the local voluntary sector and its development. Comparison with the British regeneration projects is inevitable. Here there is a requirement to 'consult' the local voluntary sector, a duty which so far has nowhere been treated very seriously, since few local authorities are aware of more than a few large philanthropic organizations in their areas. In any case, the whole developmental process in the UK is being handled in a firmly 'top-down' manner—an odd proceeding for the country which invented community development. The LisU projects make an interesting contrast with their firmly 'bottom-up' approach based on individual and social learning. Might there be some virtue in the proposition that lifelong learning in the UK now needs to include learning the lessons of democracy which British administrators taught so successfully in Germany in the years after 1945?

References

Aulerich, G. (1998), 'Bedeutung freiwilliger gemeinnuetziger Taetigkeit fuer Kompetenzentwicklung und Bewaeltigung von Arbeitslosigkeit', in *Berufliche Kompetenzentwicklung Bulletin*, 7, December 1998, and (1999) *Individuelle Lebens—und Lernverläufe unter Berücksichtigung von Strukturen des sozialen Umfelds und des freiwilligen Engagements*, QUEM Materialien No.26, Berlin, Arbeitsgemeinschaft QUEM.

Buggenhagen, P. (1997), *Lernen im sozialen Umfeld—Kompetenzentwicklung im Auf- und Ausbau regionaler Infrastrukturen*, Schwerin, Trend.

Chanan, G. (1991), *Taken for Granted: Community Activity and the Crisis in the Voluntary Sector*, London, Community Development Foundation.

Chanan, G. (1992), *Out of the Shadows: Strategies for Local Community Action in Europe*, London, Community Development Foundation.

Education and Science, Department of (1973), *Adult Education: A Plan for Development* ('Russell Report'), London. HMSO

Education, Ministry of (1948), *Further Education*, *(Pamphlet No. 8)*, London, HMSO

Elsdon, K. T. (1991), *Adult Learning in Voluntary Organisations*, Vol. 1, Nottingham, Continuing Education Press.

Elsdon, K. T. (1997), 'Voluntary Organisations: Reciprocities of Individual, Organisation and Civil Society', in Fletcher, C. L. (ed.) *The Spirit of Adult Learning: Essays in Honour of Ralph Ruddock*, Wolverhampton, University of Wolverhampton.

Elsdon, K. T., Reynolds, J. and Stewart, S. (1992–4) *Adult Learning in Voluntary Organisations*, Vols. 2–4, Nottingham, Continuing Education Press.

Elsdon, K. T., with Reynolds, J. and Stewart, S. (1995), *Voluntary Organisations: Citizenship, Learning and Change*, Leicester, NIACE.

Elsdon, K. T., with Reynolds, J. and Stewart, S. (1998), *Studying Local Voluntary Organisations*, London, Community Development Foundation.

Elsdon, K. T. and others. (2001) *An Education Service for the People?—A History of HMI and Lifelong Learning*, Leicester, NIACE.

Elsey, B. (1974), 'Voluntary organisations and informal adult education', in *Adult Education*, Vol. 46, No. 6, March.

Elsey, B. (1975), 'Adult education and the 'expressive functions' of voluntary organisations', in *Vocational Aspect of Education*, Vol. 27, No. 68, Autumn.

Home Office (1998), *Compact: Getting It Right Together*, Cm. 4100, London, Home Office Communication Directorate.

Kirchhöfer, D. (?1998), *Begriffliche Grundlagen des Programms 'Lernen im sozialen Umfeld'*, Berlin, Arbeitsgemeinschaft Betriebliche Weiterbildungsforschung.

Kossack, G. (ed.)(1997), *Lernen für den Wandel, Wandel im Lernen*, Berlin, Quem Report 50, Arbeitsgemeinschaft QUEM.

Percy, K. *et al.* (1983), *Post Initial Education in the North West of England: A Study of Provision*, Leicester, ACACE.

Percy, K. (1988), *Learning in Voluntary Organisations*, Leicester, UDACE.

21 Education, training and adult refugees in the UK and Australia

Janet Hannah

The UK and Australia are two of the 134 nations to have ratified one or both of the United Nations Geneva Convention of 1951 and the subsequent protocol of 1967 relating to the status of refugees. Both countries provide protection or resettlement for significant numbers of refugees who are identified as people who are outside their country of nationality or usual residence, and are unable or unwilling to return because of a well-founded fear of being persecuted for reasons of race, religion, nationality, membership of a particular social group or political opinion. It is estimated that the total population of refugees and asylum-seekers in the UK is somewhere between 220,000 and 300,000 (Africa Educational Trust 1998), whilst 580,000 humanitarian entrants have settled in Australia since the Second World War (Iredale *et al*. 1996).

Having left behind their homes, work, education and perhaps family and friends, refugees are highly vulnerable to isolation and dislocation from 'normal' life in their place of refuge. Satisfying the most basic of human needs such as shelter and income will be the most urgent priority for refugees and their support organizations, but once these are met, other priorities will emerge, including access to education and training (Cox 1996). Asylum-seekers and refugees are highly vulnerable to economic and social exclusion, and participation in education and training can play a crucial role in helping refugees to rebuild their lives. For those who seek temporary protection, it can provide access to a constructive and practical period of exile. For those who are adjusting to permanent citizenship in the host country, it can make a significant contribution towards resettlement.

It must be acknowledged that whilst refugees share certain common characteristics, they are not a homogeneous entity: they come from a variety of social, cultural and educational backgrounds and have diverse and specific needs. Nevertheless, research indicates that there are fundamental barriers that are likely to impact upon most, if not all, adult refugees who seek to participate in education and training. These barriers fall broadly into three categories. The first, and probably the most serious, encompasses the physical and psychological problems which many refugees experience as a result of torture and trauma. The second relates to the process of resettlement and can include language, sociocultural and economic difficulties. Finally, institutional barriers will emerge, particularly in relation to formal education, and include the poor availability of guidance, information and advice, the non-recognition of qualifications and prior learning, and the lack of institutional sensitivity and support.

The various ways in which these barriers operate, and how they are currently being addressed, is presented and analysed. The chapter concludes with suggested improvements to policy and practice.

Refugee programmes in the UK and Australia

Whilst both the UK and Australia are major host nations for refugees, their national policies towards refugees and asylum-seekers are quite different. Australia operates a planned Humanitarian Programme, the size and composition of which is determined annually by the government after consulting with the United Nations High Commissioner for Refugees (UNHCR). This Programme in 1998–99 consisted of 12,000 places divided between four component parts, as follows:

> *Refugees* as defined in the UN Convention and Protocol who have been identified by UNHCR as in need of resettlement (this category includes the Woman at Risk Programme for refugee women and their dependants); 4,000 places were allocated in 1998–99.
>
> *Special Humanitarian Program* (SHP) Those who have suffered discrimination amounting to gross violation of human rights and who have strong support from an Australian citizen or resident or a community group in Australia; 4,250 places were allocated in 1998–99.
>
> *Special Assistance Category* (SAC) Those who do not technically meet the refugee or Special Humanitarian criteria, but are nonetheless in situations of discrimination, displacement or hardship. Applicants normally require proposers to be close family members resident in Australia; 1,750 places were allocated in 1998–99.
>
> *Onshore Protection Visa Grants* are awarded to those found to need protection in accordance with the UN Convention and Protocol who apply in-country, i.e. asylum-seekers; 2,000 places were allocated in 1998–99.
>
> (Department for Immigration and Multicultural Affairs 1999a)

In contrast to the highly structured Australian programme, the UK does not operate quotas or systematically accept refugees for resettlement, except in response to specific emergencies such as the expulsion of the Ugandan Asians and, more recently, the Kosovo crisis. Instead, the vast majority of those granted refugee status in the UK make an application for asylum, and in 1997, a total of 32,500 applications were lodged, half by people already in the UK (Watson and Danzelman 1998). A decision on the application is made by the Home Office, and will fall into one of three categories:

a)   those recognised as refugees who are granted asylum. After a period of four years, refugees can apply for full British citizenship; 4,000 people were granted asylum in 1997.

b)   those not recognised as refugees under the UN definition, but neverthless recognised as in need of protection and granted *indefinite leave to remain* (ILR) or *exceptional leave to remain* (ELR). This is time-limited, but may be renewed; 3,100 people were granted leave to remain in 1997.

c)   Those refused either asylum or leave to remain. There were 28,900 refusals in 1997, but 21,100 appeals were heard in that year, 6% of which were successful.

(ibid.)

As it can take anything between a few months and several years for a decision to he made on an individual application, a high percentage of the annual figures will relate to applications made in previous years. In both the UK and Australia, the systematic collection of data relating to the backgrounds of asylum-seekers and refugees is limited to country of origin, age and sex. No further data is recorded at the time of application relating to the entrant's state of health, educational qualification or occupation. The limited data that is available has been obtained from small samples and case studies, and is therefore incomplete and of limited generalizability. Whilst there is a strong argument that not officially recording such data is consistent with a non-discriminatory approach, it denies researchers a baseline against which to monitor the extent to which refugees are successfully gaining access to education, employment, health services and social services.

However, the age of applicants is recorded, and 1997 statistics show that three-quarters of both male and female applicants in that year in the UK were less than 35 years old, and less than 5 per cent aged 50 or older (ibid.). Their relative youth makes them more likely than other age groups to be predisposed to participation in some form of education or training, and some of them will already have been studying in the UK when their application for asylum was made. In Australia, the age distribution of entrants under the humanitarian programme is more evenly spread (Department of Immigration and Multicultural Affairs 1999b).

In a study of the settlement experiences of humanitarian entrants in Australia, Iredale *et al.* found that the proportion of respondents and spouses with overseas post-school qualification was 54 per cent (1996). The equivalent figure for the UK in Carey-Wood *et al.*'s UK study is 48 per cent (1995). There would appear to be considerable variation between different nationalities with the African, Serbian and Chinese entrants in the Australian study having high levels of post-compulsory education, and the Vietnamese, Kurdish and Lebanese low levels. Overall, the sample was more highly qualified than the Australian-born average. Comparable data are not available for refugees from specific countries in the UK, but it would appear that spontaneous asylum-seekers are likely to be better educated than those arriving through UNHCR programmes (Iredale *et al.* 1996). This is probably because access to the resources required, and the opportunity to travel and seek asylum, is greater for those who are well-educated in their home country and come from higher socioeconomic backgrounds. In general, the previous educational experience and qualifications obtained by humanitarian entrants will be an important factor in determining their expectations in relation to accessing education, training and the labour market when they arrive in the host country. However, their educational backgrounds will range from those who are highly educated professionals to others who are not literate in their own language. This wide variation results in highly disparate education and training needs.

The significance of education and training

Over half of the world's refugees are children and adolescents, and considerable attention has been focused on meeting their educational needs, particularly those of children who have been permanently resettled in a third country (Ahearn and Athey 1991, Kaprielian-Churchill 1996). Children of compulsory school age have a legal entitlement to receive education (enshrined in the United Nations 1951 Convention relating to the Status of Refugees and later in the 1967 Protocol), and are likely to be educated in groups within a single defined and highly structured system. In contrast, post-compulsory education is precisely that: not compulsory, and can take many forms. Consequently, the educational needs and experience of adult refugees is relatively difficult to research, and the extent to which conclusions can be generalized is limited. Nevertheless, a number of small-scale studies have been conducted in the UK and elsewhere, all confirming the crucial role that education plays in the psychological, cultural, economic and social adjustment of adult refugees (Africa Educational Trust 1997, Dodds 1986, Hannah 1999, McDonald 1996, Refugee Education and Training Working Group n.d., Refugee Resettlement Working Group 1993).

In the early stages of establishing refugee camps, education is commonly attached a high priority by the incoming refugee communities. Using exiled teachers and other educated refugees, they often take the initiative and establish classes for the children (Dodds 1986). Such provision is considered important for a number of reasons. Structure and a degree of continuity is maintained in the daily lives of the children, providing psychological support. Community and cultural identity is maintained in an alien and perhaps hostile environment, retaining a sense of purpose and dignity in a situation which can all too often breed a sense of hopelessness and despair. The involvement of the refugees themselves in the design and delivery of education programmes for both children and adults has become increasingly recognized as an important factor in overcoming the dependency which often results from prolonged periods in refugee camps. However, those who find themselves in camps run by hostile authorities can have a very different experience. An Iraqi refugee in Australia who had spent years in the Rafha camp in Saudi Arabia recounted a time when the camp's technical college was closed as a punishment by the Saudi authorities after a riot against the appalling conditions in the camp. The experience of the camp had badly affected several of his colleagues who had also resettled in Australia (Hannah 1997). Since a higher percentage of refugees in Australia are resettled by the UNHCR, they are more likely to have spent time in refugee camps than those in the UK who are more likely to have made an individual application for asylum. However, many asylum-seekers in the UK are imprisoned if they are deemed to be illegal immigrants, or pending an appeal if their application has been refused. The experience of being incarcerated in a camp or prison is likely to have physical and psychological consequences, even under more humane regimes. This will compound and prolong the trauma already experienced in the stages leading up to the decision to flee. It is to those physical and psychological consequences, and their effects on the willingness and ability to undertake education and training that we now turn.

Physical and psychological problems

Refugees often experience physical and psychological problems emanating from the factors which prompted their flight (intimidation and torture), the circumstances of their flight (hazardous journeys) and the conditions they encounter in the host country. In some cases, the pre-arrival experience will have been so traumatic that work or study is out of the question and a lengthy period of rehabilitation involving medical care and counselling may be necessary. All new arrivals will require a period of time in which to re-orientate to the new society and culture, and 'grieve' for the pre-refugee life which has been left behind, perhaps forever. Some time may elapse before refugees are in a position to seek employment or further study, particularly if they are suffering from physical or psychological problems. Various studies of refugee resettlement substantiate this (Carey-Wood *et al.* 1995, Refugee Resettlement Working Group 1993, Reid and Strong 1987).

The after-effects of torture or trauma commonly cause physical or psychological symptoms, disrupting the ability to concentrate or study. If a refugee launches into education, training or employment too soon, the inability to cope and make progress will compound the lack of self-confidence and sense of hopelessness. To minimize the danger of this occurring, it is vital that refugees have access to adequate torture and trauma counselling and are properly advised about their readiness to undertake study or employment. In the UK, specialist medical services for those who have suffered trauma and torture is provided by the Medical Foundation for the Care of Victims of Torture. The equivalent Australian organization is the Service for the Treatment and Rehabilitation of Torture and Trauma Survivors (STARTTS) which provides specialist counselling services and employs a specialist education and employment officer to provide advice and practical support to clients seeking employment or study.

The experience of torture and trauma is likely to have repercussions for refugees who embark upon education or training. A STARTTS education and employment officer cited examples of clients who had entered college or university, but were unable to complete their courses. However, she also believed that whilst their difficulties were undoubtedly exacerbated by the experiences which led them to become refugees, other factors compounded the problem (Hannah 1997). Basically, these were problems typically experienced by students from non-English-speaking language and cultural backgrounds. She quoted the example of a client from El Salvador who had a place on a humanities degree at university. His decision to leave the course was based on his inability to adjust to the teaching and learning styles and academic expectations which proved very different to those with which he was familiar. This problem of difference in academic norms and practices is, of course, a common problem for international students in the UK and Australia, and one to which we return below in the discussion of institutional sensitivity and support.

For the vast majority of refugees, the experience of flight and arrival in a strange country with a different language and culture is likely to be traumatic. Upon arrival in the host country, the refugee becomes vulnerable to the domestic legal, economic, political and social situation. It goes without saying that a hostile environment is not conducive to physical and psychological well-being. Their perception and experience of the warmth and support with which they are received in the host country is therefore important. In both the UK and Australia, this is likely to prove ambiguous. Agencies and community groups with a specific remit to support refugees generally provide a good service, but official agencies, the media and society in general are less likely to be welcoming. Government policies that seek to deter asylum-seekers and media claims of 'bogus' applicants exploiting domestic generosity fuel a widespread atmosphere of suspicion and racism.

Resettlement problems

Australia operates a comprehensive resettlement programme for humanitarian entrants at a cost of $10.7 million in 1997–98. This includes the on-arrival accommodation (OAA) programme which provides initial short-term accommodation in self-contained flats for (normally) up to 13 weeks, and the Community Refugee Resettlement Scheme (CRRS) whereby volunteer groups help with settlement assistance such as arranging schooling. The English classes provided by the Adult Migrant English Program (AMEP) discussed below are also part of the resettlement programme. Entitlement to income support and translating and interpreting services is also immediately available (Department of Immigration and Multicultural Affairs 1999b). In the UK, settlement services are overseen by the Voluntary Services Unit (VSU) located within the Home Office, but unlike Australia, there is no comprehensive resettlement programme (Carey-Wood *et al.* 1995), although the Refugee Council and other bodies continue to lobby for its introduction (Refugee Council 1997).

It is commonly recognized that there is a 'hierarchy of needs' in relation to the resettlement of refugees (Cox 1996). In March 1997, the Australian Ministerial Council on Immigration and Multicultural Affairs agreed priorities as English-language training, access to the labour market, settlement information, access to housing and translating and interpreting services (Department of Immigration and Multicultural Affairs 1997b). These are, of course, interconnected. With the possible exception of the most unskilled occupations, access to the labour market will require a degree of language proficiency to which we now turn.

Language Proficiency

A recent study in the inner London boroughs identified the lack of proficiency in English as the main barrier to education, training and employment identified by refugees (Africa Educational Trust 1998), a finding consistent with a number of other studies (Department of Immigration and Multicultural Affairs 1996, Iredale *et al.* 1996). The ability to understand and communicate in the host country language is crucial to access and benefit from education, training and employment (Carey-Wood *et al.* 1995, Department of Immigration and Multicultural Affairs 1996b, Refugee Education and Training Working Group n.d.). This is recognized in Australia where all migrants from non-English-speaking backgrounds (NESB) are entitled to 510 hours of free English-language tuition through the Adult Migrant English Service (AMES). AMES also offers counselling for refugee (and other) clients and frequently provides advice and practical help to refugee students wishing to continue their education. Meanwhile, there is no statutory requirement to provide English-language tuition for NESB refugees arriving in the UK, and the provision of English-language tuition remains sporadic and unsatisfactory: 'We need to develop a positive policy to provide refugees and asylum seekers with an entitlement to learn English, as part of a national strategy for English speakers of other languages (ESOL)' (The Refugee Council 1996).

As well as the absence of a legal entitlement in the UK, the Refugee Education and Training Working Group (n.d.) identify other barriers in accessing adequate English-language tuition. Securing a place on a course is often problematic, as long waiting lists are common. Frequent and disruptive changes in housing, particularly amongst those in bed and breakfast accommodation, can result in long distances between home and place of study. This can result in high travel, and possibly childcare, costs which can prove prohibitive. Ability to attend classes will also be affected by the need to deal with other pressing issues such as sorting out welfare benefits and attending legal consultations. Most basically of all, there are many barriers to establishing what ESOL provision is available and appropriate to meet individual needs:

> Refugees need individual advice and counselling on their English-language needs. Refugees are not a homogeneous group and they have diverse needs. Some of these language needs are literacy, study skills, survival skills, understanding colloquial English and oral communication, English related to their work, job search skills and the opportunity to practise with English speakers.
>
> (Refugee Education and Training Working Group n.d.: 4)

It is obviously desirable that language classes be sensitive to the level and needs of the individual learner, but wider social and political factors can also impact upon their degree of success. An AMES tutor gave the example of a class containing both Bosnians and Serbs, and the difficulties this created for both staff and students (Hannah 1997). The decision was then taken to establish classes for specific refugee groups in such situations. Similarly, women from particular communities might find themselves unable or unwilling to attend courses with men and attendance at single-sex classes may be their only opportunity to study English.

In interviews with a range of organizations involved with the training and employment of refugees, 44 per cent of respondents believed that refugees faced racial discrimination in job opportunities (Africa Educational Trust 1998). Again, however, the significance of English-languages proficiency emerges as a crucial factor shaping employer attitude. Indeed, its significance can be exaggerated by potential employers, using it as an excuse not to employ refugees. Furthermore, employers were considered to have a 'linguistic bias', exaggerating the language skills required for particular types of employment (ibid.).

Sociocultural problems

Excluded from the labour market for legal, linguistic or other reasons, refugees and asylum-seekers may become dependent on welfare benefits and public housing. This concentrates refugees in poorer neighbourhoods where they become easy scapegoats for the dissatisfaction of other poor and excluded citizens who consider them to be in competition for scarce housing, health and other public resources. It is estimated that 86.5 per cent of refugees in the UK live in London, and a high proportion of those in Australia live in the Sydney metropolitan area. Furthermore, they are concentrated in the poorer areas of these cities: nine inner London boroughs and the Western suburbs of Sydney. Refugees commonly become the target of local intimidation and racist abuse, forcing them, particularly women, to maintain a low profile by rarely going out and maintaining social contact largely with members of their own ethnic community. This is exacerbated by, and exacerbates, poor English-language proficiency resulting in an inability to communicate. A vicious circle ensues in which refugees (and members of other non-English-speaking ethnic minority groups), remain separated from other local communities, inhibiting the development of English-language proficiency. Non-white refugees with a high level of English proficiency are still vulnerable to racism, but less likely to be identified as 'foreigners'. As one Somali refugee has noted: 'At the University they think I am from Birmingham and they never consider I'm from Africa' (Carey-Wood *et al*. 1995: 90).

Some refugee women will also have specific needs arising from their religious/cultural background, marital status and family responsibilities. A UK study found refugee women six times more likely than men to be widowed or divorced, and 40 per cent of the refugee women in the study were single parents. Men were much more likely to be living as single persons—50 per cent, compared to 25 per cent of the women (ibid.). A high proportion of women in both the UK and Australia have children, and many are single parents. In some cases, the practical demands of looking after a family with little financial or other support precludes any possibility of undertaking education and training. In others, cultural expectations are such that looking after the family will take priority, and the ability to undertake study outside the home will be severely constrained. These constraints have been recognized to varying degrees by voluntary and official providers. The timing of courses can be arranged so that the hours are flexible and fit in with school hours and holidays. Childcare facilities can be provided on-site, at no or minimal cost. Language tuition can be provided by a woman tutor in the family home, and women-only courses are offered by public and voluntary providers such as the Training and Further Education (TAFE) colleges in Australia and the Refugee Education, Training and Advisory Service (RETAS) in the United Kingdom. A particularly successful example of targeted provision for women refugees is that offered by the Australian National Committee on Refugee Women (ANCRW). In 1992, ANCRW started courses for refugee and humanitarian-background women who had been unemployed for at least a year. Between 1992 and 1996, over 400 women passed through the programme, undertaking six-month courses which might broadly be described as preparing them in various ways for the Australian labour market. Topics covered in such courses include job-seeking and job-keeping skills, orientation to Australian society and the business community, English language and personal development. Agreements had been reached with sympathetic local employers to provide work experience, and these occasionally led to offers of employment (Hannah 1997). The work experience element was viewed as particularly positive in helping women gain access to the labour market, and approximately 50 per cent of those completing ANCRW's courses found work soon afterwards, with another 10 per cent typically continuing their studies (ibid.).

Economic barriers

Since few refugees and asylum-seekers have savings or other private sources of income, lack of finance can be a major barrier to participation in education and training. Whilst those granted full refugee status are entitled to welfare benefits, mandatory education grants and other sources of financial support on the same basis as UK citizens, the regulations governing these entitlements are complex and can be mutually undermining. For example, the Jobseeker's Allowance (which replaced Unemployment Benefit and Income Support) allows claimants to undertake up to 16 hours a week 'guided study' in further education, and there is no restriction on hours for those unemployed for over three months. However, an offer of employment cannot be refused because the hours are incompatible with course commitments. In such cases, the onus is on the claimant to find a solution by re-arranging or giving up their studies. This has resulted in concern that refugees (and others) may find themselves with no option but to abandon their studies and accept low-status, low-wage jobs (Refugee Council 1996).

Restricted access to welfare benefits, work permits and financial support to study are deliberately designed to deter potential asylum-seekers who must be resident in the UK for at least three years to qualify for Home and European Union (HEU) status. Whilst awaiting a decision on their application, they are required to pay overseas students' fees that are commonly three times greater than those charged to HEU students. This is also the case in Australia, where the refugee and humanitarian programme is highly targeted and promotes the planned and orderly movement of people. Asylum-seekers are often perceived as 'queue-jumpers' who are fortunate enough to have the means to travel to Australia and apply in-country, 'stealing' places from the less fortunate who may have waited for years in refugee camps to be resettled under the UNHCR programme.

An Immigration and Asylum Bill currently being debated in the UK Parliament (late 1999) seeks to introduce further punitive measures that will include the partial replacement of cash welfare payments with vouchers and forcing asylum-seekers to accept accommodation outside London. As the Council for International Education has noted:

> At present, participation in learning by asylum seekers is underpinned by the support from community groups, access to legal advice and to specialist services. Without such access, there will be greater pressures on the student support resources of institutions at a cost to the public purse. If students are re-housed, mid course, they may find their travel costs prohibitive and it may become impossible to continue their course. The new proposals are likely to increase the incidence of such disruption.
>
> (Council for International Education—UKCOSA 1999: 3)

Institutional barriers

The third type of barrier commonly faced by refugees seeking access to education and training can be described as institutional, as it relates to the policies and practices of the educational authorities and institutions. High quality advice, information and guidance will increase the chances of refugees undertaking the best courses to meet their personal needs. The recognition of prior educational qualifications and learning can also make a crucial difference to the ability of refugees (and others) to access education and training at an appropriate level. Once embarked upon education or training, the degree of sensitivity and support encountered will have a major impact in determining whether the course of study is successfully completed. As discussed below, however, there remains scope for improvement in overcoming these institutional barriers.

Lack of appropriate advice, information and guidance

Various studies have confirmed that refugees have difficulty in accessing effective sources of advice, information and guidance (Africa Educational Trust 1998, Hannah 1997, McDonald 1996). Often, it is to the various voluntary and non-governmental bodies that provide advice and guidance on welfare issues in general that refugees turn when they first seek advice about access to education and training. The network of Australian Migrant Resource Centres (MRCs) employ Specialist Migrant Placement Officers (SMPOs) with a specific remit to help clients access employment, education and training. However, it is difficult for them to maintain the up-to-date specialist knowledge necessary to fully advise clients about opportunities in the broad and complex field of post-compulsory education and training. Staff from the MRCs, and others based in ethno-specific refugee projects, have reported that they believe refugees to be disadvantaged by the absence of an appropriate source of information and guidance that is general, impartial and sensitive to the circumstances and needs of refugees (Hannah 1997). In the UK, however, a number of important initiatives have been launched to address this need. These include the Refugee Education, Training, and Advice Service (RETAS) and the Refugee Education Unit, both of which are based in London.

The mission statement of RETAS states its commitment:

> To support the social and economic development of refugees and asylum seekers in the UK and at a European level by facilitating their access to education, employment and training opportunities and unlocking their potential both as individuals and members of the community.
>
> (WUS 1997: 3)

RETAS services include individual advice and guidance, and training courses in various aspects of seeking and preparing for employment in the UK.

The Refugee Education Unit 'was born out of a recognition that many refugees and asylum seekers were not able to use their time constructively' (REU 1997: 6). It is based in a community resource centre in an area heavily populated by refugees and asylum-seekers. Although it is based in this centre, the education outreach workers go out into the community to establish contact with refugees and asylum-seekers in hostels, day-centres and other places where refugees live or meet. It is interesting to note that the research and subsequent report which led to the creation of the Refugee Education Unit identified a particular need to address the education and training of young men. The report concluded that: 'the needs of young male refugees are neglected. Services for refugees tend to be targeted at families and single women' (Harker and Gamaledin-Ashami 1995: 5).

Several refugee-specific support projects have been established within further education colleges and universities. The Refugee Project at Bournville College in Birmingham was established in 1992 as a joint venture between the College, the Local Authority and the Further Education Unit. From the outset, it has focused upon the accreditation of professional refugees, facilitating the recognition and accreditation of prior qualifications. Individual and group tuition is provided, and supervised work placements are also arranged. Accreditation is the particular concern also of the Refugee Assessment and Guidance Unit (RAGU), established in 1995 at the University of North London. RAGU offers support to individuals and groups in developing a portfolio of evidence for the Accreditation of Prior Experiential Learning (APEL), an opportunity which is particularly welcomed by refugees (and other migrants) who may have difficulty in having their qualifications recognized in the UK. This in turn brings us to the issue of the non-recognition of qualifications and prior learning.

The non-recognition of qualifications and prior learning

Migrants to Australia, and non-EU migrants to the UK can face enormous problems in having their skills and qualifications recognized. A 1996 Australian government report on migrant access and equity acknowledges the discriminatory nature of the skills recognition system 'at least in outcomes' to the detriment of those 'not trained in a system developed from the British model' (House of Representatives Standing Committee on Community Affairs 1996: 53). Consequently, large numbers of migrants cannot practise their skill or profession, or have their qualifications recognized without further study. Depending upon the nature of the qualification, they are likely to have to retake courses, sometimes from the beginning.

In many cases, refugees have been unable to carry official documents confirming educational experience and qualifications with them when they fled, and it is politically impossible to obtain copies. This creates problems when applying for courses which demand previous qualifications. It is common in both the UK and Australia for trades-based courses to offer applicants the opportunity to take a test to prove their existing level of competence. Candidates may also be asked to prepare a portfolio describing what they did in the past. Applicants to university who find themselves in this situation are commonly asked for a sworn statement. If the level of qualification claimed is recognized for entry purposes, candidates may be invited to an interview, to sit an examination or otherwise make a presentation of their work. There is evidence to suggest that, in both the UK and Australia, those providing advice and guidance are not themselves adequately aware of the recognition of qualifications gained overseas. An example of this cited by McDonald is the case of a refugee with a baccalaureate who was advised that, to gain entry to a university, she must first acquire three English A-levels (1996: 28).

Lack of institutional sensitivity and support

The education and training projects discussed above are provided specifically for, or targeted at refugees. As might be expected, there would appear to be a high level of client satisfaction with such provision (Africa Educational Trust 1998, Hannah 1999, McDonald 1996). However, the transition from such targeted provision into the mainstream is likely to present new challenges and difficulties. Mainstream providers in the UK and Australia do not generally have specific policies for meeting the needs of refugees. Instead, access to support services such as counselling, study skills or language teaching is likely to be assessed on the same basis as that applied to any other student. This position may arise from a genuine desire not to separate out or stigmatize those from refugee backgrounds, but it results in an absence of any acknowledgement of the specific problems that refugee background students may face. In the words of one Bosnian refugee living in Sydney, 'treating everyone the same can be discriminatory' (Hannah 1999: 163). Whilst it is true, for example, that some problems such as panic attacks and difficulty with concentrating might affect non-refugee students, the probability of their occurring in students from refugee backgrounds is higher.

If institutions were at least officially aware of the fact that a student had a refugee background, they could, with the agreement of the student, alert the teachers and trainers to be sensitive to this. Entitlement to sensitive pastoral and learning support may also prove crucial. A counsellor employed by one of Sydney's universities reported that she 'regularly' counselled students from refugee backgrounds. By the time she saw them, however, their problems were often quite serious. Occasionally, and with the students' permission, she would act as an intermediary between the student and tutor, renegotiating deadlines or agreeing other appropriate forms of action. She was surprised at how often key personnel from the student's department were unaware that the student had a refugee background. Generally, they were sympathetic to her suggestions when informed. Not often, but nevertheless disturbingly, she also encountered tutors who argued that it was 'unfair' to make concessions as this discriminated against 'Australian' students (Hannah 1999). Similarly, refugees in the UK have complained that staff have treated them 'like children' (Africa Educational Trust 1998: 30). These examples highlight the importance of staff awareness, attitudes and behaviour, but staff training in relation to these issues is rarely made compulsory by the mainstream education providers in Australia and the UK. In view of the increasingly multicultural background of trainees and students, it would seem appropriate for providers to take more seriously the need to address the awareness, attitudes and behaviour of their staff.

Recent changes in the funding mechanisms in the UK further education sector are reported as causing problems for refugees and asylum-seekers. There have been complaints about the 'contract oriented' culture resulting in an unwelcoming atmosphere, whilst the emphasis on 'outcomes' has led to discrimination against those considered less likely to find employment at the end of a course as they would reduce its 'success rate' (ibid.).

Finally, it needs to be acknowledged that a substantial proportion of refugees in the UK and Australia have experience of education systems which are very different. In particular, the UK and Australian systems are likely to be more 'active' and 'student-centred' than those previously experienced. Adjusting to the different expectations, styles and methods of teaching and learning can therefore present difficulties to which teachers need to be sensitive. The transition is likely to be smoother if teaching staff have some knowledge and understanding of the different traditions from which the students come, and this again raises issues of staff training and staff development in a multicultural teaching environment.

Conclusion

Education and training can be a vital factor determining the extent to which refugees become successfully resettled, but these needs are still not systematically addressed in either the UK or Australia, despite the presence of a comprehensive resettlement policy in the latter country. Responsibility for providing information, advice and guidance is fragmented and unsatisfactory, although the emergence of refugee-specific provision such as the Refugee Education, Training and Advisory Service (RETAS) and Refugee Education Unit (REU) are important developments in meeting this need. English-language proficiency is central to successfully accessing education, training and the labour market and the role of the Australian Adult Migrant English Service (AMES) is exemplary in meeting the needs of non-English-speaking background migrants to that country. Again, however, this service forms part of a coordinated approach to the resettlement of migrants and refugees. In contrast, the English-language provision available in the UK is patchy and poorly coordinated, and the establishment of an equivalent to AMES would be welcome.

In the absence of a coordinated policy towards the resettlement of refugees in the UK, individual pieces of legislation and policy initiatives can work against each other to the detriment of the refugee population. The decision to disperse refugees outside of London is not being accompanied by a corresponding programme to replicate the services available there. This denies them access to London's community support networks and targeted provision for refugees, increasing their sense of vulnerability and isolation. In locations where there are high concentrations of refugees in the local population, mainstream educational providers are likely to have more awareness of their needs, and their admissions and student support services will have more experience of dealing with these. However, as argued, refugees undertaking courses at college and university have encountered problems with staff who are not always sensitive to their situation. This reinforces the importance of adequate staff training to ensure that institutional commitment to equality, multiculturalism and student-centred learning is not just rhetoric, but reality.

In both the UK and Australia, lifelong learning is recognized as an important weapon in the battle against social exclusion, and wider access to all forms of post-compulsory education has become a political priority. It has been argued in this chapter that significant barriers continue to operate, particularly in the UK. Some of these are unique to asylum-seekers and refugees and some are shared with other excluded groups. To end on a positive note, however, recent policy developments relating to post-16 education provision in the UK give some cause for optimism. In particular, the competition between education and training providers promoted by the previous government is being scaled down and the newly created Regional Development Agencies will have a responsibility to develop 'a local and regional infrastructure for planning coherent post-compulsory education and training opportunities' (Hodgson 1999: 27). It is anticipated that this will result in a 'longer-term approach to the problem of disaffection, non-participation and social exclusion' (ibid.).

References

Africa Educational Trust (AET) 1998. *Refugee Education, Training and Employment in Inner London: a baseline study*. A study commissioned by FOCUS Central London Ltd for the Refugee Training Partnership.

Ahearn, F. L. Jnr. and Athey, J. L. (eds). 1991. *Refugee Children. Theory, Research and Services*. Baltimore: Johns Hopkins University Press.

Carey-Wood, J., Duke, K., Karn, V. and Marshall, T. 1995. *The Settlement of Refugees in Britain*. Home Office Research Study 141. London: Home Office.

Council for International Education (UKCOSA). 1999. *UKCOSA Briefing No. 2*. 1999.

Cox, D. 1996. *Australia's Resettlement Services*. Canberra: Bureau of Immigration, Multicultural and Population Research.

Department of Immigration and Multicultural Affairs. 1999a. Fact sheet no. 40 *Australia's Humanitarian Programme*. Canberra: DIMA.

Department of Immigration and Multicultural Affairs. 1999b. Fact sheet no. 69. *The Resettlement of Refugees in Australia*. Canberra: DIMA.

Dodds, A. 1986. *Refugee Education: The Case for International Action*. London: International Extension College/World University Service.

Hannah, J. 1997. *Refugee participation in Further and Higher Education in Sydney*. A report to the Trustees of the Commonwealth Relations Trust.

Hannah, J. 1999. Refugee Students at College and University: Improving Access and Support. *International Review of Education*. 45(2) 153–66.

Harker, A. and Gameladin-Ashami, M. 1995. *A study of Young Male Refugees in London with Particular Reference to their Education and Training Needs*. London: City Parochial Foundation.

Hodgson, A. in Hayton, A. (ed). 1999. *Tackling Disaffection and Social Exclusion*. London: Kogan Page.

House of Representatives Standing Committee on Community Affairs. 1996. *A Fair Go for All: A Report on Migrant Access and Equity*. Canberra: Australian Government Publication Service.

Iredale, R., Mitchell, C., Pe-Pua, R. and Pittaway, E. 1996 *Ambivalent Welcome: The Settlement Experiences of Humanitarian Entrant Families in Australia*. Canberra: Bureau of Immigration, Multicultural and Population Research.

Kaprielian-Churchill, I. 1996. Refugees and Education in Canadian Schools. *International Review of Education* 42(4): 350–65.

McDonald, J. 1996. *Entitled to Learn? A Report on Young Refugees' Experiences of Access and Progression in the UK Education System*. London: World University Service.

Refugee Council. 1996. *The Education, Training and Employment of Refugees*. Factfile No. 9. London: Refugee Council.

Refugee Council. 1997. The Development of a Refugee Settlement Policy in the UK. London: Refugee Council.

Refugee Education and Training Working Group. n.d. *Refugee Education Policy for the 1990's: Towards Implementing the Refugee Education Charter*. London: World University Service and the Refugee Council.

Refugee Education Unit. 1997. *A Review of the Work of the Refugee Education Unit*. London: Praxis.

Refugee Resettlement Working Group. 1993. *Lets Get It Right in Australia*. Sydney: Refugee Resettlement Working Group.

Reid, J. and Strong, T. 1987. *The Health Care Needs of Victims of Torture in New South Wales*. New South Wales: Department of Health, Cumberland College.

Watson, M. and Danzelman, P. (1998) *Asylum Statistics, United Kingdom 1997*. 14/98. London: Home Office.

Working Group on Educational Assistance to Refugees (GEAR). 1986. *The Forgotten Overseas Students: Towards a Policy for Refugees*. London: GEAR.

World University Service (UK). 1997. *The Refugee Education, Training and Advisory Service*. London: World University Service.

22 Ageing with technology

Adult viability in a technological world

Jane McKie

This chapter will explore developments in IT (information technology; also referred to as ICT information and communications technology) within the context of lifelong learning in late nineties Britain, focusing on the convergence of representation and rhetoric that frames debates about new technologies and adult education.

Discourse about lifelong learning is driven by a prevailing recognition of the increasing viability of the adult in educational terms, and this recognition is itself framed by demographic and market trends. To sustain the coherence of learning throughout life it is necessary to abandon a rigid distinction between initial education and post-compulsory education. With the collapse of this distinction we are invited to question the conventional categories of education, work and play, and I refer to the text of a postmodern advertisement for the family Macintosh and associated Apple software as an example of the conflation of these categories. In this advertisement, conventional depictions of ageing and the life course are unsettled. Other advertisements for technological products make emblematic use of children in their texts: the image of children in the driving seat of technology becomes an alternative representation, one reflecting a form of technological modernism.

Does lifelong learning, with its attendant emphasis on flexible access and skills, its holistic and cross-disciplinary epistemologies, hold the key to adult viability in a technological world? This chapter suggests that a fuller acknowledgement of learning throughout life is compatible with a view of the ageing process rejecting ossification and stasis: the ageing adult is not necessarily resistant to novelty and change. In order to explicate the ramifications of lifelong learning further, it is first necessary to look in more detail at the contexts in which the concept is used.

Lifelong learning

At the heart of the concept of lifelong learning lies a rejection of the front-end model of education, namely the idea that education is confined to childhood, adolescence and early adulthood (Tight, 1996). Lifelong learning necessarily entails the acquisition and development of knowledge, skills and attitudes throughout the whole life of the individual; furthermore, it embraces formal, non-formal and informal educational influences. The clear division between 'work' and 'leisure' (as well as that between 'work' and 'education' commented on above) is compromised by the concept of lifelong learning:

> Structurally, the balance to be changed by the introduction of lifelong education can be seen as being that between education, work (or employment) and certain kinds of 'non-work', principally leisure and retirement. Education is being shifted from its

dominant position in early life, to be combined with work and non-work in adult life.

(Tight, 1996: 38)

I believe the erosion of these conceptual boundaries is a positive and holistic process in so far as it explicitly acknowledges the natural overlap in these processes and encourages the development of the whole individual. Work divested of pleasure is an anaemic proposition, and the same could be said of pleasureless education. Although the conceptual division between 'education' and 'leisure' is still alive and kicking in the language of academic accreditation, the boundaries between the two are arguably being eroded by the use of educational technologies that incorporate an entertainment component. To leave leisure out of the equation would be to ignore that entertainment is an integral part of the learning experience. Within the industrial logic of production 'education' sits more comfortably with 'work' than with 'play', and, until relatively recently, the legitimacy of play across generations and across situational contexts has seldom been recognized.

Learning networks

Edwards (1995, 1997) observes that the learning society has been interpreted in the following three ways: in terms of education for citizenship and active participation, as a learning market, and as learning networks. All of these interpretations have relevance to claims made for information technology, though perhaps particularly the last in the sense that the Internet (specifically, the formation of electronically-linked communities) is all about networks, as the name implies. These electronic communities may be geographically separated, even geographically far-flung. They may be formed of academics, business people and practitioners working in the same fields making extensive use of conferencing facilities and electronic bulletin boards. They may also be a group of citizens with private accounts who are linked to one another through a shared interest, through the pursuit of a game such as MUD (multi-user dungeon or domain), or simply through the desire to communicate.

Boshier *et al*. (1999) draw upon Faure's (1972) concept of lifelong education and Illich's (1971) learning webs or networks, to criticize the notion of the Internet (specifically, the World Wide Web) as utopia on the basis of US dominance in terms of sites and search engines. They describe a picture of a US centre and peripheral 'others' which, they suggest, results in a form of network colonialism rooted in the dominance of 'Californian ideology':

> The Web can be a site of education for cultural revitalization but problems arise from the dominance of the English language and the lack of recognition of non-Euroamerican 'ways of knowing'. Theorists of the postmodern have deftly shown how language constructs discourses of disempowerment or possibility. Hence, serious consequences flow from the fact the Web is dominated by the English language and US techno-rational assumptions about how things work.

(Boshier *et al.*, 1999: 280)

US dominance of the Web means that educators should be conscious of the links they provide to sites that conceal exclusive assumptions. This entails critical engagement with the Web on the part of educators and students. Additionally, the individualistic mode of interaction bears scrutiny. Although it is possible for students to work collaboratively around computer clusters, most computer users are isolated from their peers by virtue of focus on the interface. Similarly, virtual dialogue results in the possibility for the construction of virtual community, but this dialogue is not face-to-face, it is mediated. Boshier *et al.* point out that this mediation differs from the ways in which many non-EuroAmerican peoples educate themselves (1999: 282). Mediated conversations have ethical ramifications: Heim (1993) suggests that face-to-face interaction has a special immediacy that carries greater moral weight. For example, electronic conferences do not require participants to respond or log their 'attendance'. Does this constitute a form of digital voyeurism, or does it provide opportunities for new forms of passive interaction that may better suit learners' needs at different times? Both ways of construing silent presence on the Web could have application. Conflicting accounts point to the need for an exploration of the ethics of virtual interaction, an endeavour that could inform educators' selection of ICT for student use.

In considering learning networks it is also relevant to look at markets. There are markets for all forms of educational provision, as well as a considerable market for the Internet, as its rapid expansion and refinement demonstrates. The Internet is a strange beast in that it is so diffuse and multifarious. These qualities allow sub-networks and search engines to be marketed, as well as specific sites, games and vehicles for discussion. And it is itself a marketing tool. It is increasingly used to market goods and services, including online educational provision. Duke (1997) believes that a determining relationship between market and education is at odds with a philosophy of lifelong learning:

> The lifelong curriculum implies closer integration of the university with the community than the English university has typically felt comfortable with in recent times. It does not mean being 'market-driven' as the system now only supposedly is.
>
> (Duke, 1997: 66)

Arguably, involving the whole community in continuing education means exploiting dormant markets, though the nuance given here belies the dominant rationale for such an endeavour on the part of providers, one that is rooted more in social justice than economic exploitation.

Usher *et al.* (1997) assert that post-Fordist forms of organization create the demand for a multi-skilled workforce. For them, it is only in this market context that lifelong learning can be understood in all its nuances: 'Learning through life and lifelong learning have become not simply an aspect of economic instrumentalism nor an assertion of enlightened humanism but also a way of constituting meaning through consumption' (1997: 5). Consumption is no longer related to need but to an assertion of identity, of difference rather than sameness in relation to others. Field (1994) has also drawn attention to the citizen as consumer, purchasing packaged opportunities for self-study (including multimedia packages). Within a learning market education itself can be regarded as a commodity. Learning is an object to be consumed, a desire to be fulfilled.

It is clear that analysis of 'learning markets' is often expressed in neo-liberal terms. In such discourse, the individual inhabits the foreground, society the background. But the concept of lifelong learning straddles several units of analysis: the self as lifelong project (Giddens, 1992), learning networks, learning societies. Individuals do not interact with information in a vacuum. They are always operating within some context, for example the context of a specific network of relationships, and, as the focus broadens, the context of wider society. Indeed, the word 'interaction' implies relationship. How are the parameters of relationships defined and enacted in learning situations? To what extent do individuals behave autonomously and to what extent do they co-operate with and/or depend on others? I think it would be fair to say that lifelong learning is no more concerned with exclusively fostering self-direction than it is with only dictating specific programmes. In terms of rhetoric, much recent attention has been directed to ways in which individual learning opportunities might be supported with some sort of infrastructure.

Supporting lifelong learning

Networks of guidance and support are the central mission of the University for Industry (Ufi), a British initiative designed to kite-mark and disseminate a range of learning packages for adults, learndirect, a nationwide network of on-line learning services. They also form the backbone of the Government's concept of a 'National Grid' for learning (of which the Ufi is a part). Just as most British homes are served by electricity, so households will be supplied with technology-based learning opportunities. This will begin with networked schools, and gradually extend to the rest of the population. Similarly, the DfEE, in a publication called *Learning to Succeed: A New Framework for Post-16 Learning* (1999), places the Ufi at the heart of a learning society:

> The Learning and Skills Council will work with others to champion lifelong learning for all. The Council will have a clear role to play in driving up demand for learning so as to complement the impact of individual learning accounts and the Ufi and support the work of NIACE, the Campaign for Learning and broadcasters in promoting learning throughout life. The Learning and Skills Council will work closely with the Ufi to improve the overall coherence and responsiveness of education and training provision for adults and embed lifelong learning in people's daily lives.
>
> (DfEE, 1999: 9)

The 1997 Further Education Funding Council report (chaired by Helena Kennedy) suggests that the further education sector is 'the least understood and celebrated part of the learning tapestry' (Kennedy, 1997: 1). In the report, learning is identified as necessary for 'economic renewal' (and adults are acknowledged as a viable population of learners); furthermore, learning is recognized as a vehicle for social cohesion. A healthy and market-led economy has the potential to stimulate learning on an unprecedented scale. But it also has its pitfalls: Kennedy is aware of the 'growing disquiet that the new ethos has encouraged colleges not just to be businesslike but to perform as if they were businesses' (3). Further education colleges can become rivals rather than collaborators. An economic argument is therefore not sufficient: 'Justice and equity must also have their claims upon the arguments for educational growth' (6). In other words, capitalism must be 'leavened' with equal attention to reciprocity, moral obligation, duty towards community, and trust. The report emphasizes the importance of collaboration (such as a national network of strategic partnerships), and of bringing learning into the workplace (both goals of the new Ufi; Hillman, 1997). Crucially, lifelong learning does not only happen in colleges; it is the promise of a whole sector of multifarious and plural activities:

> Indeed, with the revolutionary advances of technology, bricks and mortar are increasingly becoming less significant in the whole business of learning. There are many providers and locations, including the home and the workplace, training and enterprise councils, and schools and community centres, where people expand their horizons and extend their capabilities.
>
> (Kennedy, 1997: 7–8)

Other locations for learning could include family rooms in primary schools, libraries, betting shops, snooker halls, rooms above pubs, or shopping malls. This expansion of the settings in which learning can take place is consistent with an expanded vision of learning, what Edwards (1997) refers to as a de-differentiated 'moorland' to contrast with 'fields' of study:

> Universal provision for all is a chimera, as education, training and learning differentiate and are part of wider processes of differentiation in the social formation. The possibilities exist for various forms of adaptation and challenge to the currently dominant learning market and for many and multiple ambivalent positions. Such are the constant negotiations necessary for those working on the moorland of lifelong learning.
>
> (Edwards, 1997: 186–7)

Universal educational provision may well be a chimera. But new pluralism in education combines with demographic trends, market forces, and ICT to expand contexts and approaches. In this mêlée, perennial ideas about the design of learning materials and encounters are invested with new urgency.

Learning and design

A corollary of the idea that learning is active and social is the realization that it is also contextual. Decontextualized material is more difficult to remember. And what is the impetus to learn if the material has no relevance to our lives, or does not relate in interesting ways to things we already know? Leicester and Pearce (1997), drawing on the theories of Mezirow (1990, 1994), and Brookfield (1986), believe that learning in adulthood does in some sense involve stages, but they are soft stages in which (adult) experience overlaps the learning process itself and in the formation of self as an active agent of learning. Stages in adult learning do not follow an invariable sequence; rather they map on to reflection and the aforementioned process of continuous growth, with critical reflection and self-examination being key learning processes: 'growing self-knowledge seems also to have generated greater moral maturity, and some of the students have talked about greater awareness of other people's point of view and experiences, and of their own changing, more inclusive, values.' (Leicester and Pearce, 1997: 472).

The notion of growth incorporates notions of building on (supplementing and transforming) previous experience in creative ways. It suggests something of the multidisciplinarity that is associated with the flexibility of hypermedia: the way that hot links are engineered can enable the learner to make multiple associations between sources and subjects. This is the ideal, not necessarily the reality. One must bear in mind that the sources are not exhaustive, and that they may be ideologically or culturally biased. However, it is an assumption of adult education—influenced as a 'discipline' by both pragmatism and existentialism—that a person's experience is enriched by making connections between past and present, and between self and other. This expansive process requires time for both contemplation and reflection, a factor that becomes a design consideration when applied to a formal learning situation.

For Eden *et al.* (1996), learning should be conceived of as a 'new' form of labour:

> By emphasising learning as a new form of labour . . . new educational strategies such as the integration of working and learning become necessities rather than options. Learning cannot stop with a high school diploma or an undergraduate degree. The world is constantly evolving, creating the challenge for individuals and organisations to deal with change and for schools and universities to prepare people for change.
>
> (Eden *et al.*, 1996: 40)

This is clearly an allusion to the changing nature of the marketplace. As the average age of the population increases, the profile of the labour market shifts to one of unemployment and short-term contracts, although one must be wary of generalizations: differential changes take place on the basis of class, generation, gender and ethnicity. In this climate, official rhetoric naturally adapts to incorporate notions of lifelong learning. Eden *et al*.'s paper is predominantly concerned with establishing the educational techniques that would be suitable for lifelong learning. In the light of the above, I think it is safe to suggest that, among other things, lifelong learning involves blurring the boundaries between school, work and home, that are sharply differentiated in a model of learning that incorporates the primary/secondary/tertiary distinction. Given the fluidity of these formal and informal domains, would a mix of formality/informality in method be appropriate? Eden *et al*. feel the need to strike a balance between 'instructionist' and 'constructionist' models of learning. That is, the constructionist model permits self-directed learning, but 'without guidance, learners can feel overwhelmed by an infinite number of options and a paucity of clear goals' (1996: 40). By contrast, instructionist approaches have clear and statable goals but restrict the learner's creativity. A balanced approach would therefore marry contextualized instructional support for learners coupled with the opportunity for them to solve self-selected problems. In a similar vein, Fischer (1996: 3) argues against the artificial separation between school and work:

> The previous notions of a divided lifetime—education followed by work—are no longer tenable. Learning can no longer be dichotomized, spatially and temporally, into a place and a time to *acquire* knowledge (school) and a place and a time to *apply* knowledge (the workplace). (emphasis in original)

For Fischer, lifelong learning is a 'continuous engagement acquiring and applying knowledge and skills in the context of authentic, self-directed problems' (1996: 3). This is clearly a call for a move away from top–down approaches towards student-centred problem-based learning. Overall, although Fischer is optimistic about the Internet as a forum for the production of 'new' educational design, he is wary of premature claims of this nature. New technologies should never enshrine old paradigms. Making classroom OHP transparencies available on the Web may go some way towards increasing the accessibility of information and/or expertise, but it does little to change the 'old' frameworks of instructionism, fixed curriculum, or decontextualized learning. Technology has the potential to re-engineer knowledge. To what extent this potential has been realized remains contentious, though perhaps, as Smith (1993) intimates, time will tell: 'We accept new modes and new technologies when they are justified by established needs. It takes time for them to generate new needs' (1993: 46).

Children who work, adults who play

The distinction between education, play, and work is blurred in the advertisement for the family Macintosh and compatible software: 'And when your children stop working... you can play with it.' The accompanying image is of a schoolroom; a Macintosh on a desk in the foreground supersedes a traditional blackboard in the background, and the screen displays a window featuring a clip from the Disney film *The Lion King*. In fact, there is a clear adult/child and work/play reversal. The advertising company capitalizes on the erosion of normative categories precipitated by the perceived melding of education and entertainment.

Informal education has unprecedented currency in the world of the home computer. As we have seen, for Fischer (1996), school is no longer the only place in which to acquire knowledge and the workplace is no longer the only place to apply it. Even the meanings of educational acquisition and application are rendered problematic in the light of recent cultural changes.

Work and play, acquisition and application, are presented as coexistent in the text of this advertisement:

> The family Macintosh is the ideal family computer. It comes complete with a built-in CD-ROM drive, high-speed modem and of course access to the Internet. It's designed to make a serious contribution to your children's education by making learning stimulating and enjoyable for all ages. Besides heavyweight software such as Grolier's Multimedia Encyclopaedia, you'll also find Disney Interactive's fun-packed Apple Magic Collection.
>
> And, if you can ever wrest the computer away from your children, you'll have access to all the office software you need to work from home, using the integrated package, Claris Works™.
>
> So instead of asking yourself what you can do with your Family Macintosh, you'll soon be asking what would you do without it.

Firstly, notice the 'of course' with reference to Internet access. It is now a taken for granted assumption that this is an automatic feature of contemporary computing. The very word 'access', long familiar to the world of continuing educational provision (particularly in relation to non-traditional students), now goes hand-in-hand with the Internet, although this access is usually only available to computer owners, with some institutional and community-based exceptions.

The packages available for the Family Macintosh are not frivolous: the 'heavyweight' encyclopaedia, the 'serious contribution' to your children's education. But they are not so heavy as to be a chore to interact with: Disney's Apple Magic Collection stands alongside the encyclopaedia, and the 'serious contribution' to learning is mediated through 'stimulating' and 'enjoyable' experiences. Education can be entertainment and vice versa through the mediation of digital technology. Similarly, children and adults participate in both. The irony is that you will have to 'wrest' the computer away from your children because of the fascination it exerts for all ages. The words 'education', 'desire' and 'choice' are linked in the rhetoric of both education and advertising (Field, 1994; Usher *et al.*, 1997). This public association has, in part at least, been facilitated by the popularity of interactive multimedia and games software.

Fear or anticipation?

If adults can share computer applications in terms of both learning and enjoyment, why are adults sometimes held to be reticent to use ICT? There may be some mileage in the attribution of fear of change, but as a response to developments in digital technology it is by no means uniform, nor necessarily age-related. Admittedly, prolonged association is a factor that militates against this, and children in contemporary Western society grow up with this association. However, ICT increasingly pervades the arenas in which adult learning takes place, and there are many individual adult experts and enthusiasts for something that is a relatively new phenomenon. Think of magazines like *Wired* and specialist PC monthlies that cater for an adult readership. Individual differences account for differential responses to ICT, and these differences should not be allowed to bleed into preconceptions about age-related abilities or predilections.

Fear of technology is fuelled partly by the feeling that digital development moves more quickly than we can keep up with. Following the 'explosion' of computers as tools for education and industry in the sixties, newer and more sophisticated models supplant previous models in a relentlessly modernist production line, resulting in obsolescence of the old. The rapidity with which the internal mechanism is modified in the computing industry keeps pace with sought-after realism in software and simplification of the user interface. The pressure to refine the machine is articulated as a quest for a 'face' that is amenable to purportedly 'intuitive' short-hand such as visual icons.

Technological development is thus marked in accelerated time. As new products evolve from old, the old becomes outmoded. The following extract from the narration of an advertisement for Microsoft products, postmodern in form (using collage and fast editing to present a tapestry of human/computer interaction) but modern in message, illustrates one strategy to manage consumer trepidation:

Listen . . . this stuff that we make . . .

it's powerful . . .

it makes . . . you powerful . . .

take it . . .

gather up your ideas . . .

run with them . . .

make trouble . . .

and good things will happen . . . ['make trouble' is superimposed on screen]

make some mistakes . . .

it doesn't matter . . .

just do something amazing . . .

we're in your corner . . .

and we can't wait to see what you're going to do . . . [repeat]

the world will never be the same again [repeat]

I am reminded of a 1998 TV and print advertisement for Apple products, entitled '20 icons', which uses iconic figures from the twentieth century to suggest a link between these 'crazy' innovators, artists and politicians and digital technology. In the individualistic assertion that Apple (as a company) 'recognise genius' where others see madness, the advertisement echoes the Microsoft imperative 'make trouble'. Both advertisements promulgate a vision of individuality that rests on the supposed versatility of new technological tools. Glaister (1998), in a scathing newspaper article entitled 'Rebels, but not to the core', suggests that the advertisement's aspiring 'maverick' spirit belies a unitary corporate strategy. It is a 'paean to rebellion' that is really a 'hymn to conformity':

> While probably admitting that it would not, strictly speaking, be a great idea for all its users to throw away the manual and disobey the rules, Apple recognises that corporate culture thrives on rebellion. A certain sort of rebellion. This business age is characterised by non-conformity: hot desking, portable portfolios, multi-skilling, change for change's sake . . . There is no norm, everything is open to question. As the economic cycle shortens, flexibility is the by-word for today's aspiring executive, and we embrace what has been termed 'the imperative of endless difference'.
>
> (Glaister, 1998: 7)

In the narration cited above, customer trepidation about technology is openly acknowledged: 'make trouble... and good things will happen... make some mistakes... it doesn't matter', and 'we're in your corner', which summons to mind a boxing ring. Here, it is claimed, Microsoft products provide support for the forthcoming confrontation with the status quo. While the learning environment may be unfamiliar, the words suggest that the products tolerate the mistakes. Indeed, the company actively encourages you to risk making mistakes in a spirit of non-conformity. The same advertisement also uses images of children to make links with a technological future world—'The world will never be the same again'—and in so doing draws upon the ubiquitous association between children and technology. This particular use of imagery preys on the aforementioned fear of obsolescence in the face of fast-changing technologies: the built-in obsolescence of technology itself undermines the individual's belief in their ability to 'master' the application. The central claim is that one needs technology in order to cope with the rapidity of technological change, and it is paradoxical. Technology is a contributing factor to contemporary dis-ease. But it is also the cure. Parallels can be drawn with advertisements for cosmetic products: these advertisements are themselves implicated in the creation of anxiety about ageing (the dissolution of the surface, the skin), while simultaneously marketing products that claim to stave off this inevitable dissolution.

I hope to have identified two trends in the advertising of technological hardware and software. The first conflates adults and children, work and play, in a postmodern depiction of home computer use. The second dwells on images of children to evoke the futurism associated with modernity. Although this advertisement reinforces stereotypical expectations about youth and novel technology, and the former subverts them, both interpretations feed on the same moment—a moment in which categorical distinctions between education, work and play face erosion. Tension coalesces around the deconstruction of age-related expectations in late modern Western society. I will proceed to look in more detail at prevailing conceptions of ageing and what it means to be old in order to explicate this further.

Ageing, leisure and lifestyle

It has long been acknowledged that there is a 'social clock' guiding our biographical expectations at different developmental stages. However, as age-related expectations are affected by prevailing social conditions, this clock is not irrevocably set. Meyrowitz (1984) draws attention to an increasing similarity in the modes of presentation of self and leisure-time pursuits adopted by parents and children, believing that the more informal 'uni-age' style was a result of media imagery as a major form of communication. For Featherstone and Hepworth (1990a) this is one example of the postmodern deconstruction of stages of the life course. Furthermore, 'evidence continues to accrue which disproves the necessary decline of mental, sexual and physiological capacities in old age' (1990a: 146). Thus, there is a trend away from regarding chronological age as an indicator of inevitable age norms and lifestyles.

Featherstone and Hepworth (1990a and 1990b) believe lifestyle to be one of the most important aspects of postmodern culture. Others include a playful, youthful approach to culture mediated by the media and mass spectacle, specifically the media creation, reproduction and circulation of images; and the fact that those formally excluded, such as elderly people, are increasingly recognised as valid partners:

> The emphasis upon flexibility, adaptability and self-expression long associated with youth is now being extended for forthcoming generations into old age. Here we can refer to the whole paraphernalia of consumer cultural artefacts and services. Jogging, exercise

routines, cosmetics, health foods and fashionable leisure-wear are now marketed for elderly people to sustain health, youthful energy and the spirit of self-improvement deep into old age. The consequences for relationships between the generations are momentous.
(Featherstone and Hepworth, 1990b: 273).

This is a positive view, but there needs to be a proviso: culture does not have the overarching power to render embodied development redundant. Time is indelibly inscribed on our bodies (Turner, 1995), and we still have to come to terms with the reality of physical ageing.

Wearing (1995) suggests that it may be possible to offer resistance to negative images of ageing through the discourse of leisure with its emphasis on individual abilities and interests, rather than a sole emphasis on what the individual is no longer capable of doing:

> In fact, leisure is possibly the one area in advanced industrial capitalist societies where freedom is encouraged, albeit a freedom constrained by the commodification of leisure goods and services and by ideas of legitimate leisure and pleasure (Rojek, 1985). When applied to older persons, leisure emphasizes what a person can do rather than what they are no longer physically capable of doing. Therefore, it has distinct possibilities for resistance to ageism.
>
> (Wearing, 1995: 272)

Her attention to leisure choices can be interpreted in existential terms. The image of an ageing individual as active learner and consumer can be contrasted with a self-fulfilling prophecy of under-use rooted in an emphasis on deterioration. The deficiency model is embedded in the following functional theories of ageing: 'disengagement theory' (Cumming and Henry, 1961) in which ageing is seen as a process of attenuating emotional involvements as a way of preparing for death socially and psychologically; and 'activity theory' (Havighurst, 1963) in which taking up new forms of activity in later life is a form of compensation for lost roles. This language of 'attenuation' and 'compensation' is no longer tenable.

Gilleard (1996) also considers the refashioning of older adults' identities in contemporary society. Again, the suggestion is that postmodernity offers an opportunity to redefine personal identity through the exercise of choice or agency:

> A new generation of Third Age consumers is emerging within contemporary culture. The targeting of older people in marketing and business journals, the up-market housing offering new retirement lifestyles, the distribution of holiday brochures for the 'golden years' or those 'young at heart', the emergence of 'trendy' magazines for a self-consciously older readership, the growing number of 'guru' writers reappraising and rewarding views of older lifestyles; all are evidence of a culturally emergent phenomenon, epitomised by the term The Third Age.
>
> (Gilleard, 1996: 491)

Gilleard acknowledges that the material features of class are still present, but goes on to suggest that perhaps they can be subordinated by those aspects of desire that shape identity—specifically, desire for consumer goods and services. It would be a shift in focus that managed to transcend 'structured dependency' and 'the social construction of old age' to a 'richer, more agentic view of older people both reacting to and contributing to a new pluralistic culture for later life.' (Gilleard, 1996: 493).

Drawing on Rojek (1993; 1995), Edwards (1997) suggests that leisure has been seen as a kind of 'rational recreation' associated with modernity and stability, a rational recreation of which adult education is a part. But there is also another side to the coin: 'It is that 'other' of modernity which is foregrounded in a postmodern and de-differentiated view of leisure. Leisure comes to be seen more in terms of play and desire, with a greater role attributed to social actors and an emphasis on a leisurely stance in all aspects of life' (1997: 102). This second, postmodern reading of leisure lies behind the erosion of conventional age-related expectations. While a child growing up with computers may be more familiar with them than an adult who has not been exposed to them over time, this difference in familiarity should not be confused with a difference in aptitude or ability. Tuition, enthusiasm and prolonged use are all that is required to overcome technological illiteracy, although this begs the question about the desirability of technological know-how. Network literacy is certainly being hailed as a desirable skill in nineties Britain, but uncritical acceptance is an inappropriate response to change.

Ageing with technology

If computers and computer-mediated communication are to become fixtures, adults must be able to learn flexibly enough to be able to accommodate them. The ossification of mental processes is the myth at the heart of supposed resistance to change. Adults are equally in a position to reclaim a share of the 'postmodern' processes of desire and play, not least because of the interweaving of leisure, labour and learning. Wearing (1995) maintains a rational attraction to leisure as a concept that underwrites other key social processes. Leisure could play an instrumental role in undermining implicit or explicit ageism, though one must be wary of making excessive claims on its behalf. Not everyone has the means or the ability to capitalize on the forms of leisure evoked by a vocabulary of activity. Equally, there is pleasure to be gained in reflection and repose, concepts that are in danger of being excluded from an emphasis on fitness, lifestyle and vitality. Nevertheless, I would assert that adults have reason to be optimistic on two related counts. Firstly, they are enjoying a 'new' viability, partly because of the demographic and socioeconomic changes that make a discourse of lifelong learning possible. Secondly, the text of another advertisement for technology (in this case the car; it is an advertisement for the Royal Automobile Club), reminds us of the insights age can bring:

> As technology gets older it becomes obsolete/but as humans age they become wiser. A Japanese proverb says / Cherish the old to understand the new. It is a piece of wisdom to inspire us / as we prepare to tackle the 21st century.
>
> *Hiroshe Inose, Director-General NACSIS Tokyo*

In marketing, technology may sometimes favour the young. This particular advertisement disturbs the cliché that 'the future belongs to our children'. Fischer's (1996) reconceptualization of labour must involve a rethinking of the categories of 'adult' and 'child', so that the adult is accorded fair provenance over technological products and processes in contemporary culture. I am not suggesting that all distinctions between adulthood and childhood be abandoned, or that children are merely 'little adults'. Rather I would argue for an abandonment of preconceptions about age-related abilities which themselves fuel generalizations about ageing being on the one hand about accumulation of experience and on the other about progressive resistance to experiment. In a sense, these generalizations are contradictory. Can we continue to accumulate experience without experimentation being involved, at least to some degree? Reflection on something already experienced risks a modification of the perception of that experience. Reflection is undertaken in the light of new experience. Novelty need not be 'radical' to be constituted a part of the learning process, and, by the same token, change is not necessarily felt 'radically'.

While ICT may hold no fears for those children for whom it is a part of the daily round, there may be children who are unfamiliar and hesitant in its use. Similarly, individual adults may relish using ICT, while others may avoid it. Moving the focus from the general to the particular allows one to reflect on generalizations in a new light. Nash (1996: 52) addresses the compartmentalization of work and play, and concludes with a call for reassessment of their mutuality:

> Whether an activity should be considered work or play is to be determined not only by the external description of the activity, but also by the internal spirit in which it is carried on. This is clearly seen in the way young children will often carry out in a spirit of joyous play tasks that would be regarded as work by an adult. The mental attitude determines whether the task is done because of the compulsion of the outcome or because of a free enjoyment of the activity. There is danger in many contemporary pedagogical activities because they concentrate so fully on the *results* of the work. This may induce the student to produce more in the short run, but it often leads eventually to a loss of zest, to dullness, and to boredom.

This pragmatic approach to pedagogy has much to recommend it, not least the intuition that work and play are not, and should not be, mutually exclusive. Their conflation as units of analysis has been accelerated by the advent of ICT including the Internet and the prevalence of computer games, many of which arguably marry the two. This conflation is reflected in contemporary advertisements for digital hardware and software, and is articulated in both a reassertion and subversion of stereotypes. Similarly, the logic of late capitalism in Western societies seems to offer new opportunities for identity construction, according to postmodernists. These constructions may be playful, they may draw on what are conventionally held to be 'leisure' activities (resulting in a self-sustaining burgeoning of the leisure, tourism and heritage sectors), and they may extend to individuals across a range of age groups if income and circumstance permits.

The dual trends of process-oriented Web 'surfing' and game playing, and an acknowledgement that identity is neither necessarily stable nor static but potentially malleable, invite us to consider education, play, and work—learning, leisure and labour—afresh. Historically, the devaluation of play arose when it was perceived in its irrational and capricious forms, devoid of purpose. Perhaps the move away from product towards process in the discourses of both life-long learning and new technology represents an opportunity to reclaim the irrational, the 'joyous', the purpose*less*, and, ironically, to *put play to work* in a productive fusion of modes of being: working at play, playing at work. At their worst, these discourses could merely be putting the gloss on economic rationale. Another concern rests with the extent to which we should balance process and goal as educators. Nash, following Dewey, points out that 'fooling occurs when all reference to outcome is eliminated from play', whereas drudgery occurs when the worker cares only for what is to be gained at the end of their labour. Play is a 'source of freedom' only when enriched by the authority of purpose (1966: 51). This intuition has relevance to use of the Internet, for example. It can be approached formally and informally, the pathways selected may be more or less haphazardly structured, the selection may be whimsical or serious, goals may be implicit, and learning may be incidental. I would not wish to undervalue play by suggesting that a consciously articulated purpose must always be present to render it enriching. But the balance between work and play in educational endeavour nevertheless bears further examination.

The allied discourses of lifelong learning and new technology are implicated in critical reflection on what differentiates education from play, and both from work. Perhaps even more fundamentally, they take an active part in the recent cultural reshaping of what is judged to be age-appropriate behaviour by Western societies.

References

Boshier, R., M. Wilson and A. Qayyum (1999) 'Lifelong education and the World Wide Web: American hegemony or diverse utopia?' *International Journal of Lifelong Education*, vol. 18, no. 4.

Brookfield, S. (1986) *Understanding and Facilitating Adult Learning*. Milton Keynes: Open University Press.

Cumming, G. E. and W. W. Henry (1961) *Growing Old: The Process of Disengagement*. New York: Basic Books.

DfEE (1999) *Learning to Succeed: A New Framework for Post-16 Learning*. London.

Duke, C. (1997) 'Towards a lifelong curriculum', in F. Coffield and B. Williamson (eds) *Repositioning Higher Education*. Milton Keynes: SRHE and Open University Press.

Eden, H., M. Eisenberg, G. Fischer and A. Repenning (1996) 'Making learning a part of life'. *Communications of the ACM*, vol. 39, no. 4.

Edwards, R. (1995) 'Behind the banner: whither the learning society?' *Adults Learning*, vol. 6, no. 6.

Edwards, R. (1997) *Changing Places? Flexibility, Lifelong Learning and a Learning Society*. London and New York: Routledge.

Faure, E. (1972) *Learning To Be*. Paris: UNESCO.

Featherstone, M. and M. Hepworth (1990a) 'Ageing and old age: reflections on the postmodern lifecourse', in B. Bytheway, T. Keil, P. Allatt and A. Bryman (eds) *Becoming and Being Old*. London: Sage.

Featherstone, M. and M. Hepworth (1990b) 'Images of ageing', in J. Bond and P. Coleman (eds) *Ageing in Society*. London: Sage.

Field, J. (1994) 'Open learning and consumer culture'. *Open Learning*, vol. 9, no. 2.

Fischer, G. (1996) NSF Symposium 'Learning and Intelligent Systems' (unpublished).

Giddens, A. (1992) *The Transformation of Intimacy*. Cambridge, Polity Press.

Gilleard, C. (1996) 'Consumption and identity in later life: towards a cultural gerontology'. *Ageing and Society*, vol. 16, 489–98.

Glaister, D. (1998) 'Rebels, but Not to the Core', in *The Guardian*, 27 January.

Havinghurst, R. J. (1963) Successful ageing, in R. Williams, C. Tibbitts and W. Donahue (eds) *Processes of Aging*. Atherton: New York.

Heim, M. (1993) 'The erotic ontology of cyberspace', in M. Benedikt (ed.) *Cyberspace: First Steps*. Cambridge, MA: MIT Press.

Hillman, J. (1997) 'The University for Industry'. *Open Learning Today*, issue 36.

Illich, I. (1971) *Deschooling Society*. London: Penguin Books.

Kennedy, H. (1997) *Learning Works: Widening Participation in Further Education*. Coventry: FEFC.

Leicester, M. and R. Pearce (1997) 'Cognitive development, self-knowledge and moral education'. *Journal of Moral Education*, vol. 26, no. 4.

McKie, J. (1996) 'Is democracy at the heart of IT? Commercial perceptions of technology'. *Sociological Research Online*, vol. 1, no. 4 (http://www.socresonline.org.uk/socresonline).

Meyrowitz, J. (1984) 'The adult child and the childlike adult'. *Daedalus*, vol. 113, no. 3.

Mezirow, J. (1990) *Fostering Critical Reflection in Adulthood*. San Francisco: Jossey Bass.

Mezirow, J. (1994) 'Understanding transformation theory'. *Adult Education Quarterly*, no. 44.

Nash, P. (1966) *Authority and Freedom in Education*. New York: John Wiley.

Rojek, C. (1985) *Capitalism and the Construction of Old Age*. London: Macmillan.

Rojek, C. (1993) *Ways of Escape: Modern Transformations in Leisure and Travel*. London: Macmillan.

Rojek, C. (1995) *Decentring Leisure: Rethinking Leisure Theory* London: Sage.

Smith, A. (1993) *Books to Bytes*. London: British Film Institute.

Tight, M. (1996) *Key Concepts in Adult Education and Training*. London: Macmillan.

Turner, B. S. (1995) 'Aging and identity', in Mike Featherstone and Andrew Wernick (eds) *Images of Aging*. London: Routledge.

Usher, R., I. Bryant and R. Johnston (1997) *Adult Education and the Postmodern Challenge*. London: Routledge.

Wearing, B. (1995) 'Leisure and resistance in an ageing society'. *Leisure Studies*, vol. 14, no. 4.

23 Reflections on lifelong learning and the Third Age

Alex Withnall

Emphasis on lifelong learning at national and international levels suggests that the time is ripe to launch a new debate about purpose in the provision of educational opportunities for older people. Does the ageing of populations, especially the emergence of the so-called Third Age, pose a challenge to popular notions of lifelong learning? Is it possible to develop a theory about education for older adults as some writers have attempted to do over the last few decades? This chapter begins with a critical discussion of current notions of lifelong learning. It then examines the concept of the Third Age and summarizes the debate concerning the philosophical and emerging theoretical approaches to the education of people who are post-work in the sense that they are no longer primarily involved in earning a living or with major family responsibilities—although this does not preclude the fact that they may be involved in or actively seeking some kind of paid work and/or be involved in a caring role in some capacity. This definition also recognizes that the notion of work is essentially a dynamic one and may be subject to redefinition over time. Finally, an attempt is made to argue for a new more inclusive perspective on lifelong learning for the twenty-first century.

Lifelong learning policies

Notions of the individual and collective responsibility to continue learning throughout life are certainly not new. They appear in different guises in the work of Plato, in early Chinese philosophy and in the work of Comenius. They are implicit within a number of religions, notably the Jewish faith. Discourses of lifelong learning and recurrent education which would assuredly result in an educated and democratic society appear at intervals in the writings of academics and in the philosophies of different educational practitioners and some politicians over the last few decades. However, lifelong learning as it is currently understood, at least in a European context, has taken on a new meaning as the forces of change necessitate a review of taken-for-granted understanding of the theory and practice of learning.

Edwards (1998) in a perceptive analysis, takes as his starting point the view that, in late modernity, change and uncertainty are often seen as defining characteristics of the contemporary world. He argues that different forms of change—economic, cultural, technological and demographic—have been used to promote certain priorities within the generalized growth of interest in the concept of lifelong learning and emphasis on the need to become a 'learning society' in the new millennium. He shows how these different analyses have been welded together by a variety of interests to produce a powerful discourse which has been influential in stressing the need for lifelong learning policies to support the need for economic competitiveness. Indeed, a detailed analysis of three major policy reports relevant to the development of lifelong learning in the UK reveals a strong priority accorded to vocational education and training in spite of some general rhetoric about the non-economic, personal and social benefits of lifelong learning (Tight, 1998). Vague statements about 'improvement in society' and 'personal fulfilment' also tend to permeate various recent European educational policy statements concerned with the promotion of lifelong learning issues (Withnall, 1997/8). In addition, Hodgson and Spours (1999) in a consideration of the key points of New Labour's emergent educational policy agenda for lifelong learning in the UK, point to a series of short term issues which need attention in order to stimulate lifelong learning. Once again, the focus is mainly on participation in the education and training system although the authors do comment on the longer term issues which should be considered including 'the more fundamental structural issues to face in terms of building the kind of seamless robe of provision required for a system of lifelong learning, as well as the kind of social and economic climate in which learning is valued, used and rewarded' (p. 46).

Certainly, the present UK government has acknowledged the need to 'break down barriers' to older people playing a full part in its vision of a learning society, but to date, its proposals for development and the packages of support available to adult learners suggest that people who are post-work are not genuinely part of the vision (DfEE, 1999). Indeed, older people are still largely marginalized in educational policy circles in Europe and beyond by continued emphasis on economic competitiveness in tandem with moral panics about the financial support of an ageing population which, although of major importance, tend to conceptualize later life primarily as a social problem.

The emergence of the Third Age

Why should older people merit consideration at all? The increase in life expectancy in almost every country in the world has been one of the major features of the last hundred years mainly the result of the reduction in mortality and fertility worldwide. Indeed, it is usual for gerontological texts to begin with a series of statistics illustrating how the proportion of people aged 60 and over have grown in the preceding century, estimates of the numbers living in developing countries, lists of countries with the oldest populations, etc. together with alarmist projections about future growth. It can be argued, however, that such statistics mean little when taken in isolation from issues of economic status and social policy. The bald presentation of statistical facts also disguises the diversity and heterogeneity of older populations in different countries and stands to be accused of perpetuating a 'them and us' mentality—as though older people were somehow a different species from the rest of the population rather than acknowledgeing that ageing is something which everyone experiences.

What can be said is that as the numbers and thus the visibility of older people in the population have increased, the processes of ageing have attracted attention from a range of disciplinary interests. For our purposes, it is the transformation of the institution of retirement as the result of trends in labour force participation that is of interest. Phillipson (1998) demonstrates how the meaning of retirement has evolved from a period of stability in the 1950s and 1960s when it was associated with (largely male) exit from the workforce and entry into a state old age pension scheme to a phase of considerable instability and accompanying loss of identity for people who are post-work. The age at which people leave the workforce may depend on a variety of factors—redundancy, voluntary severance, health, caring duties—or the possibilities offered by flexible retirement policies or self-employment. At the same time, increased longevity means that the post-work period is likely to be lengthy and, as Blaikie (1999) has shown, this change in the balance of life stages has largely unexplored social and cultural outcomes.

One of these is the tendency among commentators to talk of a division of the later life period into the 'young old' and the 'old old' or the 'Third Age' of active leisure and personal fulfilment and the 'Fourth Age' of descent into dependence, senility and death. In defining the Third Age as 'the crown of life', Laslett (1989) has commented that it will become a considerable and increasing part of everyone's experience and that therefore society needs to adjust to the cultural requirements of members of this group, themselves perceived as the cultural trustees of the future. Recognition of the Third Age as a new phenomenon requiring investigation in order to open up greater choice for all lay at the basis of the extensive Carnegie Inquiry into a range of aspects of life, including learning, between the ages of 50 and 74 (Carnegie UK Trust, 1993).

In examining the imagery of the Third Age, Blaikie (1999) points out how Third Agers have been encouraged to develop a new kind of retirement lifestyle in which the emphasis has shifted from issues of sickness and decline towards health, liberation and 'refurbishment'. This change of emphasis, he shows, lies with the emergence of consumer culture, particularly as businesses become aware of demographic trends and more sensitized to the mature market. Gilleard (1996), in fact, argues that contemporary consumer culture plays a part in helping older people to shape their identities at a time when the meaning of growing old is subject to revision in a time of rapid change. Indeed, a glance at any of the recent rash of 'lifestyle' magazines aimed at retired people reveals a wide spectrum of positive images and expectations unimagineable in previous older generations. However, issues of gender, class, race and ethnicity and geographical location require far more exploration in understanding how the experience of living in the Third Age is actually structured by socioeconomic and other factors such as health status, largely outside individual control.

Theoretical issues in the education and training of Third Agers

The influence of activity theory

Predictions about the burgeoning numbers of older people in all industrialized countries, the beginnings of changing patterns of retirement and the possible implications for educators of adults and other professions concerned with ageing began to attract attention in the 1970s, initially in the USA. A particular concern ever since has been to justify the post-work population as worthy of inclusion in educational policy decisions although only a somewhat limited number of attempts have been made to address the fundamental philosophical issues involved and to engage in theory building. A brief review by Withnall and Percy (1994) suggests that these attempts have been located mainly within a functionalist paradigm and derive from activity theory and from sociological theories of role change (Havighurst, 1963). The emphasis in approaches that utilize role theory, as in activity theory, is that older people must deal with role loss and adjustment to role change in retirement. Activity theory sees later life as a time of potential individual growth and renewed social relationships—life satisfaction derives from social interaction and active participation so that the post-work period can be a positive, creative and busy time. In this way, the purpose of educational activity in later life is to provide solutions to the problem of how to achieve successful ageing through the preservation of a positive, healthy and active lifestyle or through adaptation to a socially acceptable role. There is an implicit assumption that education can contribute to this process by assuring good health, well-being and personal satisfaction in later life. Activity theory thus opens the door for educators of adults to develop suitable interventions and legitimates their claims to be able to offer older people choice and opportunity for keeping their brains active and healthy, for personal fulfilment and for self-development—although this latter term surely requires further exploration (Walker, 1998).

To these ends, any debate has tended to be framed in terms of older people's participation (or non-participation) in formally organized activities (Withnall and Percy, 1994) together with discussion of appropriate provision for older people as one of a range of identified target groups often labelled as 'disadvantaged' (e.g. McGivney, 1990). It has found practical expression in the current Older and Bolder development project run in England and Wales under the auspices of the National Institute of Adult Continuing Education (NIACE). To date, this initiative has utilized a mixture of statistical and anecdotal evidence to make a strong case for increasing public investment in learning provision for older people (Carlton and Soulsby, 1999). Other initiatives along similar lines are described in Schuller and Bostyn (1992) in their work for the Carnegie Inquiry. Indeed, older people now feature in the UK government's plans for the development of its lifelong learning strategy, albeit in a very limited way, on the grounds that learning can have positive health outcomes (DfEE, 1999).

Certainly, there is some emerging medical evidence concerning the beneficial results of continued mental stimulation in later life with regard to the maintenance of good health (see Khaw, 1997 for a summary). Recent neurological research also suggests that mental training in later life can boost intellectual power, assist in maintaining mental function and help to reverse memory decline (Kotulak, 1997). However, little of this work impacts on educators of adults in a systematic way and they have tended to proceed on the basis of a range of clinically unproven assumptions. Moreover, activity theory may be far too limited to capture the complexity of older people's engagement in social activities and their participation in education. Powell Lawton (1993), drawing on a range of approaches, shows that older people continue to be complex in their orientations and relationships so that their activities also tend to be multi-dimensional. In addition, later life may bring transitions that impact on relationships, expectations, opportunities and abilities (widowhood or the deterioration or loss of some physical functions for example) and thus on willingness and capacity to participate in different types of activities at different times. Szinovacz (1992) finds it necessary to combine insights from activity theory with other theoretical perspectives in order to investigate how gender, marital status and household composition relate to post-retirement social activity patterns. Finally, activity theory implicitly castigates older people who do not wish to embrace the 'busy' ethic as in some way withdrawn or deviant. In general, research on later life has moved on and, as Katz (1996) has shown, has embraced more reliable theories and frameworks within which to examine the lived experiences of older people in their everyday environments.

The moral dimension

Apart from supposed health benefits, another approach that can be discerned in many of the writings of educational gerontologists is an emphasis on older people's rights to have access to educational opportunities. These often derive from notions of the relative deprivation and what Townsend (1981) and others have called the structured dependency characteristic of later life. This approach formed the basis of the 'educational charter for the elderly' published by Laslett (1989) who was closely involved in the genesis of the Forum on the Rights of Elderly People to Education (FREE) developed by a group of enthusiasts in the UK. Although the charter did not have the long-lasting impact intended at the time and FREE was eventually disbanded, it may be that it now warrants a re-examination in the light of more recent official concern with the ageing of populations across Europe and beyond.

The moral dimension also underpins other arguments developed by Schuller and Bostyn (1992) and Carlton and Soulsby (1999). Indeed, Schuller and Bostyn contend that older people are entitled to educational opportunities as compensation for lack of these earlier in their lives, especially since the divides of gender and class have had such a major impact on the division of educational opportunities.

Reviewing these approaches, Withnall and Percy (1994) call for something more than just the recognition of educational rights advocated from a quasi-political stance where reasoning is grounded in concepts of equality and justice. They suggest that notions of equal opportunities in the commonly understood sense of the same opportunities for all be abandoned in favour of a focus on the importance of human dignity, on the fulfilment of human potential and the promotion of fair treatment for everyone. More recently, Elmore (1999) has examined this moral dimension further through a carefully reasoned advocacy of older people's access to both instrumental and expressive education on the basis of social justice but using notions of fair equality of opportunity, access to democratic participation and the status of equal citizenship at a time when many societies are undergoing fundamental change in their social and economic structure. In this way, older people's access to education becomes a tool towards the achievement of a liberal democracy. However, it can be argued that these kinds of discussions have been conducted without reference to the wider debates about ethics and intergenerational equity which have challenged demographers and gerontologists in recent years and forced them to reconsider some long held assumptions about the sites and boundaries of their disciplinary fields.

Generativity

The theme of intergenerational recognition and reciprocity found expression both in the 1993 European Year of Older People and Solidarity Between Generations and in the 1999 United Nations Year of Older People which took 'towards a society for all ages' as its main slogan. Such an approach derives largely from the work of developmental psychologists such as Erikson (1963) who theorized that human development occurs through a sequence of eight psychosocial stages involving crisis or conflict at each stage. A major developmental crisis is said to occur in early and middle adulthood and involving the attainment of generativity—a concern with others beyond the immediate family, with future generations and the nature of the world in which these descendants will live. People who are successful in resolving this crisis are said to be able to establish clear guidelines for their lives and generally to age in a happy and productive way. Failure to achieve generativity results in stagnation in which people become preoccupied with personal needs, comforts and concerns.

The theme of generativity underpins the work of Laslett (1989) who has argued persuasively that self-fulfilment in later life implies those in the Third Age taking responsibility for themselves and their learning and also recognizing the obligation to create an interchange with younger members of society so that an equitable relationship with the future can be secured for the whole of society. Notions of generativity also inform the exploratory work of the American feminist Betty Friedan (1993) in her personal quest to give meaning to the ageing process. Much of the practical intergenerational educational work taking place in different countries, notably in the United States, bases its *raison d'être*, probably unconsciously, on the notion of generativity.

Theories of adult development and the personality changes taking place in adulthood which see progression in stages, although influential, have been largely discredited in that they take insufficient cognizance of class and gender issues and of the changing socioeconomic context. Indeed, the sheer diversity of experience in adult life makes it impossible to predict major stages. Crises may occur at any age and may be satisfactorily resolved at individual level with no major effects. Stage theories also imply a discontinuity of development whilst other psychological theories stress the continuity of personality during adulthood. It may well be then, that whilst participation in educational intergenerational activity might be relevant and rewarding for many Third Agers, the perspectives which derive from developmental psychology are inadequate in offering a useful theory which might be translated into practice.

Critical educational gerontology

The 1980s saw the emergence of a range of critical perspectives within the field of social gerontology for a range of reasons discussed in some detail by Phillipson (1998). These perspectives have begun to impinge on debates in the field of educational gerontology, especially the development of a critical educational gerontology from the mid-1980s onwards. Glendenning (1997), a staunch advocate of the need for a new paradigm that would unshackle ideas about educational provision for older people from the functionalist paradigm, argues that we need to ask a number of searching questions about such provision including why it is needed and whose interests are really being served together with a re-evaluation of existing practices and models. He advocates a more robust paradigm where a new discourse about later life might be located and identifies a pressing need firstly, to disentangle the reasons for what he sees as the marginalization and structured dependency of older people; and secondly, for education to lead older people to take charge of their lives and to become emancipated, thereby introducing a new moral dimension to the debate about educational purpose in the Third Age and beyond. That his ideas have resonated with some educators of adults can be seen in some descriptive accounts of how the possibilities of critical educational gerontology are being explored in practice (e.g. Cusack, 1999).

Glendenning has been a major influence on the development of educational gerontology in the UK and his insistence on the need for a new paradigm within which to explore major questions concerning Third Age education has enabled some accepted wisdom to be questioned and re-evaluated. However, it can be argued as Usher *et al.* (1997) have done in relation to the education of adults in general, that although an approach derived from critical theory seeks to unmask distortions and constraints, it actually runs the risk of substituting a partial and unbalanced view of human experience. The drive for emancipation and empowerment may itself become a new form of oppression. Indeed, in seeming to assume a heterogeneity among older people and seeing them as uniformly disadvantaged and committed to praxis, Glendenning appears to be making a number of unwarranted assumptions and unwittingly to be imposing a new kind of ideological constraint. For example, we have previously commented that the Third Age is increasingly characterized by widening inequalities largely determined by the socioeconomic structure and the growth of consumerism implicated with issues of gender, class, race, ethnicity and age itself. Psychological evidence concerning the impact of ageing on health status, intellectual skills and lifestyles (Stuart-Hamilton, 1994; Slater, 1995) also suggests a sharper division between the fit and active majority and the minority suffering acute or chronic illness whether mental, physical or both. It can also be argued that critical educational gerontology cannot account for the emergence of newer models of educational provision for and by older people themselves such as the Elderhostel movement in North America or University of the Third Age in the UK. It is through these movements that more middle-class Third Agers have sought to re-appropriate both knowledge and learning and, as Blaikie (1999) observes in respect of the latter, to present themselves as in the vanguard of cultural change.

The assumptions that Glendenning makes with regard to the role of educators of older people must also be subjected to scrutiny. The question of the role and responsibilities of educators of adults in general with regard to social action has long been an issue. We simply cannot assume those who teach older people to be themselves unfettered by ideological beliefs, or to possess a uniform desire or ability to encourage an emancipatory critique, to operationalize a new political lobby or even to encourage individual action on a small scale. The issues are more complex than has hitherto been acknowledged.

Lifelong learning revisited: an inclusive approach

One issue which emerges clearly from these debates is the emphasis on the notion of education in the Third Age and in later life generally. Indeed, the very field of educational gerontology, although subject to redefinition over the years and in different national contexts, suggests a definite emphasis on provider concerns rather than offering a Third Age learner perspective. Where learning is mentioned at all in relation to later life, there is little attempt to distinguish between formally provided educational opportunities and the formal and informal learning which Third Agers might undertake, much of which might be unrecognized even by older people themselves.

We have seen that, apart from the work of Glendenning, educational gerontology is largely atheoretical. A new formulation that seems to offer a way forward would be to focus on learning as discussed above, rather than on education in later life. We may begin from the proposition that, in late modernity, a conceptualization of lifelong learning as 'cradle to grave' but which nevertheless privileges vocational education and training and makes only scant reference to the post-work population, is inadequate. It may be that learning itself might be more readily located in social and cultural developments such as the growth of consumerism and in a range of social practices (Usher *et al.*, 1997). Indeed, we have examined the arguments that notions of the Third Age emerged from the growth of consumerism and that current consumer culture plays a part in helping older people refashion their identities when the old certainties of later life have been displaced. In this sense, formally provided learning opportunities for adults generally have themselves become part of the consumer culture, offering the promise of access to a particular lifestyle and often marketed as 'fun' with enjoyment as the main aim. However, for many adults, particularly those returning to learning, the actual processes of learning are more likely to be experienced as challenging, demanding and even painful. For older people, the fun element may well be provided by the social context, the chance to spend time in the company of like-minded people, to subject oneself to new experiences, to structure one's week around a focal point.

Educators of adults have long argued, of course, that learning does not have to take place in formal settings and to be structured by formal providers. The success of the University of the Third Age as it has developed in Britain and in Australia and indeed, other similar informal and self-help endeavours, has shown that some older people do not necessarily wish to buy into a lifestyle but that other factors may be important in assisting them to shape a post-work identity including taking concerted action to better their position. Learning may also be incidental, unanticipated or imposed; the plethora of publications describing the early stages of widowhood and the subsequent necessity of learning a range of unfamiliar tasks is a case in point. Alternatively, learning in later life may consist of the kind of reflection and life review which takes place in an unstructured and spasmodic way but which may lead to greater self-understanding and individual insight.

It was argued earlier that to reconstruct the Third Age as a period of lifestyle choice and opportunity is to ignore the realities of the socioeconomic structure and issues of gender and ethnicity. Certainly choice is not a straightforward issue. However, this kind of thinking suggests that what is needed is a better understanding of what learning means in the context of older people's lives, whether they make choices about learning in both formal and informal contexts in an uncertain world, and the basis on which they might do so. We also need to identify what constitutes a successful learning experience and to assess what outcomes learning has for those in the Third Age. The very heterogeneity of the post-work population and the sheer diversity of experience of different groups of older people further suggests that we need to find a way to understand the influence of different events and beliefs over the life course and to problematize their experiences as learners. The definitive questions that need to be asked are wide-ranging. For example, how do older people themselves define and understand learning post-work? What value do they place on learning (and education)? What are the contexts and discourses over the life course that have shaped their perceptions? How have they constructed and developed ideas and attitudes to learning and to education? What outcomes do formal/informal and other types of learning have for older people in the context of their own lives, and how are these outcomes experienced and described? Answers to these questions might also help us to focus on a broader issue—what are the implications for theory and for social and educational policies in general in respect of a stronger emphasis on learning in later life?

The life course approach is not without its methodological problems and is a complex task since it needs to incorporate a holistic approach to adult life covering a range of aspects, as Blaikie (1999) has observed. Indeed, the life course perspective suggests that learning activity in the Third Age and the forms it might take at different times will be influenced by a complex interplay of individual characteristics and by a variety of individual and collective experiences over a lifetime combined with genetic and environmental influences on the ageing process (Bergeman, 1997). Such an analysis, together with an exploration of differing situational experiences, opportunities and constraints throughout life including the post-work period would offer a distinctive perspective on the factors which might influence older people to continue or to take up learning activity at any stage of their post-work lives. It also provides a way of investigating the relationship between learning undertaken in formal or informal contexts and encourages reflection on that learning which is unintentional or unanticipated.

The life course approach would also help to illuminate how the opportunities or constraints of age, class, gender, race and location may combine with other factors to influence learning choices and activities in later life—or indeed, an apparent lack of them. Jarvis (1994) in beginning to address these issues has theorized about the relationship between biography and experience pointing out that they should be distinguished from each other. Jamieson *et al.* (1998) have used the life course approach on a small scale in an empirical study of a group of older people attending a residential summer school and, although offering a basic framework for understanding education in the context of retirement, admit that their study focuses on a small and atypical group of older people. In addition, they are once again adopting a provider perspective rather than a focus on learning itself.

The development and testing of a conceptual model of the reasons for participation in learning, the pathways through, and outcomes of undertaking different types of learning activity in the Third Age would enable the identification not only of the circumstances which affect opportunity and choice at different times but would also offer a clearer understanding of Third Agers' experiences as learners in a variety of settings and contexts. This would enable us to move towards a refinement and re-alignment of theory in lifelong learning by taking a more inclusive perspective. In this way, educational gerontology as it has been conceptualized to date, would become incorporated into a new theoretical perspective on lifelong learning itself (Withnall, 2000).

Researching Third Age learning

The use of methods which focus on personal meaning and help to illuminate how older people experience various aspects of daily life are currently in vogue among social gerontologists, mainly as a reaction to the medical model of ageing which focuses closely on clinical trials and on quantitative methods associated with research into health care in later life. However, in advocating the use of qualitative data from which to begin theory-building, especially the process of asking older people to reflect upon their life stories and present learning experiences, it is necessary to exercise caution. It is generally recognized by advocates of the life course method that the self cannot be a single stable identity and that life stories are necessarily subjective interpretations and evaluations that are open to change over time and in different contexts. Alternatively, it may be the case, as other scholars have argued, that life stories are social constructions that are created and sustained by social interaction and that experiences are only made real and bestowed with meaning through telling and presentation. Brandon Wallace (1994) discusses these issues at length in an overview of the use of life stories as a research tool, emphasizing the necessity for researchers to clarify their epistemological stance at the outset.

Any empirical research that seeks to ascribe meaning to learning in the context of the Third Age using a life course approach therefore must be carried out with an acknowledgement that the topic under investigation, the subjects of the research and, indeed, the stance and changing perspectives of the researchers themselves, may shape the ways in which the research develops and is interpreted and reported. Strategies may need to adapt and evolve over time. In addition, as in any research, ethical issues need consideration. The concept of research as an enactment of power relations between researchers and the subjects of the research has perplexed educational and social science researchers for some time (see Usher *et al.*, 1997 for a detailed discussion). Withnall (2000) suggests that one way to begin to confront this dilemma might be to encourage older people themselves to become researchers. Certainly, both the Senior Studies Institute at the University of Strathclyde in Scotland and the UK Pre-Retirement Association have successfully enabled groups of older people to become competent researchers; and some University of the Third Age branches have also developed considerable expertise in training their members in the research process. However, the informed consent of research informants, assurances of anonymity and issues concerned with the ownership of research would still need detailed consideration and discussion.[1]

Concluding remarks: towards a wider perspective

The emphasis in this chapter has been firstly, on the paucity of current political visions of lifelong learning—visions that rarely acknowledge the emergence of the Third Age or the importance of changing demographics in other than in a desultory way. Secondly, it has critically reviewed a range of statements of purpose about education and older adults, examined a range of perspectives and noted the general absence of theory in what has come to be known as educational gerontology. Thirdly, it has been suggested that a possible way forward in respect of the Third Age would be to change the current emphasis from education to learning and to investigate what meaning older people actually ascribe to learning by locating it within a life course perspective. In obtaining empirical data, however, it has been argued that we need a new research paradigm that would place ageing itself at the centre of the debate and which might incorporate older people themselves into the research process. In these ways, it might be possible to move towards a new and more inclusive theory of lifelong learning that would have relevance for a society experiencing demographic and other kinds of change at an unprecedented rate.

This cannot, however, be the end of the story. In talking about the Third Age and equating this period of life with choice, opportunity, creativity and personal development, to what extent do we risk denial of the 'Fourth Age'? Even if we accept ideas of Third and Fourth Ages uncritically—and it can be argued that such a division is unrealistic—do we not ignore the learning possibilities of the Fourth Age? Accounts of pioneering work carried out with very old and infirm people in nursing and residential homes through reminiscence and other activities suggest that the possibilities for learning, in all its dimensions, do not end with chronic illness or infirmity (Bornat, 1994). There is still room for exploration of residents' changing sense of self whatever the nature and extent of their disability. However, to understand that learning in later life must also incorporate acknowledgement of the finitude of existence and to accept and to prepare for death would also mean that learning would be truly 'to grave'.

In discussing Third Age learning from a mainly Eurocentric perspective, we also run the risk of failing to acknowledge demographic trends, mentioned earlier, on a global scale. We are aware from predictions that the real challenge of population ageing in the twenty-first century will come from developing nations where concepts of lifelong learning will take on different dimensions in that increased knowledge, improved skills (especially in literacy and numeracy) and access to educational opportunities are imperative if older people, especially women, are to be enabled to become fully empowered members of their communities and yet retain traditional roles as guardians of culture and tradition to be passed down to other generations. The implications for countries undergoing social and political transition are likely to engage the attention of both educators of adults and social gerontologists in years to come and to change our current understanding of the Third Age in ways that are not yet apparent. In the meantime, debate about learning in later life, informed by quality research must continue. We cannot escape from the fact that ageing is universal!

Note

1 A research project currently underway at Keele University, funded by the Economic and Social Research Council (ESRC) under its Growing Older Programme is attempting to incorporate these methods into an investigation of older people and lifelong learning (Award No. L480254049).

References

Bergeman, C S (1997) *Aging. Genetic and Environmental Influences.* Thousand Oaks, CA, Sage Publications, Inc.

Blaikie, A (1999) *Ageing and Popular Culture.* Cambridge, Cambridge University Press

Bornat, J (Ed) (1994) *Reminiscence Reviewed: Evaluations, Achievements, Perspectives.* Buckingham, Open University Press

Brandon Wallace, J (1994) Life stories. In Gubrium, J F and Sankar, A (Eds.), *Qualitative Methods in Aging Research* (pp 137–54). Thousand Oaks, CA, Sage Publications

Carnegie Inquiry into the Third Age (1993) *Final Report. Life, Work and Livelihood in the Third Age.* Dunfermline, The Carnegie UK Trust

Carlton, S and Soulsby, J (1999) *Learning to Grow Older and Bolder,* Leicester, NIACE

Cusack, S (1999) Critical educational gerontology and the imperative to empower. *Education and Ageing, 14,* 21–37

Department for Education and Employment (1999) *Learning to Succeed.* Cmd 4932. London, DfEE

Edwards, R (1998) *Changing Places?* London, Routledge

Elmore, R (1999) Education for older people: the moral dimension. *Education and Ageing, 14,* 9–20

Erikson, E (1963) *Childhood and Society*. 2nd ed. New York, Norton

Friedan, B (1993) *The Fountain of Age*. London, Jonathan Cape

Gilleard, C (1996) Consumption and identity in later life: towards a cultural gerontology *Ageing and Society*, *16*

Glendenning, F (1997) Why educational gerontology is not yet established as a field of study *Education and Ageing*, *12*, 82–91

Havighurst, R J (1963) Successful aging. In Williams, R H, Tibbitts, C and Donahue, W (Eds.), *Processes of Aging*, 1. (pp 299–320). New York, Atherton

Hodgson, A and Spours, K (1999) *New Labour's Educational Agenda*. London, Kogan Page

Jamieson, A and Stafford, J (1998) Education in a life course perspective: continuities and discontinuities *Education and Ageing*, *13*, 213–28

Jarvis, P (1992) Learning, developing and ageing in late modernity *Journal of Educational Gerontology*, *7*, 7–15

Katz, S (1996) *Disciplining Old Age: The Formation of Gerontological Knowledge*. Charlottesville, VA. And London, University Press of Virginia

Khaw, K-T (1997) Healthy ageing *British Medical Journal*, *315*, pp 1090–6

Kotulak, R (1997) *Inside the Brain: Revolutionary Discoveries of How the Mind Works*. Kansas City, Andrews McMeel Publishing

Laslett, P (1989) *A Fresh Map of Life*. London, Weidenfeld and Nicholson

McGivney, V (1990) *Education's for Other People*. Leicester, NIACE

Phillipson, C (1998) *Reconstructing Old Age*. London, Sage Publications

Powell Lawton, M (1993) Meanings of activity In Kelly, J R (Ed.), *Activity and Ageing*. Newbury Park, CA, Sage Publications

Schuller, T and Bostyn, A-M (1992) *Learning: Education, Training and Information in the Third Age*. Carnegie Inquiry into the Third Age, Research Paper No. 3. Dunfermline, Carnegie UK Trust

Slater, R (1995) *The Psychology of Growing Old*. Buckingham, Open University Press

Stuart-Hamilton, I (1994) *The Psychology of Ageing*. London, Jessica Kingsley Publishers

Szinovacz, M (1992) Social activities and retirement adaptation: gender and family variations. In Szinovacz, M, Ekerdt, D J and Vinick, B H (Eds.), *Families and Retirement* (pp 236–53) Newbury Park, CA, Sage Publications

Tight, M (1998) Education, education, education! The vision of lifelong learning in the Kennedy, Dearing and Fryer reports *Oxford Review of Education*, *24*, pp 473–85

Townsend, P (1981) The structured dependency of the elderly: the creation of social policy in the twentieth century *Ageing and Society*, *1*, pp 5–28

Usher, R, Bryant, I and Johnston, R (1997) *Adult Education and the Postmodern Challenge*. London, Routledge

Walker, J (1998) Mapping the learning of older adults *Adults Learning*, *10*, pp 14–16

Withnall, A (1997/8) Older Europeans in the learning society *Ageing International*, *24*, pp 46–63

Withnall, A (2000) The debate continues: integrating educational gerontology with lifelong learning. In Glendenning, F (Ed.), *Teaching and Learning in Later Life: Some Critical Implications*. Aldershot, Ashgate

Withnall, A and Percy, K (1994) *Good Practice in the Education and Training of Older Adults*. Aldershot, Ashgate

24 Lifelong learning

Trade unions in search of a role

John McIlroy

By the end of the twentieth century British trade unions had come to enthusiastically embrace the dominant discourse of lifelong learning. Conceptions of the learning society as intrinsically bound up with self-fulfilment, enhanced equality, enlarged democracy, qualitative social change and working-class progress were still present. They were supplementary and subordinate in trade union narratives to lifelong learning conceived as an instrument for adapting to, rather than controlling economic forces, and as a vehicle for individual employability and social mobility, while also extending flexibility to improve the competitiveness of enterprise and nation in the global market. This version of lifelong learning took economic and social relations as fixed: it aimed to make the economy work better, not transform society. It was essentially about improving the skills of the workforce: everything else was incidental or auxiliary. Under the rubric, 'A Policy Framework for Lifelong Learning' and 'The Learning Age', the Trades Union Congress (TUC) made only perfunctory reference to traditional educational goals. It had little to say about further and higher education, and nothing at all to say about the emaciated remnants of 'adult continuing education', perceived as central in earlier visions of lifelong learning. TUC statements, in contrast, were inspired by eager address of initiatives to expand vocational training couched in approbatory language and infused with repeated reference to 'work', 'skills', 'investment', 'flexibility', 'career resilience' and 'vocational qualifications'. 'Education' appears spasmodically, typically yoked to training to ennoble cramped pedagogies and vary and broaden dense economic narratives (TUC 1998a: 215–16).[1]

Attention to traditional, and still sharply relevant, purposes of labour pedagogy, vestigial and palely expressed, came a poor second to the irresistible imperatives of the market: 'At long last there is a real political will to create a learning society. There is recognition that in today's global economy ignorance costs more than education in terms of lost competition and social exclusion' (TUC 1988a: 214). During the twentieth century trade unions had made significant contributions to the expansion of the education system (Griggs 1983, Simon 1990), to the education of adults (Fieldhouse 1996) and to the education of their own members (McIlroy 1995a, 1996a). The TUC observed in a glance towards this past that, in contrast, 'there has been little union involvement in vocational training. This is changing rapidly' (TUC 1992a: 214). If the new vocationalism did not exhaust union concerns, it became by the 1990s an absorbing priority. Even reports on Employee Development Schemes (EDS), hailed as providing trade unionists with a wider range of educational opportunities (Forrester 1995), were almost exclusively concerned with skills training and intimately related to the viability of the company and its employees' position in the labour market (TUC 1999a).

This constricted and partial approach to lifelong learning was an organic component of broader union strategy, itself the product of adaptation to the traumas and transformed industrial, political and social landscapes of the final decades of the century. From 1979 unions were confronted by hostile administrations; restrictive legislation; qualitative restructuring of the labour market; a revolution in work; the burgeoning of globalization; and, affirmed in New Labour's modified Thatcherism, the ascendancy of neo-liberalism. Consequent decline in membership, recognition by employers, collective bargaining, social weight and political influence produced incremental change. By the mid-1990s there was a metamorphosis of union policy. Organized labour forsook adversarialism and corporatist ambition, embraced commitment to partnership with employers and the state, and recast their members as clients and consumers. They revamped their organizations in contemporary managerial mode and reconceived their mission as combining the eradication of conflict at work with satisfying the individual needs of members. Utilizing idealizations of the European Union (EU) model of social partnership, but settling all too often in practice for the American model of business unionism, they saw as central to their purposes the efficient delivery to capital of flexible, skilled, labour, imprinted with enterprise goals and committed to a revitalized economy, in return for increased investment in human capital, Human Resource Management (HRM) and increased employment security (McIlroy 1995b; 1998).

Within this problematic training became a central issue for unions. Put simply: 'On the one hand, training increases the range of services offered to members. On the other hand, it is part of an approach to employers which allows unions to demonstrate their ability to cooperate in a productivist strategy' (Keep and Rainbird 1995: 537). But more than this: beyond the workplace, in the public arena, unions in some ways excelled capital and even the state in their powerful definition of this deracinated version of lifelong learning and their tireless, imaginative, proselytization of its adoption as an antidote to economic decline. There were, however, problems, centring both on the unions' narrowly instrumental conception of training as lifelong learning and on their powerful prescriptions for greater state intervention and a revival of tripartism. This chapter explores the evolution and the detail of trade union approaches to lifelong learning and examines some of the difficulties they have encountered in achieving their objectives.

From tripartism to neo-liberalism

In the 1960s and 1970s the TUC, acting as spokesperson and agent for the unions, shadowed all aspects of educational policy and was viewed by the state as a respected and legitimate interest group (Simon 1991). Its stance on lifelong education was progressive, if pragmatic and untheorized, and involved attention to three main areas. First, it gave sustained support to the coordination and expansion of what it termed 'continuing education'—defined as 'all learning opportunities for adults which are taken up after full-time schooling has ceased, with priority accorded to those whose previous educational opportunities have been severely limited' (TUC 1977: 152–3). The TUC promoted a range of initiatives from the recommendations of the Russell Report in 1973 to the proposals of the Advisory Council for Adult and Continuing Education later in the decade, proposals which if implemented would have contributed to the establishment of a broad expanded system of lifelong learning integrating all kinds of education and training (TUC 1977: 151; 1979: 72–3). The support of the unions was always significant to the continuing education community but the imaginative plans for expansion of the 1970s fell victim to the economic crisis of the mid-1970s.

Second, the unions supported the creation of the national tripartite training system which developed from 1962 and whose landmarks were the Industrial Training Act 1964, which presaged the Industrial Training Boards (financed by a levy on employers), and the Employment and Training Act 1973, which created the Manpower Services Commission to oversee labour market manpower policies (Field 1996). Given the corporatist momentum of these decades, intervention by the state and the statutory involvement of organized labour was perceived as a prerequisite to transcending the inaction engendered by earlier dependence on voluntarism and employer initiatives (Ainley and Cornley 1991). The tripartite system granted unions an appreciable, though not to be exaggerated, influence over training, buttressing their historic role in the apprenticeship system. But the overall contribution it made to amelioration of Britain's economic malaise was questionable (King 1993).

Third, the unions estimated their own education schemes as constituting a significant contribution to lifelong learning. This area witnessed considerable progress in the 1960s and 1970s. By 1979 a system of annual state grants underpinned the education and training of union representatives while rights to paid release from work were introduced in the Employment Act 1975. The TUC programme was expanded to include more than 1,000 day-release courses annually. There was also substantial growth in the educational work of affiliated unions, while the long-term residential colleges for adults, long associated with the labour movement, were augmented by the addition of Northern College. Trade union education, too, had its limitations. It was centrally concerned with the role training of union officials, it neglected ordinary members and, ultimately dependent on state finance and union power, it was subject to the treacherous vagaries of economics and politics (McIlroy 1996b).

The advent of neo-liberalism thus transformed matters. The reinvented, reinvigorated stress on market competition, enterprise culture, individualism and consumer choice had as one of its specific objectives the reduction of union influence over education and training (Hall 1983). The new political and economic context debilitated the labour movement and drove revision of philosophy and policy. By the 1990s the TUC had scaled down its broader social and political role in favour of prioritizing key issues and industrial problems (Heery 1998). It had vigorously opposed from their initiation many of the changes in further, higher and adult education, including those which 'restricted publicly funded adult education to a narrow range of vocationally orientated courses' (TUC 1992a: 66). It had done so with minimal success. As the unions regrouped and retooled their educational policies the vision of an expanded integrated lifelong learning slipped from sight.

There was similar diminution of ambition as well as decline in trade union education. The number of ten-day courses fell from 1,200, with 16,000 student places in 1980, to 762 with 9,500 places in 1987 and 512 with 6,000 places in 1992 (McIlroy 1996b). Conservative governments patrolled the parameters of course content, objecting to critical approaches and securing their suppression. In a harder climate opportunities for release from work were eroded. The state grant was progressively reduced and then, between 1993 and 1996, finally phased out. Several unions closed training facilities acquired in the 1970s. The residential colleges were substantially remoulded in the image of the new vocationalism and restructured to deliver access to higher education, their evacuation of old traditions symbolized by the appointment of a management consultant as Principal of Ruskin (McIlroy 1995b).

There were broader more hopeful developments. The 1994 amalgamation of NALGO, the white collar local government union which mounted strong programmes of both trade union and vocational education, and its blue collar counterpart NUPE, also educationally inclined, provided a new impetus. The Unison Open College provided an extensive and integrated scheme of education and training, ranging from 'Return to Learn' and 'Women, Work and Society' modules to courses in economics and politics at universities as well as a rich range of vocational qualifications (Sutherland 1998). The best known EDS, that at Ford, was a management initiative and an American import. But it generated tremendous interest from trade unionists and a proliferation of similar management–union innovations with opportunities for more diverse and broader education than union representative training offered (Payne 1996).

What increasingly interested the unions, however, was the training field. Here they were passionately critical of neo-liberal deregulation and actively and energetically opposed key government initiatives, particularly training schemes for the unemployed. As training became an increasingly important instrument in state management of the economic, political and social tensions arising from industrial change and sustained high unemployment (Field 1996: 350), the unions were markedly unsuccessful in influencing the trajectory of the new schemes. Nor were they able to mount more than token education for the jobless through the TUC supported unemployment centres (Forrester 1995). Across the board their response gradually, at times imperceptibly, became critically positive. Once their initial hostile response subsided the TUC accepted and sought to influence the key innovations. As the Industrial Training Boards were phased out and replaced by the voluntary, employer-dominated Industrial Training Organisations, the TUC tenaciously pursued involvement and representation. As the government developed the system of National Vocational Qualifications (NVQs), the unions became supportive and were soon vocal advocates. When the TUC's objections to the training scheme for the long-term unemployed led the Conservatives to axe the Training Commission (the successor to the MSC) and introduce the Training and Enterprise Councils (TECs), the TUC did their best to make them work (Rainbird 1990).

By the 1990s attention to vocational training was at the centre of the TUC's concerns.

> The General Council's main objective has continued to be to maximise the influence of the trade union movement on developments in education and training ... Within that object-ive the promotion of joint action over training between trade unions and employers has been the priority task.
>
> (TUC 1992: 57)

This new imperative was stimulated by a number of factors. Weakened unions were already deploying a more collaborative posture towards management and, in contrast with traditional issues, training held the promise of partnership potential. The unions were already vigorously embracing the EU whose model of social partnership and emphasis on lifelong learning (CEC 1994) suggested a viable alternative to neo-liberalism. The development of national accreditation demanded a response. At least rhetorically the Conservatives were pledged to qualitative expansion of training. Yet research suggested reliance on employers to deliver it was naive. Moreover what training there was, was skewed towards progressive firms, privileging the more skilled and better educated, while expansion was evidently leaving training ghettos of unskilled atypical workers, often women and ethnic minorities (Keep 1989; Finegold and Soskice 1990). The space was there. The situation was defined as bristling with opportunity for the unions to demonstrate that, in contrast to management, they were alert to state exhortation; and that they could act as a responsible stimulus and helpmate to capital in developing a skilled flexible workforce, while simultaneously boosting their members' labour market value (Bacon and Story 1993).

Gradually TUC policy took shape.

> The key ingredient of Britain's economic recovery is raising the skills of our people. They are our most valuable asset. That philosophy lies at the heart of the role of the Education and Training Committee ... Much more must be done by employers and government in terms of investing additional resources in schools, colleges, TECs and company training. Much more must be done to push the employers and to be quite categoric the employers themselves must face up to their own responsibilities and it is no secret that we want a proper statutory system with a levy system.
>
> (TUC 1992a: 288–9)

Realization of this approach in the face of the Major government's continued hostility to the diminished chastened unions and apathy from employers, for whom cost conventionally took precedence over the development of the human resource, was to prove more difficult. The TUC fought back against union exclusion. They secured representation on the National Advisory Council for Education and Training Targets, the National Council for Vocational Qualifications, and Investors in People UK. Despite possessing no guaranteed institutional role and despite periodic regrets 'concerning the continued reluctance of some TECs to involve unions in training initiatives', by 1993 unions were represented, albeit slenderly, on 63 out of the 82 training councils. Four years later their tenacity was rewarded: 72 out of the 78 councils had a union director and the remainder had agreed in principle to union representation, although employer dominance endured (TUC 1993: 66; 1998a: 111).

The National Training Council proved willing to accord the TUC a significant role in publicizing the training targets. After a joint campaign with South Thames TEC to win the commitment of trade unionists to the targets aimed specifically at disadvantaged groups, similar projects were mounted with a growing number of TECs. In the context of making members aware of the evolving national accreditation system the TUC emphasized the importance of negotiating training agreements with companies which included precise objectives. Trade unions were urged to persuade employers to adopt the Investors in People standard. There was particular stress on meeting the training needs of 'the socially excluded', women, ethnic minorities, the long-term unemployed and those with special needs. Surveys affirmed the resilience of 'the training divide': those who received training were typically the already trained skilled workers and those in management and professional grades at the expense of unskilled workers while exclusion on ethnic grounds continued to constitute a problem (TUC 1992b).

Individual unions were also active. The GMB and TGWU published a joint statement which urged the need to prioritize training in bargaining agendas and a minimum of 7-days training annually for each employee (GMB/TGWU 1992). USDAW, which recruited large numbers of unskilled workers, advocated the extension of training as a matter of social justice (USDAW 1991). The work of union representatives on the EU Social Dialogue Education and Training Committee, and the Advisory Committee on Vocational Training, reinforced for trade unionists the benefits of tripartism, the necessity for a statutory framework with specific responsibilities on employers, and rights to paid leave for employees (TUC 1993: 62–3). The dual track strategy—pressing for the legislation of an alternative system while making the most of the existing one—produced by the mid-1990s the *Bargaining for Skills* project. This was intended to put unions at the centre of the drive to meet the national targets. It comprised ten projects aimed at 60 TECs, with 20 staff conducting awareness briefings for union representatives, integrating training issues in union education programmes, offering modules to management and, crucially for the TUC, building links with key company staff (TUC 1994; TUC 1995: 1–2). By 1996 more than 40 TECs were involved in *Bargaining for Skills* projects, and the TUC had agreed an 'accord' with the TEC National Council that stressed the importance of the partnership approach (TUC 1996a: 82; 1996b).

As a Labour government loomed it was difficult to estimate what the unions' new approach had achieved. Studies attested that there had been some increase in training since 1988—although not as great as official surveys suggested. Provision continued to differentiate between companies, sectors and categories of employee, and training was focused on 'core skills' rather than 'portable' transferable skills, still less on broader education (Finegold 1991; Payne 1990; Rainbird and Vincent 1996; Turner *et al.* 1992). What the unions found extremely encouraging was that there appeared to be a 'union differential' and some correlation between union recognition and the incidence of company training (Green *et al.* 1995; Winterton and Winterton 1994).

New Labour: new opportunities

In the run up to the 1997 general election, the TUC deepened and extended the search for partnership with capital and the state, stressing the centrality of training to this approach (TUC 1997a; 1997b: 31–4). For the unions lifelong learning meant emphatically lifelong job-related training: other dimensions essential to any meaningful lifelong learning were neglected or downplayed in what was increasingly an unbalanced, distorted and diluted variant driven by the TUC's institutional need to find a niche in which it could advertise the benefits of partnership. The position was encapsulated in the official report on the major 1996 conference, *Partners for Lifelong Learning*. It pithily summed up the TUC's pervasive instrumental reductionism: 'The conference was a showcase for unions' contribution to training' (TUC 1996a: 79).

The first move in relation to New Labour was an explicit attempt to achieve their most cherished and most contentious objective. Union leaders held talks with shadow ministers and forcefully proposed a statutory framework with legal obligations on employers and complementary entitlements for workers. This would effectively underpin the enfranchisement of unions as the state's agents in stimulating a training revolution. New Labour's modified neo-liberalism precluded such interference with the autonomy of capital: there was no question of 'placing specific legal obligations on employers to train the workforce' (TUC 1997: 32). The unions had to content themselves with an informal, facilitative rather than directive approach and with the commitments to individual learning accounts and the University for Industry (UfI) as grist for bargaining efforts. Under the heading 'Lifelong Learning', New Labour's Manifesto made no mention of trade unions. It was, and here it was in close accord with the TUC, a statement soaked in vocational instrumentalism. It commenced: 'We must learn throughout life to retain employment through new and improved skills ...'. Ignoring the unions, the Manifesto privileged employers and employees as individuals: 'Employers have the primary responsibility for training their workforces... But individuals should be given the power to invest in training' (Labour Party 1997: 8–9). State licensing of the unions' role would remain ad hoc and informal, circumscribed in accordance with the thrust of Labour Party policies in the 1990s (McIlroy 1998).

Nothing daunted, the TUC publicized its case with renewed vigour. Citing the *Skill Needs in Britain* survey, which claimed that only 40 per cent of employees had received any off-the-job training in 1997 while the average number of 'training days' had dropped from 5.3 to 3.2 between 1996 and 1997, they argued that the problem was enduring but soluble. The unions, if adequately supported, could make the difference. With their 'unique relationship' with their members, unions could reach the excluded, such as the 36 per cent of adults who left school at the earliest opportunity. Unions could ensure high quality training and real commitment because they knew the needs of employees as well as employers. All TUC affiliates should strive to ensure lifelong learning was one of the most important services they offered members, particularly young people (TUC 1998a: 2–3). Lobbying for a legislative framework continued and the TUC put their case to both the Department of Trade and Industry and the Department for Education and Employment (ibid: 10–11).

Although there was a formal welcome for the 1998 Green paper, *The Learning Age*, there was behind the scenes annoyance at the junking of the promised White Paper. There was a growing sense that the government which prioritized the schools, and whose gaze largely stopped at the formal education system, was unlikely to invest substantially in lifelong learning. Having accepted the Conservative's financial parameters, they saw the only source for such expenditure as transferring resources from other, more electorally crucial, sectors of education.

There was criticism by Congress delegates of the government's indecisiveness and what were perceived as essential weaknesses in its strategy.

> What a shame that the White paper on Lifelong Learning turned into a Green Paper, a discussion paper instead of an action paper, a talking shop instead of a workshop ... Many people want to welcome the Government's vision of Lifelong Learning but it is somewhat difficult to see how that vision can become a reality because of a flaw in the Government's approach. The problem is the Government's wish to rely on a voluntary approach to training. It will leave irresponsible employers free to cop out of training, to carry on poaching instead of coaching. By default the White paper (*sic*) also ignores the training support the small to medium-sized enterprise and the industries of tomorrow need.
>
> (TUC 1998b: 108)

The problem for the TUC was that the unions, debilitated by two decades of economic and political attrition lacked, in the absence of state support, the muscle to enforce training agreements on employers. This was why they returned to elaborate a position fundamental to their objectives, if currently unrealisable.

> The first steps towards a training system fit for the new millennium and a learning society must be a statutory framework, which includes a modern sectoral-based levy system. A levy grant system in sectors ... falling short of the national training targets would not penalise companies who already carry out quality training. In fact they would benefit from such a system. A sector based levy would ensure that all employers renewing their approach to training would help them recoup the genuine benefits through developing their own workforce.
>
> (ibid)

Despite what they perceived as the inadequacies of state intervention the unions energetically set about boosting their own contribution to the expansion of training. Learning accounts were welcomed although doubts were expressed about the level of government finance, their possible attraction to low paid and atypical workers, and the danger of employers utilizing them as a substitute for company investment in training. There was general enthusiasm for the UfI combined once more with worries about the level of finance it was receiving and the reliance on information technology. The TUC pitched for an extended institutional role in promoting and marketing the UfI to members and employers and urged trade unionists to negotiate agreements with employers which incorporated UfI membership; they also provided for monitoring the quality of UfI activity and maximized the use of the Learning Direct helpline (NIACE 1998). Concern at government's commitment—the initial tranche of money for learning accounts was not new money but diverted from unspent TEC funds—and assertions that 'New Labour wants lifelong learning on the cheap', were quietened, in the way of the trade union world, by the announcement in the Green Paper of the Union Learning Fund. This provided £8 million over four years to promote activity by unions in support of 'the learning society'. By the end of the century 45 projects involving 21 unions were in progress and a further 48 had received funding. These covered a range of activity from pump-priming EDS schemes to developing union links with UfI, new qualifications with NTOs and new employer-union partnerships (GMB/TGWU 1998, TUC 1999b: 99).

The majority of the Learning Fund projects involved the development of a system of union learning representatives in the workplace: they would advise members on training and educational opportunities and negotiate over implementation. The expressed aspiration was to construct a union role in advancing basic skills and managerial and professional qualifications

(*Labour Research* 1999). Unions increased their representation on those bodies at the heart of state strategy, notably the DfEE Skills Task Force, the DTI Workforce Development Working Party and the Qualifications and Curriculum Authority which replaced the National Council for Vocational Qualifications. Nonetheless, the organizational sinews of lifelong learning remained dominated by managers: employers were the primary actors, appointment of trade unionists was ad hoc, there was no return to tripartism. The 1999 White Paper, *Learning to Succeed*, was sharply criticized by the TUC on the grounds it would institutionalize employer dominance, not only in the new structures which would replace the TECs, but also over further education. The limits to New Labour's willingness to curtail employer prerogative, despite capital's record of inactivity in this area, was graphically defined by firm refusal to meet union objectives in the 1999 employment legislation. A clause in the Employment Relations Act required management to consult with unions over training but not as the unions had wanted, to negotiate with them (TUC 1999b: 97).

Emphasis on vocational training remained predominant. For example, the TUC saw EDS as stemming 'from circumstances within an organisation at a particular time—changing methods, increased competition, technological development and (they) form an important part of wider strategies for improving both organisational and individuals' employability'. The 'wider strategies' referred to centred on HRM, its revamped yet resiliently primitive Human Relations sociology striving to rhetorically eliminate conflict at work and commit employees' hearts and souls to the organization without ceding to them any real influence over the labour process or the organization itself. The TUC's unsupported assertion that those who availed themselves of EDS 'quickly move on to other learning', immediately collapsed into the unsurprising conclusion 'that (it) helps them with the skills they need to get on at work and contribute to their organisation's success' (TUC 1999a: 2–3; TUCc; Storey 1995).

But there was attention, even if much of it was rhetorical, to aspects of lifelong learning beyond 'getting on at work'. Some TUC pronouncements, while couched in the language of priorities, urged 'a new agenda for learning to support employability, citizenship and community renewal' (TUC 1998a: 109). There was understanding among Congress delegates that 'lifelong learning is an essential component of a democratic society with a profound commitment to equal opportunities', even if such sentiments were typically incursions into the now established text which continued routinely 'and that everyone has an entitlement to learning opportunities to enable them to use all their skills and talents ... lifelong learning has a major contribution to make to promoting employability and adaptability' (TUC 1998b: 31).

If there was no attempt to revive a system for adult continuing education from the attrition of local authority cuts, the remoulding of the WEA and the dissolution by the universities of their extra-mural departments, as some had hoped (Fieldhouse 1996: 398), there was concern over the future of post-16 education. Trade unionists recognized that government sound bites emphasizing its importance clouded the continued absence of adequate funding: 'The proportion of GDP spent on post-school education must rise to at least the 1979 level if we are to begin to recover what we have lost, never mind embarking on the learning revolution' (TUC 1998b: 31). The TUC General Council 'called for the further and higher education sectors to be put on a stable financial footing' and it was recognized that without a change in the disproportion between New Labour's rhetorical and financial contribution any expansion of lifelong learning would be limited and second rate:

We have endured massive increases in workloads and uncompetitive and unprofessional salaries ... We have also experienced a huge drop in the unit of resource and a dramatic worsening of staff/student ratios all of which has led inevitably to a decline in quality and standards. Expansion of this sort is worthless.

(TUC 1998b: 108)

Trade union education was imprinted with the inflections of the general approach. The traditional opposition to accreditation of union courses as inappropriate and divisive fell away in the 1990s. From 1997 all TUC courses offered credits as part of a scheme developed with the National Open College Network with a reported take-up rate of 80 per cent and 94 per cent of those registering receiving credits. The TUC argued that the 16 ONC credits at levels 2 or 3, which could be attained through their programme, was equivalent to 2 or 3 A-levels and should qualify students for university entrance. TUC commissioned research pronounced the innovation a success with 74 per cent of union representatives viewing the initiative in positive terms. It had built on taking account of students' experiential learning, had not distorted the collective ethos of courses and their objectives, and had fostered a more serious approach to work (Capizzi 1999).

The content of programmes also continued to change. There was a growth of courses dealing with computer, technological and managerial skills as well as joint courses with management. In 1999 a review of union education provision suggested the need for new modules and new strands in existing courses focusing on union collaboration with employers, joint problem-solving, understanding of business issues, corporate finance and economics. This was motivated by the argument that

> partnership requires a very different portfolio of skills from collective bargaining as traditionally understood. Joint problem-solving skills are not the same as negotiating skills and partnership also puts a premium on facilitation, brokering, listening and consulting. Furthermore greater union involvement in the organisation planning process requires an understanding of business issues and economics.

(TUC 1999b: 62)

The decline in the number of courses slowed and by the turn of the century appeared to have stabilized. The number of TUC 10-day courses fell from 394 with 4,700 students in 1993, to 330, with 3,700 students, four years later. It then increased slightly to 340 courses with 3,400 students in 1998 (TUC 1998a: 130). The application of the new vocationalism to the residential colleges continued to provoke well-argued dissension from staff at the reduction of the still intensely relevant tradition of education for collective development, social understanding and progressive political change to preparation for the labour market (Andrews, Keane and Thompson 1999).

Assessment

Trade unions have been in the forefront of advocates of the consensus approach in which lifelong learning is essentially an epi-phenomenon of economics and the learning society, collapsed into the learning enterprise, is fundamentally about improved performance and bigger profits in the global market. Education has always, inescapably, been related to the market, occupational position and the economy. What is involved under globalization is a naked impoverishing, more intimate realignment, which simplistically conflates economic necessity with the good of the enterprise and seeks to appropriate intellectual development and confine it to capitalist regeneration. Conceptions of education as empowering individuals, groups and classes, as developing critical address of society, as engendering equitable social and economic organization, as promoting new political strategies, remain. But they now play only an ancillary role. Conceptions of a diverse cultural and political working-class education which subsumes but transcends training (Fryer 1990) have been replaced by human capital approaches, differing only in their refinement and in the role and resources they offer unions, from Conservative models.

In the field of action the TUC has privileged workplace training and the socially mobile individual over education, society and class. Where it has had direct control, as in the case of union education, it has prioritized employment training while its interest in EDA is largely expressed in terms of developing workplace skills. Where it possesses influence, as in the residential colleges, it has not demurred from the growth of marketization and managerialism. Unions are not education bodies: the further they move away from work, the more difficult they find policy initiation and policy success. They can be expected to emphasize vocational training. Nonetheless, at times in the past they have embraced a broader educational agenda than is presently deployed. Within the confines of the current economic learning paradigm the unions have defined problems and solutions in powerful fashion and have taken compelling issue with the state over the necessity for stronger partnership, more resources and a firmer regulatory framework.

The TUC cannot be faulted on the dedication and energy with which this project has been pursued. Doubts as to its success stem from the restricted ambit of the project itself and the attitudes of employers, politicians and union members towards it. The problem of training, or the lack of it, is entrenched and enduring. In the mid-1990s only 10 per cent of those aged 17 were studying anything and half had not studied since they left school. Employers have failed with facility to attain National Training Targets. Despite widespread publicity, only a relative handful of workers are covered by EDS schemes while union education has sequentially declined over two decades (NIACE 1994, TUC 1999a: 2). There must be doubts as to whether qualitative progress can be made without, ironically, more sophisticated educational address of the issues at stake. Tighter thinking seems to be required, for example, on the plausible but ultimately elusive links between training and the success of the enterprise and the economy. And to what extent does education and cultivation of the intellect make a contribution prior to that of any job-related training (Jones and Hendry 1992; Shackleton 1992)? What stands out is the absence of rigorous research to underpin policy. Research, for example, which illuminates the relationship between training and education, and explores their linkages with different kinds of flexibility and employability. Some work suggests that labour flexibility in the sense of adapting to a changing economy, is facilitated more by broader educational agendas than by specific skills training (Halstead and Wright 1995). Finally, there must be doubts as to whether qualitative progress can be made without greater state intervention, support and finance (Hutton 1995).

Trade unionists' own prognostications appear justified: 'The government is continuing with the failed policy of relying on the goodwill of companies ... without the mandatory involvement of the employers there can be no successful transformation to Lifelong Learning in the workplace' (*Labour Research* 1998). But such legislation is unlikely. And unions which represent only a third of all employees, whose coverage is uneven and who exclude millions of low paid, atypical, women and ethnic minority workers are implausibly cast as substitutes for the state as catalysts of change and stimulators of training provision. Despite the much-vaunted 'union mark-up' to training, they lack, at least in general aggregate terms, the power to enforce training on reluctant, recalcitrant employers. While their ability to do this in specific favourable circumstances is likely to entrench the training divide between different groups of workers.

Training may, contrary to TUC orthodoxy, constitute a conflict issue. And strong independent unions are more likely to influence the determination of such conflict (Streeck 1992). Evidence suggests the TUC overestimates the extent to which employers are positive about accepting unions as partners and the extent to which, if they do so, unions are accorded a significant, rather than subservient role (Kelly 1996). Members still join unions for protection against management, not to resource vocational training. Unions which attempt to utilize an emphasis on generating training as a substitute for declining influence over wages and conditions, rather than as a supplement to effective performance over these issues, may find current weakness exacerbated, rather than ameliorated. After all, the business union model at the heart of partnership has played a role in ensuring that 90 per cent of American workers are outside union membership.

Even the progress recorded by unions may prove in some aspects insubstantial. For example they have largely taken at face value the NVQ system condemned by academic researchers as 'a disaster of epic proportions' (Prais 1991; Smithers 1993). The accreditation of union training courses has an element of mimicry of mainstream credentials. Tutors confide that every student who registers and attends receives credits, that if they are equivalent to A-levels they are not A-levels, and if students want to enter university they would be better off taking customized courses.[2] The unions' role in the much publicized EDS initiatives has been slender apart from 'a few well known exceptions like Ford and Peugeot' (TUC 1992a: 2). In the end, the unions' thinking and their myopic stress on skills training may itself bespeak the need to replace their unbalanced restricted model with a broader conception: an inclusive educationally based social and political lifelong learning.

Notes

1 The TUC acts in this area not only as spokesperson but in important aspects as policy-maker for its affiliated unions so that this paper concentrates on its contribution.
2 Based on discussions with tutors on union courses.

References

Ackers, P., Smith, C. and Smith, P. (eds.)(1996) *The New Workplace and Trade Unionism*, London, Routledge
Ainley, P. and Corney, M. (1991) *Training for the Future*, London, Cassell
Andrews, G., Keane, H. and Thompson, J. (1999) *Ruskin College: Contesting Knowledge, Discussing Politics*, London, Lawrence & Wishart
Bacon, N. and Storey, J. (1993) 'Individualisation of the employment relationship: implications for trade unions', *Employee Relations*, 15, 1, 3–23
Capizzi, E. (1999) *Learning that Works: Accrediting the TUC Programme*, Leicester, NIACE
Commission of the European Community (1994) *Growth, Competitiveness, Employment: The Challenge and Way Forward into the 21st Century*, Luxembourg, Office for Official Publications
Edwards, P. (ed.)(1995) *Industrial Relations: Theory and Practice in Britain*, Oxford, Blackwell
Edwards, R. (1997) *Changing Places? Flexibility, Lifelong Learning and the Learning Society*, London, Routledge
Field, J. (1996) 'Learning for work: vocational education and training', in Fieldhouse, R. and associates (1996)
Fieldhouse, R. (1996) 'British adult education: past, present and future', in Fieldhouse, R. and associates (1996)
Fieldhouse, R. and associates (1996) *A History of Modern British Adult Education*, Leicester, NIACE
Finegold, D. (1991) 'The Implications of "Training in Britain" for the analysis of Britain's skills problem', *Human Resource Management Journal*, 2, 1, 11–22
Finegold, D. and Soskice, D. (1990) 'The failure of training in Britain: analysis and prescription', in Gleeson, D. (ed.)(1990)
Forrester, K. (1995) 'Learning in working life', in Mayo, M. and Thompson, J. (eds.)(1995)
Fryer, B. (1990) 'The challenge to working class adult education', in Simon, B. (ed.) (1990)

Gleeson, D. (ed.) (1990) *Training and Its Alternatives*, Milton Keynes, Open University Press

GMB/TGWU (1992) *Training for Britain's Economic Success*

GMB/TGWU (1998) *Training for Success*

Green, F., Machin, S. and Wilkinson, D. (1995) *Unions and Training*, University of Leeds

Griggs, C. (1983) *The Trades Union Congress and the Struggle for Education, 1868–1925*, Brighton, Falmer Press

Hall, S. (1983) 'Education in crisis', in Wolpe, A. and Donald, J. (eds.) (1983)

Halstead, J. and Wright, P. (1995) *Confronting Industrial Demise: The Employment and Unemployment Experiences of Miners and their Families in South Yorkshire and North East Derbyshire*, University of Sheffield and Rotherham Metropolitan Borough Council

Heery, E. (1998), 'The re-launch of the Trades Union Congress', *British Journal of Industrial Relations*, 31, 3, 339–60

Hutton, W. (1995) *The State We're In*, London, Vintage Books

Jones, A. and Hendry, C. (1992) *The Learning Organisation: A review of Literature and Practice*, London, HRD Publishing

Keep, E. (1989) 'A "training scandal"?' in Sisson, K. (ed.) (1989)

Keep, E. and Rainbird, H. (1995) 'Training' in Edwards, P. (ed.) (1995)

Kelly, J. (1996) 'Union militancy and social partnership' in Ackers, P., Smith, C. and Smith, P. (eds.) (1996)

King, D. (1993) 'The Conservatives and training policy 1979–1992: from tripartite to a neo-liberal regime', *Political Studies*, 67, 214–35

Labour Party (1997) *New Labour: Because Britain Deserves Better*

Labour Research (1998) 'When the skills revolution comes', *Labour Research*, April

Labour Research (1999) 'A lot to learn from the unions', *Labour Research*, July

Leisink, P., Van Leemput, J. and Vilrok, J. (eds.) (1996), *The Challenge to Trade Unions in Europe*, Aldershot, Edward Elgar

McIlroy, J. (1995a) 'The dying of the light? A radical look at trade union education' in Mayo, M. and Thompson, J. (eds.) (1995)

McIlroy, J. (1995b) *Trade Unions in Britain Today*, 2nd edition, Manchester, Manchester University Press

McIlroy, J. (1996a) 'Independent working class education and trade union education and training' in Fieldhouse, R. and associates (1996)

McIlroy, J. (1996b) 'From "The Great Tradition" to NVQs: universities and trade union education at *fin de siècle*' in Wallis, J. (ed.) (1996)

McIlroy, J. (1998) 'The enduring alliance? trade unions and the making of New Labour 1994–1997', *British Journal of Industrial Relations*, 36, 4, 537–64

Mayo, M. and Thompson, J. (eds.) (1995), *Adult Learning: Critical Intelligence and Social Change*, Leicester, NIACE

NIACE (1994) *What Price the learning Society?*, Leicester, NIACE

NIACE (1998) *Partners for Learning: Opportunities for Trade Unions and the University for Industry*, Leicester, NIACE

Payne, J. (1990) *Women, Training and the Skills Shortage: The Case for Public Investment*, London, Policy Studies Institute

Payne, J. (1996) 'Who really benefits from Employee Development schemes' in Raggatt, P., Edwards, R. and Small, N. (eds.) (1996)

Prais, S. (1991) 'Vocational Qualification in Britain and Europe: theory and practice', *National Institute Economic Review*, 135

Raggatt, P., Edwards, R. and Small, N. (eds.) (1996) *The Learning Society: Challenges and Trends*, Routledge

Rainbird, H. (1990) *Training Matters: Union Perspectives on Industrial Restructuring and Training*, Oxford, Blackwell

Rainbird, H. and Vincent, C. (1996) 'Training: a new item on the bargaining agenda' in Leisink, P., Van Leemput, J. and Vilrok, J. (eds) (1996)

Regini, M. (ed.) (1992) *The Future of Labour Movements*, Sage

Shackleton, J. (1992) *Training Too Much? A Sceptical Look at the Economics of Skill Training in the UK*, London, Institute of Economic Affairs

Simon, B. (ed.)(1990) *The Search for Enlightenment: The Working Class and Adult Education in the Twentieth Century*, London, Lawrence & Wishart

Simon, B. (1999) *Education and the Social Order 1940–1990*, London, Lawrence & Wishart

Sisson, K. (ed.)(1989) *Personnel Management in Britain*, Oxford, Blackwell

Smithers, A. (1993) *Futures: Britain's Education Revolution*, Channel Four Television

Storey, J. (ed.)(1995) *Human Resource Management: A Critical Text*, London, Routledge

Streeck, W. (1992) 'Training and the new industrial relations: a strategic role for unions?' in Regini, M. (ed.) (1992)

Sutherland, J. (1998) *Workplace Learning for the 21st Century* Report of the Workplace Learning Task Group to the National Advisory Group for Continuing Education and Lifelong Learning, DfEE.

TUC (1977)

TUC (1979)

TUC (1992a) *Annual Report*, TUC

TUC (1992b) *Bargaining for Skills: a call to action*, TUC

TUC (1993) *Annual Report*, TUC

TUC (1994) *A New Partnership for Company Training*, TUC

TUC (1995) *Bargaining for Skills: A TUC initiative*, TUC

TUC (1996a) *Report of the General Council*, TUC

TUC (1996b) *Training at the Workplace: A Negotiator's Guide*, TUC

TUC (1997a) *Partners for Progress: Next Steps for the New Unionism*, TUC

TUC (1997b) *Report of the General Council*, TUC

TUC (1998a) *Report of General Council*, TUC

TUC (1998b) *Report of Congress 1998*, TUC

TUC (1999a) *Employee Development Schemes: case studies of union involvement*, DfEE

TUC (1999b) *Report of the General Council*, TUC

TUC (1999c) *Employee Development Schemes; A Negotiator's Guide*, TUC

Turner, P, Dale, I. and Hurst, C. (1992) 'Training: a key to the future', *Employment Gazette*, August, 23–5

USDAW (1991) *Training for the Future*, USDAW

Waddington, J. and Whitston, C. (1997) 'Why do people join trade unions in a period of membership decline?', *British Journal of Industrial Relations*, 35, 4, 515–46

Wallis, J. (ed.)(1996) *Liberal Adult Education: The End of an Era?*, Nottingham, University of Nottingham

Winterton, J. and Winterton, R. (1994) *Collective Bargaining and Consultation over Vocational Training*, London, DfEE

Wolpe, A. and Donald, J. (eds.)(1983) *Is There Anyone Here From Education?*, London, Pluto Press

Index